Innovations in Computer Science and Engineering

Innovations in Computer Science and Engineering

Edited by **Tom Halt**

New York

Published by Willford Press,
118-35 Queens Blvd., Suite 400,
Forest Hills, NY 11375, USA
www.willfordpress.com

Innovations in Computer Science and Engineering
Edited by Tom Halt

International Standard Book Number: 978-1-68285-131-9 (Hardback)

The publisher's policy is to use permanent paper from mills that operate a sustainable forestry policy. Furthermore, the publisher ensures that the text paper and cover boards used have met acceptable environmental accreditation standards.

Trademark Notice: Registered trademark of products or corporate names are used only for explanation and identification without intent to infringe.

Printed in the United States of America.

Contents

Preface

In my initial years as a student, I used to run to the library at every possible instance to grab a book and learn something new. Books were my primary source of knowledge and I would not have come such a long way without all that I learnt from them. Thus, when I was approached to edit this book; I became understandably nostalgic. It was an absolute honor to be considered worthy of guiding the current generation as well as those to come. I put all my knowledge and hard work into making this book most beneficial for its readers.

Rapid technological changes have led to new innovations in computer science and engineering. The ever growing need for advanced technology has fueled the research in the fields of computing, signal processing and embedded systems. This book examines various studies that are constantly contributing towards advancing technologies and brings forth new areas for future research. This book is an attempt to provide in-depth knowledge about the theory and practice of mobile computing, robotics and industrial electronics. It will provide comprehensive knowledge to the readers.

I wish to thank my publisher for supporting me at every step. I would also like to thank all the authors who have contributed their researches in this book. I hope this book will be a valuable contribution to the progress of the field.

Editor

Simulating of microstructure and magnetic properties of nanostructured Fe and Fe$_{50}$Co$_{50}$ powders by neural networks

Ali Heidari[1]*, Mehdi Delshad Chermahini[2] and Mohammad Heidari[3]

[1]Department of Civil Engineering, Shahrekord University, Shahrekord, Iran.
[2]Department of Material Science and Engineering, Kerman University, Kerman, Iran.
[3]Islamic Azad University, Aligodarz Branch, Aligodarz, Iran.

In this study, a series of experiments were performed in order to determine the effects of changing milling time on the microstructure and magnetic properties of nanostructured Fe and Fe$_{50}$Co$_{50}$ alloys by back propagation neural networks (BPN). The microstructure and magnetic properties of Fe and Fe$_{50}$Co$_{50}$ alloys were estimated using the data acquired from the experiments performed, performance values obtained were used for training a BPN whose structure was designed for this operation. The network, which has two layers as hidden layer, and output layer, has two input and five output neurons. The BPN is used for simulating the microstructure and magnetic properties of nanostructured Fe and Fe$_{50}$Co$_{50}$ alloys. The BPN method is found to be the most accurate and quick, the best results were obtained by the BPN by quasi-newton algorithms training with 12 neurons in the hidden layer. The quasi-newton algorithms procedure is more accurate and requires significantly less computation time than the other methods. Training was continued until the mean square error is less than 1e-3, desired error value was achieved in the BPN was tested with both data used and not used for training the network. Resultant of the test indicates the usability of the BPN in this area.

Key words: Nanostructured materials, mchanical alloying, microstructure, magnetic measurements, computer simulation.

INTRODUCTION

It is established that during mechanical alloying a solid state reaction takes place between the fresh powder surfaces of the reactant materials at room temperature. Consequently, it can be useful to produce alloys and compounds that are difficult and impossible to be obtained by conventional melting and casting techniques (Capdevila et al., 2001).

Pure iron is a good ferromagnetic material with a low resistivity so in some applications it leads to large eddy current losses. Alloying can be engineered to instill greater magnetic permeability and lower core losses (Koohkan et al., 2008). Cobalt in iron is unique in increasing simultaneously the saturation magnetization and Curie temperature (McHenry et al., 1999). Although

the maximum saturation magnetization (M$_S$) occurs at a concentration of 35 at % Co, equiatomic compositions offer a considerably larger permeability for similar M$_S$ (Sourmail, 2005). Recently, the effects of milling time (Delshad Chermahini et all 2009a), composition (Delshad Chermahini et al., 2009c), heating time (Delshad Chermahini and Shokrollahi, 2009) and heating rate (Delshad Chermahini et al., 2009b) on the both microstructure and magnetic properties of nanostructured Fe-Co alloys were investigated. The present paper is focused on the prediction effect of the ball milling on the structure and the magnetic properties of Fe and Fe$_{50}$Co$_{50}$ alloys, using artificial neural network.

The structure and magnetic properties of Fe and Fe$_{50}$Co$_{50}$ alloys in the experiments were adjusted by changing the milling time. Then the data obtained from the test results was used for simulating the system performance by the BPN. Recent developments in

*Corresponding author. E-mail: heidari@eng.sku.ac.ir.

Table 1. Experimental measurements.

Milling time	Fe					Fe$_{50}$Co$_{50}$				
	Cry	Mic	Lat	Coe	Mag	Cry	Mic	Lat	Coe	Mag
0.3	101	0.03	0.28669	25.0	208.1	100	0.04	0.28650	72.0	178.0
1.0	72	0.06	0.28673	27.0	208.3	68	0.08	0.28649	79.0	179.0
1.5	50	0.15	0.28677	29.0	208.5	40	0.20	0.28648	85.0	180.0
2.0	45	0.23	0.28680	30.0	208.7	35	0.33	0.28648	94.0	181.0
3.0	40	0.30	0.28686	34.0	209.0	30	0.45	0.28642	103.0	182.0
4.0	35	0.47	0.28692	33.0	209.1	25	0.63	0.28637	97.8	189.0
5.0	30	0.66	0.28698	32.0	209.2	21	0.86	0.28631	92.6	196.0
6.0	23	0.79	0.28703	31.3	209.3	17	1.00	0.28626	87.5	200.0
7.0	18	0.90	0.28707	30.6	209.4	15	1.10	0.28623	78.7	204.0
8.0	14	1.00	0.28710	30.0	209.5	12	1.20	0.28620	70.0	208.0
12.0	13	1.13	0.28719	29.3	209.7	11	1.23	0.28617	67.0	208.7
17.0	12	1.17	0.28727	28.6	209.9	12	1.23	0.28616	64.0	209.4
20.0	12	1.20	0.28730	28.0	210.0	12	1.20	0.28615	61.0	210.0
26.0	13	1.20	0.28732	27.4	210.3	12	1.18	0.28613	60.6	211.7
30.0	12	1.21	0.27834	26.7	210.6	12	1.16	0.28611	60.3	213.4
35.0	13	1.20	0.28735	26.0	211.0	12	1.15	0.28610	60.0	215.0
37.0	15	1.15	0.28736	25.1	211.2	12	1.11	0.28610	57.0	215.6
40.0	17	1.09	0.28736	24.2	211.4	13	1.06	0.28611	54.0	216.2
43.0	18	1.02	0.28737	23.1	211.7	14	1.00	0.28612	51.0	216.8
45.0	19	0.95	0.28737	22.0	212.0	15	0.95	0.28613	47.0	217.5

information technology and increased computer powers led to the development of new programming techniques.

One kind of artificial neural network is BPN. The BPN are being used in control applications, robots, pattern recognition, medicine, power systems, signal processing, social and psychological sciences. The BPN have also being used in heating (Rama Kumar and Prasad, 2006), cooling (Kanarachos and Geramanis, 1998), analysis (Swider et al., 2001), design (Heidari and Salajegheh, 2006; Heidari and Karimpor, 2008; Heidari et al., 2009) and optimization (Salajegheh and Heidari 2004a, b).

EXPERIMENTAL DETAILS

Fe (99.5%, < 10 μm) and Co (99%, < 3 μm) powders supplied by Merck were mechanically alloyed in an argon atmosphere to form Fe and Fe$_{50}$Co$_{50}$ alloy in a Fritsch planetary ball mill, whilst confined in sealed 250 ml steel containers rotated at 400 rpm for a variety of milling times. The container was loaded with a blend of balls (φ = 10 mm, mass = 4.14 g and φ = 20 mm, mass = 32.12 g). The total weight of the powder was about 23 g and the ball to powder mass ratio was about 20:1.

X-ray diffraction measurements were carried out in a Philips X'Pert High Score diffractometer using Cu K_{α} (λ = 1.5405 $\overset{\circ}{A}$) radiation over 20 - 140° 2θ. The crystallite size and lattice strain were estimated using the Williamson-Hall method:

$$B_s \cos\theta = 2(\varepsilon)\sin\theta + k\lambda/D$$

Where B_s is the full-width at half maximum of the diffraction peak, θ is the Bragg angle, ε is the internal microstrain λ is the wavelength of the X-ray, D is the crystallite size. B_s can be given as

$$B_s^2 = B_m^2 - B_c^2$$

Where B_s is the width at half-maximum of the Si powder peaks used for calibration and B_m is the evaluated width.

Lattice parameters were determined using 3 high-angle peaks in order to increase the precision of the measurements. Morphology and particle size were observed using scanning electron microscopy (Camscan mv2300). Magnetic properties were estimated using a magnetometer VSM.

The used data for this paper is prepared by the author at previous work (Delshad Chermahini et al., 2009a). The effect of milling time on the microstructure (crystallite size, microstrain and lattice parameter) and magnetic properties (coercivity and magnetization saturation) of nanostructured Fe and Fe$_{50}$Co$_{50}$ powders has been investigated. The results of this experimental study are shown in Table 1, where Cry is crystallite size, Mic is microstrain, Lat is lattice parameter, Coe is coercivity and Mag is magnetization saturation.

For each composition (Fe and Fe$_{50}$Co$_{50}$), 20 milling times are selected. The experimental results that are shown in Table 1 were conducted on the system by changing the milling time is used to train and test of the BPN (Delshad Chermahini et al., 2009a).

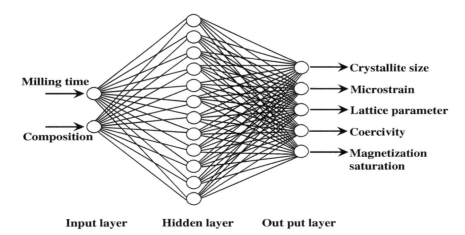

Figure 1. Architecture of the BPN used.

BACK PROPAGATION NEURAL NETWORK

Back propagation neural network resembling neural neurons of a human brain are used successfully in many science branches on modelling and control applications. The BPN can be used to learn from the training dataset the non-linear relationships between multiple inputs and outputs without requiring specific information on the fundamental mechanisms relating them. The BPN is composed of interconnected computational processing elements called neurons that process input information and give outputs. The BPN have an algorithm that can learn and decide by its own throughout the process. They have data processing units called neurons. These networks involve connections between the neurons, which have their own weights. Their total energy is calculated by multiplying data signals by these weights. Data at the neuron output is found by making use of an activation function. The BPN have structural and mathematical variations (Heidari and Karimpor, 2008; Salajegheh and Heidari, 2004a; Salajegheh and Heidari, 2004b).

Structural differences arise from the number of layers and the variations of the connections among the nodes. Generally, they have two layers as; hidden layer and output layer. Number of the layers can change and can be rebounded between the layers. This completely depends on the usage purpose of the network. Number of the nodes in the input equals to the number of data to be given to the BPN. Number of nodes at the output layer equals to the number of knowledge that will be taken from the BPN (Figure 1).

Learning capability of the BPN improves as the number of nodes and the connections increases; however, it takes more time to train. A node has many inputs while it has only one output. Nodes process these input data and feed forward to the next layer. Input data are processed as follows; each data are added up after it was multiplied by its weight and then it is subjected to activation function. Thus, the data, which will be transferred to the next layer, is obtained. The algorithm used in training the BPN, and the type of activation function used at the output of the node are the mathematical differences. Activation functions involve exponential functions and thus non-linear modeling can be achieved. Various algorithms have been developed according to the BPN purpose of usage. They can be preferred according to their convenience to the problem to be solved, and training speed. The BPN are trained with known data and then tested with data not used in training. Although training takes a long time, they make decisions very fast during operation. They are used widely in simulating non-linear systems thanks to their ability to learn, generalize, tolerate the faults and benefit from the faulty samples. In the BPN optimizes the weighted connections by allowing the error to spread from output layer

towards the lower layers, was used as the training system in training networks. The values of the training and test data were normalized to a range from -1 to 1. The formulas used in this algorithm are as follows (Heidari, 2008):

i.) Hidden layer calculation results:

$$net_i = \sum x_i w_i \tag{1}$$

$$y_i = f(net_i) \tag{2}$$

Where x_i and w_i are input data and weights of the input data, respectively. f is activation function, and y_i is result obtained from hidden layer.

ii.) Output layer calculation results:

$$net_k = \sum y_i w_{jk} \tag{3}$$

$$o_k = f(net_k) \tag{4}$$

Where w_{jk} are weights of output layer and o_k is result obtained from output layer.

iii.) Activation functions used in layers are tansig and linear (Heidari, 2008):

$$f(net_i) = \frac{1 - e^{-net_i}}{1 + e^{-net_i}} \quad \text{(tansig)} \tag{5}$$

$$f(net_i) = net_i \quad \text{(linear)} \tag{6}$$

iv.) Errors made at the end of one cycle:

$$e_k = (t_k - o_k)o_k(1 - o_k) \tag{7}$$

$$e_i = y_i(1 - y_i)\sum e_k w_{ij} \tag{8}$$

Table 2. Result of neural network with the BPN for Fe.

Milling time	Fe (Neural network)					Error = (Exp - Neu)/Exp × 100				
	Cry	Mic	Lat	Coe	Mag	Cry	Mic	Lat	Coe	Mag
1.0	74.2	0.062	0.28645	26.89	209.29	3.06	3.33	0.097	0.41	0.44
6.0	22.13	0.76	0.28702	31.82	210.61	3.78	3.79	0.004	1.66	0.63
17.0	12.34	1.16	0.28728	28.12	209.46	2.83	0.85	0.004	1.68	0.21
30.0	12.13	1.24	0.28743	25.93	211.61	1.08	2.47	0.035	4.53	0.48
40.0	16.63	1.12	0.28738	24.43	212.32	2.18	2.75	0.007	0.95	0.44
Mean relative error for the data not used in training						2.59	2.64	0.029	1.52	0.45

Where t_k is result expected from output layer, e_k is error occurred at output layer, and e_i is error occurred at hidden layer.

v.) Weights can be changed using these calculated error values according to:

$$w_{jk} = w_{jk} + \alpha e_k y_i + \beta \Delta w_{jk} \qquad (9)$$

$$w_{ij} = w_{ij} + \alpha e_i x_i + \beta \Delta w_{ij} \qquad (10)$$

Where w_{jk} and w_{ij} are weights of output and hidden layers, respectively. Δw_{jk} and Δw_{ij} are correction made in weights at the previous calculation. α is learning ratio and β is momentum, that is used to adjust weights. In this paper, $\alpha = 0.75$ and $\beta = 0.70$, are used.

vi.) Square error, occurred in one cycle, can be found by Eq. 11.

$$e = \Sigma\ 0.5 \| t_k - o_k \|^2 \qquad (11)$$

vii.) The completion of training the BPN, relative error (RE) for each data and mean relative error (MRE) for all data are calculated according to Eqs. 12 and 13, respectively.

$$RE = \left(\frac{100\ (t_k - o_k)}{t_k} \right) \qquad (12)$$

$$MRE = \frac{1}{n} \sum_{i=1}^{n} \left(\frac{100\ (t_k - o_k)}{t_k} \right) \qquad (13)$$

Where n is the number of data.

RESULTS AND DISCUSSION

Thirty out of forty experiments results used in training and the other 10 experiments were used to test of the BPN. Square error condition of less than 1e-3 was tried to be realized in training and it was achieved for the BPN. The various training algorithm (Heidari, 2008) is used for training the BPN. All weights were corrected and repeated after the calculation of each data set. The best algorithm for this problem is the quasi-Newton algorithms. This is the type of problem for which the quasi-newton algorithms is best suited. A personal computer Pentium 4 is used and the computing time is calculated in clock time. The BPN with twelve hidden neuron reached to desired error value after repeating 4.23 s.

No more the BPN having hidden layer neurons other than this number was tested since the desired error value was reached by this the BPN. Relative error values were calculated for the data used and not used in training according to Equations 12 and 13. Crystallite size, micro-strain, lattice parameter, coercivity and magnetization saturation error values of these (RE, MRE) found by artificial neural network with the BPN as well as. The test and RE values can be seen in Tables 2 and 3. Crystallite size, micro-strain, lattice parameter, coercivity and magnetization saturation predicted by the BPN and the experimental results were compared in Figures 2 - 6. Apses of the graphic shows the values measured, and estimated by the BPN. The regression value (R^2) of the output variable values between the experimental values and the values estimated by the BPN were also calculated.

Figure 2 shows the changes in crystallite size. The BPN learned the data not used in training with a MRE of 2.19% and a regression value of 0.9881. The change in microstrain is shown in Figure 3. Mean relative error of the BPN in these values is 2.42% and regression value is 0.9804. The lattice parameter is shown in Figure 4. The BPN learned the data not used in training with a MRE of 0.025% and a regression value of 0.9992. The coercivity is shown in Figure 5. The BPN learned the data not used in training with a MRE of 1.41% and a regression value of 0.9955. The magnetization saturation is shown in Figure 6. The BPN learned the data not used in training with a MRE of 0.31% and a regression value of 0.9979.

CONCLUSION

Microstructural and magnetic properties estimation was made according to the experimental values by using the BPN. Results of 30 experiments out of 40, which were conducted at laboratory conditions, were used to train the

Table 3. Result of neural network with the BPN for $Fe_{50}Co_{50}$.

Milling time	$Fe_{50}Co_{50}$ (Neural network)					Error = (Exp - Neu)/Exp × 100				
	Cry	Mic	Lat	Coe	Mag	Cry	Mic	Lat	Coe	Mag
2.0	36.21	0.34	0.28645	93.23	181.44	3.46	3.03	0.011	0.82	0.24
5.0	20.62	0.84	0.28613	91.81	195.91	1.81	2.32	0.063	0.85	0.05
20.0	12.11	1.19	0.28611	62.15	210.83	0.92	0.83	0.014	1.89	0.39
37.0	12.17	1.09	0.28612	56.91	215.29	1.42	1.80	0.007	0.16	0.14
43.0	13.81	0.97	0.28614	52.43	216.7	1.36	3.00	0.007	2.80	0.05
Mean relative error for the data not used in training						1.79	2.20	0.020	1.30	0.17

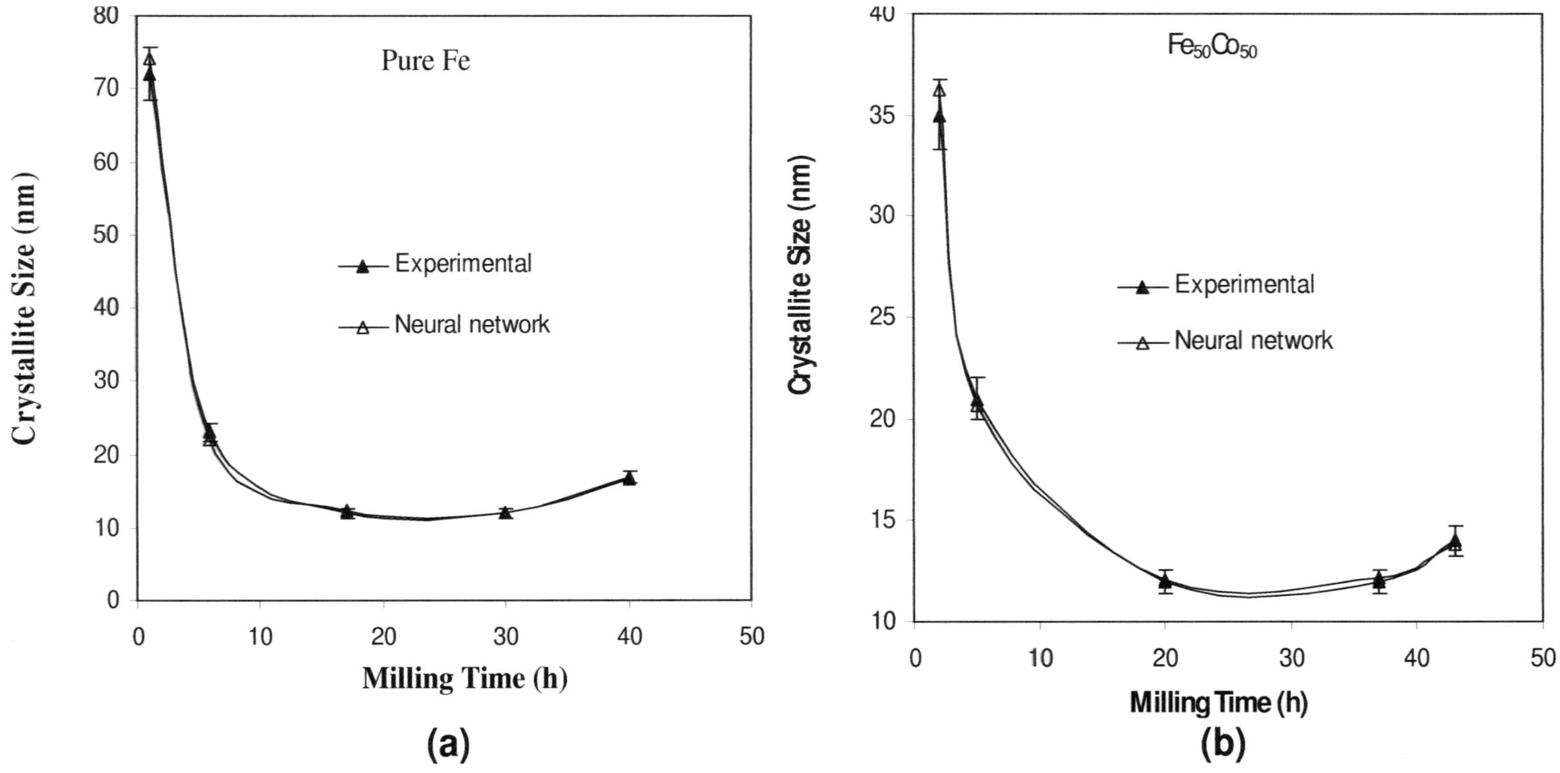

Figure 2. (a) The crystallite size of pure Fe from the experimental data, and the one obtained from neural network. **(b)** The crystallite size of $Fe_{50}Co_{50}$ from the experimental data, and the one obtained from neural network.

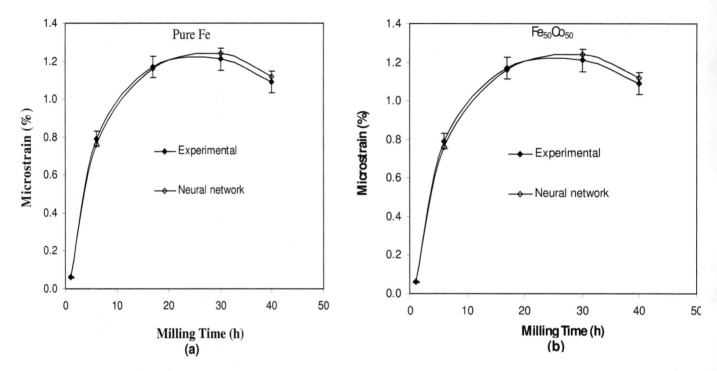

Figure 3. (a) The microstrain of pure Fe from the experimental data, and the one obtained from neural network. (b) The microstrain of $Fe_{50}Co_{50}$ from the experimental data, and the one obtained from neural network.

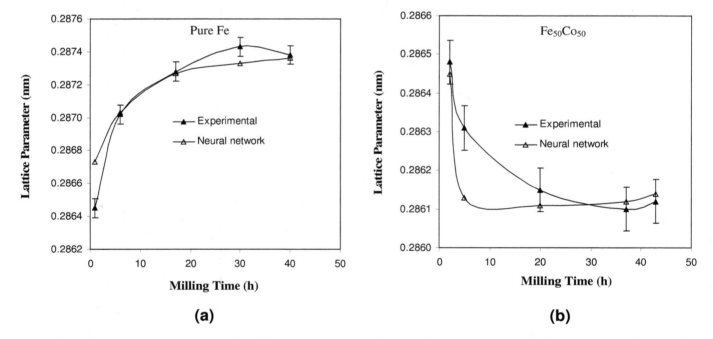

Figure 4. (a) The lattice parameter of pure Fe from the experimental data, and the one obtained from neural network. (b) The lattice parameter of $Fe_{50}Co_{50}$ from the experimental data, and the one obtained from neural network.

BPN and the other 10 were used to test the BPN. Mean relative errors of the test of artificial neural network were found to be 2.19% for crystallite size, 2.42% for microstrain, 0.025% for lattice parameter, 1.41% for coercivity and 0.31% for magnetization saturation. Multiple determination coefficient found by the BPN were 0.9881 for crystallite size, 0.9804 for microstrain, 0.9992 for lattice parameter, 0.9955 for coercivity and 0.9979 for

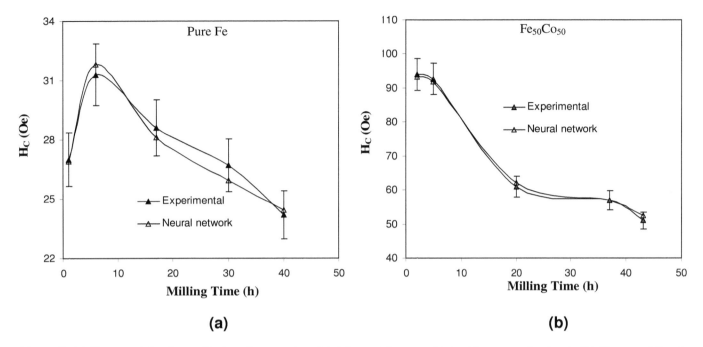

Figure 5. (a) The coercivity of pure Fe from the experimental data, and the one obtained from neural network. (b) The coercivity of $Fe_{50}Co_{50}$ from the experimental data, and the one obtained from neural network.

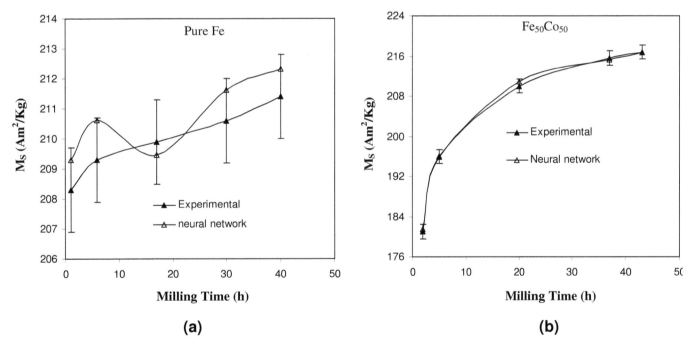

Figure 6. (a) The magnetization saturation of pure Fe from the experimental data, and the one obtained from neural network, (b) The magnetization saturation of $Fe_{50}Co_{50}$ from the experimental data, and the one obtained from neural network.

magnetization saturation. These results showed that the BPN gave a good estimation of results and it can be used in performance estimation of microstructural and magnetic properties with appropriate network architecture and training set.

REFERENCES

Capdevila C, Miller U, Jelenak H, Bhadeshia HKDH (2001). Strain heterogeneity and the production of coarse grains in mechanically alloyed iron-based PM2000 alloy, Mater. Sci. Eng. A., 316: 161–165.
Delshad Chermahini M, Sharafi S, Shokrollahi H, Zandrahimi M

(2009a). Microstructural and magnetic properties of nanostructured Fe and $Fe_{50}Co_{50}$ powders prepared by mechanical alloying, J. Alloys Comp., 474: 18-22.

Delshad Chermahini M, Sharafi S, Shokrollahi H, Zandrahimi M, Shafyei A (2009b). The evolution of heating rate on the microstructural and magnetic properties of milled nanostructured $Fe_{1-x}Co_x$ (x = 0.2, 0.3, 0.4, 0.5 and 0.7) powders, J. Alloys Comp., (in press).

Delshad Chermahini M, Zandrahimi M, Shokrollahi H, Sharafi S (2009c). The effect of milling time and composition on microstructural and magnetic properties of nanostructured Fe–Co alloys J. Alloys Comp., 477: 45-50.

Delshad Chermahini M, Shokrollahi H (2009). Milling and subsequent thermal annealing effects on the microstructural and magnetic properties of nanostructured $Fe_{90}Co_{10}$ and $Fe_{65}Co_{35}$ powders, J. Alloys Comp., 480: 161-166.

Heidari A (2008). Artificial neural network (theory and application with MATLAB), Nazeran, Esfahan, (in Farsi).

Heidari A, Heidari M, Rahmani S (2009). Modelling Absorption Heat Transformer Powered by Back Propagation Neural Network, J. Eng. Tech. Res. (Submitted).

Heidari A, Karimpor M (2008). Earth pressures and design of narrow MSE walls by neural network, 3rd International Conference on Bridge, Tehran, Iran.

Heidari A, Salajegheh E (2006). Time history analysis of structures for earthquake loading by wavelet networks, Asian J. Civil Eng, 7: 155-168.

Kanarachos A, Geramanis K (1998). Multivariable control of single zone hydronik heating system with neural networks, Energy Convers. Manage., 39: 1317-1328.

Koohkan R, Sharafi S, Shokrollahi H, Janghorban K (2008). Preparation of nanocrystalline Fe–Ni powders by mechanical alloying used in soft magnetic composite, J. Manage. Magn. Mater., 320: 1089-1094.

McHenry ME, Willard MA, Laughlin DE (1999). Amorphous and nanocrystalline materials for applications as soft magnets, Prog. Mat. Sci., 44: 291-433.

Rama Kumar BVN, Prasad BVSSS (2006). A combined CFD and network approach for a simulated turbine blade cooling system, Indian J. Eng. Mater. Sci., 13: 20-31.

Salajegheh M, Heidari A (2004a). Optimum design of structures against earthquake by discrete wavelet neural network, 7th International Conference on Computational Structures Technology, Lisbon, Portugal.

Salajegheh E, Heidari A (2004b). Optimum design of structures against earthquake by adaptive genetic algorithm using wavelet networks, Struc. Multi. Optim., 28: 277-285.

Sourmail T (2005). Near equiatomic FeCo alloys: Constitution, mechanical and magnetic properties, Prog. Mater. Sci., 50: 816-880.

Swider DJ, Browne MW, Bansal PK, Kecman V (2001). Modeling of vapour-compression liquid chillers with neural networks, Appl. Therm. Eng., 21: 311-323.

Clustering analysis: A case study of the environmental data of RAMA-Toluca

Miguel Sánchez Sotelo[1], Rosa María Valdovinos Rosas[1]*, Roberto Alejo Eleuterio[2], Edgar Herrera[3] and Eduardo Gasca[4]

[1]Universidad Autonóma del Estado de México, Centro Universitario Valle de Chalco, Hermenegildo Galena No.3, 56615, Valle de Chalco, México.
[2]Tecnológico de Estudios Superiores de Jocotitlan, Carr. Toluca-Atlacomulco Km 44.8, 50700, Jocotitlan, México.
[3]Instituto Nacional de Investigación Nuclear ININ, Carr. Mexico-Toluca s/n, 52750, La Marquesa, Mexico.
[4]Instituto Tecnológico de Toluca, Av. Tecnológico s/n, 52140, Metepec, Mexico.

Recently, the climatic analysis has been widely studied with artificial intelligence tools. The importance of this topic is based on the environment impact produced for natural variations of the data on a certain ecosystem. In this paper, a first study of the meteorological parameters obtained with the Automatic Network of Atmospheric Monitoring (by its abbreviation in Spanish, RAMA) of Toluca, Mexico, is exposed. The study period is from 2001 to 2008. RAMA-Toluca includes seven monitoring stations located in the Toluca Valley. Using clustering algorithms, the experimental results establish the base for determining the days of distribution in clusters, which could be oriented to the natural cluster that the days have in climatic seasons. However, the results show a different situation than the awaited one. With this, the bases for future work are in the climatic analysis context in Toluca Valley.

Key words: Clustering analysis, environmental data, RAMA-Toluca, days of distribution.

INTRODUCTION

The environmental data analysis is one topic that, in the last decades, has had importance in the scientific community. In this scope, studying the climatic change is the main environmental problem. The impact of this change has been foreseeable on the hydric resources, the productive ecosystems, the bio-diversity, the infrastructure, the public health and generally, on the diverse components included in the development process (Staines, 2007), which threatens the healthy environment and the quality of life.

In the Mexican State, particularly, in the metropolitan zone of the Toluca Valley (MZTV), it is possible to see that, when a rural place has been over-passed to an industrialized place, due to the continuous process of urbanization, the natural resources are devastated, and several environmental problems, like: bad use of the ground and reduction of the agricultural and forest border, invasion of protected natural areas, deforestation, erosion processes, forest fires, residues burnt in open-cast, pollution emissions by industries and damaged vehicles, are found (http://www.edomex.gob.mx/medioambiente).

For this reason, several artificial intelligence (AI) techniques are proposed to discover and conduct patterns of climate parameters in the MZTV. The AI is a discipline for developing software and hardware which can emulate the human actions, for example, manipulation of knowledge, generating conclusions, explaining the human reasoning and conducting it as if it was a human.

Clustering is the generic name of a great variety of techniques, useful for finding non-obvious knowledge in large data sets (Kotsiantis and Pintelas, 2004). There are two technique groups: The non-hierarchic techniques or the partition one and the hierarchic techniques. The first

*Corresponding author. E-mail: li_rmvr@hotmail.com.

Abbreviations: RAMA, by its abbreviation in Spanish, Automatic Network of Atmospheric Monitoring; AA, Adaptive Algorithm; TC, Toluca Center; SL, San Lorenzo Tepatitlan; SM, San Mateo Atenco.

one separates the data set in k groups, and the second one forms a set of several differentiation levels (MacKay, 2003). We can find different useful methods for determining the quality of clusters (Bolshakova et al., 2005). These methods use numerical measures on the clustering results by inferring the quality and describing the situation of a certain pattern inside the cluster.

Several studies are developed for handling this problem. Some studies, in which the climatic change was studied, were: Secretaria del medio ambiente (2007) and Parra-Olea et al. (2005). In general, the proposals consider a regional study of the climatic changes (Travasso et al., 2008) for projecting, regionally, the global predictions of the climate models available and to identify the effects of these changes (Gutierrez and Pons, 2006; Tebaldi and Knutti, 2009). On the other hand, there are several researchers that use either data mining (Steinbach et al., 2002; Atem et al., 2004) or clustering methods in different ways. For example, for discovering ecosystem patterns (Steinbach et al., 2001; Kumar et al., 2001), and improving the algorithm behavior (Gutiérrezr and Rodríguez, 2004), proposals were made on the weighted clustering method for analyzing infrequent patterns, or extreme events in the weather forecasts.

Based on the exposed patterns given previously, the object of this study was to analyze and discover the information that was inside the data bases provided by RAMA-Toluca. In particular, we analyzed the meteorological variables using clustering algorithms, for identifying the grouping in each year of the studied period (2001 – 2008). That is to say, we can know the distribution of the days between the groups and, in consequence, the seasons identified by the clustering methods. The paper is organized as follows: The clustering methods used in the study are exposed, followed by a description of the cluster validation algorithms which allow a corroboration of the group quality. Then the study zone and the meteorological parameters evaluated are given in detail, after which the experimental results are shown. Finally, the concluding remarks and the open lines of study are given.

CLUSTERING METHODS

The clustering process consists of a division of the data set in groups with similar objects. For measuring the similarity between objects, usually we use different distance measures, which are subsequently described in this work.

Adaptive algorithm

The adaptive algorithm (AA) is an incremental heuristic method which uses two parameters: distance threshold for creating groups (t) and a T fraction which determines the total confidence ( ). The main function of the algorithm is to create groups based on t (weighted by). However, the first group settles down arbitrarily. The main processes of the AA are the following (Bow, 1992):

(i) The first group is determined arbitrarily.

(ii) When a sample was assigned to a certain group, the cluster center must be recalculated. This process can show that some samples change the cluster.
(iii) It is possible that the samples of a certain cluster change due to the iterative process.
(iv) The algorithm ends when there are no reassignments. At this time, the partition is considered stable.

K-means algorithm

K-means is a partition algorithm. In this way, similar samples are in the same cluster, and dissimilar samples are in different clusters (MacKay, 2003). In the process, the algorithm needs to define a unique parameter k. K defines the number of groups that will be found in the data set. For this, the K-means uses an iterative process, which starts by defining a sample prototype (centroid) as a cluster representative and is defined as the average of their samples. Next, the sample is assigned to the close centroid using a metric, commonly known as the Euclidean distance. Later, the centroid is recalculated using the new group formed. This process continues until a criterion is obtained, for example, the epochs number, no more replacements, etc (Garre et al., 2007).

The algorithm is faster and efficient; nevertheless, it has several limitations, such as, the a-priori knowledge about the cluster number inside the data set.

Validation algorithms

The cluster analysis consists of the clustering result evaluation, in order to find the partition that better fits the data (Halkidi et al., 2001). When the conglomerates were created, we needed to verify their quality through validation of algorithms (Bolshakova et al., 2005).

Cohesion

The cohesion can be defined as the sum of the proximities regarding the prototype (centroid) of a cluster (Bolshakova et al., 2005). The cohesion is given by:

$$Cohesion\ (Ci) = \sum_{x \notin C_i} proximity\ (x, C_i) \qquad (1)$$

Where x is the sample contained in cluster i; Ci, is the centroid of cluster i; and proximity is the squared Euclidean distance.

Separation

The separation between two clusters can be measured by the proximity of the prototypes (centroids) of two clusters. The separation is given by the next equation:

$$Separation\ (Ci) = proximity\ (C_i, C) \qquad (2)$$

Where Ci is the centroid of cluster i; C, is the general prototype (centroid) and *proximity* can be any metric (Tan et al., 2006).

Silhouette coefficient

This method combines two methods, which are cohesion and

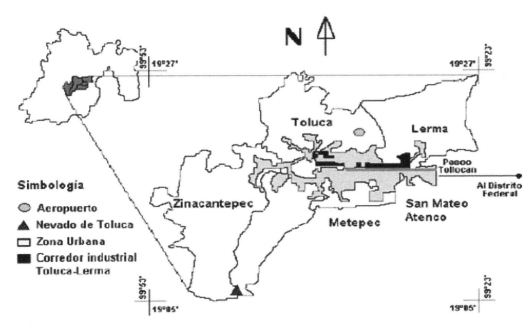

Figure 1. ZMVT Location (Extracted from Secretaria de medio ambiente, 2007).

Table 1. Samples by station and year.

Station	2001	2002	2003	2004	2005	2006	2007	2008	Total
CE	8627	8746	8528	8567	8104	6910	5546	2661	57689
SL	8171	8639	8692	8549	8441	7973	4087	7761	62313
SM	8213	8480	8478	8535	7909	8316	7828	595	58354

separation. The following steps explain the coefficient operation for a single object (Halkidi et al., 2001).

i.) For the i-'th object, the distance average is calculated for all objects that are in the same cluster, which is called value ai.
ii.) For i-'th object and any cluster that is empty, the distance average is calculated for all the objects in the next cluster. Finding the minimum value, regarding all clusters, is called bi.
iii.) For i-'th object, the silhouette coefficient is si = (bi - ai)/max(ai,bi). Where max(ai, bi) will be the maximum value between ai and bi.

The silhouette coefficient can vary between -1 and 1, and the maximum value of the coefficient is 1 when ai = 0. A negative value is undesirable because this corresponds to the case when ai is the average distance between the points in the cluster, and it is also greater than bi, which is the minimum average distance to the points of the other clusters. The best result desired is when the silhouette coefficient is positive ($ai < bi$) and when ai is close to 0.

To calculate the silhouette coefficient average (of one cluster), we take the coefficient average of all the points inside the cluster. A general measurement of a conglomerate can be obtained by calculating the silhouette coefficient average of all the points (Tan et al., 2006).

Study zone

In the ZMVT, the air quality has been measured since 1993 with 7 monitoring stations, and it includes seven municipalities in three zones which are shown in Figure 1. The monitoring stations store environmental data. For this research, the meteorological variables studied are: TMP (temperature), HR (relative humidity), PA (atmospheric pressure), RS (solar radiation), VV (wind speed) and DV (wind direction).

The data present several problems related to the monitoring station. These problems complicate their study, some or which are: faults in the sensor or its hard movements that are provoked by the wind or other causes. Some meteorological values are inconsistent with the reality (for example, a temperature of 80 °C in winter) that the values are not captured completely (lost data). When the RAMA administrator identifies some of these problems, it marks the record for his later consideration.

In this way, the solution found was to choose the average value between the last and next real data for each feature. With this, we obtain a value in the real rank. On the other hand, when a sample loses more than 50% of the information, it is considered as noise and as such, it is eliminated.

The data, used for the study, were provided by 3 monitoring stations that showed different characteristics like: a great record number and a little lost of information. The monitoring stations are: Toluca Center (TC), San Lorenzo Tepatitlan (SL) and San Mateo Atenco (SM). Table 1 shows the number of samples by station and the number patterns per year in each station.

EXPERIMENTAL RESULTS

Here, the results of the clustering algorithms studied on

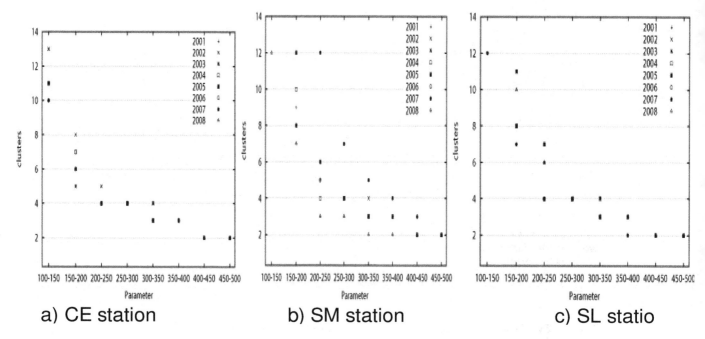

a) CE station   b) SM station   c) SL statio

Figure 2. Cluster number using the adaptive algorithm.

the data base provided by RAMA-Toluca are shown. Firstly, the data were filtered and, next, the clustering algorithms were applied: k-means and adaptive algorithm.

Some specifications for the k-means algorithm are the next: the initial seed was chosen randomly. The k value where k =2, 3, 4 for each data base (Table 1). On the other hand, for the adaptive algorithm, different thresholds by the data base were applied, and they were: 100 - 150, 150 - 200, 200 - 250, 250 - 300, 300 - 350, 350 - 400, 400 - 450, and 450 - 500, for the threshold and T-value, respectively. Figure 2 showed how the samples were grouped and how many groups were formed. The validity of the conglomerates quality, using the silhouette coefficient, is displayed in Figure 3. In Figures 2 and 3, it is possible to observe that when the clusters number is diminished, the quality is greater. This indicates that the best clustering is when the algorithm finds two clusters. On the other hand, Table 2 includes the samples grouped in each clustering results (in the case of two clusters).

The figures reflect the convergence existing between these two clustering algorithms, when both of them are found in the two groups. Regarding the groups' samples, it is possible to observe that one of the groups is bigger than the other one with almost a double quantity of the samples.

Conclusions

Throughout the year, the climate changes according to the cultural season. The hypothesis establishes that there

are four seasons in one year. For this reason, we expect to find four conglomerates in the data set provided by RAMA-Toluca, because of the similarities between the samples of each season. Nevertheless, with the analysis exposed here, it was possible to identify that with the meteorological data analyzed, the clustering algorithms found only two great groups. In order to validate the quality of the clusters, the silhouette coefficient, cohesion and separation were used.

The preliminary results, exposed here, could indicate that in the meteorological data studied, the values of the samples of each year have similar features, mainly, of two seasons. In addition, due to the insignificant differences from each conglomerate, it is possible to suppose that, any climatic variation could happen before the year 2001.

With these results, it is possible to establish the bases of future works in this important topic, but several questions needs an answer: Is the cluster number equal to the season number? Is the behavior due to the climatic change? For answering these questions and obtaining a wider analysis, we came in contact with meteorological experts. During this time, we were in touch with the environmental engineering group of the Technological Institute of Toluca and Environment Secretariat in Toluca for improving the analysis. As such, we are sure that in a future work, we are going to expose the new analysis.

About the research in process, we are working with the unsupervised neural network SOM (Tan et al., 2006) for comparing several scenarios, for example, between 2001 and 2002 to 2008. The linear regression and correlation analysis is done by another study in process that would

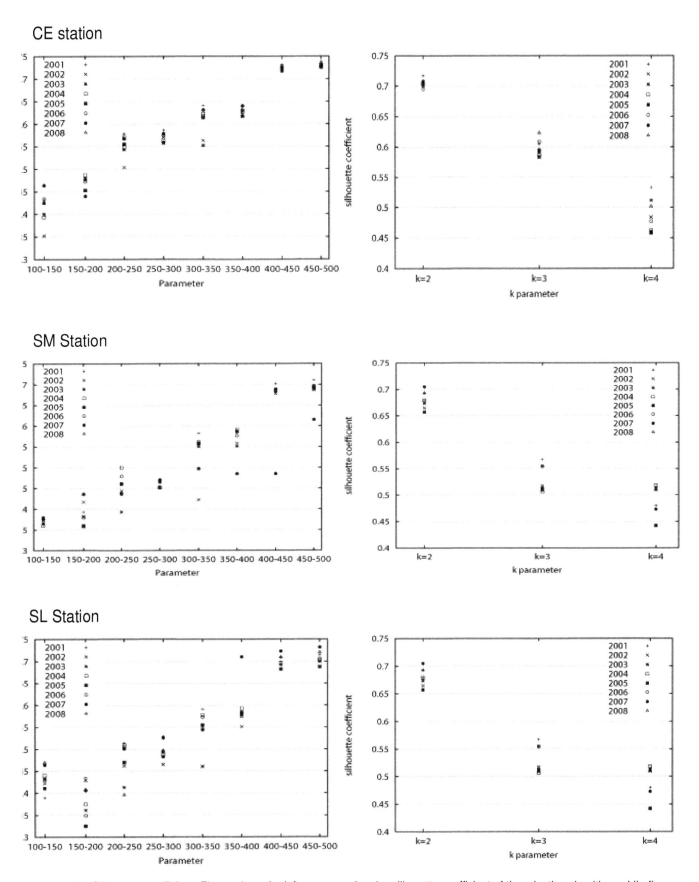

Figure 3. The Silhouette coefficient. Figures from the left correspond to the silhouette coefficient of the adaptive algorithm, while figures from the right are the silhouette coefficient of the k-means algorithm.

Table 2. Samples grouped by cluster.

Algorithm	Year	SL		SM		CE	
		Cluster 1	Cluster 2	Cluster 1	Cluster 2	Cluster 1	Cluster 2
Adaptive	2001	6451	1719	6638	1575	6832	1795
	2002	6894	1745	6930	1550	6832	1795
	2003	6924	1768	6898	1580	6781	1747
	2004	6865	1684	6959	1576	6856	1711
	2005	6757	1684	6402	1507	6474	1630
	2006	6475	1498	6790	1526	5539	1371
	2007	3263	824	6215	1613	4419	1127
	2008	6305	1356	512	83	2067	594
K-means	2001	2207	5964	2241	5972	2193	6434
	2002	2294	6345	6294	2186	6572	2174
	2003	2346	6346	6233	2245	6387	2141
	2004	2306	6243	2272	6263	2141	6426
	2005	2254	6187	2116	5793	6057	2047
	2006	5953	2020	6161	2155	1845	5066
	2007	3098	989	6293	1535	1407	4139
	2008	5933	1728	427	168	753	1908

soon be finished.

The open lines point to the study of other data bases with information of more years and of the other states or countries. Also, it is possible to include the analysis of other years and other climatic data bases, as well as to use other algorithms such as ISODATA and DBSCAN (Martín et al., 1996). In the same way, we analyze the convenience of including other validation methods and studying methods for handling the lost data.

ACKNOWLEDGMENTS

This work has been partially supported by grants: INV-2010-XX (from the Spanish 2010-UJI promotion plan), Reactor operation UR-001 (from the ININ), PROMEP 103.5/09/4195 (from the Mexican SEP), 2933/2010U (from the UAEM) and SDMAIA-010 (from the TESJO project).

REFERENCES

Atem OI, Luengo F, Cofiño AS, Gutíerrez JM (2004). Grid oriented implementation of selforganizing maps for data mining in meteorology. In: In meteorology, in grid computing. Proc. of 1st European Across GRIDs Conference, pp. 163–170.

Bolshakova N, Azuaje F, Cunningham P (2005). An integrated tool for microarray data clustering and cluster validity assessment. Bioinformatics, 21(4): 451–455.

Bow ST (1992). Pattern Recognition and Image Preprocessing Marcel Dekker Inc.

Garre M, Cuadrado JJ, Sicilia MA, Rodriguez D, Rejas R (2007). Comparison of different algorithms from clustering in the cost estimation in the development of software. Revista Española de Innovación, Calidad e Ingeniería del Software, 3(1): 6–22.

Gutiérrezr JM, Cofiño AS, Cano R, Rodríguez MA (2004). Clustering methods for statistical downscaling in short-range weather forecasts. Monthly Weather Rev., 132(9): 2169-2183.

Gutierrez JM, Pons MR (2006). Numerical modeling of climate change: Scientific basis, uncertainties and projections for the iberian peninsula. Cuaternario Geomorfología, 20(2-4): 15-28.

Halkidi M, Batistakis Y, Vazirgiannis M (2001). On clustering validation techniques. J. Intelligent Inf. Syst., 17(2-3): 107–145.

Kotsiantis, SB, Pintelas PE (2004). Recent advances in clustering: A brief survey. WSEAS Transactions on Infor. Sci. Appl., 1: 73–81.

Kumar V, Steinbach M, Tan P, Klooster S, Potter C, Torregrosa A (2001). Mining scientific data: Discovery of patterns in the global climate system. In Proc. of the Joint Statistical Meetings.

MacKay DJC (2003). Information Theory, Inference, and Learning Algorithms. Cambridge University Press.

Martín E, Hans PK, Jörg S, Xiaowei X (1996). A density-based algorithm for discovering clusters in large spatial databases with noise. In Proc. of the 2nd International Conference on Knowledge Discovery and Data Mining (KDD-96), pp. 226–231.

Parra-Olea G, Martínez-Meyer E, Pérez-Ponce G (2005). Forecasting climate change effects on salamander distribution in the highlands of central Mexico. Biotropica, 37(2): 202–208.

Secretaria del medio ambiente (2007). Aire Limpio: Programa para el Valle de Toluca 2007-2011. Edomexico.

Staines F (2007). Cambio climático: interpretando el pasado para entender el presente. Ciencia Ergo Sum, 14(4): 345–351.

Steinbach M, Tan P, Vipin K, Klooster S, Potter C, Torregrosa A (2002). Discovery of climate indices using clustering. In: In Proc. of the 9th ACM SIGKDD International Conference on Knowledge Discovery and Data Mining, pp. 24–27.

3

Construction and adjustment of differential polynomial neural network

Ladislav Zjavka

Faculty of Management Science and Informatics, University of Žilina, Univerzitná 8215/1, 010 01 Žilina, Slovakia.
E-mail: lzjavka@gmail.com.

Artificial neural networks in general are used to identify patterns according to their entire relationship, responding to related patterns with a similar output of applying absolute values of variables. However, a lot of real data contain some unknown relations of variables. Learning of these dependencies could be a new way of modelling complex systems instead of usual time series prediction based on pattern similarity. Differential polynomial neural network, which constructs a differential equation of fractional terms using multi-parametric polynomial functions, is a new type of neural network developed by the author. Its functionality is based on principles, which are applied in human brain learning. The brain does not utilize absolute values of variables, but relative ones, which are created by time-delayed dynamic periodic activation functions of biological neurons. They take part in differential equation composition as partial derivative terms, describing a relative change of particular dependent variables.

Key words: Polynomial neural network, dependence of variables identification, differential equation approximation, rational integral function, modelling of complex system.

INTRODUCTION

Artificial neural networks (ANN) are trained to classify certain patterns into groups, and then they are used to identify the new ones, which were never presented before. If ANN is trained, for example, to identify a shape, it can correctly classify only the incomplete or similar patterns as compared to the trained ones (Kvasnička et al., 1997), but in a case the shape is moved or its size is changed in the input matrix of variables the neural network identification will fail. The principal lack of the ANN identification in general is its disability of input pattern generalization. It utilizes only the absolute values of variables, but these can differ enormously, while their relations may be the same. ANN is in principle a simplified form of polynomial neural network (PNN), whose combinations of variables are missing. These partly describe the data relations in polynomials through exponential functions, created by multiplications.

A trial should be made in looking at the vector of the input variables as a no "pattern", but a bound dependent point set of N-dimensional space. Likewise, the ANN classified the patterns, while the study tried to identify any unknown relations of the data variables. The response of this neural network should be the same for all patterns (dependent sets), whose variables are performed with the

trained dependence. It does not matter what values they become, a multi-parametric non-linear function can describe their relations to each other. So, if neural network creates such a compound function, its neurons must apply some n-parametric polynomial functions to catch the partial dependence of its n-inputs. The biological neural cell (Figure 1) applies a similar principle and its dendrites collect signals that come from other neurons, but unlike the artificial neuron, the signals already interact in single branches (dendrites). This could be modelled with multiplications of some inputs in polynomials (PNN). Subsequently, these weighted combinations are summed in the cell of the body and are transformed using time-delayed dynamic periodic activation function (the activated neural cell generates a series of time-delayed output pulses, in response to its input signals) (Beňušková, 2002). The period of this function depends on some combinations of input variables and seems to represent the derivative part of a partial derivation of an entire polynomial (as a term of differential equation).

Polynomial neural network for dependence of variables identification (or differential polynomial neural network – D-PNN, because it constructs a differential equation)

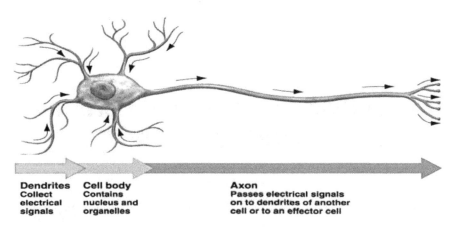

Figure 1. Biological neural cell.

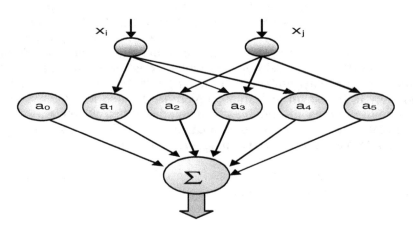

Figure 2. GMDH polynomial neuron.

describes a functional dependence of input variables that are not entirely patterns as ANN are. This could be regarded as a pattern abstraction, similar to the ones utilized by the brain, in which identification is not based on values of variables, but only relations of these. D-PNN forms its functional output as a generalization of input patterns.

GMDH polynomial neural network

General connection between input and output variables is expressed by the Volterra functional series, a discrete analogue of which Kolmogorov-Gabor polynomial (1) is:

$$y = a_0 + \sum_{i=1}^{m} a_i x_i + \sum_{i=1}^{m}\sum_{j=1}^{m} a_{ij} x_i x_j + \sum_{i=1}^{m}\sum_{j=1}^{m}\sum_{k=1}^{m} a_{ijk} x_i x_j x_k + .. \qquad (1)$$

m – number of variables
$X(x_1, x_2, ... , x_m)$ - vector of input variables

$A(a_1, a_2, ... , a_m), ...$ - vectors of parameters

This polynomial can approximate any stationary random sequence of observations and can be computed by either adaptive methods or the system of Gaussian normal equations (Ivakhnenko, 1971).

The starting point of the new neural network type D-PNN development was the GMDH polynomial neural network, created by a Ukrainian scientist Aleksey Ivakhnenko in 1968. When the back-propagation technique was not known yet, a technique called Group Method of Data Handling (GMDH) was developed for neural network structure design and parameters of polynomials adjustment. An attempt was made for it to have a resemblance with the Kolmogorov- Gabor polynomial (1) by using low order polynomials and (2) every pair of the input values (Galkin, 2000):

$$y' = a_0 + a_1 x_i + a_2 x_j + a_3 x_i x_j + a_4 x_i^2 + a_5 x_j^2 \qquad (2)$$

The GMDH neuron has two inputs and its output is a quadratic combination of 2 inputs, totalling 6 weights (Figure 2). Thus, GMDH network builds up a polynomial

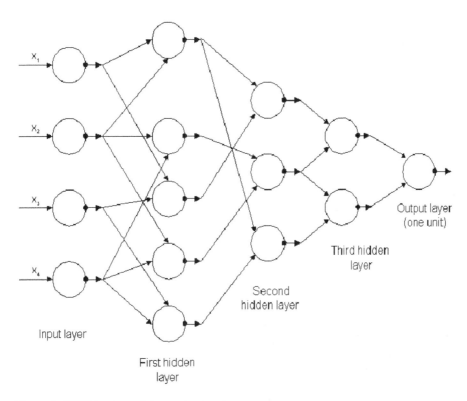

Figure 3. GMDH polynomial neural network.

(actually a multinomial) combination of the input components. The typical GMDH network (Figure 3) maps a vector input x to a scalar output y', which is an estimate of the true function of f(x) = y. Each neuron of the polynomial network fits its output to the desired value y for each input vector x from the training set. The manner in which this approximation is accomplished is through the use of linear regression (Galkin, 2000).

In the hope to capture the complexity of a process, this neural network attempts to decompose it into many simpler relationships, each described by a processing function of a single neuron (2). It defines an optimal structure of the complex system model, identifying non-linear relations between input and output variables. Polynomial neural network (PNN) is a flexible architecture, whose structure is developed through learning. The number of layers of the PNN is not fixed in advance, but it becomes dynamically meaningful that this self-organising network grows over the trained period (Oh et al., 2003).

Differential equation approximation

The basic idea of the author's D-PNN is to approximate a differential equation (3), which can define relations of variables (Hronec, 1958), with a special type of root fractional multi-parametric polynomials; for example Equations (4) and (5):

$$Y = a + \sum_{i=1}^{n} b_i \frac{\partial u}{\partial x_i} + \sum_{i=1}^{n} \sum_{j=1}^{n} c_{ij} \frac{\partial^2 u}{\partial x_i \partial x_j} + ... = const. \quad (3)$$

$u = f(x_1, x_2, ... , x_n)$ - function of input variables
$a, B(b_1, b_2, ..., b_n), C(c_{11}, c_{12}, ...)$ - parameters.

Elementary methods of the differential equation (DE) solution express the solution in special elementary functions – polynomials (such as Bessel's functions or power series). Numerical integration of differential equations is based on their approximation using:

(a) Rational integral functions.
(b) Trigonometric series.

The most simplest way for this integration have been selected using the method of integral analogues, by replacing mathematical operators in equations with a ratio of pertinent values (Kuneš et al., 1989).

$$y_i = \frac{\left(a_0 + a_1 x_1 + a_2 x_2 + a_2 x_3 + a_4 x_1 x_2 + a_5 x_1 x_3 + a_6 x_2 x_3 + a_7 x_1 x_2 x_3\right)^{1/3}}{\left(b_0 + b_1 x_1 + b_2 x_2 + b_3 x_1 x_2\right)^{1/2}} \quad (4)$$

$$y_i = \frac{\left(a_0 + a_1 x_1 + a_2 x_2 + ... + a_n x_n + a_{n+1} x_1 x_2 + ...\right)^{1/n}}{\left(b_0 + b_1 x_1 + ...\right)^{1/m}} \quad (5)$$

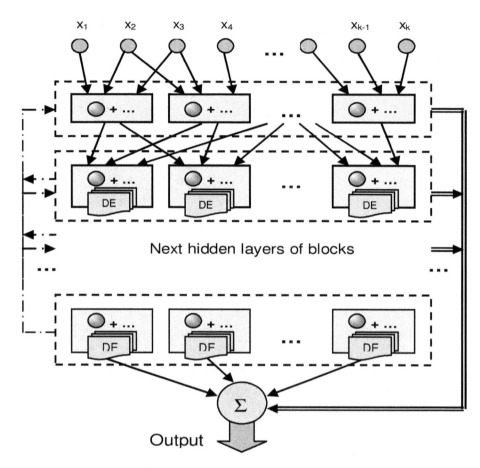

Figure 4. Differential polynomial neural network.

n – combination degree of n-input variables of the numerator.
m – combination degree of denominator ($m<n$).

The fractional polynomials (4 and 5), which can describe a partial dependence of n-input variables of each neuron, are applied as terms of the DE (3) composition. They partly create an unknown multi-parametric non-linear function, which codes relations of input variables. The numerator of Equations (4) and (5) is a polynomial of complete n-input combination degree of a single neuron and it realizes a new function z of formula (6). The denominator of Equations (4) and (5) is a derivative part, which gives a partial mutual change of some neuron input variables and its polynomial combination degree m is less than n. It arose from the partial derivation of the complete n-variable polynomial by competent variable(s). In general, it is possible to express this approximation in formula (6) (Hronec, 1958):

$$Y = w_0 + w_1 \frac{\partial z}{\partial x_1} + w_2 \frac{\partial z}{\partial x_2} + ... + w_n \frac{\partial z}{\partial x_n} + w_{n+1} \frac{\partial z}{\partial x_1 \partial x_2} + ... = const \quad (6)$$

z – function of n-input variables

w_i – weights of terms

Each layer of the D-PNN consists of blocks of neurons. Block contains derivative neurons, one for the variables combination of each fractional polynomial (4) and (5), thereby defining a partial derivative dependent change of some input variables (Figure 4). The root functions of denominators are lower than n, according to the combination degree which take the polynomials of neurons (4) and (5) into competent power degree. Neurons do not affect the block output but are applied only for the total output calculation (DE composition). Each block also contains a single polynomial (without the derivative part), which forms its output entrance into the next hidden layer. Each neuron has 2 vectors of adjustable parameters (a and b) and each block contains 1 vector of adjustable parameters of the output polynomial. Inputs of constant combination degree ($n=2,3,...$) forming particular combination of variables, enter each block, where they are substituted into polynomials. Therefore, it is necessary to adjust not only the polynomial parameters, but the D-PNN's structure too. This means some neurons, in terms of role of the DE, have to be left out.

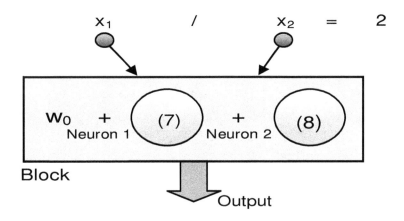

Figure 5. Identification of a constant quotient of 2 variables ($x_1 = 2x_2$).

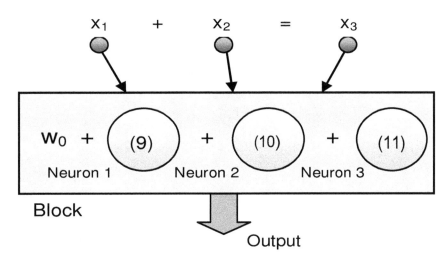

Figure 6. Identification of the sum dependence.

Following the examples, simplicity is assumed only for linear dependencies of variables. If there is an occurrence of a non linear dependence in the input data, square power exponent variables would likely extend the combination polynomials and could be applied also as competent derivative terms.

Identification of simple dependencies of variables

When considering a very simple dependence of the 2-input variables, multiplicity is constant (for example = 2). D-PNN will contain only 1 block of 2 polynomial neurons (7) and (8) as terms of DE (Figure 5). As the input variables do not change constantly, it is necessary to add both terms (fractional polynomial of derivative variable x_1 and x_2) in the DE (block). D-PNN will learn this relation according to samples of the training data set by means of genetic algorithm (GA).

$$y_1 = w_1 \frac{(a_0 + a_1 x_1 + a_2 x_2 + a_3 x_1 x_2)^{\frac{1}{2}}}{b_0 + b_1 x_1} \tag{7}$$

$$y_2 = w_2 \frac{(a_0 + a_1 x_1 + a_2 x_2 + a_3 x_1 x_2)^{\frac{1}{2}}}{b_0 + b_1 x_2} \tag{8}$$

Consider a more complicated dependence, where 2 variables depend on the 3rd variable. For example, the sum of the first 2 variables equals the 3rd one ($x_1 + x_2 = x_3$). This task seems to be very simple, but it is rather difficult for D-PNN to learn it. The complete DE (for derivatives 1 and 2-combinations of block) consists of 6 terms (neurons), but only 3 of them will be enough for the derivative terms x_3 (9), $x_1 x_3$ (10) and $x_2 x_3$ (11). If other terms (neurons) are added, the D-PNN will work amiss (Figure 6).

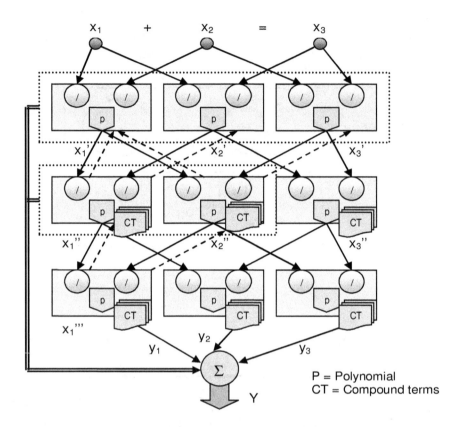

Figure 7. Multi-layered D-PNN with 2-variable combinations of blocks.

$$y_1 = w_1 \frac{(a_0 + a_1 x_1 + a_2 x_2 + a_3 x_3 + a_4 x_1 x_2 + \ldots + a_7 x_1 x_2 x_3)^{1/3}}{b_0 + b_1 x_3} \qquad (9)$$

$$y_2 = w_2 \frac{(a_0 + a_1 x_1 + a_2 x_2 + a_3 x_3 + a_4 x_1 x_2 + \ldots + a_7 x_1 x_2 x_3)^{1/3}}{(b_0 + b_1 x_1 + b_2 x_3 + b_3 x_1 x_3)^{1/2}} \qquad (10)$$

$$y_3 = w_3 \frac{(a_0 + a_1 x_1 + a_2 x_2 + a_3 x_3 + a_4 x_1 x_2 + \ldots + a_7 x_1 x_2 x_3)^{1/3}}{(b_0 + b_1 x_2 + b_2 x_3 + b_3 x_2 x_3)^{1/2}} \qquad (11)$$

This 3-variable dependence is described by more complicated exponential functions. The D-PNN as well is charged by the possible 2-sided change of input variables. For example *1+9=10* is the same sum as *9+1=10*. The 2-combination polynomials of numerators, which could improve the D-PNN functionality, can also be applied. The principal phase of its adjustment resides in the elimination of some neurons (in terms of DE).

Multi-layered D-PNN

It is possible to solve this problem of multi-layered D-PNN with 2-combination blocks of variables. Even though, in this way, more mistakes can occur by identification, more

complex DE would be created (that is, much more terms arise). However, it can be clearly seen that the D-PNN operates. If the sum of the first two variables is less than it should be, the output of the D-PNN is less than the desired round and the other hand round. So, it is shown that a separating plane is detached from the relative "classes", which have the same characteristic (dependence); likewise, it is current by ANN's pattern identification. The problem of the multi-layered D-PNN construction reside creates every partial combination term for a complete DE in utilizing some fixed low combination degrees (*2, 3*), while the amount of variables is higher.

Each block of the D-PNN takes part in the total network output calculation (forms the partial DE terms) and utilizes its basic and extended neurons with back connected blocks of previous layers. The single adjustable polynomial (Figure 7) without a derivative part creates the block output (applied in the next hidden layer), but the neurons are applied only for the total DE composition. The blocks of the 2nd and the following hidden layers extend the basic DE terms (neurons) using their additional neurons, outputs and inputs of back connected blocks of the previous layers to create compound terms (Figure 7) of the DE. Consider for instance the 1st block of the last hidden layer, which takes its own neurons as 2 basic terms (12) of the DE (6).

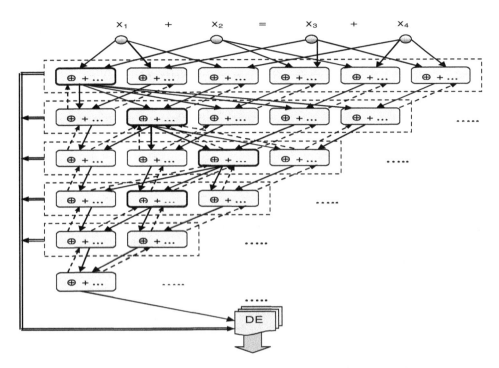

Figure 8. One of the "wedge" networks of the 4-variable 2-combination block D-PNN.

Subsequently, it creates 4 extended terms of the 2nd (previous) hidden layer, using reverse output polynomials and inputs of bound blocks. It joins these 2 blocks and creates 4 fractional terms of the DE for 4 derivative input variables of 2 previous blocks, for example (13).

$$y_1^1 = w_1 \frac{\sqrt{{}^1x_1'''}}{2*(b_0 + b_1 x_1'')} = w_1 \frac{\left(a_0 + a_1 x_1'' a_2 x_2'' + a_3 x_1'' x_2''\right)^{1/2}}{2*(b_0 + b_1 x_1'')} \qquad (12)$$

$$y_3^1 = w_3 \frac{\sqrt{\dfrac{{}^3x_1'''}{2*x_2''}}}{2*(c_0 + c_1 x_1')} \qquad (13)$$

$$y_7^1 = w_7 \frac{\sqrt{\dfrac{\dfrac{{}^7x_1'''}{2*x_2''}}{2*x_2'}}}{2*(d_0 + d_1 x_1)} \qquad (14)$$

The back connection of the previous layer(s) is realized through the output polynomials of the linked 2nd (or 1st) layer opposite the blocks, forming fractional parts in numerators of formulas (13) and (14). Likewise, terms can be created for the 1st hidden layer (14). The 3 linked blocks, forming 8 terms of the DE were attached to the layer and were performed well by a recursive algorithm. The multiplication of "2*" (or higher) in the denominators of formulas (12), (13) and (14) is applied in decreasing

the D-PNN's total output value. It was not every term that was used in the complete DE; some of them were necessarily left out. This indicates "0" or "1" in the neurons of blocks and is easy to use them as genes of GA.

Construction of "wedge" networks of the D-PNN

It can be seen that the D-PNN (Figure 7) substantially consists of 3 overlaying "wedge" networks (WN), each going back out from the blocks of the last hidden layer and gradually attaching to the derivative variables of previous layers.

The D-PNN of the 4 dependent input variables using 2-combination blocks will have totally 6 blocks of all input combination couples in the 1st hidden layer. It could have at first 6 hidden layers at the back of the 1st layer derivative input variables (from the last hidden layer blocks) and several overlaying WNs partly in the layer (Figure 8). The number of layers can be brought down to 4 and this decreases the number of combination blocks of WNs too. The number of combinations for each variable increases enormously in the next hidden layer. This had caused problems, which were solved by applying WNs, as only some of the blocks were created and used. Each block of the 1st hidden layer was taken as a dominant one and the 2nd layer blocks are created from its WN as a combination with the rest of its WN blocks. This way, the number of all WN blocks decreases in the next hidden layer until it reached just 1 block. Some WN

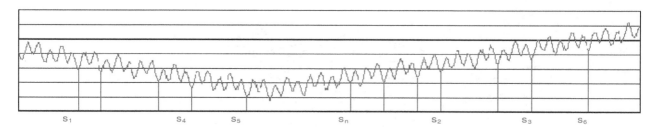

Figure 9. Example of a search space.

layers overlay each other and so the blocks can be used several times by different WNs (Figure 7). Block inputs of the 2nd and the following layers can be subsequently reconnected and this could compensate the missing combination blocks and WNs. However, it is better to preserve the rough structure of each WN, which warranted the best results. The connections of the complete 1st hidden layer blocks are fixed.

ADJUSTMENT OF THE D-PNN

Genetic algorithm

GA can perform the search of the fittest input combinations of higher layer blocks using permutation encoding of chromosomes, for example:

2nd layer: 12 15 23 24 26 34 35 4 5 ...
3rd layer: 13 14 18 19 23 25 36 3 10 ...

Only some of the entire possible DE terms can be applied. GA can again find their fittest combination using binary encoding of them and crossover operation for example:

0 1 0 0 1 0 1 0 1 ...

If too many DE terms (or WNs) are employed, an effect of "overlearning", could be shown when the dependence generalization "slides off" (turns) into pattern identification (which is undesirable). The total output error of training data set decreases, but the dependence generalization is not reached. Terms of higher layer blocks seem to influence strongly the right dependence identification.

Exact parameter calculation

The adjustment is another problem that will be solved besides the D-PNN's construction. A trial could be made to calculate the precise polynomial parameter change according to total and partial output errors. This method requires exactly the rules of the DE term's behaviour to know. The Hebb's delta rule (Kvasnička et al., 1997) has

been applied by the DE term parameter adjustment. So, the bigger the values of the input variables of a term, the bigger its polynomial parameter change (+ or − according to the output error) will be. The parameter change must be given relatively to the absolute wide range of the input variables' values and with regard to nominator or denominator setting in fractions, for example, (15), (16) and (17) - for basic neurons of the 1st block of the D-PNN's last hidden layer (Figure 7). This way, the total output error can be brought down to certain limit, but the effect of dependence generalization is not shown finally (or slightly). There might be some other unknown principles of the DE term's functionality applied.

$$\partial_0 = \frac{a_0}{\dfrac{\sqrt{a_3 x_1^{''} x_2^{''}}}{b_0 + b_1 x_1^{''}}} \tag{15}$$

$$\partial_2 = \frac{x_2^{''}}{\dfrac{a_3 x_1^{''} x_2^{''}}{b_0 + b_1 x_1^{''}}} \tag{16}$$

$$\partial_3 = \frac{\sqrt{x_1^{''} x_2^{''}}}{b_0 + b_1 x_1^{''}} \tag{17}$$

Evolution strategy

Parameters of polynomials are represented by real numbers, in which initial values are randomly generated from the interval of *0.5* and *1.5*. A chromosome is a sequence of their values, which can be easily mutated. Polynomial outputs can not be a negative value, but parameters can. Evolution strategy (ES) creates descendants usually by modification (mutation) of only 1 individual; because it need not use the operation of crossover. Problem solving can be expressed as looking for the minimum of error (fitness) function of a search space (Figure 9) (Obitko, 1998). There can arise many local solutions, caused by plenty of possible combinations of block inputs that are composed of DE terms (only some of them may be employed). The study's ES is based on evolving 1 individual, whose parameters are in the 1st generation (cycle), mutated only randomly with decreasing learning coefficients. As a result, each cycle creates a solution that is finished with high probability in a local error minimum. These local solutions, form "learning schemes" (LS), give directions of parameter changes in the next generations. Fitter solutions (with lower error) can arise for each LS in the next generation and can replace the existing older LS. LS define the particular parameter changes that are applied simultaneously on the actually modified 1 individual (18), besides its mutation. So each actual individual utilises the existing partial local solutions of LS to find a better (global) error minimum.

$$X_{act} = X_{act} + E * (X_{lsi} - X_{act}) \qquad (18)$$

$X(a_1, a_2,..., a_n)$ - vectors of parameters; act=actual, $lsi=$ i-th LS; $E = <0, 1>$ - learning rate

Evolution algorithm

Difference evolution algorithm (DEA) was developed for optimizing real parameter functions. The main difference between DEA and GA is that GA gives more importance to crossover operation, while DEA's main operation is based on the differences of randomly sampled pairs of solutions in the population. DEA generates new parameter vectors by adding the weighted difference vector between 2 population members and a 3rd member. If the resulting vector yields a lower objective function value, the newly generated vector replaces the vector that it was compared with. Like other evolutionary algorithms, the performance of DEA deteriorates with the increase in dimensionality of the objective function. $D = 10\sim20$ can be applied to individuals of each population $P(x_1, x_2, ..., x_D)$. Each individual from the current population is presented as N-dimensional vector, when N corresponds to the number of required variables. The core of DEA is built in the strategy of creating mutation vector $u(u_1, u_2, ..., u_n)$. The most frequent strategy applies weighted difference from randomly chosen solutions (19), to each random individual from target population P. Another strategy can generate mutation vector u from the best solution x_{min} in the previous and present population (20). Control factor F is entered from interval $[0, 1]$ (Hájek, 2010).

$$u = x_{r1} + F(x_{r2} - x_{r3}) \qquad r_1 \neq r_2 \neq r_3 \neq i \qquad (19)$$

$$u = x_{min} + F(x_{r1} - x_{r2}) \qquad r_1 \neq r_2 \neq min \neq i \qquad (20)$$

After creating a mutation u (called perturbed or "noise"

vector), it is possible to make y_i (trial vector) a descendant from parents u and x_i using crossover operation according to following Equation (21).

$$y_{j,i} = \begin{cases} u_j & if\ rand_j \leq CR \ \lor \ j = k \\ x_{j,i} & otherwise \end{cases} \qquad (21)$$

Variable $j = 1, 2, ..., n$, $k \in \{1, .., n\}$ is a random parameter's index chosen for each i, whereas CR (frequency of crossing) is from interval [0, 1]. This last parameter represents a probability of crossover that influences the generation of the perturbed individual u, by controlling the amount of genes, which will be changed from the target individual x_i to the trial one y_i (Ali et al., 2009).

$$X_{i,G+1} = \begin{cases} Y_{i,G}\ if\ f(Y_i) \leq f(X_i) \\ X_{i,G} & otherwise \end{cases} \qquad (22)$$

The population for the next generation is selected from the target individual x_i in the current generation and its corresponding trial vector y_i. Each individual of the trial population is compared with its counterpart in the current population (22). The one with the lower objective function value will survive from the tournament selection to the population of the next generation. As a result, all individuals of the next generation are as good as better than their counterparts in the current generation. In DEA, the trial vector was not compared to the individuals in the current generation, but was compared only against 1 individual, which was its counterpart (Ali et al., 2009).

DEA can be simply described as follows:

1. Create 'initial' random population $P(x_1, x_2, ..., x_d)$
2. Create 'mutation' vector $u(u_1, u_2, ..., u_n)$
3. Create 'new solution' y_i by combining parents u and x_i
4. If $f(y_i) <= f(x_i)$, then replace x_i by y_i (f = target function)
5. Repeat until the stop condition □

There is no need considering the output of the D-PNN, so it is adjusted to an average random value according to the initial parameters. Same applies to all samples of the training data set. Then the response to all input vectors, performed with the trained dependence of variables, should follow the same trend too. The output error of all training data samples (22) must be computed relatively to the present average output value (y_{Avg}), as omission of neurons (DE terms) and reconnecting inputs of blocks influence its computation. The omitted neuron (term) would always decrease it without employing the denominator of (22).

Table 1. Responses to random input vectors with dependent variables.

Input vector	Output
10 + 42 = 6 + 46	3.901
20 + 2 = 21 + 1	4.142
45 + 20 = 38 + 27	3.994
2 + 40 = 38 + 4	3.896
25 + 13 = 8 + 30	3.926
17 + 3 = 4 + 16	3.898

Table 2. Responses to random independent input vector variables.

Input vector	Output	Input vector	Output
58 + 10 < 24 + 54	3.845	57 + 17 > 15 + 49	4.205
22 + 40 < 37 + 35	3.691	21 + 26 > 6 + 31	4.612
29 + 50 < 51 + 38	3.740	52 + 32 > 4 + 70	5.632
22 + 53 < 51 + 34	3.704	58 + 41 > 3 + 86	6.345
59 + 60 < 36 + 93	3.874	32 + 32 > 51 + 3	7.687
24 + 39 < 44 + 29	3.745	41 + 10 > 34 + 7	4.667
36 + 56 < 54 + 48	3.747	49 + 41 > 55 + 25	4.265
39 + 26 < 56 + 19	3.788	50 + 33 > 9 + 64	4.738
34 + 10 < 6 + 48	3.756	14 + 44 > 19 + 29	4.151
21 + 54 < 28 + 57	3.654	52 + 6 > 20 + 28	4.173

$$E = \frac{1}{M}\sum_{i=1}^{M}\frac{(y_i - y_{Avg})^2}{y_{Avg}} \to \min \qquad (22)$$

The advantage of the D-PNN is its ability to be trained only with small input-output data samples (likewise, the GMDH polynomial neural network does) to learn any dependence. The training data set can consist of the following 6 input vectors, for example:

{1 + 22 = 20 + 3}, {16 + 1 = 2 + 15}, {34 + 3 = 30 + 7}, {60 + 30 = 42 + 48}, {5 + 25 = 2 + 28}, {2 + 5 = 4 + 3}

A separating plane detaching relative "classes" (Tables 1 and 2), which are of the same characteristic can be noticed (if the sum of the 1st couple is less than the 2nd one, the output is less and opposite). The searching space contains a great amount of local error solutions, which DEA can finish easily. This problem is caused by a lot of possible combinations of block inputs and is composed of DE terms (only some of them are employed), whose selection is a critical phase of the D-PNN's construction, besides the simultaneous parameter adjustment of DEA. The three previously described algorithms will be alternated by D-PNN's formation as follows:

1. Construction: GA searching of input combinations of blocks (repeat until an improvement is seen).
2. Selection: GA searching of the fittest DE term combination (repeat until improved performance).
3. DEA parameter and weight adjustment (repeat until it reached the desired error value, <).

In the beginning, the study was predominated by the 1st GA of the D-PNN's construction, while it was subsequently followed by the 2nd GA of the DE term selection and finally, by the adjustment of the DEA. Weights of terms are initialised with value *1.0* and adjusted likewise by the parameters of polynomials in separate cycles of DEA.

CONCLUSION

D-PNN is a new neural network type designed by the author, and can be used to identify any unknown dependencies of data set variables (but not the entire patterns as the ANNs do). Like the brain, it does not utilize absolute values of variables, but relative ones. This identification could be regarded as a pattern of abstraction (or generalization), similar to that utilized by the human brain according to data relations. However, it applies the approximation with time-delayed periodic activation functions of biological neurons in high dynamic system of behaviour (Beňušková, 2002). D-PNN constructs a differential equation, which describes a system of dependent variables, with rational integral polynomial functions. The problem of the partial differential terms' composition of the multi-layered D-PNN is inherent in the method of creation of all possible combinations (compound fractions) and the realization of a partial derivation (describing a dependence) of some input variables (through fractional or periodic functions).

Relations of some data variables describe a lot of complex systems, in that D-PNN could model their behaviour and utilise the unknown generalized relations of data. DE approximation would better describe the states of a complex system with dependent variables than a common time-series prediction, which is based on pattern similarity. Only linear dependencies of variables have been assumed for simplicity in the examples presented. If there is an occurrence of a non-linear dependence of the input data, it is likely that the square power exponent variables would be attached to combinations of the extended polynomials and applied also as competent derivative terms. A real data example might solve the weather forecast based on some trained data relations, which are used for calculating the next state of a system.

REFERENCES

Ivakhnenko AG (1971). Polynomial theory of complex systems. IEEE Trans. Syst., 1: 4.

Oh SK, Pedrycz W, Park BJ (2003). Polynomial neural networks architecture: analysis and design. Comput. Elect. Eng., 29(6): 703-725.

Kuneš J, Vavroch O, Franta V (1989). Principles of modelling. SNTL Praha (in Czech), p. 78.

Beňušková Ľ (2002). Neuron and brain. Cognitive sciences. Calligram Bratislava (in Slovak), p. 12.

Galkin I (2000). Polynomial neural networks. Materials for UML 91.531 Data mining course, University Mass Lowell. http://ulcar.uml.edu/~iag/CS/Polynomial-NN.html.

Hronec J (1958). Differential equations II. Publ. SAV, Bratislava (in Slovak), p. 8.

Kvasnička V, Beňušková Ľ., Pospíchal J, Farkaš I, Tiňo P, Kráľ A (1997). An introduction to the theory of neural networks. Bratislava, Iris (in Slovak), p. 54.

Obitko M (1998). Genetic algorithms. Hochshule fur Technik und Wirtschaft Dresden. http://labe.felk.cvut.cz/~obitko/ga.

Hájek J. (2010). Adaptation of an evolutionary algorithm in modeling electric circuit. Czech Technical University Publishing House, Prague. Acta Polytechnica, 50(1): 14-18.

Ali M, Pant M, Singh VP (2009). An improved differential evolution algorithm for real parameter optimization problem. Int. J. Recent Trends Eng., 1(5).

4

Implementation of a one-lead ECG human identification system on a normal population

Tsu-Wang (David) Shen[1]*, Willis J. Tompkins[2] and Yu Hen Hu[3]

[1]Department of Medical Informatics, Tzu Chi University, Hualien, Taiwan 701, Sec. 3, Jhong-Yang Rd., Hualien, 97004, Taiwan.
[2]Department of Biomedical Engineering, University of Wisconsin, Madison, WI, USA.
[3]Department of Electrical and Computer Engineering, University of Wisconsin, Madison, WI, USA.

The electrocardiogram (ECG) is not only a very useful diagnostic tool for clinical purposes, but also is a potential new biometric tool for human identification. The ECG may be useful as a biometric in the future, since it can easily be combined with other biometrics to provide a liveness check with little additional cost. This research focused on short-term, resting, Lead-I ECG signals recorded from the palms. A total of 168 young college volunteers were investigated for identification as a predetermined group. Fifty persons were randomly selected from this ECG biometric database as the development dataset. Then, the identification algorithm developed from this group was tested on the entire database. In this research, two algorithms were evaluated for ECG identification during system development. The algorithms included template matching and distance classification methods. Signal averaging was applied to generate ECG databases and templates for reducing the noise recorded with palm ECG signals. When a single algorithm was applied to the development dataset, the identification rate (that is, rank one probability) was up to 98% (49 out of 50 persons). However, when the prescreening process was added to construct a combined system model, the identification rate increased to 100% accuracy on the development dataset. The combined model formed our ECG biometric system model based on results from the development dataset. The identification rate was 95.3% when the same combined system model was tested on the entire ECG biometric database.

Key words: Biometrics, biometric liveness tests, electrocardiogram (ECG), ECG features, identification, template matching, distance classification.

INTRODUCTION

Biometric techniques provide one strategy for identity verification. Biometrics use anatomical, physiological or behavioral characteristics that are significantly different from person to person and are difficult to falsify. Several biometric systems that have been used commercially for human identity verification are facial geometry, fingerprints, and voice analysis. Unfortunately, these biometric systems may be deceived without liveness check (Willmore, 2002). ECG analysis (Tompkins, 1993; Webster, 1998) is not only a very useful diagnostic tool for clinical proposes, it is also potentially a good biometric for human identification. The ECG differs from person to person because of the position, size, and anatomy of the heart even among normal people. In addition, age, sex, relative body weight, chest geometry, and various other factors create ECG variants among persons with the same cardiac conditions (Simon and Eswaran, 1997). However, modeling those physiological conditions to ECG biometric features are extremely complicated. For instance, ECG features explain only 25.3% of the variability of the BMI (Shen et al., 2005).

Recently applying ECG for biometric identity recognition has drawn more attention in the research community which is expected to be more universal and

*Corresponding author. E-mail: tshen@mail.tcu.edu.tw.

be hard to mimic. Some pioneer studies showed that it is possible to identify people with a one-lead ECG signal on a small population (<30). Biel et al. (1999; 2001) and Israel et al. (2005) used principle components analysis (PCA) method and our previous research applied correlation coefficients to identified 20 arrhythmia persons from the MIT/BIH database (Shen et al., 2002). Current studies have involved various approaches. Khalil et al. (2008) found the most unique signature bearing parts on QRS Complex of ECG for human identification by applying the high-order Legendre Polynomials. Wang et al. (2008) proposed a combined model on autocorrelation (AC) in conjunction with discrete cosine transform (DCT). Also, the discrete wavelet transform was applied for extracting ECG features from wavelet coefficients. Their experimental results demonstrated that the proposed approach worked well for normal 35 subjects, but the accuracy is reduced on 10 arrhythmia patients (Chiu et al. 2009).

It is challenge to applied ECG identification on arrhythmia patients. The previous work by Agrafioti shows that abnormal ECG or ECG with arrhythmia may affect morphological changes of the signal (Agrafioti, 2009), so their proposed method discards PVC windows to increase the robustness. This may alter the classification decision and performance especially when the system had never been trained with such data. Chen et al. introduce complexity-based approach to deal with abnormal ECG for biometric identification purpose (Chen et al. 2007).

In this article, not only is one-lead ECG analysis for human identification investigated with a larger sample size, but also, all of the one-lead ECG signals are recorded from the subjects' palms. Our database indicates that, even though two people are very similar in size, age, and sex, their ECGs are different. Figure 1 shows an example of two persons with the exact same age, sex, weight and height who have completely different ECG patterns.

Background and significance

The ECG fiducial point detection is essential for temporal feature extraction and template generation. Several digital signal processing technologies were utilized on raw ECG signals to detect PQRST fiducial points, including digital filtering, Pan and Tompkins method, first derivative ECG method (that is, dECG) (Kamath, 2007), and the zero-crossing method. In order to accomplish ECG analysis, it is obvious that the R point is the major landmark which needs to be detected first. After digital filtering to limit the ECG bandwidth from 0.01 to 50 Hz, a reliable, real-time QRS detection algorithm is essential to apply. Pan and Tompkins method (Pan, 1985) was used in this research to determine all the R points in order to calculate R-R intervals.

Once the R point is found, the Q and S points are limited within the 150 ms period which is centered by the R point. In addition, the T wave is complete within a 400 ms period backward from the R point, and the P wave is a 200ms advance from the R point. By using these statistical data with the first derivative ECG, the P, Q, S, and T points can be detected by searching minimum (valley) or maximum (peaks) of all the zero-crossing points within the certain window period $[t_{left} : t_{right}]$. For example, to detect P points, t_{left} and t_{right} were set at 200ms and 40ms advance from R points.

The details are described as following equations:

$$[x \quad y]_{Q,S} = \min_{Q,S \, points} \{ ECG(find(dECG[t_{left} : t_{right}] = 0)) \} \cdots \; (1)$$

$$[x \quad y]_{P,T} = \max_{P,T \, points} \{ ECG(find(dECG[t_{left} : t_{right}] = 0)) \} \cdots \; (2)$$

where $ECG(t)$ is the de-noised ECG waveform, and $dECG(t)$ is the first derivative of the $ECG(t)$ waveform $dECG(t)$ combines with zero-crossing method to detect PQST points. After fiducial points are correctly detected, each ECG heart beats is segmented for identification. Henceforth, biometric features are able to be extracted and interested ECG templates are created with 50 points before and after P and T points. In this research, template matching, distance classification, and combined models were investigated for ECG-based human identification.

Template matching method

Signals are correlated if the shapes of the waveforms of two signals match one another. The correlation coefficient provides a quantitative measure of how similar the signals look. It is important to note that the amplitude differences of two signals do not affect the correlation coefficient. The equation for the correlation coefficient is:

$$r_{xy} = \frac{\sum_{n=1}^{N} \{x(n) - \bar{x}\} \{y(n) - \bar{y}\}}{\sqrt{\sum_{n=1}^{N} \{x(n) - \bar{x}\}^2 \sum_{n=1}^{N} \{y(n) - \bar{y}\}^2}} \quad \cdots \quad (3)$$

where the value of r_{xy} varies between 1 and −1 depending on the degree of similarity of the shapes of x and y.

LDA distance classification

The distance in R space can be represented as the

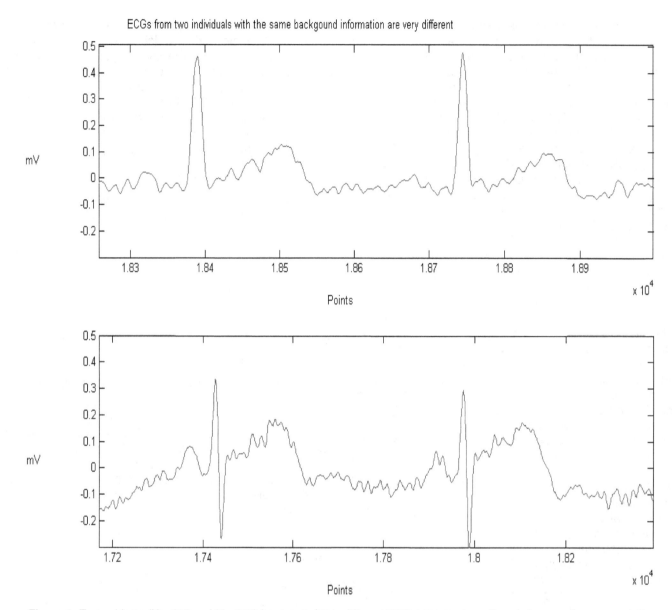

Figure 1. Two subjects (No. 217 and No. 225) have completely different ECG patterns, even though they are the same gender (female), age (21 years old), weight (56.7 kg; 125 lb), and height (170 cm; 5' 7"). The units on the *x* axis are sample data point numbers. The sampling rate of these ECG signals is 500 sps. The units on the *y* axis are millivolts.

similarity between feature vectors x^p and x^q in the Euclidean metric system by:

$$d(x^p, x^q) = \sqrt{\sum_{i=1}^{R} (x_i^p - x_i^q)^2} \; \ldots \quad (4)$$

However, in the feature space, not all the features are equally weighted. So, this relation can be adjusted by adding a weight vector $w = [w_1, w_2, ..., w_R]$.

$$d(x^p, x^q) = \sqrt{\sum_{i=1}^{R} w_i (x_i^p - x_i^q)^2} \; \ldots \quad (5)$$

The smaller the value of $d(x^p, x^q)$ the closer the distance between vector x^p and x^q. And the distance between two classes, called S_L and S_K, can be described by:

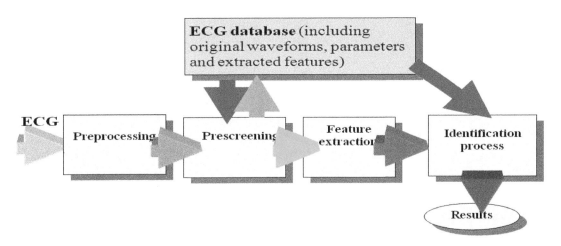

Figure 2. System structure for human identification.

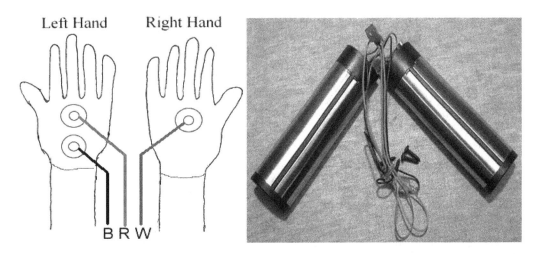

Figure 3. Disposable electrodes were attached to each subject's palms; The measurement layout can be implemented by using dry metal electrodes.

$$D(S_L, S_K) = \frac{1}{m_L \cdot m_K} \sum_{x^p \in S_L} \sum_{x^q \in S_K} d(x^p, x^q) \ \dots$$ Where

m_L and m_K are the numbers of feature vectorin S_L and S_K.

System structure

In this research, Lead I ECG signals were recorded from the palms of 168 young college volunteers. Figure 2 shows the block diagram of the human identification system.

EXPERIMENTAL SETUP

Unlike the MIT/BIH database (Goldberger et al., 2000) of ECG signals from cardiology patients, this research focuses on normal,

healthy persons. Short-term, resting, Lead-I ECG signals were measured from 168 individuals (113 females and 55 males) to create our ECG biometric database. The ranges of age, weight and height were 19 to 52 years, 45 to 118 kg and 155 to 208 cm, respectively. The interquartile ranges (IQR) of age, weight, and height were 3 years, 13 kg and 15.2 cm, respectively. The subjects' ECG signals were measured and collected with an ECG data acquisition unit (BIOPAC Student Lab PRO system, MP30 with software), electrodes (disposable silver-silver chloride electrodes from BIOPAC Systems, Inc.), and computers (IBM-compatible PCs).

For the lead recording, two electrodes were placed on the left palm and one electrode was placed on the right palm as shown in Figure 3. These subjects were in a resting position and sitting upright, and they were asked to relax with their palms open and resting on their legs. The ECG was recorded for 90 s at a sampling rate of 500 sps for the enrollment process. A calibration procedure was applied by the acquisition software (BIOPAC Student Lab PRO system).

Three sets of ECG databases were generated during enrollment. Because this research surveyed a normal healthy population, all ECG signals were from college students with similar background,

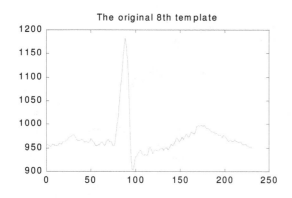

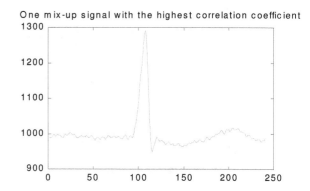

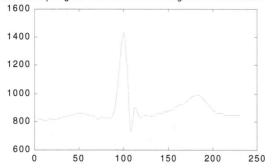

Figure 4. Two similar ECG signals can yield a false positive if only template matching is applied.

such as   age   and education background. Fifty individuals (33 females and 17 males) were randomly chosen from the database for the system development dataset. Then 20 sequential normal heartbeats were randomly selected by our computer program from each of the 50 individuals in this investigation to form a 1000-beat group as our original ECG database. Next, signal averaging was applied on each 20-heartbeat group to create 50 mean averageheartbeats and 50 median average heartbeats as our second and third databases.

Five methods were used to generate real-time ECG templates (or testing ECG signals). The testing ECG signals were randomly selected from different time slots in the group databases; that is, there is no temporal overlap between the ECG templates and the group database. Five normal heartbeats were picked from each person as testing ECG signals (or real-time ECG templates). Then, each five-beat group was transformed to five different templates by applying signal averaging methods (Tompkins, 1993) for partly eliminating both outliner beats and high frequency interferences: (1) A single heartbeat (randomly chosen without a signal average), (2) A signal-averaged heartbeat using a five-heartbeat-mean method, (3) A signal-median heartbeat using a five-heartbeat-median method, (4) A signal-averaged heartbeat using a three-heartbeat-mean method, and (5) A signal-median heartbeat using a three-heartbeat-median method. Only one heartbeat was contained in each template. Finally, five input template sets were built.

Preprocessing

ECG preprocessing included selection of appropriate beats and removal of various artifacts. Baseline wander, dc shift, power-line noise, and high-frequency interference were removed (Maglaveras, 1998; Haykin, 2001; Ma et al., 1999). Standard ECG machines have a bandwidth of 0.05 to 150 Hz. However, the noise was so severe for a palm ECG that the signal was band limited to the frequency range between 1 and 50 Hz.

Prescreening

Template matching was used as a prescreening tool. The template (or real-time input) was matched by all the members of the determined group. Correlation coefficients showed to what extent two signals were similar between each template and the pre-determined database. In order to reduce the group size for the identification process, a certain threshold, typically between 0.92 and 0.95, was set on the correlation coefficient to eliminate those members that were not likely candidates. In addition, the maximum size of the candidate group was limited to 10% of the whole sample size. Template matching is limited in its ability to distinguishing among waveforms which are very similar because it ignores amplitude information, which is part of the essential information for identification. An example is shown in Figure 4. ECG machines from all manufacturers use a standard amplitude calibration and a standard bandwidth, so the amplitude and appearance of the ECG should be the same for a particular individual regardless of when it recorded or what ECG machines it is recorded on.

Improvement of the template matching method

Our goal was to find the best match result of databases and templates. Recursively, the template matching method was applied among the three database sets and five template sets, resulting in a total of fifteen dataset matches. Twelve of these dataset matches are two-single-heartbeat matches, and three dataset matches are 20-to-single-heartbeat matches. Our previous study showed the

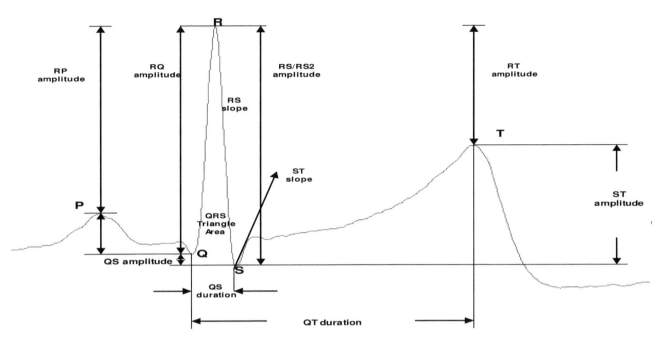

Figure 5. Potential features for classification.

Table 1. Seventeen selected features used for classification.

	Selected features		Selected features		Selected features
1	RQ amplitude	8	RS amp./TS amp.	15	Angle Q
2	QS duration	9	RS2 amplitude	16	Angle R
3	RS amplitude	10	PQ amplitude	17	Angle S
4	ST amplitude	11	QS amplitude		
5	QT duration**	12	RP amplitude		
6	RS slope	13	RT amplitude		
7	QRS triangular Area	14	ST slope		

**The definition of QT duration is different from the clinical definition of QT interval. The QT duration is the time delay between the Q and T point. It has to be normalized with heart rate if not a resting ECG (as is QT interval).

procedure used to obtain 20-to-single-heartbeat matches (Shen, 2002, 2005).

Feature extraction

The 17 ECG features shown in Figure 5 and Table 1 were extracted from ECG waveforms. For comparing among features with different units, all features were normalized using:

$$\text{Normalized feature} = \frac{feature-\min}{\max-\min} \dots \quad (7)$$

Where max and min represent the maximum and minimum values among 17 features, which came from the development dataset.

These features were selected for identify verification purposes, so some of them may not be meaningful for clinical diagnosis. Most features were extracted from the QRS complex because this

waveform is most easily recognized, easy to detect, essential for life, and stable with different heart rates.

The QT time duration depends on heart rate, so normalization must be applied to make sure the QT measurements are usable. One of the commonly used techniques is Bazett's formula, in which the QT interval is adjusted for heart rate by dividing it by the square root of the R-R interval. However, this formula has been criticized for being inaccurate with fast heart rates (Al-Khatib et al., 2003). Our experimental data showed that the Bazett formula fits better with resting heart rate status than the Framingham linear regression equation. In addition, RS2 amplitude is defined as amplitude from point R to the point after 0.024 s delay. An exhaustive test was used to eliminate the bad features or to diminish their weights in order to enhance the identification rate.

Identification process

To avoid misidentification, distance classifications were used in the

Table 2. Template matching results with different template and /or database sets.

Template database	Single heartbeat*** (%)	Five-heartbeat mean (%)	Five-heartbeat median (%)	Three-heartbeat mean (%)	Three-heartbeat median (%)
Twenty heartbeats	42-45/50 (84-90)	45/50 (90)	45/50 (90)	43/50 (86)	44/50 (88)
Mean heartbeat	46/50(92)	49/50 (98)	49/50 (98)	48/50 (96)	48/50 (96)
Median heartbeat	43-45/50 (86-90)	49/50 (98)	49/50 (98)	48/50(96)	48/50 (96)

*** By randomly choosing a single heartbeat as an input template, the results vary with the heartbeat we chose. So, the results are unstable and highly dependent on the chosen heartbeat.

identification process after selecting the possible candidates using the template-matching prescreening. Seventeen features were used for distance classification. The class of an input template can be found by calculating the minimum distances between the feature vectors in an input template and all pre-selected candidates.

Equations (5) to (7) show the mathematical method for finding the distance relationship between two feature vectors and between classes. This method was selected in a combined model for the identification process and used in conjunction with the prescreening process to increase the accuracy of identification.

RESULTS

The template matching method used five different types of template sets to match three different types of database sets. The 15 matching results in Table 2 show that it is not a good idea to pick a single heartbeat randomly as a template because the performance is unstable and highly dependent on the chosen heartbeat. The more heartbeats for signal average processing can provide performance improvement. However, for trade-off on signal quality and system access time, we suggest to capture 5 to 6 continuous heart beats for template making. The entire ECG identification expects to be done within 10 seconds. The best matching results giving 98% accuracy (49 out of 50) occurred when five-heartbeat templates were matched with databases which use averaged heartbeats from 50 to 20-heartbeat groups. That is, the signal averaging approach provided much better template matching performance when the averaged heartbeats were applied to both templates and databases. The templates with more averaged heartbeats offered better performance on the palm ECG biometric system but required more computation time. Even though the signal averaging method removes some high frequencies (Tompkins, 1993), the overall identification rate was still increased. That is, signal averaging removed more interference while preserving biometric traits. Also, there was no difference in using the mean or median as a noise reduction method for template matching.

Without using the entire ECG waveforms, the distance classification calculates the distance from a template feature vector to database feature vectors as described in Equation (6). Exhaustive tests were utilized to determine the appropriate weight vector $w = [w_1, w_2, ..., w_R]$ by

ranking these features. The features were eliminated earlier by exhaustive tests; the lower numbers of weights were set. Four levels of weights were used on 17 features. They are 0, 0.2, 1 and 2. However, system performance drops when too many features are assigned to zero (that is, removed). After the weight vector $w = [w_1, w_2, ..., w_R]$ was determined, a 98% (49 out of 50) identification rate was found as the overall performance. In addition, no training process is needed to use distance classification.

The combined system model was investigated using template matching plus LDA distance classification. In Figure 6, the combined system model which unites the template matching method and distance classification was investigated.

There is no training process in this model, so it needs much less time than the previous combined model (DBNN) (Shen, 2005). Hence, the model is more suitable than DBNN for use on a large population.

In the predetermined group with 10, 20, and 50 persons, a 100% identification rate (rank one probability) was also achieved. The rank one probability represents that the identified subjects matched their own templates at the top rank over the entire database. Moreover, the combined system model was further tested in the predetermined group with 100 and 168 people to get 96% and 95.3% identification rates respectively. Figure 7 show that the classification error rate (CER) increased when the number of people in the predetermined group increased. This phenomenon in which the numerical error rate increases when the number of group members increase is fairly typical. The statistical explanation and real data evidence according to the fingerprint biometric can be found in the NIST report to Congress (NIST, 2004).

DISCUSSION

Unlike a clinical ECG database with 12-lead records including limb and thoracic signals, this research focused on palm ECG signals. The ECG recorded from the palms has more noise than the ECG recorded from the torso, but the waveform morphologies are the same as the Lead I ECG. The electromyogram (EMG) interference and baseline wander become more significant when ECGs are recorded from palms; that is, the signal-to-noise ratio

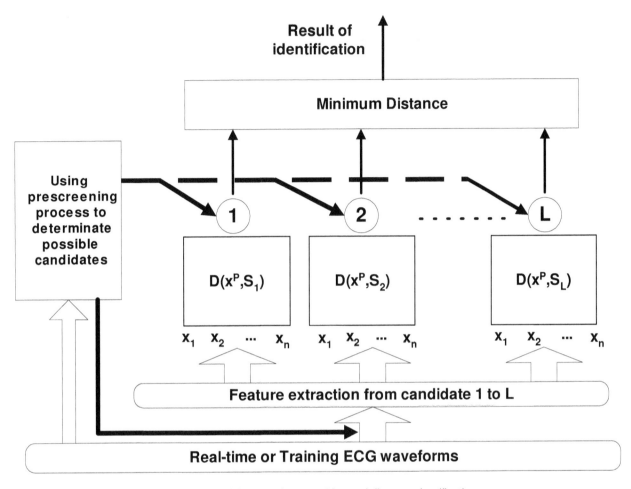

Figure 6. ECG identification model by combining template matching and distance classification.

(SNR) of the palm ECG signal is lower than of the chest ECG signal. However, the big advantages for palm ECG are easy to access, to combine with fingerprint/palm biometrics, and to use mental/dry electrodes. The signal averaging method successfully increased the signal-to-noise ratio thereby improving system performance. However, signal averaging introduces low-pass filtering if the averaged heartbeats are not aligned perfectly, and some identifying features may be distorted by such filtering. Fortunately, benefits gained from reducing interference are much greater than the disadvantages of feature losses using the signal averaging method. Hence, those modified features in the filtered frequency band are insignificant in comparison to the interference from noise.

The feature, angle Q, is not a useful feature because of serious measurement problems. According to Sherwood (1997) and Dubin (2000), Q deflection is small and sometimes absent. Our exhaustive tests confirmed this statement because in our experiments, the accuracy rate always improved if the feature, angle Q, was dropped.

For comparison of identification methods, the major advantage of our combined model (Figure 7) is that no

training process needed permitting this technique to be implemented in real-time systems applied to a large population.

Conclusions

This research concentrates on measurements of palm ECG signals from 50 normal healthy persons for human identification. For the combined system model, the identification rate (i.e., rank one probability) was 100% in the predetermined group and 95.3% (160 out of 168 persons) when the same combined system model was tested on the entire ECG biometric database. Based on these results, the Lead-I ECG can be viewed as a potential new biometric for human identity verification. More filter development is desirable for future analysis of palm ECG signals to preserve biometric attributes while improving the signal-to-noise ratio. In addition, the long-term changes of an individual's ECG signals and their implications for implementing a practical biometric system also need to be investigated.

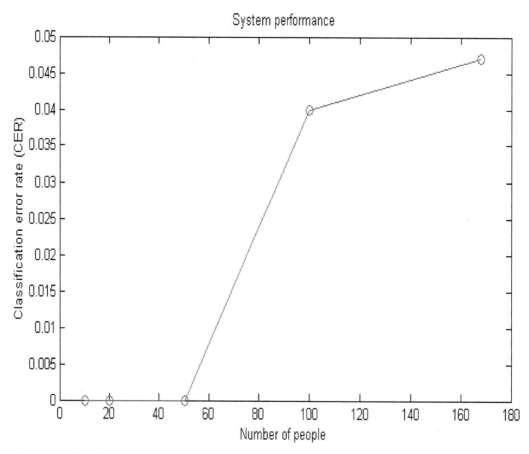

Figure 7. Classification error rate (CER) increased when the number of people in the predetermined group increased.

FUTURE WORK

In this research, only static ECG identification was studied. The current waveform analysis and recognition on ECG biometrics may not be robust on exercise ECGs with unavoidable heart rate increase. Hence, more heartbeat resistance features may come from time-frequency, frequency and other signal decomposition methods. More exquisite equipment and advanced artificial intelligent algorithms would be very helpful to discover other significant ECG features for future human identification.

REFERENCES

Agrafioti F, Hatzinakos D (2009). ECG biometric analysis in cardiac irregularity condition, SIViP, 3: 329-343.

Al-Khatib SM, LaPointe NMA, Kramer JM, Califf RM (2003). What clinicians should know about the QT interval, JAMA, 289: 2120-2127.

Balakrishnama S, Ganapathiraju A (1998). Linear discriminant analysis – A brief tutorial, Institute for Signal and Information Processing, Department of Electrical and Computer Engineering, Mississippi State University, pp. 1-8.

Biel L, Pettersson O, Philipson L, Wide P (1999). ECG analysis: A new approach in human identification, IMTC/99. Proc. of the 16th IEEE Instrumentation and Measurement Technology Conference, 3: 557-561.

Biel L, Pettersson O, Philipson L, Wide P (2001). ECG analysis: A new approach in human identification, IEEE Trans. on Instrumentation and Measurement, 50 (3): 808-812.

Chen S, Thakor NV, Mower MM (2006). Ventricular fibrillation detection by a regression test on the autocorrelation function." Med. Biol. Eng. Comput., 25: 241-249.

Chen SW (2007). Complexity-measure-based sequential hypothesis testing for real-time detection of lethal cardiac arrhythmias, EURASIP J. Advanc. Signal Process., 2007: Article ID 20957.

Chiu CC, Chuang CM, Hsu CY (2009). Discrete wavelet transform applied on personal verification with ECG signal, International Journal of Wavelets, Multiresolution and Information Processing (IJWMIP), 7 (3): 341-355.

Dubin D (2000). Rapid interpretation of EKG's, V ed. Cover Publishing Company, Tampa, Florida, Pp. 368-369

Goldberger AL, Amaral LAN, Glass L, Hausdorff JM, Ivanov PCh, Mark RG, Mietus JE, Moody GB, Peng CK, Stanley HE (2000). PhysioBank, PhysioToolkit, and PhysioNet: Components of a New Research Resource for Complex Physiologic Signals. Circulation, 101(23): e215-e220.

Haykin S (2001). Adaptive filter theory. 4th Ed., New Jersey: Prentice-Hall, pp. 313-322

Israel SA, Irvine JM, Cheng A, Wiederhold MD, Wiederhold BK (2005), ECG to identify individuals. Patt. Recog., 38: 133-142.

Kamath C, Ananthapadmanabhayuyu TV (2007). Modeling QRS Complex in dECG. IEEE Trans. Biomed. Eng., 54(1): 156 - 158.

Khalil I, Sufi F (2008). Legendre Polynomials based biometric authentication using QRS complex of ECG. In: Intelligent Sensors, Sensor Networks and Information Processing, 2008. ISSNIP 2008. Int. Conf., on, pp. 297-302.

Ma WK, Zhang YT, Yang FS (1999). A fast recursive-least-square adaptive notch filter and its applications to biomedical signals, Med. Bio. Eng. Compt,, 37: 99-103.

Maglaveras N (1998). ECG pattern recognition and classification non-linear transformations and neural networks: a review. Int. J. Med. Inf., 52: 191-208.

NIST report to Congress (2004). http://www.itl.nist.gov/iad/894.03/fing/pact1102.pdf.

Pan J, Tompkins WJ (1985). A real-time QRS detection algorithm. IEEE Trans. Biomed. Eng. BME, 32(3): 230-236.

Shen TW, Tompkins WJ (2005). Biometric Statistical Study of One-Lead ECG Features and Body Mass Index (BMI), 27th Annual International Conference of the IEEE Engineering in Medicine and Biology Society (EMBC05), pp. 1529-1533.

Shen TW (2005). Biometric Identity Verification Based on Electrocardiogram (ECG), Ph.D. Dissertation, University of Wisconsin, Madison.

Shen TW, Tompkins WJ, Hu YH (2002). One-lead ECG for identity verification, 2nd Joint Conference of the IEEE Engineering in Medicine and Biology Society and the Biomedical Engineering Society, pp. 62-63.

Tompkins WJ (1993). Biomedical Digital Signal Processing, Prentice-Hall, p. 368.

Webster JG (1998). Medical instrumentation, application and design. New York: Wiley, pp. 1-72.

5

A feature preserved mesh simplification algorithm

Jiacai Wang[1], Lirong Wang[2*], Jinzhu Li[3] and Ichiro Hagiwara[1]

[1]Department of Mechanical Science and Engineering, Tokyo Institute of Technology, Japan.
[2]Institute of Advanced Integration Technology, Shenzhen Institute of Advanced Technology, Chinese Academy of Science, China.
[3]Insigma China, Beijing, China.

Large-volume mesh model faces challenge in rendering, storing, and transmission due to large size of polygon data. Mesh simplification is one of solutions to reduce the data size. This paper presents a mesh simplification method based on feature extraction with curvature estimation to triangle mesh. The simplified topology preserves good geometrical features in the area with distinct features, that is, coarse simplified mesh in the flat region and fine simplified mesh around the areas of crease and corner. Sequence of mesh simplification is controlled on the basis of geometrical feature sensitivity, which results in reasonable simplification topology with less data size. This algorithm can decrease the size of the file by largely simplifying flat areas and preserving the geometric feature as well.

Key word: Mesh simplification, feature extraction, curvature estimation.

INTRODUCTION

Nowadays, product design based on reverse engineering is popularly due to the fast development of three-dimension (3D) measurement technology like 3D laser or CMM (coordinate-measuring machine) scanning systems. Measured representation of a 3D model is usually described in a million triangle mesh data. On the other hand, in traditional computer-aided design (CAD) modeling systems, high-level geometric primitive surfaces initially defined by versatile modeling operations like extrusion, constructive solid geometry and freeform deformations are usually be tessellated into lowest common form of polygonal mesh for display rendering. Complex triangle meshes face challenge in real-time rendering performance, storage capacities and transmission. In order to effectively operate complex mesh, typically triangular meshes, mesh simplification has emerged to dispatch meshes from a complex level to a simplified level (Li et al., 2005).

In recent years, automatic simplification to highly detailed mesh model has received increasing attention in the research field such as real-time rending of large-scale terrain, surface reconstruction in reverse engineering and rapid prototyping. Several kinds of simplification algorithms such as vertex or triangle decimation to remove vertices or triangle and re-triangulating the surrounding mesh, vertex clustering to condense vertices in certain cell into one vertex, vertex pair contraction and iterative edge contraction have been studied since the 1990s. Iterative edge collapse is a kind of simplification approach that tries to preserves volume geometric properties by collapse control. Progress mesh (PM) representation is a kind of iterative edge collapse based mesh simplification method developed by Hoppe (1996), in which an energy function to describe the complexity and fidelity of mesh is used to track simplification quality. This method requires many vertex distance evaluations and it reduces the computational speed. Other edge contraction based simplification, such as quadric error metrics (QEM) based simplification algorithm proposed by Garland (1997), use QEM to choose the edge to be simplified and the new vertex after contraction. Recent years some new mesh simplifications are developed. introduce a kind of simplification of surface mesh using Hausdorff envelope, in which two tolerance areas defined by an approximation of Hausdorff distance in percentage of the minimal bounding box size of the initial surface mesh are used to control mesh simplification and

*Corresponding author. E-mail: wanglr97@hotmail.com

optimization in order to preserve the geometry of the surface. A mesh optimization algorithm based on neural network of Growing Neural Gas mode is presented to obtain a simplified set of vertices representing the best approximation of 3D object in (Noguera et al., 2009). Tang et al. (2007) develope a mesh simplification algorithm based on surface moments and volume moments defined to the original mesh to simplify mesh in an edge collapse scheme. Boubekeur and Alexa (2009) introduced a fast simplification algorithm based on stochastic vertex sampling. The stochastic sampling depends on local feature estimator of normal information, and mesh simplification starts from selecting vertices and re-indexing triangles to be clustered. Nate and Jihad (2010) proposed a novel top-down mesh simplification approach, in which simplification is carried out by a series of carving operation of iteratively removing tetrahedral to topological complex mesh. González et al. (2009) present a user-assisted mesh simplification method applied to triangle mesh converted from CAD models. This mesh simplification can be conducted to the whole models with a single level of detail, and some simplified parts can be modified or refined furtherly in different levels of detail according to user's demanding.

In this paper, feature extraction based mesh simplification is investigated. During simplification, edge-weight based on edge-collapse simplification is carried out, which is more efficient than energy minimization based on optimization mesh algorithm in PM introduced by Hoppe (1996). An algorithm to control simplification sequence is defined by an edge-weight using average curvature. As a result, less simplification is carried out on the surface part near to the sharp geometrical feature like corner; and the surface part without distinguished geometrical feature like flat surface will be largely simplified with large-scale mesh. This way, the geometrical feature can be preserved by ordering control of edge-collapse.

GEOMETRICAL FEATURE EXTRACTION

The estimating intrinsic geometric feature of polygonal mesh is an important stage in laser range scanning, scientific computing, computer vision, medical imaging and so on. There are two classified groups to extract geometric feature from polygonal mesh, volumetric-based method to utilize global characteristics of 3D object and boundary-based method to describe an abject based on distinct local properties of its boundary and their relationship. In boundary-based methods, curvature range image data. Comparison of Gaussian and mean estimation is important to features recognition, segmentation and registration to polygonal mesh. Great effort had been invested in computing curvature from realcurvature estimation methods on triangular mesh are investigated by Magid et al. (2007). A curvature

estimation scheme for triangle meshes using biquadratic Bezier patch demonstrates to be good at dealing with irregular shape presented in Razdan and Bae (2005). In the computer vision literature, one can find some approaches for depth images that can handle features correctly and extract the feature lines. Guy and Medioni (1997) extract surfaces, feature lines and feature junctions from noisy point clouds, and space around the point cloud is discretized into volume grid. Gumhold et al. (2001) adopted the algorithm used by Guy and Medioni (1997) but avoided the discretization into a volume grid, in order to allow efficient handling of non-uniformly sampled point clouds. Kodani et al. (2003, 2004) investigated a method to select only points located on feature lines after classifying all points on feature lines like edges and tips appearing on smooth surface. The average curvature estimation presented in Kodani et al. (2003, 2004) was adopted by Wang et al. (2008) to extract feature point. In this research, the extraction of feature point is carried out on the basis of average curvature estimation.

In cloud point of a mesh, for each data point p_i, a set N_i of neighbor data points are gathered from its neighboring graph. The number of neighbor points depends on the point density and noise level of the dataset. The following two quantities are extracted from the set of neighboring points:

$$c_i = \frac{1}{|N_i|} \sum_{q=N_i} q \tag{1}$$

$$C_i = \sum_{q \in N_i} (q - c_i)(q - c_i)^T \tag{2}$$

where c_i is center location of the neighbor point set of q, and C_i is the correlation matrix.

The eigenvectors $\{e_0, e_1, e_2\}$ of the correlation matrix C_i and corresponding eigenvalues $\{\lambda_0, \lambda_1, \lambda_2\}$ with $\lambda_0 \leq \lambda_1 \leq \lambda_2$ can be calculated by using Equation 2.

The average curvature can be estimated from the least square fitted plane given by (e_0, c_i). Figure 1 shows a two dimensional projection of the data point p with its tangent plane degenerated to the horizontal line. The distance of a point to its tangent plane is:

$$d = \left| e_0^t (p - c_i) \right| \tag{3}$$

Curvature estimation from fitted plane and average neighbor distance μ is shown in Figure 1. The curvature

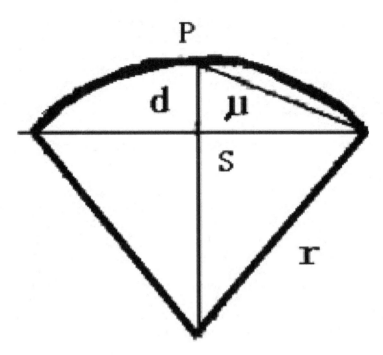

Figure 1. Curvature estimation.

radius, as shown in Figure 1, intersects the tangent plane at approximately the average neighbor distance μ. From $s^2 = \mu^2 - d^2$ and $s^2 = r^2 - (r - d)^2$, the curvature $k = 1/r$ computes to $2d/\mu^2$ and is a good criterion for detecting feature point of crease and corner points. Curvature estimation k_i for each data point p_i with distance d_i from the fitted plan can be defined as:

$$k_i = \frac{2d}{\mu^2} \qquad (4)$$

By computing the maximum curvature estimation $k_{\max}$ of all data points, the normalized curvature is defined as:

$$w_{ki_i} = \frac{k_i(p)}{k_{\max}}$$

$$(5)$$

where w_{ki} is in the range of [0,1]. When w_{ki} near to 1, the possibility of that point to be considered as a crease on

corner point is highly; and when W_{ki} near to 0, the neighboring region around that point is approaching to a flat plane. Here the corner points are regarded as the feature points. The extraction of feature points depends on the point density and data noise.

MESH SIMPLIFICATION

Geometrically, triangle mesh consists of a set of vertices. A set of triangles can be used to describe a piecewise linear surface by connecting subset of the vertices together in an order. In this research, edge collapse transformations are carried out on the initial mesh M^n, and a coarser approximation of M^0 is obtained after N operations of simplification, as described as $M^n \xrightarrow{Ecol_{n-1}} \cdots \xrightarrow{Ecol_1} M^1 \xrightarrow{Ecol_0} M^0$. Edge collapse transformation of $Ecol(V_t, V_s)$ to collapse the edge $V_t V_s$, as shown in Figure 2, unifies 2 adjacent vertices V_t and V_s into a new vertex V'_s. The vertex V_t and the two adjacent triangles of f_l and f_r vanish. Then the neighborhood faces around V'_s are rearranged, and the geometrical information of $(V_t, V_s, V_f, V_r, V'_s)$ is recorded as a sequence of vertex splitting record. The new point can located on the one position on edge $V_t V_s$ defined by user.

Sequence of edge collapse transformation, validity check of collapse transformation and curvature control are important influences on quality of the simplified approximating meshes in order to keep typical topology features of the original model and to achieve acceptable approximations as required. Edge collapse may potentially introduce undesirable inconsistency, degeneracy into the mesh, like holes or degenerated lines or vertex.

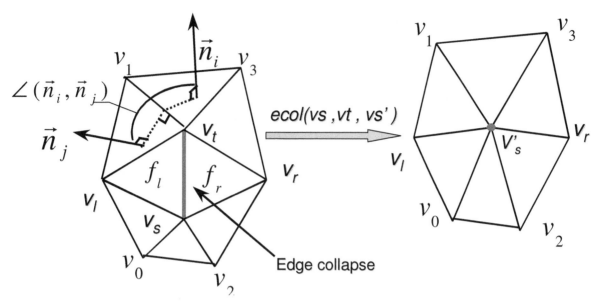

Figure 2. Collapsed edge based mesh simplification.

Figure 3. An example with no validity check.

As shown in Figure 3, the simplification result is very bad if there is no any simplification control during simplification (see comparison with Figure 5 (a).

In this research, sequence of edge collapse algorithms are investigated by random and edge weight methods. Edge weight based simplification is to define a weight to each edge, and the edge with the smallest weight will be collapsed firstly. Edge weight is defined as:

$$\omega_{t,s} = l_{t,s} \, \overline{w}_k \qquad (6)$$

where $l_{t,s}$ is the Eulerian distance between vertex v_t and

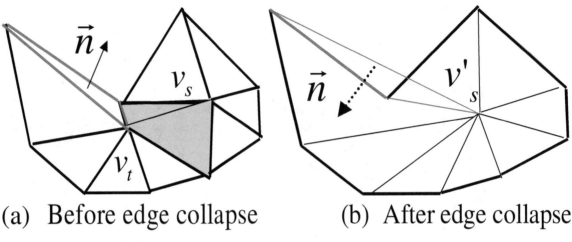

(a) Before edge collapse   (b) After edge collapse

Figure 4. Normal direction inverse.

v_s of the collapse edge. $\overline{w}_k$ is the average normalized curvature of vertex v_t and v_s, that is:

$$\overline{w}_k = (w_{kt} + w_{ks})/2 .$$

Three different validity checks are carried out: normal direction check, sliver triangle check and non-manifold edge control. As show in Figure 4, after edge collapse, the triangle with red side folds over onto itself, and the normal direction is inversed. This will result in a crease on the simplified model, regarded as flipped face. Sliver triangle control is conducted by check criteria of $Q = \dfrac{4\sqrt{3}\delta}{l_0^2 + l_1^2 + l_2^2}$, where δ is the triangle area after edge collapse, which can be calculated by $\delta = \sqrt{x(x-l_0)(x-l_1)(x-l_2)}$, l_0, l_1 and l_2 are the edge length of the triangle, $x = \dfrac{l_0 + l_1 + l_2}{2}$. When $Q \to 1$, the triangle approaches to an equiangular triangle; and when $Q \to 0$, the triangle is degenerated into a triangle whose vertices are collinear. Non-manifold edge control, is conducted by check criteria of $v_0 \neq v_1$ and $v_2 \neq v_3$, here v_0, v_1, v_2, v_3 are the vertices of the neighboring faces surrounding f_l and f_r, as shown in Figure 2. In this research, the faces adjacent to discontinuous boundary are prohibited to involve in edge collapse. Moreover, after one edge-collapse, a edge-collapse sequence algorithm is investigated, in which vertex sequence is updated by the added new vertex and edge

weight defined in Equation (6). This collapse can be cancelled if the validity check is not passed.

The simplification process is terminated under condition of simplification ratio, $R_s = \dfrac{N - N_m}{N} \times 100\ \%$, where N and N_m are the number of triangle mesh in the original model and after edge collapse, respectively. During simplification procedure, the calculated simplification ratio is compared with a given initial ratio defined by user. If it is smaller than the given ratio, the simplification procedure continuous, or the simplification procedure ends. In some cases, if no candidate edge to be collapsed under the initial simplification control parameter is found, the simplification is terminated, even though the simplification ratio did not reach the initial value.

CASE STUDY

A GUI (graphics user interface) of mesh simplification and refinement has been developed based on C++. In the following example, sliver triangle control parameter of Q is set to 0.5, and the change region of normal direction is within 60°. Figure 5 (b) illustrates the simplified models of Stanford Bunny by using the presented feature sensitivity simplification algorithm. It shows that the mesh on the flat area is largely simplified, such as the area of belly. On the other side, the mesh in the region with a small curvature, such as the areas of ears, is not significantly simplified, and the geometric topology in these areas is preserved. Figure 5 (c) is the simplification results by using the commercial software RAPIDFORM, in which the feature in the area of ears is lost with serious distortion. Comparisons of the simplification results by using the presented method and commercial software RAPIDFORM indicates that the proposed mesh simplified algorithm can keep more

Points: 2904, triangles: 5805, file size: 1204KB

(a) Original model

Points: 12033, triangles: 4063, file size: 724KB   Points: 1182, triangles: 2361, file size: 421KB

(b) Simplified mode

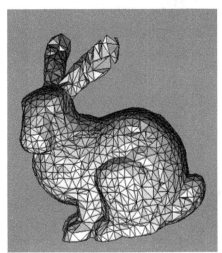 

Points: 2201, triangles: 4353, file size: 1105KB   Points: 1406, triangles: 2767, file size: 703

(c) Simplified model by commercial software RAPIDFORM

Figure 5. Simplifications of Bunny model.

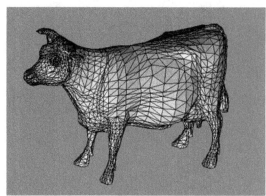

Points: 2904, triangles: 5805, file size: 1204KB

(a) Original model

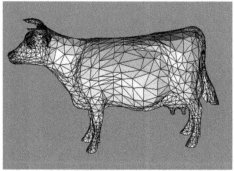

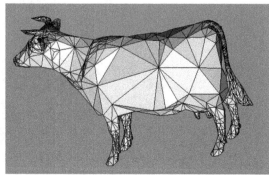

Points: 2033, triangles: 4063, file size: 724KB   Points: 1182, triangles: 2361, file size: 421KB

(b) Simplified mode

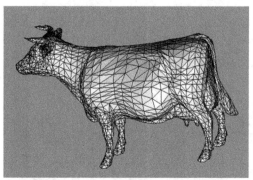

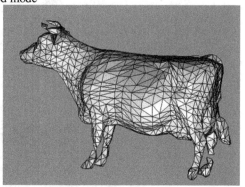

Points: 2259, triangles: 4518, file size: 1151KB   Points: 1240, triangles: 2464, file size: 628KB

(c) Simplified model by commercial software RAPIDFORM

Figure 6. Simplification of a cow model.

accurate topology in the area with small curvature than the uniform mesh algorithm in RAPIDFORM. Figure 6 illustrates the simplified result of another example of a cow model. The areas with distinct feature in horn, eyes, leg and tail demonstrate highly preserved topology than the simplified model by RAPIDFORM. But the body parts are too coarse to reflect the original geometry. More effort will be done to balance the simplifications in the areas with different curvature.

Conclusions

This research investigates a geometric topology preserved mesh simplification algorithm for large-scale triangle mesh model. The presented mesh simplification approach can help to reduce the simplified model size at a large-scale keeping geometrical feature under the edge-weight based simplification sequence control. A coarse mesh model can be obtained by mesh simplification, which can reduce disk and memory requirements and speed up visualization and transmission. Moreover, this research can also be applied into 3D streaming technology for web based collaborative product development, real-time rending, rapid prototyping and more. Further improvement will be carried out to control simplifications around the area near geometrical feature, and to improve the smooth topology between flat and feature areas.

ACKNOWLEDGEMENT

This research is supported by Industrial Technology Research Grant Program of 06A11010a, from New Energy and Industrial Technology Development Organization (NEDO) of Japan.

REFERENCES

Boubekeur T, Alexa M (2009). Mesh Simplification by Stochastic Sampling and Topological Clustering. Comput. Graphics, 33: 241-249.

Garland M, Heckbert P (1997). Surface Simplification Using Quadric Error Metrics. Proceeding of SIGGRAPH'97, pp. 209-216.

González C, Gumbau J, Chover M, Ramos F, Quirós R (2009). User-assisted Simplification Method for Triangle Meshes Preserving Boundaries. Comput.-Aided Des., 41: 1095-1106.

Gumhold S, Wang X, Macleod R (2001). Feature Extration from Point Clouds. Proceeding of the 10 International Meshing Roundtable, Sandia national Laboratories, pp. 293-305.

Guy G, Medioni G (1997). Inference of surfaces, 3d curves and junctions from sparse, noisy 3d data. IEEE Trans. Pattern Anal. Mach. Intell., 19(11): 1265-1277.

Hoppe (1996). Progressive Meshes. Proceedings of SIGGRAPH'96, pp. 99-108.

Kodani T, Manabe T, Taniguchi T (2004). Detection of Feature Lines from Point Clouds and Surface Generation of 3D Domain. Proc. Comput. Eng. Confer., 9: 773-776.

Kodani K, Manabe T, Taniguchi T (2003). Surface Generation from Point Cloud on Surface of 3D Domain. Proc. Comput. Eng. Confer., 8: 837-840.

Li DW, Lu WF, Fuh JYH, Wong YS (2005). Collaborative computer-aided design – research and development status. Comput.-Aided Design, 8(1): 17-30.

Magid E, Soldea O, Rivlin E (2007). A Comparison of Gaussian and Mean Curvature Estimation Methods on Triangular Meshes of Range Image Data. Comput. Vision Image Understanding, 107: 139-159.

Nate H, Jihad ES (2010). Carving for topology simplification of polygonal meshes. Comput.-Aided Des., 42: 67-75.

Noguera JV, Tortosa L, Zamora A (2009). Analysis and Efficiency of the GNG3D Algorithm for Mesh Simplification. Appl. Math. Comput., 197: 29-40.

Razdan A, Bae MS (2005). Curvature Estimation Scheme for Triangle Meshes Using Biquadratic Be´zier Patches. Comput.-Aided Design, 37: 1481-1491.

Tang H, Shu HZ, Dillenseger JL, Bao XD and Luo LM (2007). Moment-based Metrics for Mesh Simplification. Comput. Graphics, 31: 710-718.

Wang LR, Xu F, Wang JC, Hagiwara I (2008). Efficient Iterative Closest Point Algorithm for Measured Surface Registration. The 6th International Conference on Vibration Engineering (ICVE'2008), 4-6 June, Dailian, China.

6

Hybrid mixed handover for call blocking probability analysis in wireless ATM network

Parag Jain[1,2]* and S. C. Gupta[3]

[1]Bhagwant University, India.
[2]Computer Applications Department, Roorkee Institute of Technology, Roorkee, India.
[3]Department of Electronics and Computer, Indian Institute of Technology, Roorkee, India.

This paper focuses on the problem of congestion control in wireless ATM network based on new Hybrid Scheme proposed by the authors to solve the hand off/hand over problem in ATM-based PCN, which aims to give handover calls high priority over new calls. It presents a non-disruptive handoff protocol with dynamic channel reservation for wireless ATM networks. The analytical results are verified by a simulation study, which has shown that a non-disruptive handoff with dynamic channel reservation does achieve much lower blocking probability under high traffic load and significantly reduce the average waiting time during handoff. The improvement reflects remarkable reduced percentage of FTP due to handover failure, when we use our proposed Hybrid Scheme.

Key words: Wireless ATM, network, call blocking.

INTRODUCTION

In wireless ATM, network congestion can occur when a number of Base Stations can simultaneously send packets to the same switch in the network. Bursty communication requires dynamic bandwidth allocation, which may be difficult to allocate in practice. Bandwidth management is crucial for maintaining communication in the wireless networks. Two types of probabilities may be defined as QoS parameters in wireless networks as follows:

Forced termination probability (FTP)

In wireless networks, when a mobile user (MU) travels from one cell to another, the connection handover takes place between the new and previous cell. The forced termination probability (FTP) is the probability that an original call is eventually not completed because of an unsuccessful handover attempt (Ramaswami and Parhi, (2003).

Connection/call blocking probability (CBP)

The connection/call blocking probability (CBP) is the probability that a new connection/call request is rejected. The reason for rejection is generally the unavailability of the sufficient resources which are required to meet the demands made by the connection/call. One of the most obvious merits of a wireless network (Siv and Kumar, 2004) is the total traffic it carries, it is the amount of traffic admitted to the wireless/cellular network as opposed to the offered load. In light traffic conditions, the carried traffic can be taken to be equal to the offered traffic. However, in general, the carried traffic is less than the offered load because of blocking of calls and handover failures.

To support network-wide handoff, new and handoff call requests will compete for connection resources in both the mobile and clustered networks. Handoff calls require a higher congestion related performance, that is, blocking probability, relative to new calls because forced terminations of ongoing calls due to hand-off call blocking are generally more objectionable then new call blocking from the subscriber's perspective (Oliver and Victor, 1997).

This paper focuses on the problem of congestion control in wireless ATM network. This is a practical fact that frequent handoff in PCN introduces the phenomena of congestion. After studying the currently used schemes, it is clear that there is some room for improvement for conventional handoff ordering schemes.

*Corresponding author. E-mail: paragjain2k1@rediffmail.com.

Handover initiated in PCN, a new channel (Kyasanur and Vidya, 2005) has to be granted to handover request for successful handover. To keep FTP to desired minimum values, handover algorithm should avoid blocking handover request due to lack of resources, that is, radio and wired links. In our proposed Mixed Handover Scheme, this has been achieved by giving handover high priority over initiating calls. After applying proposed scheme there is a remarkable reduction in FTP at the cost of tolerable CBP.

LITERATURE REVIEW

To deal with initial access and handoff problem, several strategies are reported in the literature (Guerreroand and Aghvami, 1999; Kulavaratharasah and Aghvami, 1998) as: Non-prioritized; Reserved Channel; FIFO Priority; Measurement-Based Priority; and Subtracting Schemes. Queuing of handover requests is made possible by the existence of the time interval the mobile terminal (MT) spends in the handover area, where it is physically capable of communicating with both the current and next base terminal stations (BTSs). In queuing handover, if all channels of a cell are occupied, calls originating within that cell are blocked and the handover requests to that cell are queued. FIFO is queuing discipline, in which, the call first queued, will be first served. A Measurement-Based Prioritized Scheme is proposed in Tekinay and Jabbari (1992) according to the scheme a queued MT gains a higher priority as its power ratio decreases from the handover threshold to the receiver threshold. The MTs waiting for a channel in the handover queue are sorted continuously according to their priorities.

Signal prediction priority queuing (SPPQ), which uses both received signal strength (RSS) and the change in RSS to determine the priority ordering of an MT. In order to optimize the system for the minimum number of dropped handovers, the handover that would be terminated next should be the first to be handed over.

Another scheme called reserved channel scheme (RCS), gives handover calls a higher priority than new calls. In RCS, a number of wireless channels, called guard channels, are exclusively reserved for handover calls, and the remaining channels, called normal channels, can be shared equally between handover and new calls. In Oliver and Victor (1997) the objectives of dynamic reserved channel scheme (DRCS) are to satisfy a desired dropping of the probability of handover calls, to reduce the blocking probability of new calls, and to improve the channel utilization. Similarly a flexible channel assignment scheme is proposed in (Tajima and Imamura, 1999). In the subtracting scheme (SRS) certain channels are allowed to temporarily divide into two channels at half the original rate to accommodate handover calls. This subtracting occurs when all the channels occupied at the moment of handover arrival.

When subtracting channel is released, it forms into an original full-rate channel by combining with another subtracted channel (Kulavaratharasah and Aghvami, 1998).

DESIGN SCHEME FOR MIXED HANDOVER

The author presents a mixed handover scheme, which aims to give handover calls higher priority than new calls. The Mixed Scheme combines two priority schemes namely Handover Queuing Scheme and Reserved Channel Scheme (bandwith reservation). In this work, first in, first out (FIFO) and measurement based priority scheme (MBPS) queuing discipline (Tekinay and Jabbari, 1992) and Reserved Channel Scheme (RCS) is used, and achieves a remarkable reduction in FTP. The network resources are limited due to physical limitation of wired link and frequency interference in radio link.

Consequently, as FTP decrease, the blocking probability of new calls increases. Careful implementation of handover algorithm leads to minimum FTP and keeps blocking probability to the objective value. The various steps used in the proposed Mixed Scheme are as follows:

Admission control

In the proposed scheme, a new call is admitted only if number of free channels is more than number of guard channels; otherwise, the new call is blocked. Handover calls are admitted if any channel is free. If all the channels are occupied, then the handover is queued using queuing discipline like FIFO and MBPS queuing schemes. Handover requests are blocked only if it is waiting in the queue for free resource, and the tolerance time period elapsed before granting a free resource.

This reflects the natural boundary of the queue size. Queuing scheme gives the priority to handover calls by keeping them waiting for resources to be freed, and give them priority over the new calls, while, RCS gives priority to the handover calls by preventing new call to use certain number of channels, which are reserved exclusively for handover calls. The mixed scheme, combines the priority from the both schemes, and gains a higher priority for handover calls (Hadj et al., 2009).

EXPANSION OF ATM BASED NETWORK

Cellular mobile systems employ channel assignment, whereas ATM-based clustered networks may employ statistical multiplexing and statistical bandwidth assignment (Kesidis, 2007).Since statistical bandwidth assignment can be mapped into per call equivalent bandwidth assignment, the concept of guard channel, that is, RCS can be directly applied to set aside reserved bandwidth for handover calls.

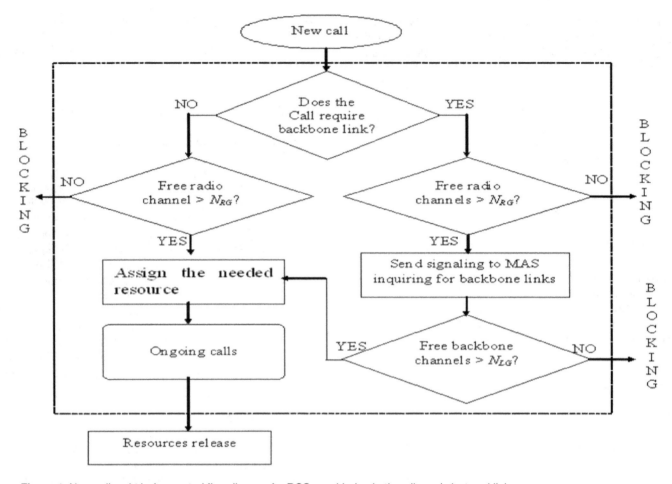

Figure 1. New calls admission control flow diagram for RCS considering both radio and clustered links.

ADMISSION CONTROL OVER CLUSTERED NETWORK

New calls may need to use the clustered network to communicate with other call parties, served by different Mobile ATM Switch (MAS). A new call is admitted only if radio and clustered resources are available, otherwise, the new call is blocked. Figure 1 show flow diagram for Call Admission Control over radio and clustered links respectively. The handover calls, may also need to use a clustered link, in this case, RCS may be applied for both radio links and clustered links, as stated in Oliver and Victor (1997). Each cell is served by BTS, which has NR radio channels to serve MT in the cell. Number NRG of radio channels, can be reserved to serve handover requests. On the other hand, each clustered link has NL channels, number in channels in a clustered link, is relatively larger than the number of channels in a BTS. As at the radio channels, NLG guard channels can be reserved to serve handover calls, that request clustered link. The number of guard channels should be determined carefully in both radio and clustered links; this number depends on the traffic patterns (Tekinay and Jabbari,

1992) and network topology.

Queuing the handover request, which is used in considering radio link only, can be used in the extension to ATM-based network. The idea is that when resources are needed to serve handover are not available, is to queue handover request instead of blocking the handover call, the queuing is limited by a time interval, during which some resources are expected to be freed, so handover request can be served. If handover request needs a clustered link, then it is queued if radio resources are not available or clustered link resources are not available.

SIMULATION MODEL

In this study, a simulation model is proposed in which multiple cells connected by MAS. The cells are connected by fixed clustered network. PCN architecture based ATM switches proposed in Low (2000). Simulation model can work with any channel assignment strategy. However, the results are obtained using Fixed Channel Assignment (FCA).

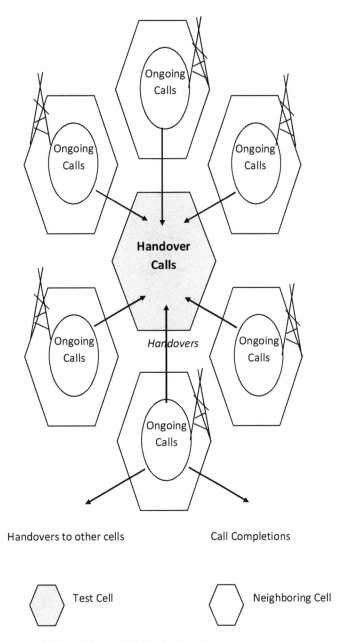

Figure 2. Simulation model for single cell.

TRAFFIC MODEL

Traffic in a cell consists of new calls initiated inside the cell and handovers arriving to the cell from the neighboring cells. New calls and handovers follow Poisson distribution. The offered load (that is, traffic) is variable; to obtain different points, while the fraction of total traffic due to the handover is kept fixed. Call duration is assumed to be exponential.

When a new call is originated in a cell and assigned a channel, the call holds until it is completed in the cell or handed over to another cell as the mobile moves out of the cell, Figure 2 shows traffic flow into a cell. MT stays in

the coverage area of a cell for a period of time (dwell time) that is exponentially distributed, and then it moves to one of surrounding cells.

The probability of requiring a handover depends on the cell coverage area, the MT movement, and the call duration. A call handover must be directed to one of the neighboring cells. The probability of each neighboring cell receiving the call depends on the amount of common boundary area and mobile direction (Oliver and Victor, 1997). In simulation model, we consider typical hexagonal cell, and we assume that the neighboring cells receive the handover with an equal probability of 1/6 for each.

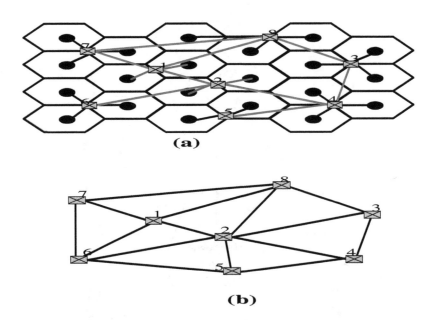

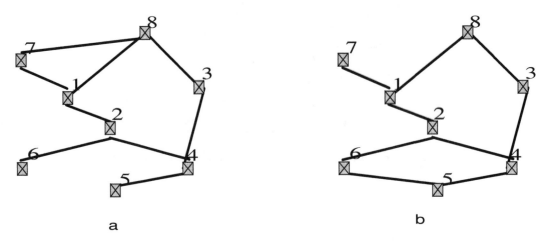

Figure 3. An ATM based cellular network. (a) An ATM based architecture. (b) Corresponding H graph of the PCN architecture.

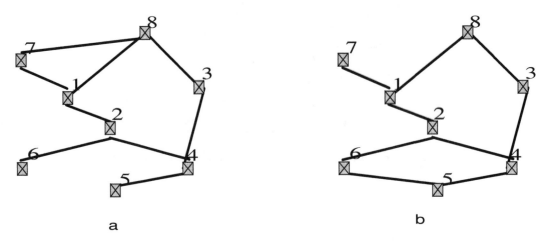

a   b

Figure 4. Different possible clustered network connections.

ENVIRONMENT DESCRIPTION

Each microcell has a BS to serve the MT within the cell. The geographical area is partitioned into a set C= {C1, C2,..., Cn} of n disjoint clusters, each cluster consists of a set of microcells. An ATM switch is allocated within each cluster and each BS in this cluster is connected to one of the ports of this switch. The ATM switch offers the services of establishing / releasing channels for the MTs in the cluster, also this switch should have routing/rerouting capabilities. Two neighboring clusters can be interconnected via the associated ATM switches. The links between ATM switches are called clustered links, and the links between ATM switch and BS are called local links.

An ATM-based topology could be represented by an undirected graph H = (V,F); where each vertex vi in V stand for a cluster Ci (or an ATM switch) and an edge ei,j is in F if clusters Ci and Ci are adjacent in the given network. Figure 3 shows an ATM based PCN topology, which consist of 21 cells, attached to 8 ATM switches, which connected by 9 clustered links. In Low (2000), they have given PCN with different number of cells and ATM switches configuration. Corresponding H graph of Figure 3(a) is shown in Figure 3(b).

Constructing a clustered network between MASs could be done in different ways. Depending on the geographical area, the cost of the clustered link, and traffic patterns. Figures 4(a) and 4(b) show different possible clustered network for the graph in Figure 3(b).

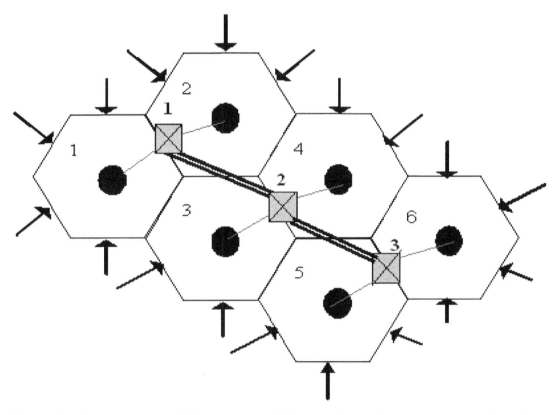

Figure 5. Simulation environment ATM-based cellular PCN. Arrows indicate handover from surrounding cells; mobile ATM switch.

MT engaged in a call or data transfer within the same cluster will consume two local links, one for each local link between base station and the associated switch. For intercluster communication, clustered links will be allocated in addition to local links. The channel occupied will depend on the communication path being assigned.

SIMULATION ENVIRONMENT

In the simulation, we have simulated the traffic in six cells as a part of full network. From Figure 5 we consider the ATM switches 1, 2 and 3. BTS 1 and BTS 2 form a cluster, and connected to ATM switch 1, BTS 3 and BTS 4 form a cluster and connected to ATM switch 2, similarly for ATM switch 3. ATM switches 1 with 2, and 2 with 3 are connected by clustered links; this configuration is illustrated in Figure 5. To eliminate the boundary effect, wraparound topology is used. Traffic in the clustered link is from: calls between (BTS1 or BTS2), (BTS3 or BTS4) and (BTS5 or BTS6), and vice versa. Load from other parts of the network that may use this link in its communication. The number of channels available in this clustered network is relatively larger than that of each BTS radio channels. The initiated and handover calls in the cells, have Poisson rate as described above.

Simulation parameters

The simulation parameters used for the purpose are as follows:

(a) NR: Number of radio channels in each cell.
(b) NRG: Number of radio guard channels in each cell.
(c) λo: New call arrival rate.
(d) λhi: Handover call arrival rate.
(e) ρ: The offered load which is $\lambda o + \lambda hi$.
(f) tc: New call holding time.
(g) th: Handover call holding time.
(h) tq: Maximum tolerable time in the queue.
(i) NL: Number of clustered channels in each clustered link.
(j) NLG: Number of clustered guard channels in each clustered link.
(k) Pcell: Probability of in cell call.
(l) Pcluster : Probability of in cluster call.
(m) Pbacbone: Probability of out cluster call.

RESULTS

In this study, simulation results are obtained to evaluate the proposed Mixed Scheme. Simulation program was

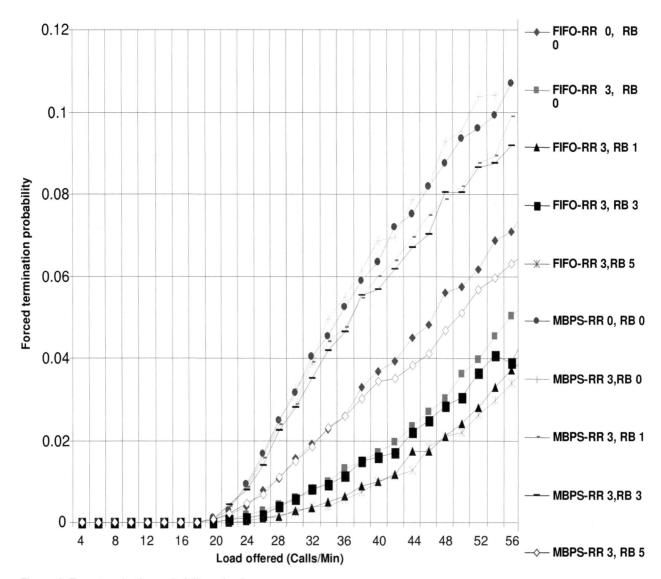

Figure 6. Force termination probability vs.load.

run using default values of simulation parameters to obtain the results. 10000 calls were sampled in one arbitrary cell of the simulation environment.

Calls may require a fixed part of the network to complete their connections. The default values for the simulation parameter are defined as follows (Ebersman and Tonguz, 1999).

NR = 30 Radio channels in each cell,
NRG = 3 Reserved Radio channels in each cell,
tc = 60 s average of new call holding time,
th = 30 s average of handover call holding time,
tq =   10 s average time in the handover queue.

Handover has 50% of the total traffic. The offered load varies from 4 calls/min to 60 calls/min, which is considered as overload traffic to the system.

Forced termination probability

From Figure 6 it is clear that pure FIFO (that is, for RR 0, RB 0) and pure MBPS (that is, for RR 0, RB 0) schemes have maximum FTP with no reserved channel at the radio link and back bone link. Reserved channels at radio link (FIFO-RR 3, RB 0, and MBPS-RR 3, RB 0) improve the performance a little bit. MBPS with 3 reserved radio channels and 5 reserved clustered channels (MBPS, RR 3, RB 5) has the least FTP. FIFO scheme with 3 reserved radio channels and 5 reserved clustered channels (FIFO, RR 3, RB 5), has little improvement over (MBPS, RR 3, RB 3). FTP for (FIFO, RR 3, RB 3) is significantly higher than (FIFO, RR 3, RB 5). As mentioned before, MBPS and FIFO with 3 reserved radio channels and zero reserved clustered channels have significant higher FTP than the other described schemes, this shows the

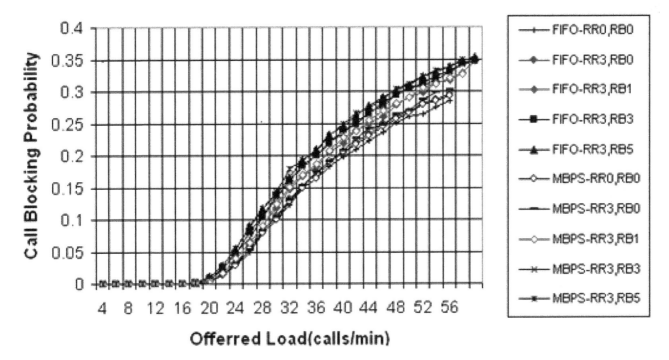

Figure 7. Call blocking probability vs. load.

importance of using reserved channels on the clustered network links. There is significant improvement when MBPS queuing discipline is used over FIFO queuing discipline, this is clear when we use the same number of reserved channels on clustered link and radio link for both schemes.

Call blocking probability

The call blocking probability (CBP) is the probability that the new calls finds all the channels busy, and blocked. It is important to keep track of the blocking probability, to see how much various scheme yields blocking probabilities. Figure 7 gives the CBP behavior of mixed and non mixed (FIFO and MBPS) schemes. It is clear that all the mixed schemes have more blocking probability at higher offered load. Increase in Call Blocking Probability is always the price we have to pay for decrease in Forced Termination Probability. All mixed schemes, which is basically queuing and reservation, approximately have the same blocking probability with minor differences. This shows a trade-offs between the handover forced termination and new call blocking.

Improvement in FTP due to reserving channels at clustered link

The improvement study carried out to show how much improvement is achieved by using the mixed scheme in

the comparison to the other schemes. The improvement reflects the reduced percentage of FTP due to handover failure. The improvement of scheme S1 over S2 is calculated as follows:

Improvement (S1, S2) in %= (f (S2) - f (S1))/ S2 * 100

where f (S) is the FTP by using scheme S, substitute S1 and S2 for various schemes.

Figure 8 shows improvement of Mixed Scheme (that is, using reserved channels with MBPS and FIFO), with respect to pure FIFO (RR 0, RB 0). The figure shows a significant improvement when 3 or 5 channels are reserved in clustered link. The maximum improvement is achieved by the schemes FIFO (RR 3, RB 5) and MBPS (RR 3, RB 5), which is 100 to 80% at moderate offered load and 70 to 50% at higher load.

Increase in CBP due to reserving channels at clustered link

As consequence of reduction in FTP, an increase in new CBP is introduced. The number of resources is limited (that is, radio channels) as more channels are assigned to serve handover request, blocking probability will increase. We have studied how the Mixed Scheme introduces increase in CBP, in comparison to other schemes. The increased blocking reflects the percentage increase in CBP due to non-availability of resources of

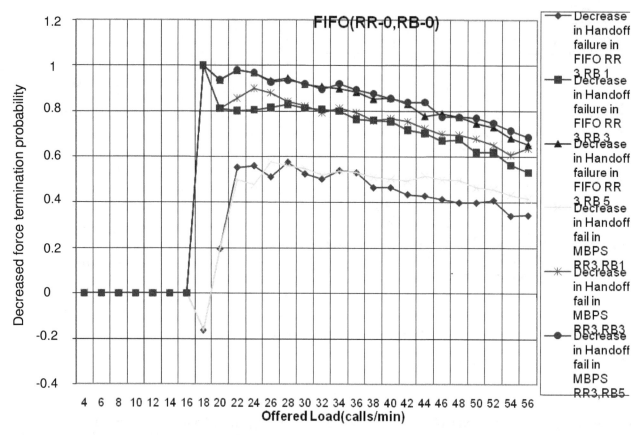

Figure 8. Decreased force termination probability wuth respect to pure FIFO(RR-0,RB-0.

scheme S1 over scheme S2, the increase in CBP is calculated as follows:

Blocking increase (S1, S2) in %   = (b(S1) - b(S2))/ S1 *100

where b(S) is the CBP by using scheme S, substitute S1 and S2 for various schemes.

Reserving channels on clustered link leads to slight increase in CBP. Figure 9 explores the increase in CBP in Mixed Scheme with respect to (w.r.t.) Pure FIFO (RR 0, RB 3). At low offered load (that is, in initial staghe) the increment in CBP is zero, which indicates that all the schemes have same performance. As the moderate load is offered to the network the increase in CBP suddenly raises up-to 100% for some duration, and than reduces to 30% gradually.

CONCLUSION

This paper focuses on the problem of congestion control in wireless ATM network. This is a practical fact that frequent handoff in PCN introduces the phenomena of congestion. After studying the currently used schemes, it

is clear that there is some room for improvement for conventional handoff ordering schemes. A simple new Hybrid Scheme is proposed to solve the hand off/ hand over problem in ATM-based PCN, which aims to give handover calls high priority over new calls. From simulation results, we find that using reserved channels at radio and clustered links, there is remarkable reduction in Forced Termination Probability (100 to 80% at moderate offered load and 70 to 50% at higher load). The price paid for using reserved channels is increase in Call Blocking Probability 75 to 25% approximately for moderate loads and 25 to 15% (approx.). This occurs because there is finite capacity for the network, and keeping more handoffs calls from being lost will result in more originating calls being lost because there are insufficient resources to handle them. We can draw the following conclusions to improve QoS for a better congestion management: Queuing discipline that serve first the handover requests, MBPS shows a considerable improvement over FIFO. However, queue discipline that depends on more measurement, and may be also on traffic patterns can lead to more accurate decision on which handover request should be served first. When reservation is applied on both radio and clustered channels, it leads to significant decrease in FTP with increase in CBP. This reflects the important of applying

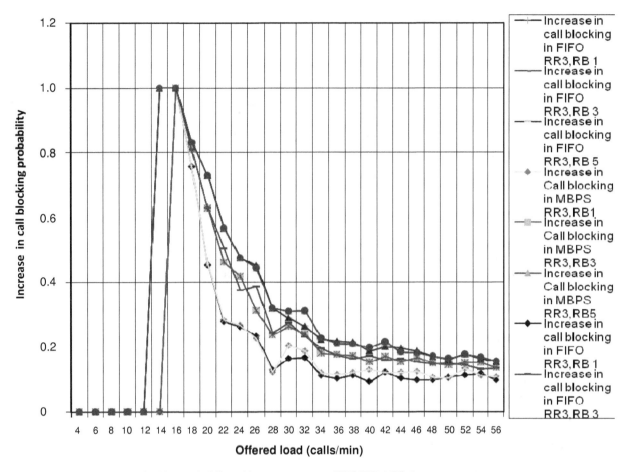

Figure 9. Increase in call blocking probability with respect to pure FIFO(RR-0,RB-0.

reservation scheme on both radio and clustered links and establishes a trade-offs also. Suddenly changes in the values of probabilities shows there is a need of careful determination/ implementation of reserved channels at radio as well as clustered levels. Consideration of traffic pattern and offered load is also important.

REFERENCES

Ebersman HG, Tonguz OK (1999). Handoff ordering using signal prediction priority queuing in personal communication systems." IEEE Trans. Veh. Technol., 48(1): 20-35.

Guerrero LO, Aghvami AH (1999). A prioritized handoff dynamic channel allocation strategy for PCS." IEEE Trans. Veh. Technol., 48(4): 1203-1215.

Hadj G aoued boukelif UK (2009). Proposed "A New Authentication Scheme For Wireless ATM Networks (WATM)"ACTA Electrotech., 50(2).

Kesidis (2007). Analysis of ATM Communication system." John Wileys.

Kulavaratharasah MD, Aghvami AH (1998). Teletraffic performance evaluation of microcellular personal communication networks (PCNs) with prioritized handoff procedures " IEEE Trans. Veh. Technol., 37(2): 92-103.

Kyasanur and Vidya (2005). Capacity of Multichannel Wireless N/W : impact of number of Channel interface." ACM Mobicom. p.21.

Low CP (2000). An efficient algorithm for link allocation problem on ATM-based personal communication network." IEEE JSAC, 18(7): 1279 -1288.

Oliver TW, Victor CM (1997). Adaptive resource allocation for prioritized call admission over an ATM-based wireless PCN." IEEE JSAC, 15(7): 1208-1225.

Ramaswami and Parhi (2003). Distrubuted Scheduling of Broadcast in ATM radio N/W." IEEE/ACM. p.23

Siv RM, Kumar M (2004). AD HOC "Wireless Networks Architecture and Protocols." Pearson Education.

Tajima J, Imamura K (1999). A strategy for flexible channel assignment in mobile communication systems." IEEE Trans. Veh. Technol., 48(1): 137-152.

Tekinay S, Jabbari B (1992). A measurement-based prioritization scheme for handovers in mobile cellular network." IEEE JSAC, 10(8): 1343-1350.

7

Sample reduction using recursive and segmented data structure analysis

R. H. Laskar*, F. A. Talukdar, Biman Paul and Debmalya Chakrabarty

Department of Electronics and Communication Engineering, National Institute of Technology, Silchar, India.

Support vector machine (SVM) is one of the widely used machine learning algorithms because of its salient features such as margin maximization and kernel substitution for classification and regression of data in a high dimensional feature space. But SVMs still face difficulties in handling large datasets. This difficulty is because of solving quadratic programming problems in SVMs which is costly, especially when dealing with large sets of training data. The proposed algorithm extracts data points lying close to the cluster boundaries of large data set, which form a much reduced but critical set for classification and regression. Inspired by the difficulties associated with SVM while handling large data sets with nonlinear kernels, the presented algorithm preselects a subset of data points and solves a smaller optimization problem to obtain the support vectors. The method presented reduces the data vectors by a recursive and segmented data structure analysis on the data vectors used to train the SVM. As this method is independent of SVM and precedes the training stage of SVM, it reduces the problem suffered by most data reduction methods that choose data based on repeated training of SVMs. Experiments using line spectral frequency (LSF) data vectors for voice conversion application show that the presented algorithm is capable of reducing the number of data vectors as well as the training time of SVMs, while maintaining good accuracy in terms of objective evaluation. The subjective evaluation result of the proposed voice conversion system is compared with the state of the art method like neural networks (NNs). The results show that the proposed method may be used as an alternative to the existing method for voice conversion.

Key words: Support vector machine, clustering based support vector machine, Mahalanobis distance, ward's linkage.

INTRODUCTION

Support vector machines (SVM) (Burges, 1998a; Vapnik, 1998g) play an important role in many areas such as pattern recognition, image processing, and many classification and regression problems. This is because of its salient properties such as margin maximization and kernel substitution for classifying the data in high dimensional feature space. Neural networks (NNs) (Haykin, 2003a) and Gaussian mixture models (GMMs) (Barrobés, 2006) are being used for classification and regression for many years. The performance of NNs depends on the training data size and network structures (Ellis et al., 1999b). As the network structure increases the training time also increases. GMM uses first and second order statistics and mixture weights, and hence, may not describe the complex distribution of the dataset appropriately. The number of mixtures should be low when there is no much data available to train the system (Mesbahi et al., 2007b).

The network structure for NNs and the number of mixtures for GMMs needs to be captured empirically. Unlike the back-propagation algorithm used to train NNs, the kernel based SVM follows the structural risk minimization problem and operates only in batch mode. The SVM with radial basis function network (RBFN) kernel best fits on the data, when number of data is large. SVMs have a small number of tunable parameters as it deals with the boundary points and is capable of finding the global solution (Burges, 1998a; Vapnik, 1998g). However, with increase in the number of data point, the limitation of SVMs becomes significant in the aspect of

---

*Corresponding author. E-mail: rabul18@yahoo.com.

scalability. Quadratic programming (QP) algorithms (used in SVM) are too time-consuming and memory-consuming in the case of a large number of data points.

The time-complexity and memory insufficiency problems associated with training the SVMs with large training dataset called for the need of reduced support vector machine that uses a subset of complete dataset to reduce the time-complexity and memory insufficiency problems. Many algorithms for reduction of training dataset have been proposed from time to time with their own merits and demerits (Wang et al., 2008).

Decomposition of the QP problem into several sub-problems can be used to provide a better solution to quicken SVMs training time, so that overall SVMs training time may be reduced. The time complexity can be reduced from $O(N^3)$ to $O(N^2)$ when the number of data points N is large (Wang et al., 2008). Active learning has also been applied in SVMs to select a small number of training data from the whole dataset (Hsu et al., 2002; Thong et al., 2000c; Schohn et al., 2000b). Another method uses repetitive use of SVM to find the final SVM is the incremental learning (Mitra et al., 2000a). Some random selection methods also prevail to reduce the training dataset but the probability distribution of the whole dataset is not taken into consideration in this method (Lee et al., 2001b; Watanbe et al., 2001d).

Dividing the overall quadratic programming (QP) problem of SVM into multiple QP sub-problems may quicken to solve QP problem without any extra matrix storage (Platt, 1999d). But it does not lead to a linear programming approach to reduce the complexity of the problem. The complexity may be further reduced by using Iterative Re-weighted Least Square (IRWLS) algorithm, which approximates the QP problem to a linear programming problem. The IRWLS algorithm is more computationally efficient than QP algorithms both in time and memory requirement for SVM (Pérez-Cruz et al., 2005).

Clustering based SVM (CB-SVM) (Yu et al., 2003b) method considers the clustering information in reducing the training dataset for SVM training. A clustering approach adopted in Wang et al. (2008) based on Ward's linkage is a hierarchical clustering algorithm that gives ellipsoid clusters for the complete dataset. The reduction uses Mahalanobis distance of every point within the cluster from the center of each cluster.

The data points in the vicinity of center of each cluster are removed to get reduced training dataset. But, Mahalanobis distance uses covariance matrix of the data points within a cluster. Covariance matrix is an $N \times N$ matrix, where N is number of data points whose covariance is to be calculated.

Almost all the existing methods proposed to improve the scalability of SVMs may either need to train SVMs/ repeatedly train SVMs or select randomly, select pseudo randomly or scan the whole dataset for many times to get the reduced dataset or by chunking method (Collobert et al., 2001a). These methods do not give the optimum distribution of data set and, their efficiency is still limited by the training speed of the SVMs and the scale of the dataset. Instead of using the above methods to train the SVMs, an approach proposed in Wang et al. (2008), which is based on the structure of the dataset, and is modified by recursive and segmented use of the algorithm on the dataset so that the limitation of the approach for handling large amount of data can be overcome.

The sample reduction by data structure analysis (SR-DSA) algorithm (Wang et al., 2008) was used for classification of both synthetic and real world datasets. The dataset used in Wang et al. (2008) has 2000 samples for training and 2000 samples for testing.

The proposed sample reduction using recursive and segmented data structure analysis (SR-RSDSA) which is based on SR-DSA algorithm is applied to regression problem for mapping the vocal tract characteristics of a source speaker according to that of a target speaker in a voice conversion system.

VOICE CONVERSION SYSTEM

The phenomenon of voice conversion (VC) (Barrobés, 2006; Lee, 2007a; Mesbahi et al., 2007b; Kain et al., 1998d; Stylianou et al., 1998f) is to modify a source speaker's utterance, as if spoken by a specified target speaker. The main aim of voice conversion is to design a system that can modify the speaker specific characteristics of the source speaker keeping the information and the environmental conditions, contained in the speech signal intact. In our day-to-day life, individuality in one's voice is one of the most important aspects of human speech communication. Our main objective is to design a SVM model for voice conversion which can maintain the target speaker's identity in the synthesized speech signal. Various potential applications of voice conversion are: customization of Text-To-Speech (TTS) system, developing speaker recognition and speaker verification systems in security and forensic applications, movie dubbing, animation, karaoke etc., hence the motivation for our work.

In the area of speech signal processing, isolating the characteristics of speech and speaker from the signal is a challenging problem. As the speaker identity lies in all the acoustic cues with varying degree of importance, so it is not possible to modify all the speaker specific characteristics to design a voice conversion system. The vocal tract characteristics carry the most significant information related to the identity of a particular speaker (Kuwabura et al., 1995).

The vocal tract characteristics are represented by various acoustic features, such as formant frequencies, formant bandwidths, spectral tilt (Kuwabura et al.,1995), linear prediction coefficients (LPCs) (Abe et al., 1988a), cepstral coefficients (Stylianou et al., 1998f), line spectral frequencies (LSFs) (Arslan, 1999a), refection coefficients (RCs) (Rao et al., 2007c) and log area ratios (LARs) (Rao et al., 2007c). For mapping the speaker-specific features between source and target speakers, various models have been explored in the literature. These models are specific to the kind of features used for mapping. For instance, GMMs (Barrobés, 2006; Stylianou et al., 1998f), vector quantization (VQ) (Abe et al., 1988a), fuzzy vector quantization (FVQ) (Rao et al., 2007c), linear multivariate regression (LMR) (Baudoin et al., 1996), dynamic frequency warping (DFW) (Baudoin et al., 1996), radial basis function networks (RBFNs) (Baudoin et al., 1996), feed forward neural network (Desai et al., 2010; Srinivas et al., 2009; Rao et al., 2007c) are widely used for mapping the vocal tract characteristics.

Feature extraction and database preparation

The basic shape of the vocal tract can be characterized by the gross envelope of linear prediction (LP) spectrum. LPC parameters are obtained using the LP analysis. LSFs are derived from LPCs, which are obtained from time aligned frames (overlapping frame of 20 ms) of source and target speakers sentences. LSFs are used to describe the vocal tract characteristics, as it possesses good interpolation property. For deriving the mapping function for voice conversion, the system has to be trained with LSFs extracted from the source and the target speaker's speech signal. For this purpose, we have taken 100 parallel sentences (for training) and 30 parallel sentences (for testing) from the Arctic database of Carnegie Mellon University (CMU ARCTIC database - 0.95-release). Two male (BDL and RMS) and two female (CLB and SLT) speakers are used for this study. The CMU ARCTIC database is recorded at 16 kHz with 16 bit resolution.

To capture the relationship between the vocal tract shapes between the source and the target speakers, it needs to associate the time aligned vocal tract acoustic features of the source and the target speakers. Dynamic time warping (DTW) algorithm is used to derive the time aligned vocal tract acoustic features. Thus the database for both the source and the target speakers are prepared which consists of time-aligned 10th dimensional LSF vectors. The database contains 56054 LSF vectors for training and 23846 LSF vectors for testing the system.

Training and testing the VC system

The training of the VC system is done through VQ, NNs, and GMMs. In this paper we have used support vector regression for training the system. For a given set of input and output vectors, the goal of regression is to fit a mapping function which approximates the relation

between the data points and is used later to predict the output feature space from a given new input feature space. As the database contains 10th dimensional, 56054 LSFs vectors for training, it may not possible to train the VC system with large amount of data. The SVM algorithm (Gunn, 1998c) can handle 4000 vectors and SVMTorch (Collobert et al., 2001a) can take 20000 vectors for training. The conventional methods for training the SVMs, in particular decomposition methods like SVM-Light, LIBSVM and SVMTorch handle problems with large number of features quite efficiently, but their super-linear-behavior makes their use inefficient or even intractable on large datasets (Joachim, 1999c). The algorithms mentioned in Collobert et al. (2001a), and Gunn (1998c), SVM-Light or LIBSVM needs to be applied for each dimension of the output vectors and leads to uni-dimensional regression problem. As, both the input and output feature vectors are multi-dimensional, therefore, SVM multiregressor (MSVR) (Fernandez, 2004a) is used in this study. The M-SVR can capture a nonlinear regression model which can approximate a vector-valued nonlinear function between the input and output acoustic spaces. The M-SVR can handle 4000 vectors during training, so a new algorithm named SR-RSDSA is proposed to reduce the number of training vectors to be applied to M-SVR.

Synthesis of target speaker's speech signal

The target speaker's LSF vectors corresponding to new LSF vectors (for test sentences) of the source speaker are obtained by the mapping function captured during the training phase. These predicted LSF vectors are converted to LPCs which gives the modified vocal tract characteristics of the target speaker. The modified vocal tract characteristics are excited by the source residual signal to get the target speaker's speech signal.

SUPPORT VECTOR MACHINES

Given m training pairs $(x_1, y_1), (x_2, y_2), \ldots, (x_m, y_m)$ where, $x_i \in R^d$ is an input vector labeled by $y_i \in \{+1, -1\}$ for $i = 1, \ldots, m$. SVMs (Burges, 1998a; Vapnik, 1998f) search for a separating hyper-plane with largest margin, which is called an optimal hyper-plane $w^T x + b = 0$. This hyper-plane can classify an input pattern according to the following function:

$$f(x) = sgn(w^T x + b) \tag{1}$$

$$sgn(k) = \begin{cases} +1 \ if \ k \geq 0 \\ -1 \ if \ k < 0 \end{cases} \tag{2}$$

In order to maximize the margin for linearly separable cases, we need to find the solution for the following quadratic problem:

$$min \frac{1}{2} \| w \|^2 \qquad (3)$$

subject to:

$$y_i(w^T x_i + b) \geq 1 \quad \forall i = 1,2,\ldots\ldots,m \qquad (4)$$

In fact, there are many linearly non-separable problems in the real world. In order to solve these problems related to linear SVMs, we have to modify the previous method by introducing non-negative slack variables $\xi_i \geq 0$, $i = 1,\ldots\ldots,m$. The non-zero $\xi_i > 0$, are those training patterns that do not satisfy the constraints in Equation (4). The optimal hyper-plane for this kind of problem could be found by solving the following quadratic programming problem:

$$min \frac{1}{2} \| w \|^2 + C \sum_{i=1}^{m} \xi_i \qquad (5)$$

subject to:

$$y_i(w^T x + b) \geq 1 - \xi_i, \quad \forall i = 1,2,\ldots,m \qquad ($$

$$\xi_i \geq 0 \qquad (7)$$

The problem is usually posed in its Wolfe dual form with respect to Lagrange multipliers $\alpha_i \in [0,C]$, $i = 1,2,\ldots\ldots,m$, which can be solved by standard quadratic optimization packages. The bias b can be easily calculated from any support vector x_i satisfying $0 < \alpha_i < C$. The value of α_i should be such that the support vectors can train the system effectively. If $\alpha_i = C$, then this will lead to over fitting of the system as there will be too many support vectors to handle. So for an efficient modeling, $\alpha_i's$ should be optimal. The discriminative function is therefore given by

$$f(x) = sgn(w^T x + b) = sgn(\sum_{i=1}^{m} \alpha_i y_i x_i^T x + b) \qquad (8)$$

A typical SVM regression problem is to find a non linear function that is well learned by a linear learning machine in a kernel induced feature space while maintaining all the main features that characterize the maximal margin algorithm. This non linear function will then try to predict output vectors when the SVM is subjected to new input vectors. In a typical classification or regression task, only a small number of $\alpha_i's$ greater than zero are considered. The training vectors respective to $0 < \alpha_i < C$, are called support vectors, as $f(x)$ depends on them exclusively.

For some problems, improved classification or regression can be achieved using non-linear SVMs (Burges, 1998a; Vapnik, 1998f). The basic idea of nonlinear SVMs is to map data vectors from the input space to high-dimensional feature space using a non-linear mapping ϕ, and then proceed for classification or regression using linear SVMs.

However, the nonlinear mapping ϕ is performed by employing kernel functions $K(x_i, x)$, which obeys Mercer's conditions (Burges, 1998b), to compute the inner products between support vectors $\Phi(x_i)$ and the data vector $\Phi(x)$ in the feature space. Typical kernel functions include the radial basis function network

(RBFN) $(\exp(-\frac{|x-x_i|^2}{2\xi^2}))$, the polynomial learning machine $((x^T x_i + 1)^p)$ and two-layer perceptron $(\tanh(\beta_0 x^T x_i + \beta_1))$ (Haykin, 2003a). For an unknown input pattern x, we have the following discriminative function:

$$f(x) = sgn\left(\sum_{i=1}^{m} \alpha_i y_i K(x_i^T x) + b\right) \qquad (9)$$

In this paper, we have used RBFN kernel to project the data into feature space as RBFN implicitly calculates the bias b.

To capture the nonlinear mapping function, M-SVR (Fernandez et al., 2004a) algorithm, an approach based on IRWLS (Pérez-Cruz, 2005) algorithm is used in this study. The M-SVR was applied for non-linear channel estimation in multi-input and multi-output (MIMO) system. It is observed that M-SVR based approach provides better results in terms of bit error rate (BER) and complexity in comparison to radial basis function network (RBFN) as well as uni-dimensional support vector regression based approach.

The M-SVR is a generalization of SVR to solve the problem of regression estimation for multiple variables. The uni-dimensional regression estimation is regarded as finding mapping between an incoming vector $x_i \in R^d$ and an observable output $y_i \in R$ from a given set of i.i.d. sample $(x_i, y_i), i = 1,2,\ldots,m$. If the observable output is a vector $y_i \in R^Q$, it needs to solve the multi-dimensional regression estimation problem (Fernandez et al., 2004a). For voice conversion system, both d and Q are 10; that motivates us to use M-SVR algorithm to capture the nonlinear mapping function between the acoustic spaces of two speakers.

SAMPLE REDUCTION

Here a discussion on finding the structural information in the given dataset is carried out followed by Mahalanobis distance calculation. Thereafter, we have discussed on some of the modifications in the algorithm (Wang et al., 2008) for data segmentation and recursive reduction. The proposed algorithm for sample reduction using recursive and segmented data structure analysis (SR-RSDSA) is presented afterwards.

Data structure analysis

For many applications, whether classification or regression, data appears in homogenous groups and this structural information can provide us the basis to select the data points that are likely to be the support vectors thereby reducing the training time of the SVMs significantly.

The structure of the data is defined as the units inside which the data points are considered to share the same dispersion (Wang et al., 2008). For the purpose of investigating the structure of given dataset, hierarchical clustering (Jain et al., 1988b; Salvador et al., 2004b) is adopted to detect the clusters in each individual class. For linear SVMs, hierarchical clustering is performed in input space, and for nonlinear SVMs, in the kernel space. Specifically speaking, data points are clustered in an agglomerative manner (Jain et al., 1988b; Salvador et al., 2004b) which is described as follows:

1. Initialize each point as a cluster and calculate the distance between every two clusters.
2. While more than one cluster remains.
a. Find the closest pair of clusters.

b. Merge the two clusters.
c. Update the distance between each pair of clusters.

Hierarchical clustering approaches (Jain et al., 1988b; Salvador et al., 2004b), (single-linkage clustering, complete-linkage clustering and Ward-linkage clustering) differ in the way of finding the closest pair of clusters. The Ward-linkage clustering gives clusters that are compact and ellipsoidal, which offers a meaningful basis for the computation of the covariance matrix. If U and V are two clusters with means $\bar{U}$ and $\bar{V}$, respectively, the Ward's linkage $W(U,V)$ between clusters U and V can be calculated as (Wang et al., 2008).

$$W(U,V) = \frac{|U|.|V|}{|U| + |V|} . \| \bar{U} - \bar{V} \|^2 \qquad (10)$$

Initially, each pattern is one cluster. The Ward's linkage of two patterns x_i and x_j is (Wang et al., 2008):

$$W(x_i, x_j) = \frac{\| x_i - x_j \|^2}{2} \qquad (11)$$

When two clusters A and B are being merged to a new cluster A', to be more computationally efficient, the Ward's linkage between A' and cluster C, that is, $W(A',C)$ can be conventionally derived from $W(A,C)$, $W(B,C)$, and $W(A,B)$, in the following way (Wang et al., 2008):

$$W(A,C) = \frac{(|A| + |C|)W(A,C) + (|B| + |C|)W(B,C) - |C|W(A,B)}{|A| + |B| + |C|} \qquad (12)$$

In the high-dimensional implicit kernel space, the hierarchical clustering is still applicable:

(1) The Ward's linkage between $\Phi(x_i)$ and $\Phi(x_j)$, that is, the images of patterns x_i and x_j, can be calculated by (c.f. Equation 10).

$$W(\Phi(x_i),\Phi(x_j)) = \frac{1}{2} [K(x_i,x_i) + K(x_j,x_j) - 2K(x_i,x_j)] \qquad (13)$$

(2) Reference (Wang et al., 2008) shows when two clusters A^Φ and B^Φ merge to a new cluster A'^Φ, the Ward's linkage $W(A'^\Phi, C^\Phi)$ between A'^Φ and C^Φ can be conveniently calculated by

$$W(A'^\Phi, C^\Phi) = \frac{(|A^\Phi| + |C^\Phi|)W(A^\Phi,C^\Phi) + (|B^\Phi| + |C^\Phi|)W(B^\Phi,C^\Phi) - |C^\Phi|W(A^\Phi,B^\Phi)}{|A^\Phi| + |B^\Phi| + |C^\Phi|} \qquad (14)$$

During hierarchical clustering, the Ward's linkage between clusters to be merged increases as the number of clusters decreases. A curve namely the merge distance curve is drawn to represent this process. This curve is used to find the knee point (Wang et al., 2008), that is, the point of maximum curvature to determine the number of clusters.

Mahalanobis distance

As the Mahalanobis distance is calculated by utilizing the mean and variance of data statistics, it implicitly contains the data structural information. Therefore, it is more reasonable to use the Mahalanobis distance, instead of the Euclidean distance, as the distance metric. It gives the distance of a test point within the cluster from the mean of the cluster divided by width of the ellipsoid in that particular direction. It is scale invariant which means that the result will not change if all the dimensions are scaled equally.

Let X be a $n \times m$ matrix containing m random observations $x_i, i = 1,2, \ldots \ldots ,m$. Let μ be the mean of the m data points and σ be the covariance, then, the Mahalanobis distance is given by

$$d^2(x_i,X) = (x_i - \mu)^T \sigma^{-1}(x_i - \mu) \qquad (15)$$

If the covariance matrix is singular, it is difficult to directly calculate the inverse of σ. Instead, we can calculate the pseudo inverse σ^+ to approximate σ^{-1} as $\sigma^+ = A^T G^{-1} A$, if the Eigen-structure of the real symmetric and positive semi-definite matrix σ is $A^T G A$. Then the Mahalanobis distance from a sample x_i to the population X is:

$$d^2(x_i,X) = (x_i - \mu)^T A^T G^{-1} A(x_i - \mu) \qquad (16)$$

Data segmentation

The method proposed in Wang et al. (2008) suffered from the computational complexity and memory insufficiency, due to calculation of covariance matrix and its inverse. Thus, the covariance matrix formed should be small so as to avoid memory insufficiency, which required limited amount of dataset that machine can handle. This limitation forbids the algorithm to be applied for large datasets.

To apply this algorithm for very large dataset, a small modification can be done. The data set may be divided into many segments with each having maximum number of data points whose covariance matrix and inverse of covariance matrix can be computed by avoiding the memory insufficiency problem. Then, applying the clustering algorithm to the segmented data set followed by calculation of Mahalanobis distance for the same set may help the algorithm to work for large dataset.

Recursive reduction

The data reduction obtained using the process of clustering by Ward's linkage followed by calculating the Mahalanobis distance may not be able to reduce the data to sufficient extent for large dataset. Moreover, due to segmentation chances are there that data points which form a cluster for whole dataset may not result in cluster formation for segmented data. These data points have to be kept intact because we are not sure about its contribution to support vectors. The clustering of the data is shown in Figure 1, and the corresponding reduced data set those may be the candidates for SVMs are shown in Figure 2.

The above mentioned two limitations are overcome using many stages of reduction. This recursive reduction not only reduces the dataset for training but also considers chance of the weakly clustered points in a particular stage to form cluster in subsequent stages.

ALGORITHM

The algorithm as shown in Figure 3 is based on repetitive use of the

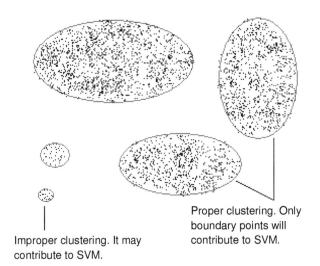

Improper clustering. It may contribute to SVM.

Proper clustering. Only boundary points will contribute to SVM.

Figure 1. Proper clustering and improper clustering.

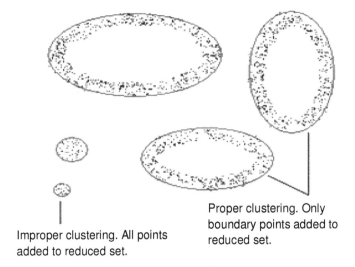

Improper clustering. All points added to reduced set.

Proper clustering. Only boundary points added to reduced set.

Figure 2. Reduced dataset using Mahalanobis distance.

following steps until the desired subset of dataset is obtained. The first iteration (stage or recursion) results in reduction of data to certain extent. But there may not be proper clustering of many data points because the whole data set is not considered due to memory limitation. These weakly clustered points may form proper cluster in the subsequent stages.

1.) Divide the complete training dataset into small subsets (sequentially or randomly) such that each subset contains maximum amount of data for which covariance matrix and its inverse computation does not lead to memory insufficiency problem. As the covariance matrix is an $N \times N$ data matrix for N points. This computation is a limitation to the approach if the whole set of points is fed for data reduction.
2.) If the dataset is linearly separable, the following operations can be done in the input space. If the dataset is not linearly separable, the following operations have to be done in kernel space as it becomes linearly separable in high-dimensional kernel space. Hence, for non-linearly separable dataset, it has to be projected in the kernel space.

3.) Cluster the data using hierarchal clustering technique using Ward's linkage using properly chosen cutoff distance for clustering. Hierarchal clustering using Ward's linkage takes into account the covariance of the data points and results in the formation of ellipsoidal clusters. Cutoff is properly chosen so that there is optimum amount of clustering. If the cutoff or merge distance is very less there will be many different cluster with few data points in each cluster and there would not be any assurance that the points at the vicinity of the center of the cluster shall not contribute to SVM. If cutoff is too large, the whole dataset may be clustered in single cluster. To select the optimum number of clusters the knee point of the curve between the numbers of clusters formed vs. cutoff or merge distance is chosen (Wang et al., 2008).
4.) For each cluster formed:

(a) If there is significant number of data points in the cluster, Mahalanobis distance of each point within the cluster from the mean (center of the cluster) of the data points of the cluster is calculated. η is chosen such that $1 > \eta > 0$ η is multiplied with maximum Mahalanobis distance calculated for each data points within the cluster from the center of the cluster. Thereafter, the points with Mahalanobis distance less than $\eta * MAX(d_i)$ from the center are discarded.
(b) If there is very few numbers of points in the cluster, then there is no assurance that the points would contribute to SVM or not. The data is kept as it is with the hope that it might form cluster with the points that are present in the other subsets of data that were not considered at once. If left unaltered, these points may result in formation of cluster in the next stage when the above process is repeated for reduced dataset obtained for the present stage.

TESTING AND RESULTS

The M-SVR algorithm along with the SR-RSDSA is used for mapping the vocal tract characteristics of a source speaker according to that of a target speaker. LSFs derived from LPCs are used to represent the vocal tract characteristics. The training dataset contains 56054 LSF vectors. It is divided into number segments with each segment contains 2000 LSF vectors and the last segment may have less number of vectors, if number of data points is not perfectly divisible by 2000. The cutoff is chosen to be 1.1542 for male to female and 1.154 for male to male voice conversion. The value of η has been taken to be 0.8 for both the speaker combinations.

Figures 4 and 5, show the desired, predicted and source LSF vector for a particular frame of a test sentence using the above algorithm. The figures indicate that the predicted LSF vector closely follows the deisred LSF vector. The LSFs are closely related to formant frequencies and most significant information lies in the lower order formants (Barrobés, 2006; Kuwabura et al., 1995). It is observed that the proposed method for voice conversion based on M-SVR and SR-RDSA algorithm can predict the lower order LSFs more closely as compared to higher order LSFs.

The mean-square-error (MSE) is an objective measure used to evaluate the performance of the VC system. It is evaluated for the complete set of test LSF vectors.

The MSE between the desired and predicted LSF

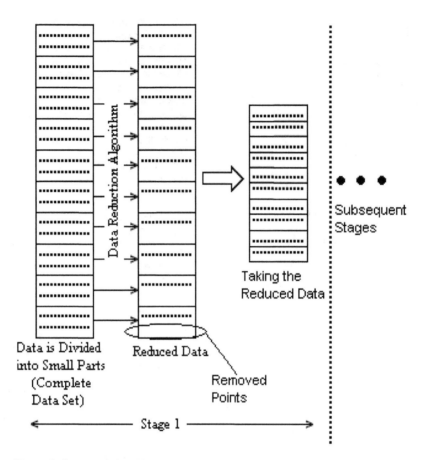

Figure 3. Proposed algorithm.

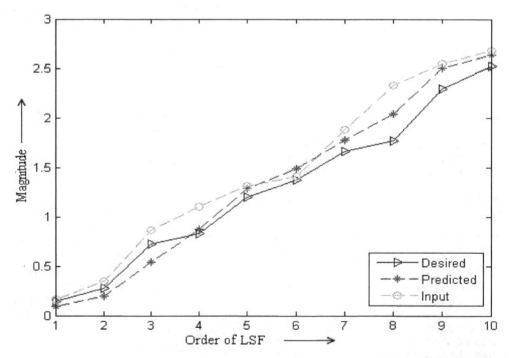

Figure 4. Desired, predicted and input LSF vector (for a particular frame of speech signal) showing the performance of the algorithm for male to female conversion. MSE is found to be 0.4 for the complete test set.

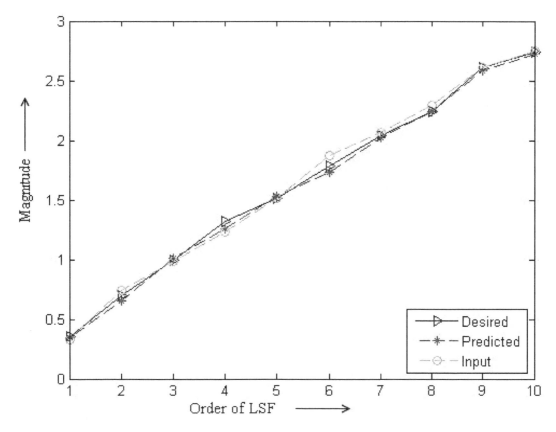

Figure 5. Desired, predicted and input LSF vector (for a particular frame of speech signal) showing the performance of the algorithm for male to male conversion. MSE is found to be 0.3 for complete test set.

Table 1. Performance evaluation interms of MOS for Voice Conversion System using M-SVR and LSF feature vectors.

Source	Target	MOS (proposed)	MOS (NN) Desai et al. (2010), Srinivas et al. (2009)
Male1	Female1	3.51	3.50
Male1	Male2	3.10	3.40

vectors is found to be 0.4 for Male 1 (BDL) to Female 1 (CLB) conversion and 0.3 for Male 1 (BDL) to Male 2 (RMS) conversion respectively.

Mean opinion score (MOS) is a subjective evaluation method used to judge the performance of a VC system. It is evaluated in a 5-point scale. The rating 5 indicates the excellent match between the original target speaker speech and the synthesized speech (that is, synthesized speech is close to the original speech of the target speaker). The rating 1 indicates very poor match between the original and synthesized utterances, and the other ratings indicate different levels of deviation between 1 and 5.

The MOS for two different speaker pair transformation is shown in Table 1. The MOS obtained using the proposed system is compared with the state art voice conversion system designed using NN and GMM (Desai et al., 2010; Srinivas et al., 2009). It may be observed from Table 1 that the proposed VC system may be used as an alternative to the existing method used for voice conversion. It is also observed that cross-gender voice conversion provides better result as compared to intra-gender voice conversion. It may due the wide differences in the vocal tarct characteristics between the two speakers belonging to different genders. The VC system designed in Desai et al. (2010), Srinivas et al. (2009) made use of CMU arctic database. However, in the design of VC system in Desai et al. (2010) Srinivas et al. (2009), mel frequency cepstral coefficients (MCEPs) is used as acoustic features to represent the vocal tract characteristics and artificial neural network (ANN) is used to train the VC system. The design of VC system using same set of acoustic features with different training algorithms may provide a better framework to evaluate the performance of the system.

Conclusion

In this paper, data reduction for SVM using recursive and segmented data structure analysis has been proposed. The data segmentation is achieved by dividing the dataset sequentially with each segment containing maximum data set,whose covariance matrix and inverse of the covariance matrix can be calculated by avoiding memory insufficiency problem. Ward's linkage is used for hierarchal clustering so as to get compact and ellipsoidal clusters. Mahalanobis distance has been used for calculation of distance metric. Recursive reduction has been used to reduce the dataset to the desired level of reduction. M-SVR has been used for training with the reduced dataset obtained by the proposed algorithm. The predicted data points have been found to be accurate enough for the voice conversion applications. As the speaker information lies in all the acoustic features with varying degree of importance, thereby suitably transforming the other speaker specific features such as the source characteristics (shape of the glottal pulse), pitch contour, duration patterns and energy profiles may improve the performance of the system. The proposed algorithm can be applied to other data reduction application by carefully choosing the cutoff or knee point during the hierarchical clustering process.

REFERENCES

Abe M, Nakamura S, Shikano K, Kuwabura H (1988a). Voice Conversion Through Vector-Quantization. Proc. ICASSP., pp. 655-658.

Arslan LM (1999a). Speaker Transformation Algorithm using Segmental Codebooks (STASC). Speech Commun., (28): 211-226.

Barrobés HD (2006). Voice Conversion applied to Text-to-Speech Systems, PhD Thesis, Universistat Politecnica de Catalunya, Barcelona, pp. 35-94.

Baudoin G, Stylianou Y (1996). On the transformation of the speech spectrum for voice conversion. Proc. of ICSLP., pp. 1405-1408.

Burges C (1998a). A Tutorial on Support Vector Machines for Pattern Recognition. Data Min. Knowl. Discov., 2: 121-167.

Burges CJC (1998b). A Tutorial on Support Vector Machines for Pattern Recognition. Kluwer Academic Publishers, Boston, Netherlands, pp. 18-20.

Collobert R, Bengio S (2001a). SVMTorch: Support Vector Machines for Large Scale Regression Problems. J. Machine Learn., pp. 143-160.

Desai S, Black AW, Yegnarayana B, Prahallad K (2010). Spectral Mapping using Artificial Neural Network for Voice Conversion. IEEE Trans. Audio Speech Lang. Process., 18(5): 954-964.

Ellis D, Morgan N (1999b). Size matters: An Empirical Study of Neural Network Training for Large Vocabulary Continuous Speech Recognition. Proc. ICASSP, Phoenix, pp. 1-4.

Fernandez MS, Cumplido MP, García JA, Cruz FP (2004a). SVM Multi-regression for Nonlinear Channel Estimation in Multiple-Input Multiple-Output Systems. IEEE Trans. Sig. Process., 52(8): 2298-2307.

Gunn SR (1998c). Support Vector Machines for Classification and Regression. Technical Report, Department of Electronics and Computer Science, University of Southampton.

Hsu CW, Lin CJ (2002). A Comparison of Methods for Multiclass Support Vector Machines. IEEE Trans. Neural Netw., 13(2): 415-425.

Haykin S (2003a). Neural Networks - A comprehensive foundation. Prentice Hall of India, pp. 23-270.

Jain AK, Dubes R (1988b). Algorithms for Clustering Data, Prentice-Hall, New Jersey.

Joachims T (1999c). Making Large-Scale SVM Learning Practical. In B. Scholkopf, C. Burges, A. Smola (Eds.), Advances in Kernel Methods — Support Vector Learning. MIT Press, Cambridge, M.A, pp. 169-184.

Kain A, Macon M (1998d). Spectral Voice Conversion for Text-to-Speech Synthesis. Proc. ICASSP, (1): 285-288.

Kuwabura H, Sagisaka Y (1995). Acoustic Characteristics of Speaker Individuality: Control and Conversion. Speech Commun., 16: 165-173.

Lee K-S (2007a). Statistical Approach for Voice Personality Transformation. IEEE Trans. Audio Speech Lang. Process., 15: 641-651.

Lee YJ, Mangasarian OL (2001b). RSVM: Reduced Support Vector Machine. Proceedings of 1st SIAM International Conference on Data Mining, Chicago, pp. 325-361.

Mesbahi L, Barreaud V, Boeffard O (2007b). GMM-based Speech Transformation System under Data Reduction. Proceedings of 6th ISCA Speech Synthesis Workshop (SSW6), pp. 119-124.

Mitra P, Murthy CA, Pal SK (2000a). Data Condensation in Large Databases by Incremental Learning with Support Vector Machines, Proc. Int. Conf. Patt. Recognit. (ICPR2000), Barcelona, pp. 712-715.

Pérez-Cruz F, Bousoño-Calzón C, Artés-Rodríguez A (2005). Convergence of the IRWLS procedure to the support vector machine solution. Neural Comput., 17(1): 7-18.

Platt J (1999d). Fast Training of Support Vector Machines using Sequential Minimal Optimization. In: B. Scholkopf, C. Burges, A. Smola (Eds.), Advances in Kernel Methods - Support Vector Learning. MIT Press, Cambridge, MA, pp. 185-208.

Rao KS, Laskar RH, Koolagudi SG (2007c). Voice Transformation by Mapping the Features at Syllable Level. LNCS Series, Springer. 4815: 479-486.

Salvador S, Chan P (2004b). Determining the Number of Clusters/Segments in Hierarchical Clustering/Segmentation Algorithms. Proc. 16th IEEE Int. Conf. Tools with AI., pp. 576-584.

Schohn G, Cohn D (2000b). Less is More: Active Learning with Support Vector Machines. Proc. of 17th Int. Conf. Machine Learn. (ICML'00), pp. 839-846.

Srinivas D, Ragavendra E V, Yegnarayana B, Black A W, Prahallad K (2009). Voice Conversion using Artificial Neural Networks. Proc. ICASSP, Taiwan, pp. 3893-3896.

Stylianou Y, Cappe Y, Moulines E (1998f). Continuous Probabilistic Transform for Voice Conversion. IEEE Trans. Speech Audio Process., (6): 131-142.

Thong S, Huang DK (2000c). Support Vector Machine Active Learning with Applications to Text Classification. Proc. 17th Int. Conf. Machine Learn. (ICML'00), pp. 999-1006.

Vapnik V (1998f). Statistical Learning Theory, Wiley, New York.

Wang D, Shi L (2008). Selecting Valuable Training Samples for SVMs via Data Structure Analysis. Neurocomputing, 71: 2772-2781.

Yu H, Han J, Chang KC (2003b). Classifying Large Datasets using SVMs with Hierarchical Clusters. Proc. Int. Conf. Knowl. Discov. Data Min. (KDD'03), pp. 306-315.

8

Design of fuzzy PD-controlled overhead crane system with anti-swing compensation

Shebel Asad*, Maazouz Salahat, Mohammad Abu Zalata, Mohammad Alia and Ayman Al Rawashdeh

Department of Mechatronics, Faculty of Engineering Technology (FET), Al Balqa Applied University (BAU), P. O Box 15008. Amman - Jordan.

This work aimed to find a proper control strategy to transfer loads using overhead cranes. The proposed control strategy, which is Fuzzy PD-based, should take into account two main factors. First, the time needed to move the payload from the initial pick up point to the destination point that must be minimized. Secondly, the oscillation of the payload must be reduced to prevent hazards for people and equipment in the work place. The current work, presents a comparative analysis of fuzzy PD based control basing on classical PD approach. A simplified model has been derived. The proposed control techniques have been designed and validated with MatLab. Numerical comparative results have been obtained and discussed.

Key words: Crane, position control, anti-swing compensation, fuzzy PD- based control.

INTRODUCTION

One of the current trends in industry is that cranes became larger and higher. So they supposed to be faster in order to achieve acceptable transfer times. Unfortunately, cranes with large structures that are moving at high speeds are associated with undesirable payload oscillations resulting from the system dynamics.

Cranes can be classified in terms of their mechanical structures and dynamics into three types: Overhead, rotary, and boom cranes. Overhead crane (OHC) is a common type of cranes used to transfer the payload from one position to desired position. A gantry crane incorporates a trolley which moves along the track and translates in a horizontal plane.

In such cranes system, the load suspended from the trolley by cable is subject to swing caused by improper control input and disturbances. The failure of controlling crane may cause accident and may harm people and the surroundings. Therefore, such crane control must be able to move the trolley adequately fast and to suppress the payload swing at the final position. This is so-called anti-

swing control.

In the present work, a Fuzzy PD (Proportional-Derivative) has been designed basing on classical PD approaches to ensure a robust and smooth position control of the carte (trolley position) with the presence of another fuzzy-based anti-swing compensator. The proposed model has been validated with MatLab/Simulink, fuzzy logic and virtual reality toolboxes Numerical comparative results have been obtained to be found very accepted.

To understand the overhead crane system, a simplified dynamic model has been derived that encounters the reality and complicities might be found with such type of cranes.

The main feature of the derived model is its capability to match real system's nonlinearity (trolley position and swinging angle).

DERIVATION OF A SIMPLIFIED DYNAMIC MODEL FOR OHC

The first step in deriving the equations of motion using the Lagrangian approach is to find the positions of the

*Corresponding author. E-mail: shebel_asad@hotmail.com.

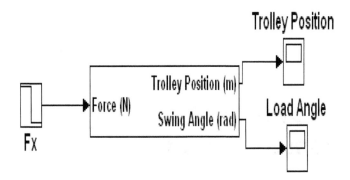

Figure 1. Presents the configuration of the approximated model of OHC.

load and position of the trolley with respect to the reference point, then the kinetic and potential energies and dissipation function of the whole system would be found. Finally, the equations of motion are as given in 1 and 2 (Moustafa et al., 2009; Abdel-Rahman et al., 2003).

$$\ddot{\theta} = -\left[\frac{F_x \cos\theta + (M+m)g\sin\theta + mL\dot{\theta}^2 \sin\theta \cos\theta}{L(M + m\sin^2(\theta))}\right]$$

(1)

$$\ddot{x} = \left[\frac{F_x + mg \sin(\theta)\cos(\theta) + mL \dot{\theta}^2 \sin(\theta)}{L(M + m\sin^2(\theta))}\right]$$

(2)

Equations (1) and (2) represent a nonlinear mathematical model of the overhead crane. Where; F_x is the applied mechanical force in Newton, θ is the swinging angel of the payload in radians, m is the payload mass, M is the trolley mass, x is the trolley position and L is the robe length in meters.

Approximation of the full model

The aforementioned derived model given in Equations 1 and 2 is an extremely nonlinear dynamic model. The nonlinear model could be approximated to simplify the progress of modeling in order to be used for numerical-control purposes (Kiviluoto, 2009).

Before the model linearization, a hypothesis for safe and smooth operation will be assumed and the swing angle would be kept small. As given in set of Equation (3).

$$\left.\begin{array}{l} \sin(\theta) \approx \theta \\ \cos(\theta) \approx 1 \\ \dot{\theta}^2 \approx 0 \end{array}\right\}$$

(3)

With this assumption, the simplified model of motion for the overhead crane system can be obtained as in Equation 4:

$$\left.\begin{array}{ll} x \ (Trolley \quad position \ ): & (M+m)\ddot{x} + mL\ddot{\theta} = F_x \\ \theta \ (Swing \quad angle \ ): & \ddot{x} + L\ddot{\theta} + g\theta = 0 \end{array}\right\}$$

(4)

State space representation of the system

After the simplification, Equation 4 can be re-written in state space representation as in Equation 5, and the equation of motion could be then obtained as shown in Equation 6:

$$x = \begin{bmatrix} x_1 \\ x_2 \\ x_3 \\ x_4 \end{bmatrix} = \begin{bmatrix} x \\ \dot{x} \\ \theta \\ \dot{\theta} \end{bmatrix} = \begin{bmatrix} Trolley \quad position \\ Trolley \quad velocity \\ Swing \quad angle \\ Rate \_ Swing \quad angle \end{bmatrix}$$

(5)

$$\dot{x} = \begin{bmatrix} \dot{x}_1 \\ \dot{x}_2 \\ \dot{x}_3 \\ \dot{x}_4 \end{bmatrix} = \begin{bmatrix} \dot{x} \\ \ddot{x} \\ \dot{\theta} \\ \ddot{\theta} \end{bmatrix} = \begin{bmatrix} 0 & 1 & 0 & 0 \\ 0 & 0 & \frac{m}{M}g & 0 \\ 0 & 0 & 0 & 1 \\ 0 & 0 & \frac{M+m}{ML}g & 0 \end{bmatrix} \begin{bmatrix} x_1 \\ x_2 \\ x_3 \\ x_4 \end{bmatrix} + \begin{bmatrix} 0 \\ \frac{1}{M} \\ 0 \\ -\frac{1}{ML} \end{bmatrix} F_x$$

(6)

Output equation ($y = Cx + Du$) is as given in Equation 7,

$$y = \begin{bmatrix} 1 & 0 & 0 & 0 \\ 0 & 0 & 1 & 0 \end{bmatrix} \begin{bmatrix} x \\ \dot{x} \\ \theta \\ \dot{\theta} \end{bmatrix}$$

(7)

From the previously described equations, it can be understood that the load (swing) angle (in other words, vibration that could be occurred) depends on the applied force F_x, the trolley and load's mass, the gravitational force and the length of the rope. The final simplified model can be built as shown in Figure 1,

With a model, shown in Figure 1, the trolley position would move to "infinity", while the load swinging is within -0.07 to 0.07 radians. So, since the trolley is non-stop at any location, it seems to be necessary if the input to be modified in order to make the trolley stop, or in the worse condition, the trolley needs to be stopped at "somewhere".

This will lead naturally to select a rectangular or "bang-bang" forcing function as an input vector. It seems that there is no mechanism or factor that makes the trolley

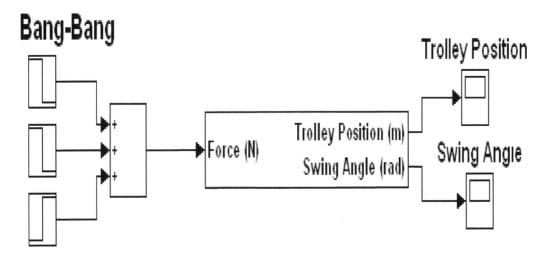

Figure 2. New system configuration.

stop (because the system model took an ideal situation). Regarding on this, this input has been introduced in order to cope with this condition. In other point of view, this type of input is well known as a time-optimal solution (Fang et al., 2003; Uchiyama, 2009). Regarding on this matter, modification of the selection of input shape has been done. This involves changing in system's block diagram, as well as the input itself only. Figure 2 shows the new Simulink block diagram and the input force applied to the system.

Validation of the simplified model

The effect in variation of input force, length of the hoisting rope, trolley mass and load mass on the dynamic behavior of the overhead crane are investigated. The comparative results are as shown in Figure 3.

Figure 3 shows the response of the system in term of trolley position and swing angle when different input forces applied to the system (0.2, 1 and 5 N).

We notice that when the input force is increase from 1 to 5 N, the trolley is able to travel more distance where it can reaches around 2.8 m from its initial position. However the vibration of the trolley is greater. The magnitude of the load swing also increased to around 0.8 rad. But the frequency of the load remains the same. When input force decreased from 1 to 0.2 N the trolley will only be able to reach around 0.12 m from its initial position. The magnitude of the load swing is decreased to approximate 0.033 rad. However the frequency of the load swing remained the same.

From Figure 3c, we can see that the magnitude (0.2 rad) and frequency of the swing angle is greater. Trolley still can reach at 0.58 m at 2 s although the length of the

hoisting rope decreased from 0.3 to 0.2 m. However the fluctuation of the trolley increased with shorter rope. This is due to the load oscillation increased when the rope is shorter.

As shown from Figure 3d when the load mass increased from 0.8 to 1.5 kg which means that the load mass is greater than the trolley mass the trolley (m < M) cannot reach more than 0.4 m and vibrate with obvious fluctuation, and the swing angle has high magnitude (0.09 rad) and frequency after the input force taken off.

CONTROL DESIGN

Proposed control structure

The structure of the proposed controller for the overhead crane system is shown in Figure 4. The proposed controller consists of fuzzy logic controllers for both position and anti-swing control respectively.

The objective of the proposed fuzzy logic controllers is to control the payload position X(s) so that it moves to the desired position $X_{ref}(s)$ as fast as possible without excessive swing angle of the payload θ(s). Here, the design of fuzzy logic control is based on a classical control approach (proportional derivative control mode PD). It shows that fuzzy logic controller is a controller that may realize the skill of human operators and the design rules describe the subjective fuzziness of operators' experiences instead of the use of mathematical model of the plant as modern control theory approaches.

Fuzzy PD controllers

Fuzzy PD controllers are physically related to classical PD controller. The parameters settings of classical and fuzzy controllers are based on deep common physical background. The introduced method considerably simplifies the setting and realization of fuzzy PD controllers (Pivoňka, 1999, 1998; Pivoňka et al., 1998). A classical ideal PD controller is described as noted in Equation 8.

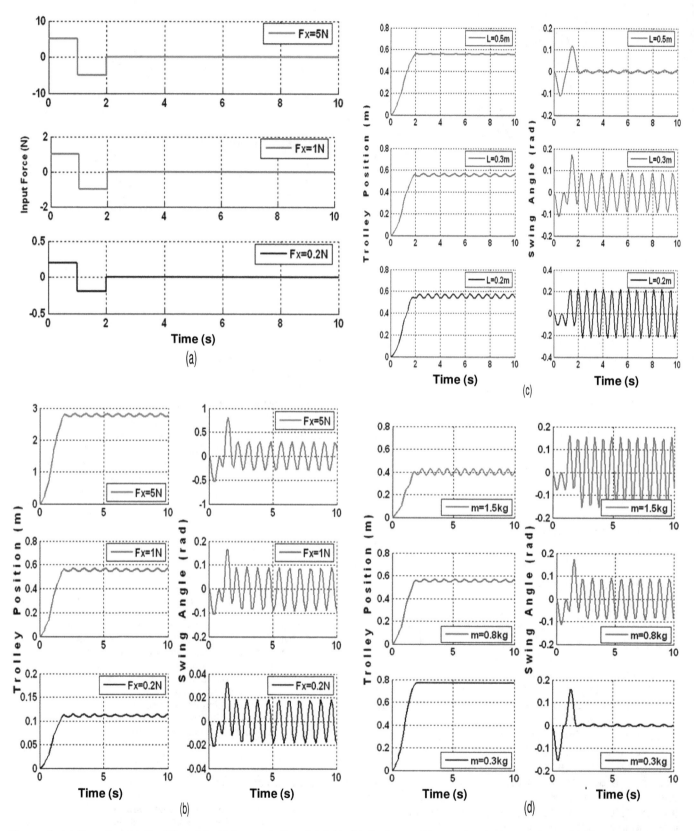

Figure 3. (a) Bang-bang with different input forces 1, 5 and 0.2 N. (b) Trolley position and swinging angle at different Fx. (c) Trolley position and swinging angle with different rope length (L= 0.2, 0.3 and 0.5 m). (d) Trolley position and swinging angle with different load masses (m= 0.3, 0.8 and 1.5 kg).

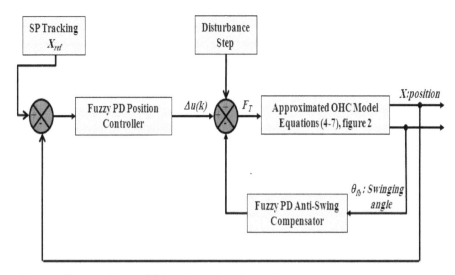

Figure 4. Proposed fuzzy PD-based overhead control system.

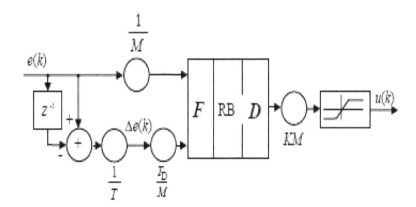

Figure 5. Fuzzy PD controller structure with the normalized universe range.

$$u(t) = K (e(t) + T_D . e'(t)) \tag{8}$$

We would like to know when the action value is equal to zero, that is why we can write:

$$e(t) + T_D . e'(t) = 0 \tag{9}$$

The solution of Equation (9) is

$$e'(t) = -e(t)/T_D \tag{10}$$

The Equation (10) depends only on the derivation time constant of the PD controller and its physical meaning is similar to Equation (4) for the PI controller. If we transfer the Equation (8) to the discrete form, we get an equation of the discrete PD controller

$$u(k) = K (e(k) + T_D \Delta e(k)) \tag{11}$$

Where $\Delta e(k) = (e(k) - e(k-1))/T$ and T is the sample period. In the next step we map the rule base to the discrete state space $\Delta e(k)$, $e(k)$. We initiate the scale M for the universe range, $M > 0$. This scale sets ranges for the error and the change-in-error. After extending the Equation (11) we get

$$u(k) = KM (e(k)/M + T_D . \Delta e(k)/M) \tag{12}$$

We apply fuzzification to input variables and after defuzzification we get the equation

$$u(k) = KM \, D\{F\{e(k)/M + T_D \Delta e(k)/M\}\} \tag{13}$$

The realization of Equation 13 of the fuzzy PD controller is depicted in Figure 5.

The adjustment of fuzzy controllers may be considerably simplified when fuzzy controller with a unified universe is used. The parameters to be tune then have their physical meaning and fuzzy

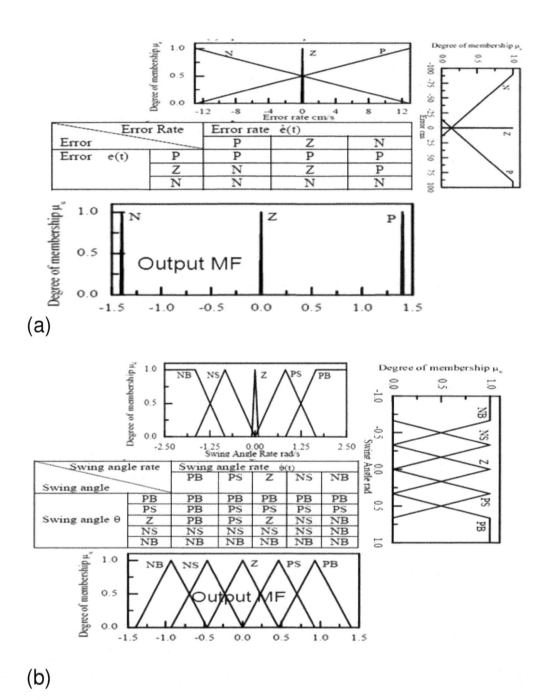

Figure 6. (a) Fuzzy sets for the proposed fuzzy PD-based position control (b) and either anti-swing compensator.

controller can be approximately adjusted using known rules for classical PD controllers. Suitable choice of inference method can ensure behavior, which is close to one of classical PD controller for both the tracking problem and the step disturbance rejection (Pivoňka, 1998; Pivoňka et al., 1998). The fuzzy sets are, as shown in Figure 6, assumed to have initially symmetrical layout and Ziegler - Nichols method, tunes the parameters of the proposed fuzzy PD-based position controller and either anti-swing compensator.

SIMULATION RESULTS

The aforementioned model concerning the fuzzy PD-based overhead crane system has been designed and validated with MatLab/Simulink. The obtained comparative results for both fuzzy PD and classical PD, given in Figure 7, have been extracted with considering the tracking problem and the step disturbance rejection.

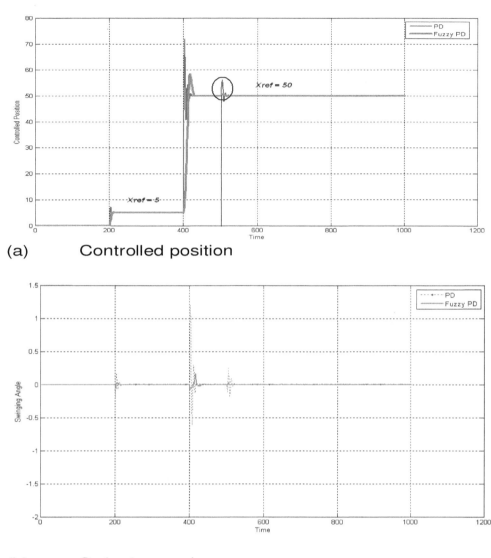

(a)　　　Controlled position

(b)　　　Swinging angle

Figure 7. Simulation comparative results of the proposed Fuzzy PD and classical PD at set point tracking (X_{ref}) and step disturbance effect (as shown inside the defined ellipse).

As concluded from Figure 7a, it could be seen that the performance of the closed loop control system using Fuzzy PD, when tracking the reference position X_{ref}, is being enhanced with modification in dynamic state comparing with classical PD control structure.

While the effect of the swing angle has been well eliminated using the proposed Fuzzy PD-controlled structure comparing with classical PD one (Figure 7b).

COMPARATIVE ANALYSIS

Table 1 summarizes the net comparative results shown previously in Figure 7.

Where a comparative study for conventional PD controller with fuzzy PD one had been affected, then the comparative results are found at different set point values (X_{ref}).

When considering: rising time in seconds, maximum overshoot, maximum overshooting in case of disturbance submission and steady-state error, it could be conclude that the overall steady state and dynamic performance of the proposed Fuzzy PD controlled plant seems to be better than that it was with classical approach (PD).

These results that are being summarized in Table 1 have been validated at different carte positions (for example, 5, 25 and 50).

Table 1. Comparative analysis for fuzzy PD and classical PD-based overhead crane system.

X_{ref}	Controller	Rising time (s)	Maximum over shoot (m)	Maximum over shoot for the disturbance (m)	Steadystate error $\pounds_{ss}$
5	PD	3.5	7.15	56	0.05
	Fuzzy PD	10	5.025	50.6	$\pounds_{ss} < 0.0001$
25	PD	3.5	36	31	0.01
	Fuzzy PD	11.32	29.75	25.7	0.0001
50	PD	3.42	71	11	0.5
	Fuzzy PD	10	5.025	5.025	0.0002

CONCLUSION

It could be noticed the fuzzy PD-based control approach has enhanced the robustness and reduced the settling time. The sensitivity of the closed-loop response against an effectiveness parameter variation and disturbances has been also modified.

The used method with the unified universe of discourse, stated in this article, considerably simplifies setting of fuzzy PD controllers. It allows approximate adjustment of controller's parameters according to well-known methods for PD controller synthesis. If the universe has non-linear membership function layout then the results can have better behaviour than the classical PD controller. The fuzzy PD controller can be programmed like a unified block in a controller and therefore work consumed on an implementation to the particular control system.

REFERENCES

Moustafa AF, Trabia B, Ismail IS (2009). Modelling and control of an overhead crane with a variable length flexible cable. Int. J. Comput. Appl. Technol., 34(3): 216-228.

Abdel-Rahman EM, Nayfeh AH, Masoud ZN (2003). Dynamics and control of cranes: Rev. J. Vib. Control, 9(7): 863-908.
Fang Y, Dixon WE, Dawson DM, Zergeroglu E (2003). Nonlinear coupling control laws for an underactuated overhead crane system. IEEE/ASME Trans. Mechatron., 8(3): 418-423.
Kiviluoto S (2009). Modelling and control of vertical oscillation in overhead cranes. M.Sc. Thesis. Helsinki University of Technology, Espoo, Finland, pp. 50-63.
Uchiyama N (2009). Robust control for overhead cranes by partial state feedback." Proceedings of the Institution of Mechanical Engineers, Part 1. J. Syst. Control Eng., 223(4): 575-580.
Pivoňka P (1999). Physical Background of Fuzzy PI and PD Controller. IFSA Eighth International Fuzzy Systems Association World Congress. Taipei, Taiwan, pp. 635–639.
Pivoňka P (1998). Fuzzy PI+D controller with a normalized universe. European Congress EUFIT'98. Aachen, Germany, 2: 890–894.
Pivoňka P, Findura M (1998). The alternative realization of fuzzy controllers. Automatizace. Czech Republic, 41(10,11,12): 31–38.

9

Commodity futures market mechanism: Mathematical formulation and some analytical properties

F. Laib[1]* and M. S. Radjef[2]

[1]CEVITAL Group, Algiers, Algeria.
[2]LAMOS laboratory, Department of Operational Research, University of Bejaia, Algeria.

This paper deals with the internal structure of a commodity futures market. We proposed a mathematical model representing the mechanism of this market. The model shows the links between market components (transactional prices, transactional quantities, open interest) and traders' states (position, position's average price, potential wealth andrealized wealth). Later, we stated and demonstrated some analytical properties of thismodel. This paper is not dealing with classical economic concepts like arbitrages, market equilibrium etc., rather it focuses on exact mathematical relationships between market platform components. Amongst our main findings is an exact relationship between open interest variation and transactional quantities. Indeed, this result indicates that if transactional quantity is tiny then open interest has 50% chance to not change and 25% chance to either increase or decrease, whereas when transactional quantity is big enough, then there is 75% chance for open interest to increase and 25% chance to decrease.

Key words: Commodity futures market, market microstructure, trader's position, open interest, market average price, market analytical properties.

INTRODUCTION

Our motivations in carrying out this work are two folds. First, we noticed that in technical literature of futures markets, a large array of results are found by empirical methods (Karpoff, 1987; Erband Harvey, 2006; Miffreand Rallis, 2007; Wang and Yu, 2004), whereas we wanted to provide exact results with full mathematical proofs. Secondly, to automatize price negotiation in the futures market, it is necessary to have a detailed mathematical model of this platform, therefore our model can be used in the automatization process.

The Santa Fe stock market simulator was designed in the 1990's (Palmer et al., 1994; LeBaron, 2001; LeBaron et al., 1999). It is a computer model intended to reproduce the behavior of a stock market platform and its empirically some properties of the stock market and explain some related phenomena like financial bubbles, crashes and band wagon practices observed in real markets (Arthur et al., 1997; Boer-Sorban, 2008;

Johnson, 2002). In a sense, our work can be viewed as an extension of the Santa Fe simulator, with two exceptions: (1) We are dealing with the *futures* market whereas the Santa Fe was focusing on the *stock* market, and (2) As a starting step, we managed to model only the futures market platform functioning and study some analytical properties of its components, without including the behavior of its agents, which is the subject of forthcoming worksagents. This simulator was used extensively to study.

Our market model was used as an underlying structure for applications in automatizing price negotiation of a futures market in case of one-producer-one-consumer (Laib and Radjef, 2011) and many-producers-many-consumers (Laib and Radjef, 2010).

Nowadays, futures market is a major part of commercial exchanges like CBOT, ICE and LIFFE. The essential instrument traded in this market is a *futures contract*. This is a binding agreement between the exchange, a buyer and a seller. Main terms of the transaction (technical specifications of the commodity, delivery time and locations, etc.) are fixed in the contract,

---
*Corresponding author. E-mail: fodil.laib@cevital.com

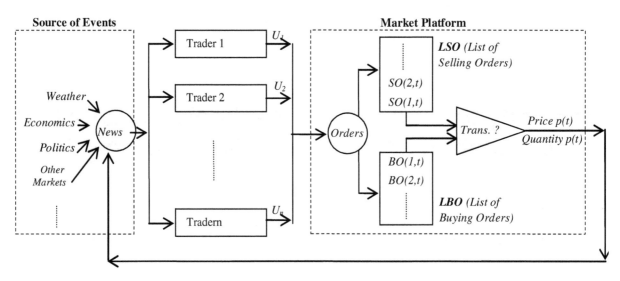

Figure 1. Flowchart of traders' orders.

only price remains negotiable. The price is fixed at present time, but delivery of the commodity occurs after contract expiry (months or years later).The buyer of the contract has a *long* position, whereas the seller has a *short* position. The buyer can sell her contract before its expiry, otherwise she must deliver the underlying commodity; the seller can buy back her contract before its expiry, otherwise she must take delivery of the underlying commodity (Catania and Alonzi, 1998; Hull, 2002; Teweles and Jones, 1999).

The majority of studies on futures markets were conducted from astochastic perspective where time series were analyzed in order to discover empirical relationships between market phenomena (Bodie and Rosansky, 1980; Chanand, 2006; Erband, 2006; Karpov, 1987; Levy et al., 1994; Miffre and Rallis, 2007; Wang and Yu, 2004). In practice, market analysts and traders use extensively *technical analysis* and *fundamental analysis* to forecast price moves and monitoring market trends (Murphy, 1999; Szakmary et al., 2010). Other works, like Shelton (1997) and Howard (1999), used game theory tools in an attempt to suggest wining trading strategies for traders.

The remainder of this study is organized into mathematical formulation and main findings. In mathematical formulation of the futures market platform, we outline the most important variables like transactional prices and quantities, traders' states and the updating process. At instant $t_j \in T$, each trader $i \in N$ is characterized by a position $y_i(t_j)$, position'savarage price $x_i(t_j)$, potential wealth $w_i(t_j)$, realized wealth $W_i(t_j)$, and total wealth $l_i(t_j)$. The market as a whole is characterized by the instantaneous transactional price

and quantity, $[p(t_j), q(t_j)]$, the open interest $y(t_j)$ and the market average price $\bar{p}(t_j)$ measures, with t_j belonging to the time horizon T. The last section provides our main findings which are analytical relationships between the above mathematical measures of the market model. One of the properties on the open interest change seems to have an interesting practical interpretation for market analysis purposes. Indeed, this result indicates that if transactional quantity is tiny then open interest has 50% chance not to change and 25% chance to either increase or decrease, whereas when transactional quantity is big enough then there is 75% chance for open interest to increase and 25% chance to decrease.

MARKET STRUCTURE

Here, we present a mathematical model formulating the functioning of the futures market platform. As shown on Figure 1, a set $N = \{1, ..., n\}$ of traders are trading a specific commodity futures contract, with a life duration T. Traders get information from different sources, then they establish their market orders U_i, with $i \in N$. The orders are sent either to the list of selling orders (LSO) or the list of buying orders (LBO) depending on their type. Sale orders of the LSO are sorted in the ascending order of *ask*prices, and buy orders of the LBO are ordered in the descending order of *bid*prices; this guaranties the fact that the best saleorder is always at the top of the LSO and the best buy order is at the top of the LBO.

We assume that daily marke t sessions of the futures

contract, since the first trading day until last business day, are grouped into a compact interval $[0, T]$ which is discretized into a set of instants:

$$\mathbf{T} = \{t_0, \cdots, t_m\} \text{ with } t_0 = 0,\ t_m = T,\ t_j = t_{j-1} + h,\ j = 1, \cdots, m,$$

h is the discretization pace (h should tend to zero to reflect reality). At instant t_j, at most one order can be received and processed. Explicitly, if an order is received at t_j, then it will be directed to the corresponding list of orders, sorted in that list, then an attempt to generate a transaction follows; all these four elementary events take place during the same period $[t_j, t_j + h[$.

Price fixation

Order $u_i(t_j)$, issued by trader $i \in N$ at instant $t_j \in \mathbf{T}$, has the following structure:

$$U_i(t_j) = [u_{i1}(t_j), u_{i2}(t_j)],$$

where u_{i1} is the ask price in case of a sale order (respectively the *bid* price in case of a buy order).

Thus $u_{i1} \in \mathbf{R}^+$; and u_{i2} is the number of contracts to sell in case of a sale order (respectively the number of contracts to buy in case of a buy order). In case of a sale order, we add conventionally a minus sign to u_{i2} to distinguish it from a buy order, therefore $u_{i2} \in \mathbf{Z}$ in general.

At each instant, an attempt is made to generate a transaction between the best sale order with the best buy order which are respectively at the top of LSO and LBO. At t_j, the first elements of LSO and LBO are respectively:

$$SO(1, t_j) \equiv U_s(\tau_s) = [u_{s1}(\tau_s), u_{s2}(\tau_s)],$$

$$BO(1, t_j) \equiv U_b(\tau_b) = [u_{b1}(\tau_b), u_{b2}(\tau_b)],$$

at instant $\tau_s \leq t_j$; and the best buy order is $U_b(\tau_b)$ issued by trader b at instant $\tau_b \leq t_j$. A transaction will occur at instant t_j if $u_{s1}(\tau_s) \leq u_{b1}(\tau_b)$, and $u_{s2}(\tau_s) \neq 0$ and $u_{b2}(\vartheta_b) \neq 0$ simultaneously. In this case, the transactional price $p(t_j)$ will be:

$$p(t_j) = \begin{cases} u_{b1}(\tau_b), & \text{if } \tau_s < \tau_b, \\ u_{s1}(\tau_s), & \text{if } \tau_b < \tau_s. \end{cases} \tag{1}$$

Transactional price is determined in this way in order to favor the trader who issued her order first. The number of contracts $q(t_j)$ sold by trader s to trader b in this transaction will be:

$$1 = min\{u_{b2}(\tau_b);\ |u_{s2}(\tau_s)|\}. \tag{2}$$

Otherwise, no transaction will take place at instant t_j, and we set:

$$p(t_j) = p(t_{j-1}) \text{ and } q(t_j) = 0. \tag{3}$$

If a transaction has occurred at instant t_j, then t_j is a *transactional time*, otherwise it is a *non-transactional time*.

Traders' states

The trading activity of futures contracts starts at t_0 and finishes at t_m. At each instant, $t_j \in \mathbf{T}$, the state of each trader can be described by the following components:

1. $y_i(t_j)$: Is the *position* of trader i, representing the number of contracts she has bought or sold.
2. $x_i(t_j)$: Is the average price of the position $y_i(t_j)$ of trader i.
3. $w_i(t_j)$: Is the potential wealth (profit or loss) of trader at t_j. It represents the amount of money that she would gain or loss if she closes her position at the current instant t_j. This amount is the difference between the real worth of her position and its current worth value, that is:

$$w_i(t_j) = y_i(t_j)[p(t_j) - x(t_j)]. \tag{4}$$

4. $W_i(t_j)$: Is the realized, or closed, wealth (profit or loss) of trader i since the beginning of the game at t_0 until t_j. Component $W_i(t_j)$ is updated only when trader i closes entirely, or partly, her position. If, at t_j, she closes

$|d'(t_j)|$ contracts from her old position then her accumulated realized wealth will be:

$$W_i(t_j) = W_i(t_{j-1}) + d(t_j)[p(t_j) - x_i(t_{j-1})]$$

5. $J_i(t_j)$: Is the total wealth of trader i at t_j, defined by:

$$J_i(t_j) = J_i^0 + W_i(t_j) + w_i(t_j),$$

(6)

where J_i^0 is the initial wealth of trader i, that is, the amount of cash shown at the beginning of the game.

We set J^0 as the global wealth of all traders:

$$J^0 = \sum_{i=1}^{n} J_i^0.$$

(7)

At the starting time t_0, all components of each trader are flat, that is:

$$ _0) = W_i(t_0) = 0, \quad i = 1, ..., n.$$

(8)

Note 2.1

In order to simplify further our notations and avoid lengthy expressions, we drop the letter t_j when no confusion is possible, hence we set:

$$(t_j), \ y_i \equiv y_i(t_j), \ W_i \equiv W_i(t_j), \ w_i \equiv w_i(t_j), \ J_i \equiv J_i(t_j)$$

To make reference to the state of any dynamical variable at the prior instant t_{j-1} we use instead the apostrophe notation ('), that is:

$$p' \equiv p(t_{j-1}), \quad x_i' \equiv x_i(t_{j-1}), \quad y_i' \equiv y_i(t_{j-1}),$$

These notations will be used interchangeably.

Updating traders' states

Consider a step forward in the trading process passing from t_{j-1} to t_j, and let us examine as follows the two possible cases.

Case of no transaction

If no transaction has occurred at t_j, then relation (3) will hold, and all the components of each trader will remain unchanged, that is for every $i \in N$ we have the following:

$$y_i = y_i', \qquad x_i = x_i',$$

(8a)

$$w_i = w_i', \qquad J_i = J_i'.$$

(8b)

Case where a transaction has occurred

If instant t_j is a transactional time, then a transaction has occurred between a buyer b and a seller s, exchanging q contracts. In this event, an update of the price and traders'components is necessary. The transactional price p and quantity q are given by (1) and (2) respectively.

All traders except the buyer b and the seller s, will only update their potential wealth, in other words, for traders $i \in N\backslash\{b, s\}$, formulas (8a) will apply, but their potential wealthcomponent w_i will evolve with time because the price has changed, that is

$$w_i = y_i(p - x_i), \ i \in N\backslash\{b, s\}.$$

(9)

Obviously, for these traders, their total wealth component J_i,given by (6), should also be recalculated since itdepends on w_i.

States of the buyer b and seller s are updated according to the following two lemmas. Mathematical proofs of these lemmas are given in appendix A, and $1_{[\cdot]}$ is the *conditional function* defined by $1_{[c]} = 1$ if condition c is satisfied, otherwise $1_{[c]} = 0$.

Lemma 2.1

If t_j is a transactional time, then components of the buyer b are updated as follows:

$$y_b = y_b' + q,$$

$$x_b = \frac{y_b' x_b' + qp}{y_b' + q} 1_{[y_b' \geq 0]} + p 1_{[-q < y_b' < 0]} + x_b' 1_{[y_b' < -q]},$$
(10)

$$W_b = W_b' + (p - x_b')\left(y_b' 1_{[-q < y_b' < 0]} - q 1_{[y_b' \leq -q]}\right),$$
(11)

$$W_b = W_b' + (p - x_b')\left(y_b' 1_{[-q < y_b' < 0]} - q 1_{[y_b' \leq -q]}\right),$$
(12)

$$w_b = (p - x_b')\left(y_b' 1_{[y_b' \geq 0]} + (y_b' + q) 1_{[y_b' < -q]}\right).$$
(13)

Lemma 2.2

If t_j is a transactional time, then components of the seller s are updated as follows:

$$y_s = y_s' - q,$$
(14)

$$x_s = \frac{y_s' x_s' - qp}{y_s' - q} 1_{[y_s' \leq 0]} + p 1_{[0 < y_s' < q]} + x_s' 1_{[y_s' > q]},$$
(15)

$$W_s = W_s' + (p - x_s')\left(y_s' 1_{[0 < v_s' < -}\right.$$
(16)

$$w_s = (p - x_s')\left(y_s' 1_{[y_s' \leq 0]} + (y_s' - q) 1_{[y_s' > q]}\right).$$
(17)

Remark 2.1

Components J_b and J_s are calculated using formula (6) by substituting i with b and s, respectively.

MATHEMATICAL PROPERTIES

In the literature, it is well-known that a futures market is a zero-sum game (Teweles and Jones, 1999), though this was stated in plain words, we did not find any mathematical formula on this issue. Using the model suggested previously in 'market structure', we can describe this property by:

$$\sum_{i=1}^{n} y_i(t_j) = 0 \quad \text{and} \quad \sum_{i=1}^{n} J_i(t_j) =$$
(18)

The first relation follows directly from (10) and (14) since for every transaction there is a buyer and a seller. The second result reflects the fact that total wealth of all traders is constant and that what was lost by some traders is gained by others (Remark 3.2).

Hereafter, we present three new classes of properties. Mathematical proofs are given in appendix A.

Traders' components properties

We show herein that the state variables w_i, W_i and J_i, of trader i at instant t_j, can be identified by knowing only their values at the prior instant t_{j-1}, the market price p and the transactional quantity q, of the current transaction, if any.

Property 3.1

$\forall t_j \in \mathbf{T}$, potential wealth w_i of trader i, defined by relation (4), can be obtained by the following formula:

$$w_i = w_i' + y_i'(p - p'),$$
(19)

for any trader $i \in N$, except if $i = b$ and $y_b < 0$, or if $i = s$ and $y_s > 0$.

Property 3.2

$\forall t_j \in \mathbf{T}$ and $\forall i \in N$, total wealth J_i given by relation (6), can be written in terms of J_i' in the following way

$$J_i = J_i' + y_i'(p - p').$$
(20)

This formula facilitates the calculation of total wealth J_i
This formula facilitates the calculation of total wealth J_i as it necessitates only prior wealth J_i' and position y_i'.

Remark 3.1

Consider the summation of (20) over all traders:

$$\sum_{i=1}^{n} J_i = \sum_{i=1}^{n} J_i' + (p - p') \sum_{i=1}^{n} y_i.$$

Since $\sum_{i=1}^{n} y_i = 0$, then $\sum_{i=1}^{n} J_i = \sum_{i=1}^{n} J_i'$ for all $t_j \in \mathbf{T}$, that is, the sum of the wealth of all traders is constant in time. This confirms that *Property* 3.2 is not in disagreement with earlier established results on futures markets second term of (18)).

Remark 3.2

If time t was continuous over the interval $[0, T]$, v then total wealth of trader i can be described by the following differential equation:

$$\dot{J}_i(t) = y_i(t)\dot{p}(t), \qquad i = 1, ..., n$$

This result is obtained by the integration of relation (20) over $[0, T]$.

Property 3.3

$\forall\, t_j \in \mathbf{T}$ and $\forall\, i \in N$, realized wealth W_i can be written as

$$W_i = W_i' + w_i' + y_i'(p - p') - w_i. \tag{21}$$

Open interest properties

Open interest measure $y(t_j)$ is a popular concept in futures markets. Stated in simple terms, it represents the numberof contracts held by all traders having *long* positions at instant t_j, which is also equal to the absolute number of contractsheld by traders with *short* positions.

Definition 3.1

Open interest $y(t_j)$ is calculated as follows:

$$y(t_j) = \sum_{i=1}^{n} y_i(t_j) 1_{[y_i(t_j)>0]} = -\sum_{i=1}^{n} y_i(t_j) 1_{[y_i(t_j)<0]}.$$

The value and sign of the change in open interest are monitored continuously by traders and analysts as it helps them assessing the behavior of the market and forecasting its future move.

Property 3.4

At instant $t_j \in \mathbf{T}$, open interest y can be calculated in the following way:

$$y = y' + A - B, \tag{22}$$

where

$$A \equiv A(t_j) = q\, 1_{[y_b' > -q]} + y_b' 1_{[-q < y_b' \leq 0]}, \tag{23}$$

$$B \equiv B(t_j) = q\, 1_{[y_s' > q]} + y_s' 1_{[0 < y_s' \leq q]}, \tag{24}$$

That is y depends only on transactional quantity q and the state of the system at the previous instant t_{j-1}. The term $A(t_j)$ represents the number of contracts added by the buyer to the open interest, and $B(t_j)$ indicates the number of contracts deducted by the seller from the open interest.

Property 3.5

$\forall\, t_j \in \mathbf{T}$, open interest $y(t_j)$ can be calculated by

$$y(t_j) = \sum_{k=0}^{j} [A(t_k) - B(t_k)]. \tag{25}$$

Property 3.6

Let $\Delta y(t_j)$ be the change in open interest at a transactional time t_j, defined by:

$$\Delta y = y - y'.$$

For a specified value of q, and allowing to the values of y_b' and y_s' to vary over the set of integer numbers, then

Table 1. Values and signs of Δy.

	Values of Δy				Signs of Δy		
	$y'_b \leq -q$	$-q < y'_b \leq 0$	$y'_b > 0$		$y'_b \leq -q$	$-q < y'_b \leq 0$	
$y'_s > q$	$-q$	y'_b	0	$y'_s > q$	<0	≤ 0	0
$0 < y'_s \leq q$	$-y'_s$	$q + y'_b - y'_s$	$q - y'_s$	$0 < y'_s \leq q$	<0	Any	≥ 0
$y'_s \leq 0$	0	$q + y'_b$	Q	$y'_s \leq 0$	0	>0	>0

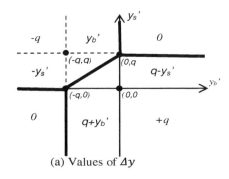

(a) Values of Δy

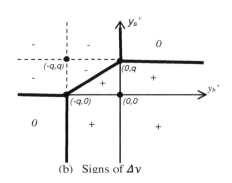

(b) Signs of Δv

Figure 2. Values and signs of Δy.

the values and signs of Δy in each possible case are given in Tables 1

Remark 3.4

The results of Table 1 can be further displayed graphically on a 2-dimension space with $(0,0)$ as origin, the horizontal X-axis representing y'_b versus the vertical Y-axis for y'_s. This is shown on Figures 2a and b.

Figure 2a shows the values of Δy for each point $(y'_b, y'_s) \in Z^2$. Inside the square delimited by the points $(0,0)$, $(-q, 0]$, $(-q, q)$ and $(0, q)$, the value of Δy is calculated by Formula (40); this square corresponds to case 5 of Table 1 (Appendix A). In addition to the two zones where $\Delta y = 0$, all the points belonging to the thick lines correspond also to $\Delta y = 0$.

On the other hand, Figure 2b shows the signs of Δy for each point $(y'_b, y'_s) \in Z^2$. Inside the triangle delimited by the points $(0,0)$, $(-q, 0)$ and $(0, q)$, the sign of Δy is positive. All the points of the triangle $(-q, 0)$

, $(-q, q)$, $(0, q)$ correspond to a negative Δy. The points belonging to the common segment $(-q, 0)$, $(0, q)$ of these two triangles satisfy $\Delta y = 0$.

Property 3.7

Assume that M is the biggest number in the set of positive integer numbers (in theory, M stands for $+\infty$). At a transactional time, the probability $\pi(\cdot)$ of the events are:

$$\pi(\Delta y = 0) = \frac{1}{2} - \frac{q}{2M},$$

$$\pi(\Delta y > 0) = \frac{1}{4} + \frac{q}{2M}\left(1 + \frac{q}{4M}\right),$$

$$\pi(\Delta y < 0) = \frac{1}{4} - \frac{1}{8}\left(\frac{q}{M}\right)^2.$$

Property 3.8

At a transactional time, assuming that q can vary from 1 to M, then we have the following limits on the probabilities of each event:

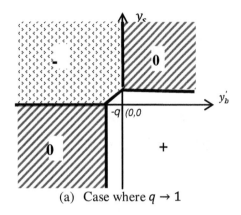
(a) Case where $q \to 1$

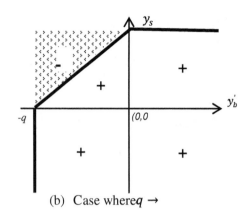
(b) Case where $q \to$

Figure 3. Limits of $\pi(\Delta y)$.

$$\lim_{q \to 1} \pi(\Delta y = 0) = \frac{1}{2}, \quad \lim_{q \to M} \pi(\Delta y = 0) = 0$$

$$\lim_{q \to 1} \pi(\Delta y > 0) = \frac{1}{4}, \quad \lim_{q \to M} \pi(\Delta y > 0) = \frac{7}{8}$$

$$\lim_{q \to 1} \pi(\Delta y < 0) = \frac{1}{4}, \quad \lim_{q \to M} \pi(\Delta y < 0) = \frac{1}{8}$$

Graphical visualization: The results of *Property* 3.8 are illustrated graphically on Figures 3a and b.

Figure 3a illustrates the case where q is small enough ($q \to 1$). The dotted area represents the zone where $\Delta y < 0$, the blank area corresponds to $\Delta y > 0$, and the two symmetrical dashed areas materialize the points (y_b', y_s') for which $\Delta y = 0$. From a rough observation, we note that the two dashed zones occupy almost half of the plane, confirming the fact $\lim_{q \to 1} \pi(\Delta y = 0) = \frac{1}{2}$.
Whereas, the blank and dotted zones, each of them fill approximately one quarter of the plane, hence $\lim_{q \to 1} \pi(\Delta y > 0) = \frac{1}{4}$ and confirming that limits $\lim_{q \to 1} \pi(\Delta y < 0) = \frac{1}{4}$ respectively. We observe also that the blank zone is slightly larger than the dotted zone, showing that:

$$\pi(\Delta y < 0) < \frac{1}{4} < \pi(\Delta y > 0).$$

Figure 3b illustrates the case where $q \to \infty$. We readily observe that the two dashed zones are no longer visible on this plane, hence confirming that $\lim_{q \to M} \pi(\Delta y = 0) = 0$. On the other hand, the blank

zone spreads over a greater space, approximately equal to $7/8$, proving that $\lim_{q \to M} \pi(\Delta y > 0) = \frac{7}{8}$, and inversely, the dotted zone is smaller than before and occupies only $1/8$ confirming that $\lim_{q \to M} \pi(\Delta y < 0) = \frac{1}{8}$.

Contribution to market analysis: *Property* 3.8 can bring further insight to market analysts. Indeed, after a transaction has occurred, open interest y could either increase, or decrease or stagnate; this is reflected by the sign of Δy. This change depends on the transactional quantity q, and the buyer's prior position y_b' and the seller's prior position y_s'; all possible cases are given in Table 1. For instance, if the buyer was long or flat before the transaction, that is, $y_b' \geq 0$.,and the seller was short or flat, that is, $y_s' \leq 0$, then for any value of q, open interest will increase as a result of this transaction.

If the transactional quantity is small enough ($q \to 1$), then it is more likely that open interest will stagnate after the transaction rather than increase or decrease, since the event $\Delta y = 0$ has about 50% chance to occur, whereas the events $\Delta y > 0$ and $\Delta y < 0$ have only about 25% chance for each to occur.

By contrast, if transactional quantity is big enough, then it is more likely that open interest will increase; in fact, this should happen in 75% of cases, and the possibility to see open interest decreases is only 25% in this case. Noticeably, in this case, open interest should not stagnate as the probability of the event $\Delta y = 0$ is almost

stagnate as the probability of the event $\Delta y = 0$ is almost zero.

Market average price

Definition 3.2

We define *market average price* $\bar{p}$ at instant t_j by

$$\bar{p}(t_j) = \frac{\sum_{k=0}^{j} p(t_k)q(t_k)}{\sum_{k=0}^{j} q(t_k)}, \tag{26}$$

which is simply the weighted average price of all the transactions since the starting time t_0 until t_j.

Property 3.9

In the particular case where

$$y(t_k) = y(t_{k-1}) + q(t_k), \quad \forall\, k = 0\,...\,j, \tag{27}$$

Then

$$\bar{p}(t_j) = \frac{\sum_{i=1}^{n} x_i(t_j)y_i(t_j)\mathbf{1}_{[y_i(t_j) > 0]}}{y(t_j)}. \tag{28}$$

The aforementioned property links market average price to open interest and traders' components. That is, Formula (28) allows computing market average price at instant t_j using only the knowledge available at this instant.

CONCLUSION AND PERSPECTIVES

Our study showed that a futures market platform has rich analytical properties. We derived the most basic of them, and we believe that many other features remain to be explored and stated in a mathematical framework. A more important issue is to bring practical interpretation of these properties as it was done with *Property* 3.8. In addition, some results has to be generalized, this is the case of *Property* 3.9 on the market average price that needs to be extended to the case where condition (27) is no more satisfied.

On the other hand, the mathematical model of the futures market platform as stated herein has already a theoretical game format, though a discussion over the game equilibrium is lacking. This could be achieved by introducing trading strategies for trading agents as it was

done by Arthur et al. (1997) for the stock market. Additionally, the continuous-time version of the model can be considered as pointed out in *Remark* 3.2.

REFERENCES

Arthur WB, Holland JH, LeBaron B, PalmerR, Taylor P (1997). Asset pricing under endogenous expectations in an artificial stock market. In: Arthur WB, Durlauf S, Lane D (Eds.).The Economy as an Evolving Complex System II. Addison-Wesley, Reading, MA, pp. 15-44.

Bodie Z, Rosansky VI (1980). Risk and return in commodity futures. Fin. Anal. J., 36(3): 27-39.

Boer-SorbanK (2008). Agent-based simulation of financial markets.PhD thesis, Erasmus University Rotterdam.

Catania PJ, Alonzi P (1998). Commodity trading manual, Chicago Board of Trade, IL.

Chan WH, Young D (2006). Jumping hedges: An examination of movements in copper spot andfutures markets, J. Futures Markets, 26(2): 169-188.

Erb CB, Harvey CR (2006). The strategic and tactical value of commodity futures. Fin. Anal. J., 62(2): 69-97.

Howard M (1999). The evolution of trading rules in an artificial stock market. in Computing in Economics and Finance 1999, series by Society for Computational Economics, No. 712, 1999, http://econpapers.repec.org/paper/scescecf9/712.htm.

Hull JC (2002). Fundamentals of futures and options markets.Pearson Education Inc., Upper Saddle River, New Jersey, 4-thedition.

Johnson PE (2002). Agent-based modeling: What I learned from the artificial stock market. Soc. Sci. Comput. Rev., 20(2): 174-186.

Karpoff JM (1987). The relation between price changes and trading volume: a survey. J. Finan. Quant. Anal., 22: 109-126.

Laib F, Radjef MS (2010). Operating futures market by automated traders. 5th International Conference on E-Commerce, Irsh Island.

LeBaron B (2001). A builder's guide to agent based financial markets, Quant. Fin., 1(2): 254-261.

LeBaron B, Arthur WB, Palmer R (1999). Time series properties of an artificial stock market. J. Econ. Dyn. Control, 23: 1487-1516.

Levy M, Levy H, Solomon S (1994). A microscopic model of the stock market: cycles, booms, and crashes. Econ. Lett., 45(1): 103-111.

Miffre J, Rallis G (2007). Momentum strategies in commodity futures markets. J. Banking Fin., 31(6): 1863-1886.

Murphy JJ (1999). Technical analysis of the financial markets. NY Institute Finance, New York.

Palmer RG, Arthur WB, Holland JH, LeBaron B, Tayler P (1994). Artificial economic life: A simple model of a stock market, 75: 264-274.

Laib F, Radjef MS (2011). Automated traders in commodities markets: Case of producer–consumer institution. Expert Systems with Applications (2011), http://dx.doi.org/10.1016/j.eswa.2011.05.091

Shelton RB (1997). Gaming the market: applyinggame theory to generate winning trading strategies. John Wiley & Sons Inc., New York.

Szakmary AC, Shen Q, Sharma SC (2010). Trend-following trading strategies in commodity futures: are-examination. J. Banking Fin., 34(2): 409-426.

Teweles RJ, Jones FJ (1999). The futures game: who wins? who loses? and why? McGraw-Hill, New York.

Wang C, Yu M (2004).Trading activity and price reversals in futures markets. J. Banking Fin., 28(6): 1337-1361.

APPENDIX

Appendix A: Mathematical proofs

Proof of lemma2.1 (Updating buyer's components)

Buyer b has bought q new contracts during transactional time t_j, her current position y_b will become:

$$y_b = y_b' + q.$$

(29)

Since she had added new contracts to her old position, the average price x_b of her new position should be updated. However, this update will depend on the value of her previous position y_b'. Below, we examine the four possible cases, 1-i to 1-iv, corresponding respectively to (i) $y_b' \geq 0$, (ii) $-q < y_b' < 0$, (iii) $y_b' = -q$, and (iv) $y_b' < -q$. In each case, we determine the analytical expressions of x_b, w_b and W_b.

Case i: When $y_b' \geq 0$. In this case, buyer's new average price x_b on her new position will be:

$$x_b = \frac{y_b' x_b' + qp}{y_b' + q}.$$

(30)

In this case, her realized wealth will remain unchanged because she has not closed any contract of her old position, thus:

$$W_b = W_b'.$$

(31)

Her potential wealth w_b should be updated because the price has moved from p' to p, that is:

$$w_b = y_b(p - x_b).$$

(32)

Substituting (29) and (30) in (32), we obtain:

$$w_b = y_b'(p - x_b').$$

(33)

Case ii: When $-q < y_b' < 0$. In this case, at instant t_j, buyer bought q new contracts with a price p. This buying operation can be viewed as two consecutive buying operations:

a. she had bought $|y_b'|$ contracts with a price p, then
b. she bought $q - |y_b'|$ contracts with a price p.

When she executed operation (a) she had closed her short position y_b' that she had sold before with a price x_b', and realized a net profit or loss equal to $|y_b'|(x_b' - p)$. Adding this amount to the old realized wealth W_b', the new realized wealth will become:

$$W_b = W_b' + |y_b'|(x_b' - p) = W_b' + y_b'(p - x_b').$$

When she executed operation (b), she had acquired a long position $y_b = q - |y_b'| = q + y_b'$ with a price $x_b = p$ and the potential wealth of this position is $w_b = y_b(p - x_b) = 0$. This is true because the new position $y_b = q - |y_b'|$ was established at the current price p, therefore it has not yet any potential wealth.

Case iii: When $y_b' = -q$. In this case, when the buyer bought the q new contracts, she had closed entirely her short position, hence she realized a net profit or loss equal to $|y_b'|(x_b' - p)$. Adding this amount to her previous realized wealth, will yield:

$$W_b = W_b' + |y_b'|(x_b' - p) = W_b' + q\,(p - x_b').$$

In this case, her new position is $y_b = y_b' + q = 0$, thus we consider its average price as $x_b = 0$, having a zero potential wealth, $w_b = y_b(p - x_b) = 0$.

Case iv: When $y_b' < -q$. In this case, when the buyer bought the q new contracts, she had closed q contracts in her old short position, hence she realized a net profit or loss equal to $q(x_b' - p)$. Adding this amount to her previous realized wealth W_b' will result in:

$$W_b = W_b' - q(p - x_b').$$

After this operation, there will remain $y_b = y_b' + q < 0$ contracts in the possession of the buyer. This is a part of her old position that she had sold with an average price x_b'. As these contracts are still in her hand at instant t_i, hence $x_b = x_b'$, and the potential wealth of this position is $w_b = y_b(p - x_b) = (y_b' + q)\,(p - x_b')$.

Summary: In order to write in a single line the functions x_b, W_b, and w_b for the four cases 1-i to 1-iv, we will use the conditional function formulation shown as follows:

$$x_b = \frac{y_b'x_b' + qp}{y_b' + q}\,1_{[y_b' \geq 0]} + p\,1_{[-q < y_b' < 0]} + x_b'\,1_{[y_b' < -q]},$$

$$W_b = W_b' + (p - x_b')\left(y_b'\,1_{[-q < y_b' < 0]} - q\,1_{[y_b' \leq -q]}\right)$$

However, we have showed that in both cases 1-ii and 1-iii that potential wealth $w_b = 0$. In the remaining cases 1-i and 1-iv, we know that $w_b \neq 0$, hence we can assert that potential wealth w_b can be written as:

$$w_b = (p - x_b')\left(y_b'\,1_{[y_b' \geq 0]} + (y_b' + q)\,1_{[y_b' < -q]}\right).$$

Proof of lemma 2.2 (updating seller's components)

After selling q contracts, the position of the seller s will be:

$$y_s = y'_s - q.$$

(34)

We examine the four possible cases subsequently, 2-i to 2-iv, corresponding respectively to (i) $y'_s \leq 0$, ii) $0 < y'_s < q$, (iii) $y'_s = q$, and (iv) $y'_s > q$. In each case, we determine the analytical expressions of x_s, w_s and W_s.

Case i: When $y'_s \leq 0$. In this case, seller's new average price x_s on her new position, $y_s = y'_s - q$, will be:

$$x_s = \frac{y'_s x'_s - qp}{y'_s - q}.$$

(35)

Her realized wealth will remain unchanged because she has not closed any contract from her old position, thus:

$$W_s = W'_s$$

(36)

Her potential wealth, w_s, should be updated due to the price move from p' to p, that is:

$$w_s = y_s(p - x_s).$$

(37)

Substituting (34) and (35) in (37), we obtain:

$$w_s = y'_s(p - x'_s).$$

(38)

Case ii: When $0 < y'_s < q$. In this case, the action of the seller can be viewed as two consecutive selling operations:

a. she had sold y'_s contracts with a price p, then

b. she sold $q - y'_s$ contracts with a price p.

When she executed operation (a) she had closed her long position y'_s that she had bought before with a price x'_s, and realized a net profit or loss equal to $y'_s(p - x'_s)$. Adding this amount to the old realized wealth W'_s, will yield the new realized wealth:

$$W_s = W'_s + y'_s(p - x'_s).$$

When she executed operation (b), she had acquired a short position $y_s = -(q - y'_s) = y'_s - q$, with a price $x_s = p$, and the potential wealth of this position is $w_s = y_s(p - x_s) = 0$.

Case iii: When $y'_s = q$. In this case, she had closed entirely her long position, hence she realized a net profit or loss equal to $y'_s(p - x'_s)$. Adding this amount to her previous realized wealth will yield:

$$W_s = W'_s + y'_s(p - x'_s) = W'_s + q(p - x'_s).$$

In this case, her new position $y_s = y'_s - q = 0$, thus we consider its average price as $x_s = 0$, and $w_s = y_s(p - x_s) = 0$.

Case iv: When $y'_s > q$. In this case, she had closed q contracts in her old long position, hence she realized a net profit or loss equal to $q(p - x'_s)$. Adding this amount to her previous realized wealth W'_b will result in

$$W_s = W'_s + q(p - x'_s).$$

After this operation, there will remain $y_s = y'_s - q > 0$ contracts in the possession of the seller. This is a part of her old position that she had bought with an average price x'_s. As these contracts are still in her hand at instant t_j, hence $x_s = x'_s$, and the potential wealth of this position is $w_s = y_s(p - x_s) = (y'_s - q)(p - x'_s)$.

Summary: In order to write on a single line, the functions x_s, W_s, and w_s of the four cases 2-i to 2-iv, we will use the conditional function formulation shown as follows:

$$x_s = \frac{y'_s x'_s - qp}{y'_s - q} 1_{[y'_s \le 0]} + p 1_{[0 < y'_s < q]} + x'_s 1_{[y'_s > q]}.$$

$$W_s = W'_s + (p - x'_s)\left(y'_s 1_{[0 < y'_s < -q]} - q 1_{[y'_s \ge q]}\right).$$

However, we have shown that in both cases 2-ii and 2-iii, we have $w_s = 0$. In the remaining cases 2-i and 2-iv, we know that $w_s \ne 0$, hence we can assert that potential wealth w_s can be written as

$$w_s = (p - x'_s)\left(y'_s 1_{[y'_s \le 0]} + (y'_s - q) 1_{[y'_s > q]}\right).$$

Proof of property 3.1

We will prove this property case by case.

(a) Case where $i \in N\{b, s\}$. At instant t_j, we know that $x_i = x'_i$ and $y_i = y'_i$, therefore,

$$
\begin{aligned}
w_i &= y_i(p - x_i) = y'_i(p - x'_i) \\
&= y'_i(p - p') + y'_i(p' - x'_i) = y'_i(p - p') + w'_i.
\end{aligned}
$$

(b) Case where $i = b$. If $y'_b \ge 0$, hence we should be in case 1-i of lemma 1's proof, then from (33) and following the same reasoning as case (a), we show readily this result.

(c) Case where $i = s$. If $y'_s \le 0$, hence we should be in case 2-i of lemma 2's proof, then from (38) and following the same reasoning as case (a), we show this result.

Proof of property 3.2

We will prove this property case by case.

(a) For every $i \in N\backslash\{b,s\}$, we know that relations (8a) and (19) apply, therefore we can write total wealth J_i defined by (6) as follows:

$$J_i = J_i^0 + W_i + w_i = J_i^0 + W_i' + w_i' + y_i'(p - p') = J_i' + y_i'(p - p').$$

(b) If $i = b$, we make use of Formulas (12) and (13) in the following development:

$$
\begin{aligned}
J_b &= J_b^0 + W_b + w_b \\
&= J_b^0 + W_b' + (p - x_b')\left(y_b' 1_{[-q<y_b'<0]} - q 1_{[y_b'\leq-q]}\right) + (p - x_b')\left(y_b' 1_{[y_b'\geq0]} + y_b 1_{[y_b'<-q]}\right) \\
&= J_b^0 + W_b' + (p - x_b')\left(y_b' 1_{[-q<y_b'<0]} - q 1_{[y_b'\leq-q]} + y_b' 1_{[y_b'\geq0]} + y_b 1_{[y_b'<-q]}\right) \\
&= J_b^0 + W_b' + (p - x_b')\left(y_b' 1_{[y_b'>-q]} - q 1_{[y_b'\leq-q]} + y_b 1_{[y_b'<-q]}\right) \\
&= J_b^0 + W_b' + (p - x_b')\left(y_b' 1_{[y_b'>-q]} - q 1_{[y_b'\leq-q]} + y_b \left[1_{[y_b'\leq-q]} - 1_{[y_b'=-q]}\right]\right) \\
&= J_b^0 + W_b' + (p - x_b')\left(y_b' 1_{[y_b'>-q]} + (y_b - q) 1_{[y_b'\leq-q]} - y_b 1_{[y_b'=-q]}\right),
\end{aligned}
$$

but we already know that $1_{[y_b'=-q]} = 1$ if only if $y_b' = -q$, in this event, $y_b = y_b' + q = 0$, hence $y_b 1_{[y_b'=-q]} = 0$, is always true. Now we resume the last expression of J_b, after erasing this zero term, we obtain:

$$
\begin{aligned}
J_b &= J_b^0 + W_b' + (p - x_b')\left(y_b' 1_{[y_b'>-q]} + (y_b - q) 1_{[y_b'\leq-q]}\right) \\
&= J_b^0 + W_b' + (p - x_b')\left(y_b' 1_{[y_b'>-q]} + (y_b' + q - q) 1_{[y_b'\leq-q]}\right) \\
&= J_b^0 + W_b' + (p - x_b')\left(y_b' 1_{[y_b'>-q]} + y_b' 1_{[y_b'\leq-q]}\right) \\
&= J_b^0 + W_b' + y_b'(p - x_b') \\
&= J_b^0 + W_b' + y_b'[(p - p') + (p' - x_b')] \\
&= J_b^0 + W_b' + y_b'(p' - x_b') + y_b'(p - p') \\
&= J_b^0 + W_b' + w_b' + y_b'(p - p') \\
&= J_b' + y_b'(p - p').
\end{aligned}
$$

(c) If $i = s$, then following the same approach then case (b), we can show easily that:

$$J_s = J_s' + y_s'(p - p').$$

Hence, relation (20) holds true for all traders and in all cases.

Proof of property 3.3

If relation (6) was applied at instant t_{j-1}, it would yield to

$$J_i' = J_i^0 + W_i' + w_i'.$$

On the other hand, from (6) we can extract the expression of W_i shown as follows:

$$W_i = J_i - J_i^0 - w_i$$

Now substituting the term J_i by its expression given in (20) will result in:

$$
\begin{aligned}
W_i &= [J_i' + y_i'(p - p')] - J_i^0 - w_i \\
&= [(J_i^0 + W_i' + w_i') + y_i'(p - p')] - J_i^0 - w_i \\
&= W_i' + w_i' + y_i'(p - p') - w_i.
\end{aligned}
$$

Proof of property 3.4

We have:

$$
\begin{aligned}
y &= \sum_{i \in N} y_i \, 1_{[y_i>0]} \\
&= y_b 1_{[y_b>0]} + y_s 1_{[y_s>0]} + \sum_{i \in N\backslash\{b,s\}} y_i \, 1_{[y_i>0]} \\
&= y_b 1_{[y_b>0]} + y_s 1_{[y_s>0]} + \sum_{i \in N\backslash\{b,s\}} y_i' \, 1_{[y_i'>0]},
\end{aligned}
$$

we write this as:

$$y = Q_1 + Q_2 + \sum_{i \in N\backslash\{b,s\}} y_i' 1_{[y_i'>0]}, \tag{39}$$

where

$$
\begin{aligned}
Q_1 &= y_b 1_{[y_b>0]} = (y_b' + q)1_{[y_b'+q>0]} = (y_b' + q)1_{[y_b'>-q]} \\
&= y_b' 1_{[y_b'>-q]} + q\,1_{[y_b'>-q]} = y_b'\left(1_{[y_b'>0]} + 1_{[-q<y_b'\le 0]}\right) + q\,1_{[y_b'>-q]} \\
&= y_b' 1_{[y_b'>0]} + A,
\end{aligned}
$$

and

$$
\begin{aligned}
Q_2 &= y_s 1_{[y_s>0]} = (y_s' - q)1_{[y_s'-q>0]} = (y_s' - q)1_{[y_s'>q]} \\
&= (y_s' - q)\left(1_{[y_s'>q]} + 1_{[0<y_s'\le q]} - 1_{[0<y_s'\le q]}\right) = (y_s' - q)\left(1_{[y_s'>0]} - 1_{[0<y_s'\le q]}\right) \\
&= y_s' 1_{[y_s'>0]} - q\,1_{[y_s'>0]} - y_s' 1_{[0<y_s'\le q]} + q\,1_{[0<y_s'\le q]} \\
&= y_s' 1_{[y_s'>0]} - q\left(1_{[y_s'>0]} - 1_{[0<y_s'\le q]}\right) - y_s' 1_{[0<y_s'\le q]} \\
&= y_s' 1_{[y_s'>0]} - q1_{[y_s'>q]} - y_s' 1_{[0<y_s'\le q]} \\
&= y_s' 1_{[y_s'>0]} - B.
\end{aligned}
$$

Substituting Q_1 and Q_2 in Formula (39), we obtain:

$$
\begin{aligned}
y &= y_b' 1_{[y_b' > 0]} + A + y_s' 1_{[y_s' > 0]} - B + \sum_{i \in N \setminus \{b,s\}} y_i' 1_{[y_i' > 0]} \\
&= A - B + \sum_{i \in N} y_i' 1_{[y_i' > 0]} \\
&= y' + A - B.
\end{aligned}
$$

Proof of property 3.5

By definition, we know that $y(t_0) = 0$ because $y_i(t_0) = 0, \; \forall i \in N$, thus (25) holds true for t_0. Now, assuming that at instant t_{j-1} relation (25) holds, that is:

$$
y(t_{j-1}) = \sum_{k=0}^{j-1} [A(t_k) - B(t_k)],
$$

Hence

$$
\begin{aligned}
y(t_j) &= y(t_{j-1}) + A(t_j) - B(t_j) \\
&= \sum_{k=0}^{j-1} [A(t_k) - B(t_k)] + A(t_j) - B(t_j) \\
&= \sum_{k=0}^{j} [A(t_k) - B(t_k)].
\end{aligned}
$$

Proof of property 3.6

Note that if t_j is a non-transactional time, then $y = y'$, therefore $\Delta y = 0$. Thereafter, we are dealing with transactional times only. From (22), we deduce that:

$$
\begin{aligned}
\Delta y &= y - y' = A - B \\
&= \left(q 1_{[y_b' > -q]} + y_b' 1_{[-q < y_b' \leq 0]} \right) - \left(q 1_{[y_s' > q]} + y_s' 1_{[0 < y_s' \leq q]} \right)
\end{aligned}
$$

Table 1 summarizes the calculation for each case: Case (1) corresponds to $y_b' > 0$ and $y_s' > q$, case (2) corresponds to $y_b' > 0$ and $0 < y_s' \leq q$, and so on. For each case, we compute the values of A and B, then we calculate the difference $\Delta y = A - B$, and the last column of the table shows the sign of Δy in each case.

Case (5) of Table 1, where $-q < y_b' \leq 0$ and $0 < y_s' \leq q$, necessitates further analysis to determine the sign of Δy. In this case, we know that

$$
\Delta y = q + y_b' - y_s'. \tag{40}
$$

Table 1. Calculation of Δy.

Case	y_b'	y_s'	$A =$	$B =$	$\Delta y = A - B$	Sign of Δy
1		$y_s' > q$	q	q	0	0
2	$y_b' > 0$	$0 < y_s' \leq q$	q	y_s'	$q - y_s$	≥ 0
3		$y_s' \leq 0$	q	0	q	> 0
4		$y_s' > q$	$q + y_b'$	q	y_b'	≤ 0
5	$-q < y_b' \leq 0$	$0 < y_s' \leq q$	$q + y_b'$	y_s'	$q + y_b' - y_s'$	Any
6		$y_s' \leq 0$	$q + y_b'$	0	$q + y_b'$	> 0
7		$y_s' > q$	0	q	$-q$	< 0
8	$y_b' \leq -q$	$0 < y_s' \leq q$	0	y_s'	$-y_s'$	< 0
9		$y_s' \leq 0$	0	0	0	0

For this case (5), we can show easily that $-2q < y_b' - y_s' < 0$, hence $-q < q + y_b' - y_s' < q$, therefore Δy could be positive, negative or nil, depending on the values of y_b' and y_s'; we have the following

1. $\Delta y > 0 \Rightarrow q + y_b' > y_s'$,
2. $\Delta y < 0 \Rightarrow q + y_b' < y_s'$,
3. $\Delta y = 0 \Rightarrow q + y_b' = y_s'$.

This completes the proof of this property.

Proof of property 3.7

Assuming that M is the biggest positive number, then from Figure 1 (Appendix A), we observe that any couple (y_b', y_s') belonging to the square delimited by the points $(-M, -M)$, $(-M, M)$, (M, M), and $(M, -M)$; this square has an area of $4\,m^2$ -units.

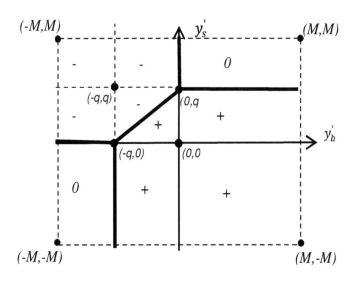

Figure 1. Calculation of $\pi(\Delta y)$.

In this square, we have:

1. Two symmetrical zones where $\Delta y = 0$, with a total area of $2M(M - q)$ square-units, hence:

$$\pi(\Delta y = 0) = \frac{2M(M - q)}{4M^2} = \frac{1}{2} - \frac{q}{2M}$$

2. One zone where $\Delta y > 0$ formed by four sub-zones: One square of M^2 -units, two symmetrical rectangles of $2Mq$ square-units, and a triangle of $\frac{q^2}{2}$ square-units; therefore:

$$\pi(\Delta y > 0) = \frac{M^2 + 2Mq + \frac{q^2}{2}}{4M^2} = \frac{1}{4} + \frac{q}{2M} + \frac{q^2}{8M^2} = \frac{1}{4} + \frac{q}{2M}\left(1 + \frac{q}{4M}\right)$$

3. One zone where $\Delta y < 0$ formed by four sub-zones: One square with $(M - q)^2$ -units, two symmetrical rectangles with $2Mq$ square-units, and a triangle of $\frac{q^2}{2}$ square-units. We can also consider this zone as being formed by a bigger square $(0,0)$, $(-M,0)$, $(-M,-M)$ and $(0,M)$, having an area of M^2 square-units, from which we deducted the triangle $(0,0)$, $(-q,0)$, $(0,q)$ having an area of $\frac{q^2}{2}$ square-units, thus:

$$\pi(\Delta y < 0) = \frac{M^2 - \frac{q^2}{2}}{4M^2} = \frac{1}{4} - \frac{1}{8}\left(\frac{q}{M}\right)^2$$

Proof of property 3.8

Assuming that M is bigger enough ($M \equiv +\infty$), then:

$$\lim_{q \to 1} \frac{q}{M} = 0, \quad \text{and} \quad \lim_{q \to M} \frac{q}{M} = 1$$

Applying these two limits we show easily *Property* 3.8.

Proof of property 3.9

Condition (27) means that, since instant t_0 till t_j, no trader is closing a part of her old position, that is, any trader who bought before continues to buy and any trader who sold before continues to sell. In a mathematical form, if s_k and b_k are respectively the seller and buyer at a transactional instant t_k, then:

$$y_{s_k}(t_{k-1}) \le 0, \text{ and } y_{b_k}(t_{k-1}) \ge 0, \qquad \forall k = 0 \dots j.$$

In this case, open interest $y(t_k)$ at any instant t_k is growing by the amount of the transactional quantity $q(t_k)$, therefore:

$$y(t_j) = y(t_{j-1}) + q(t_j) = \sum_{k=0}^{j} q(t_k).$$

Assuming that (28) holds true at t_{j-1}, that is:

$$\bar{p}(t_{j-1}) = \frac{\sum_{k=0}^{j-1} p(t_k)q(t_k)}{\sum_{k=0}^{j-1} q(t_k)} = \frac{\sum_{i=1}^{n} x_i(t_{j-1})y_i(t_{j-1}) 1_{[y_i(t_{j-1})>0]}}{y(t_{j-1})}, \tag{41}$$

And let us show this remains true at t_j. We already know that:

$$\bar{p}(t_j) = \frac{\sum_{k=0}^{j} p(t_k)q(t_k)}{\sum_{k=0}^{j} q(t_k)} = \frac{\sum_{k=0}^{j-1} p(t_k)q(t_k) + p(t_j)q(t_j)}{\sum_{k=0}^{j-1} q(t_k) + q(t_j)} \tag{42}$$

$$= \frac{\sum_{i=1}^{n} x_i(t_{j-1})y_i(t_{j-1}) 1_{[y_i(t_{j-1})>0]} + p(t_j)q(t_j)}{y(t_{j-1}) + q(t_j)} \tag{43}$$

We know that when passing from instant t_{j-1} to t_j, the components of all traders will remain the same, except the components of the buyer b and the seller s need to be updated, that is $x_i(t_j) = x_i(t_{j-1})$ and $y_i(t_j) = y_i(t_{j-1})$ for all $i \in N \setminus \{s, b\}$. This is true in case of a transactional time. In case of a non-transactional time, components of all traders will remain the same. Now resuming the apostrophe notation, we obtain:

$$\bar{p} = \frac{\sum_{i \in N \setminus \{b\}} x_i y_i 1_{[y_i>0]} + x_b' y_b' + p\,q}{y' + q} \tag{44}$$

Note that the components of the seller s do not appear above because we are in the case where $y_s' < 0$, therefore $1_{[y_s>0]} = 0$.

1. If t_j is not a transactional time, that is, $q = 0$, $y = y'$, $y_b = y_b'$ and $x_b = x_b'$, then from (44) will result

$$\bar{p} = \frac{\sum_{i \in N} x_i y_i 1_{[y_i>0]}}{y}, \tag{45}$$

which completes the proof.

2. If t_j is a transactional time, and since $y_b' \geq 0$ then $y_b = y_b' + q > 0 \Rightarrow 1_{[y_b>0]} = 1$ and

$$x_b = \frac{x_b' y_b' + p\,q}{y_b} \Rightarrow pq = x_b y_b - x_b' y_b'. \tag{46}$$

Substituting pq by $x_b y_b - x_b' y_b'$ in (44) will readily complete the proof.

10

Scenario based performance analysis of reliant ad hoc on-demand distance vector routing (R-AODV) for mobile ad hoc network

H. S. H. Jassim[1]*, S. K. Tiong[1], S. Yussof[2], S. P. Koh[1] and R. Ismail[2]

[1]College of Engineering, Universiti Tenaga Nasional, KM 7, Jalan kajang puchong, 43009 Kajang, Selangor, Malaysia.
[2]College of Information Technology, Universiti Tenaga Nasional, KM 7, Jalan kajang puchong, 43009 Kajang, Selangor, Malaysia.

A mobile ad-hoc network (MANET) is a peer-to-peer wireless network, that is, nodes can communicate with each other without the use of infrastructure. Besides, nodes are free to join and/or leave the network at anytime, move randomly and organize themselves arbitrarily. Due to this nature of MANET, there could be some malicious and selfish nodes that try compromise the routing protocol functionality and make MANET vulnerable to security attacks which lead to unreliable routing. The current work presents a reliant ad hoc on-demand distance vector routing (R-AODV) based on trusted and shortest path and compare to AODV trust framework to which have been used to overcome the mentioned problem as well. The performance differentials are analyzed using various metrics which are packet delivery fraction, average end-to-end delay, and normalized routing load. The algorithm is implemented and simulated using NS2. The performance differentials are analyzed using various metrics which are packet delivery fraction, average end-to-end delay, and normalized routing load. The results revealed that the developed R-AODV exhibits good performance. Moreover, the proposed routing mechanism is competitive, as compare to trust ad hoc on-demand distance vector (TAODV).

Key words: Reliability, mobile ad-hoc network (MANET),routing protocol.

INTRODUCTION

Mobile ad-hoc network (MANET) composes only of nodes. These nodes do not have fixed infrastructure or any centralized controller such as access point or server to determine the route of the paths. Thus, each node, in an ad hoc network, has to rely on each other in order to forward packets. Therefore, there is a need to use a specific cooperation mechanism to forward packet from hop to hop before it reaches a required destination by using routing protocol (Perkins and Royer, 2003). Examples of available routing protocols for MANET are ad hoc on-demand distance vector (AODV) (Perkins and Royer, 2003), destination sequenced distance vector

(DSDV) (Venugopal et al., 2008), and dynamic source routing (DSR) (Johnson et al., 2007). The main aim of those routing protocols is to find the shortest path in the source-destination routes selection (Buruhanudeen et al., 2007). These routing protocols can be attacked by blackhole (Tamilselvan and Sankaranarayanan, 2007; Seungjin et al., 2004; Irshad and Shoaib, 2010), denial of service DoS (Gupta et al., 2002; Aad et al., 2008), and wormhole (Khalil et al., 2005). These attacks may influence the routing of packets. Therefore, in MANET, misbehaviour nodes, due to selfish or malicious reasons, can significantly degrade the performance of MANET.

Due to security issues that can occur on MANET, researchers have proposed many mechanisms to prevent and reduce the risk. Most of these mechanisms are focused on how to protect the data transmission network such as access control (Miguel et al., 2010), and key

*Corresponding author. E-mail: Hothefa@uniten.edu.my.

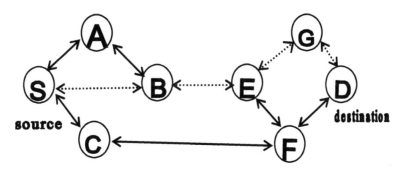

Figure 1. An example of broadcasting RREQ and unicasting RREP between source node S and destination, D.

management (Adams et al., 2005). Meanwhile, there are some works which focused on how to makes MANET routing protocols discover routes in a secure method e. g. trust models mechanisms (Meka et al., 2006; Xiaoqi et al., 2004). Most of the optimizations, in routing protocols, are limited to improving the path resilience and the reliability of packet delivery with secure route. However, current ad-hoc routing protocols have not fully addressed the performance issues related to the security by considering the shortest path.

The current work proposes an implementation of trust mechanism in the ad hoc on-demand distance vector routing protocol (AODV). The new mechanism is called as reliant ad hoc on-demand distance vector routing (R-AODV) that considers both trust and shortest path in making routing decision. Meaning route will be selected based on the trust value assign to each node with the hop count. The performance of R-AODV is compared with AODV trust framework which uses route trust as a metric for the source node to make such informed route selection decisions.

RELATED WORKS

To enhance the performance of routing protocols in MANET, a lot of approaches have been presented so far. The approaches can be mainly classified into two groups: Reliability based approaches (Amir, 2008), efficiency and security based approaches (Tamilselvan and Sankaranarayanan, 2007; Seungjin et al., 2004; Irshad and Shoaib, 2010; Miguel et al., 2010; Adams et al., 2005; Meka et al., 2006). There are quite a number of excellent protocols in terms of efficiency however lacking of the security consideration. Meanwhile, there are good protocols in terms of security too but do not significantly consider network efficiency. In this work, both aspects were considered in designing a new routing protocol. This work present a simple and reliable protocol called a reliant ad hoc on-demand distance vector routing (R-AODV) which simply considering the shortest and the trusted path. The proposed protocol was implemented

using network simulation software ver. 2. Similar routing protocol proposed by Meka et al. (2006) has been chosen for comparison in order to evaluate and bench mark the performance of proposed R-AODV protocols under different simulation scenarios.

Review of ad hoc on-demand distance vector routing protocol (AODV)

The most common ad-hoc protocol is the ad hoc on-demand distance vector (AODV) routing protocol (Perkins and Royer, 2003). It is capable of both unicast and multicast routing. It is on demand algorithm, meaning that it builds routes between nodes only when the source node needs it (Gorantala, 2006). Also it is a method of routing messages between mobile computers which allows these mobile computers, or nodes, to pass messages through their neighbours to nodes with which they cannot directly communicate. When one node needs to send a message to another node that is not its neighbour, it broadcasts a route request (RREQ) message. The RREQ message contains: The source, the destination, the lifespan of the message and a sequence number. Once node 1's neighbours receive the RREQ message, there are two options; they will forward the message if they know a route to the destination or they can send a route reply (RREP) message back to the source node if they are the destination. Figure 1 shows an example of broadcasting RREQ and unicasting RREP messages between source and destination nodes. Each node has its own routing table which maintains the following information: Next-hop, sequence number, hop count and information about all other nodes in the network. When a source node wants to send a data packet to some other destinations nodes in the network, it will first check its routing table to see if any valid route to the destination exists. If a valid route exists, the source node will send the packet to the next hop found in the source routing table. In the case where there is no existing valid route in the source routing table, the source node will initiate a route discovery process, by broadcasting a RREQ message. The RREQ message contains:

1. The source IP address and current sequence number.
2. The destination IP address and destination sequence number (destination sequence number is the last known destination sequence number for this destination).
3. A broadcast ID.

Once intermediate node receives the RREQ message, it will first check if it has an active route, or if the existing destination sequence number value saved in its routing table is smaller than the destination sequence number in RREQ message. If so, it rebroadcasts the RREQ message from its interfaces but using its own IP address in the IP header of the message and the TTL in the IP header will be decreased by one, while the hop count field in the broadcast RREQ–message is incremented by one to account for the new hop through the intermediate node. Nevertheless, if a route already exists in the source IP address and the source sequence number in the RREQ message is greater than the destination sequence number, then the source IP addresses that have been saved in the node's routing table or the sequence numbers are equal, but the hop count as specified by the RREQ message is now smaller than the existing hop count in the routing table. As such, the intermediate node will create or update a reverse route to the Source IP Address in its routing table (Perkins and Royer, 2003).

AODV supports multicast and unicast traffic and it shows only one route to every destination, which constitutes a restrictive characteristic (Johnson et al., 2007). In order to establish routes, routing messages need to be exchanged between the nodes. These messages, routing table and the operations of AODV are described subsequently.

AODV route messages

Route request message (RREQ): A RREQ message is broadcasted by the source node that wants to reach an unknown destination node. A route can be determined when the RREQ message reaches either the destination itself, or an intermediate node that has route to the destination.

Route reply message (RREP): A RREP message is unicasting back to the source node. Since each node receiving the request caches a route back to the source of the request, the RREP message can be unicasted back from the destination node to the source node

Route error (RERR): Nodes monitor the link status of next hops in active routes. When a link break in an active route is detected, a RERR message is used to notify other nodes that the loss of that link has occurred. The

RERR message indicates which destinations are now unreachable due to the loss of the link.

Routing table in AODV

In AODV, each node maintains information about other nodes in the network using a routing table. Each routing table entry contains the following information: Destination IP address and destination sequence number, valid destination sequence number flag, network interface, hop count (number of hops needed to each destination), next hop, and lifetime (Expiration time for this route table entry) (Perkins and Royer, 2003).

Reliant on-demand distance vector routing protocol (R-AODV)

AODV can be modified to select a path (called the BestPath (BP)) during the route discovery cycle based on both trust and the number of hops (trusted and shortest path). When the route request and route reply (R-RREQ and R-RREP) messages in R-AODV are generated or forwarded by the nodes in the network, each node appends its own trust to the trust accumulator (trust summation accumulator S(t)) on these route discovery messages. Each node also updates its routing table with all the information contained in the control messages. As the R-RREQ messages are broadcasted, each intermediate node that does not have a route to the destination forwards the R-RREQ packet after appending its trust to the trust accumulator in the packet which is computed by

$$S[t] = \sum_{i=1}^{n} trust_{value}(i) \qquad (1)$$

where: n is number of hop counts received in one path, $S(t)$ is the trust summation accumulator, and $trust_{value}(i)$, trust value of neighbouring nodes in the routing table.

Hence, at any point, the R-RREQ packet contains a list of all the nodes visited with their trust value added to trust summation accumulator $S(t)$.

Whenever a node receives an R-RREQ packet, it will check the updates of the route to the source node. It then checks for the *BestPath, (Bp)*, for intermediate nodes which is computed by:

$$BestPath(Bp) = \frac{S[t]}{\sqrt{Hop_{count} \cdot Hop_{count}}} \qquad (2)$$

where *BestPath (Bp)* is the best path computed based on both trust and hop count from source to destination, and Hop_{count}, the hop count included in the request message.

If the B*estPath (Bp)* to any of the intermediate nodes is greater than the previously known *BestPath (Bp)* to that node, the routing table entry is updated for that node and a new trust value computed by Equation 3 is assigned.

$$trust_{value\_new} = \frac{S[t]}{Hop_{count}}$$

$$(3)$$

where $trust_{value\_new}$ is new trust value that will be updated in the routing table.

The concepts of our reliant AODV were presented subsequently.

Route discovery

The goal of this work is for the source node to select a secure route with less hop count to a destination node. The source node, S, broadcasts a route discovery message (R-RREQ) to its neighbours which contains:

S broadcasts R-RREQ:
<Source_Addr, Source_Seq#, Broadcast_ID, Dest_Addr, Dest_Seq#, Hop_Count, S(t), Bp>

Similar to RREQ messages in AODV, when a node receives an R-RREQ message, it sets up a reverse path back to the source by recording the neighbour from which it receives the R-RREQ message. Meanwhile, when the node receives the R-RREQ message, it will check whether it is the destination or not, if so, it will update the routing table for that node and generate an R-RREP message. But if the receiving node is an intermediate node, it attaches the trust value in its routing table to the trust summation accumulator *S(t)* in the message. Upon receiving the message, a node verifies the *BestPath (Bp)* in the routing table with the new *BestPath (Bp)* value attached in the message. If the new *BestPath (Bp)* is bigger than the one in the routing table, the node then updates the routing table.

Route reply

After receiving the R-RREQ message, the destination node creates a route reply message (R-RREP), signs it and unicasts the reply massage back to the source over the reverse path. The destination node, creates the R-RREP message, and sends it back to its neighbour. The route reply message contains:

D unicasts R-RREP:

<Source_Addr,   Dest_Addr,   Dest_Seq#,   Hop_Count, Lifetime, S(t), Bp>

SIMULATION AND RESULTS ANALYSIS

In the simulation, the MAC layer used was the IEEE 802.11 MAC protocol with distributed coordination function (DCF) (Borgia et al., 2003). The MAC layer used Request-to-send (RTS) and clear-to send (CTS) control frames for unicast packet to reduce packet collisions resulting from the hidden node problem. For the radio model, Lucent's WaveLAN (Tuch, 1993; Anastasi, 2003) parameters were used in the simulation. WaveLAN had the transmission range of 250 m and the channel capacity of 2 Mb/s. The simulated nodes were allowed to move randomly according to the random waypoint mobility model (IEEE, 1997). Besides, constant bit rate (CBR) was used as the traffic model and traffic pattern that consisted of maximum 5 CBR sources were initiated randomly by time in the simulation. The parameters that were specified when randomizing the communication pattern were the number of wanted sources, the packet size, the rate of sending and the simulation time. Each of the nodes began transmitting at randomly chosen location inside the simulation area. When the simulation started, the nodes remained stationary during a period of pause time (seconds). The nodes would then select random destination in the simulation area and moved towards that destination.

Three different scenarios were simulated and for each scenario, three performance metrics are measured. For each simulation, there are four test cases:

1. The normal AODV protocol and the network nodes do not drop any packet (AODV-wo-drop).
2. The normal AODV protocol and the network nodes drop data packets based on the trust value given to the node (AODV-w-drop).
3. The proposed R-AODV protocol and the network nodes drop data packets based on the trust value given to the node (R-AODV-w-drop).
4. Related method presented by Meka et al. (2006) called a trust-based framework which uses route trust as a metric for the source node to make such informed route selection decisions.

The performance of the four test cases of routing protocol will be compared. The result of test case (1) represents the behavior of a normal AODV in a perfectly trusted MANET. On the other hand, the result of test case (2) and test case (3) represent the respective behavior of the normal AODV and the proposed R-AODV under the condition that the nodes in MANET may drop packets while the result of test case (4) represents AODV trust framework (AODVTF) under the condition that the nodes in MANET may drop packets.

Table 1. Simulation parameters for scenario 1.

Number of nodes	65 -105 nodes
Simulation time	900 seconds
Map size	500 × 500 m
Max speed	25 m/s
Mobility model	Random way point
Traffic type	Constant bit rate (CBR)
Packet size	512 bytes
Connection rate (Nominal radio range)	4 pkts/s
Pause time	0 s
Number of connection	5

Theoretically, it is expected that the proposed R-AODV routing protocol will achieve higher packet delivery rate compared to the normal AODV in the situation where the nodes can drop packets. Of course, the highest packet delivery rate is achieved when the nodes do not drop packets at all (test case (1)). When it comes to end-to-end delay, it is expected that R-AODV protocol will have slightly higher delay compared to AODV due to the possibility that it may take a longer path which is more trusted. The normalized routing load for R-AODV also is expected to be slightly higher compared to that of AODV due to the fact that it will generate more messages if a longer path is chosen.

Scenario 1 performance and analysis

In the simulation of scenario 1, nodes are free to move arbitrarily; thus, the network topology which is typically multihop may change randomly and rapidly at unpredictable times. In this simulation, the number of nodes was varied and they were equally distributed within 500 × 500 m area and the transmission range is 250 m while the simulation period is 900 s. Nodes are increased by 10 for each new simulation until the number of nodes reaches 105. The maximum speed was fixed to 25 m/s and the pause time was 0 s for every simulation. The simulation parameters for this scenario are shown in Table 1.

After each route discovery, nodes will update their routing table based on the highest trust value with less hop count replied. Hence the operation of sending packets will be distributed according to the best path selected in the routing table. Thus, the packet drop rate due to nodes misbehaviours will be reduced. Figure 2 illustrates that AODV has higher packet delivery without drop effect while R-AODV obtained about 10% higher than AODV with drop which obtained about 60% of packet delivery. R-AODV is much better than AODV with drop and AODVTF except when the number of node is small. R-AODV seems very close to AODV with drop in small number of node. The reason is that there is small

number of nodes travel in big simulation area, 500 × 500 m. R-AODV seems very close to AODVTF in term of packet delivery fraction in this scenario because they are depending on the trusted path. R-AODV shows much better performance in terms of packet delivery fraction in scenario 1.

Packet delivery fraction of the four test cases is shown in Figure 2. In scenario 1, AODV without drop performed particularly well, while the packet delivery fraction of R-AODV is better than that of AODV with drop regardless of the degree of mobility. The reason is that R-AODV node selects a new and trusted route in the route discovery procedure by using the best path mechanism to transmit data packets to destination. The use of trusted route reduces the possibility of route breakdown caused by packet drop. Therefore, R-ADOV was dropping less number of packets compared to AODV with drop and AODVM with drop while Figure 3 shows the average end-to-end delays for scenario 1 of all the four test cases. The results for the four test cases are almost similar except in AODVTF with drop which has longer delay compared to another three case. In R-AODV, high average end-to-end delay is caused by the selection of best path mechanism. Another reason is that R-AODV has trust value and best path value in the routing control message. These values was computed subsequently during the routing discovery process according to selection path mechanism proposed in (section 3), which cause a slightly longer delay. Theoretically, the expected result for R-AODV should be very high in terms of average end-to-end delay. However, the experiment result of R-AODV showed good performance in term of average end-to-end that might be due to the best path mechanism in R-AODV which is also based on less hops count.

Figure 4 illustrates the normalized routing load of all the four test cases. In this scenario, AODV without drop effects performed particularly well. The result for the four test cases show that R-AODV has higher percentage of normalized routing load because R-AODV depends on the trusted path which may have more hops count compared to the original AODV without drop and AODV with drop which depend on the shortest path only. As a

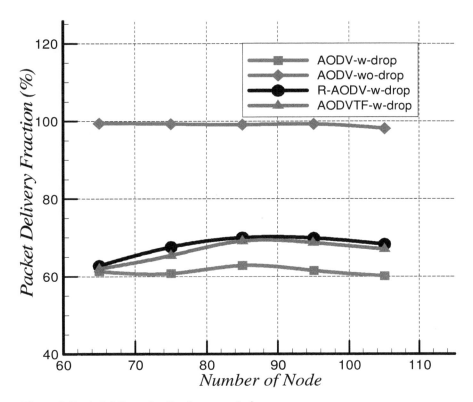

Figure 2. Packet delivery fraction for scenario 1.

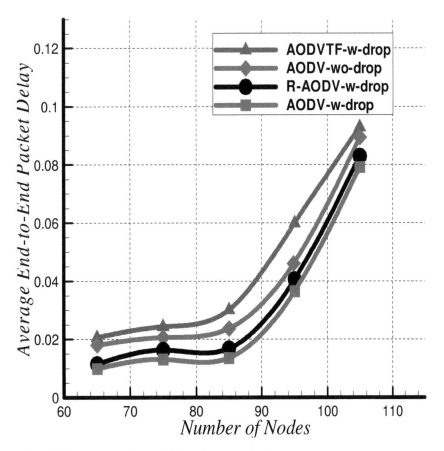

Figure 3. Average end-to-end delays for scenario 1.

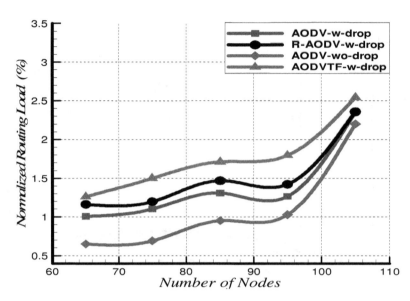

Figure 4. Normalized routing load for scenario 1.

Table 2. Simulation parameters for scenario 2.

Number of node	50 node
Simulation time	900 s
Map size	500 × 500 m
Max speed	25 m/s
Mobility model	Random way point
Traffic type	Constant bit rate (CBR)
Packet size	512 bytes
Connection rate (Nominal radio range)	4 pkts/s
Pause time	0, 25, 50, 75, 100, 125 (s)
Number of connection	5

result, R-AODV will generate more TRREQ and TRREP messages. Theoretically, the expected result for R-AODV should be very high in terms of normalized routing load compare with the other two test cases due to the selection of best path mechanism which depends on the trusted path. However, the experiment result of R-AODV in terms of normalized routing shows that R-AODV performed well with a slightly higher normalized routing load compared to AODV with drop effects.

Scenario 2 performance and analysis

In scenario 2, 50 nodes are fairly distributed within 500 × 500 m area with transmission range is 250 m. Besides, the pause time is varying from 0 to 125 and the simulation period is 900 s. Nodes are allowed to go up 25 m/s which are a reasonably maximum speed. The simulation parameters for this scenario are shown in Table 2.

Figure 5 illustrates the packet delivery fraction of all the four test cases. In this scenario, when pause time is set to 20 which is close to 0 (continuous motion), each of them obtained lower packet delivery fraction. The reason is changing of the topology of network, caused by high motion of nodes due to less pause time. As the pause time reaches 100 (no motion), packet delivery fraction for R-AODV with drop is increased due to the stable network. In summary, for node equal to 50, high values of pause time and simulation area 500 × 500 m, R-AODV with drop effects shows much better performance in the terms of packet delivery fraction compared to AODV with drop.

Figure 6 shows the average end-to-end delay for scenario 2 for all the four test cases. The break in routes in the four test cases lead to nodes discovering new routes which lead to longer end-to-end delay while the source packets are buffered at the source during route discovery. Simulation area plays a role in affecting the performance of the four test cases due to the far distance

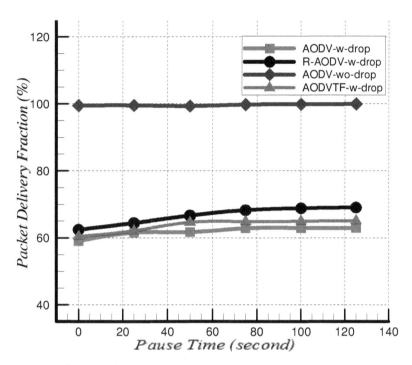

Figure 5. Packet delivery fraction for scenario 2.

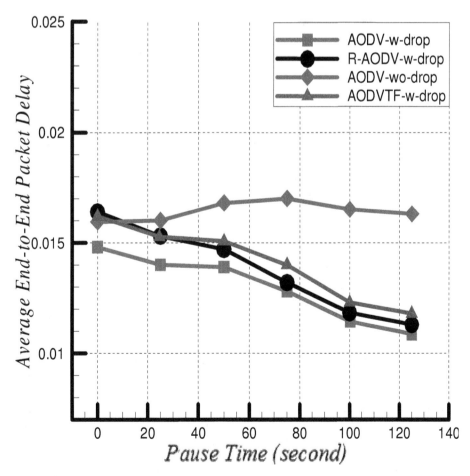

Figure 6. Average end-to-end delay for scenario 2.

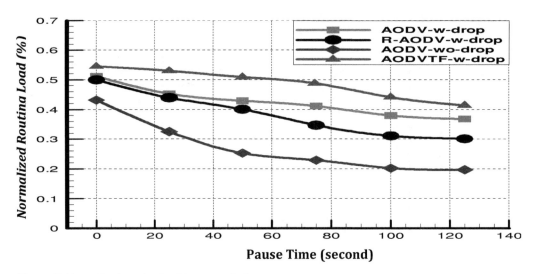

Figure 7. Normalized routing load for scenario 2.

between nodes. In this case, the packet may take longer time in buffering till the next motion. Therefore, all the four test cases may have higher average end-to-end delay. In theory, R-AODV with drop should have very high average end-to-end delay compared to the other two test cases due to the trusted path that has been selected by best path mechanism. This experiment showed that R-AODV with drop has a slightly higher average end-to-end delay compared to AODV with drop. The gap between R-AODV with drop and AODV with drop in end-to-end was reduced when the values of the pause time were increased. R-AODV with drop in scenario 2 shows good performance in term of average end-to-end delay.

Figure 7 illustrates the comparison between the four test cases in terms of normalized routing load. In R-AODV, source node may select the trusted path to destination node which may have much of hop count compared to normal AODV which select the shortest path only. As a result, R-AODV may have much TRREQ and TRREP messages. Sources nodes may have routes break to destination. In this case, nodes need to send RRER message to notify other nodes about that routes break. Hence, nodes have to discover new routes by sending other RREQ messages. Once these RREQ messages received, destinations will generate RREP message. Theoretically, R-AODV should have very high normalized routing load caused by these messages. However, R-AODV with drop in this simulation experiment if this scenario showed better performance in term of normalized routing load compared to AODV with drop.

In this scenario, at pause time equal to 0 (continuous motion), each of the four test cases shows high routing normalized load due to routes break or change in route directory caused by the high motion of nodes. Hence, when the pause time increased to reach no motion, normalized routing load was lower due to the stability of

nodes motion. In summary, for fix number of nodes equal to 50 and small spaces, for example 500 × 500 m, R-AODV perform very well and show excellent performance in terms of normalized routing load.

Scenario 3 performance and analysis

In this scenario, 50 nodes are equally distributed in 500 × 500 m area with 250 m as transmission range. Nodes are free to move arbitrarily; thus, the network topology which is typically multihop may change randomly and rapidly at unpredictable times. In this scenario, the mobile nodes move with a speed which varied between 25 to 105 m/s while the pause time was 20 s. The simulation parameters for this scenario are shown in Table 3.

Figure 8 shows the comparison between the four test cases in term of packet delivery fraction. In this scenario, as the maximum speed of node is low, the packet delivery fraction will be higher because the nodes in the network border move slowly toward the network center and the load density of the network center does not change very much. Therefore, the four test cases performed much better when the maximum speed is low, AODV without drop performed particularly well while AODV with drop packet obtained very low percentage of packet delivery fraction. R-AODV with drop obtained almost 70% of packet delivery fraction which is higher than AODV with drop by almost 10%. R-AODV with drop shows much better performance in the terms of packet delivery fraction compared to AODV with drop.

Theoretically, pause time equal to 20 s (almost continuous motion) with varied movement speed will generate unstable network. Therefore, the expected result for R-AODV should be very high in term of average end-to-end delay. The experimental results in this scenario showed that R-AODV has a slight delay due to

Table 3. Simulation parameters for scenario 3.

Number of nodes	50 nodes
Simulation time	900 s
Map size	500 × 500 m
Maximum speed	25-105 m/s
Mobility model	Random way point
Traffic type	Constant bit rate (CBR)
Packet size	512 bytes
Connection rate (Nominal radio range)	4 pkts/s
Pause time	20 s
Number of connection	5

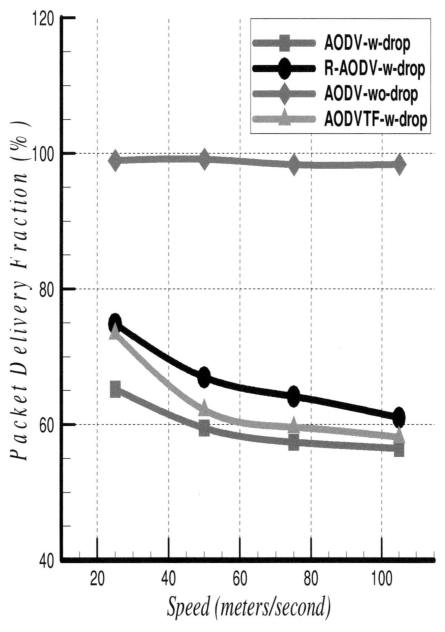

Figure 8. Packet delivery fraction for scenario 3.

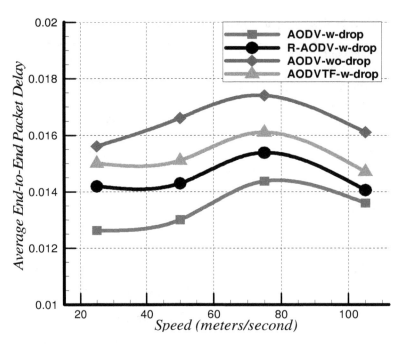

Figure 9. Average end-to-end delay for scenario 3.

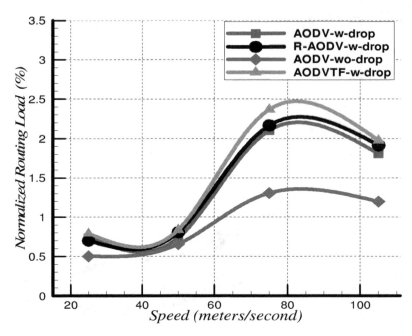

Figure 10. Normalized routing load for scenario 3.

unstable network as shown in Figure 9. On the other hand, R-AODV shows good performance in term of average end-to-end delay.

Theoretically, the source node in AODV without drop and AODV with drop need few RREQ and RREP messages to discover the new route to destination because the routing discovery in these two test cases is based on the shortest path while source node in R-AODV may need much of TRREQ and TRREP messages to discover the new route to the destination. As a result, the expected result for R-AODV with drop should be very high in term of normalized routing load. This experiment showed that R-AODV with drop has a slightly higher normalized routing load compared to AODV with drop as shown in Figure 10. Therefore, R-AODV showed good performance in terms of normalized routing load.

CONCLUSION AND FUTURE WORKS

In this paper, we proposed a new MANET routing algorithm called reliant-AODV (R-AODV) which is basically an extension to the AODV routing protocol that incorporates a trust mechanism to enhance its reliability. The proposed algorithm was implemented and simulated using the NS-2 network simulator. In the simulation used, each node is given a trust value and this value is associated with the possibility of the node to perform a packet drop. With the inclusion of trust mechanism, it is expected that using R-AODV would result in a higher percentage of successful data delivery as compared to AODV. However, it is also expected that due to the extra processing done and the possibility that the packets may take a longer route. Besides, the normalized routing load and end-to-end delay are anticipated to be increase too. Based on the simulation result, the use of R-AODV does provide a higher percentage of successful data delivery. Meanwhile, the simulation has also shown that the impact to normalized routing load and end-to-end delay is very minimal. Therefore, it can be concluded that R-AODV does provide enhanced reliability with minimal impact to performance.

In the future works, research will be carried out to optimize the reliant-AODV routing algorithm and establish some fast response mechanisms when malicious behaviours of attackers are detected. Then, the trust model will be farther applied into other application such as key management. A detailed simulation evaluation will be conducted in terms of packet delivery fraction, message overhead, and security analysis.

REFERENCES

Aad, Hubaux J, Knightly WE (2008). Impact of Denial of Service Attacks on Ad Hoc Networks. Networking. IEEE/ACM Trans., pp. 791- 802.

Adams W, Davis N, Hadjichristofi (2005). A Framework for Key Management in a Mobile Ad-Hoc Network. Proceedings of the International Conference on Information Technology Coding and Computing (ITCC 05), pp. 568-573

Amir Pirzada A (2008). Reliable Routing in Ad Hoc Networks Using Direct Trust Mechanisms. School of Computer Science and Software Engineering. The University of Western Australia. Crawley, 6: 131-157.

Anastasi G, Borgia E, Conti M (2003). IEEE 802.11 ad hoc networks: performance measurements. Icdcsw., 23rd International Conference on Distributed Computing Systems Workshops (ICDCSW'03), p. 758.

Borgia E, Anastasi G, Conti M (2003). IEEE 802.11 ad hoc networks: protocols performance and open issues. Ad hoc Networking. IEEE Press Wiley. New York, pp. 21-26.

Buruhanudeen S, Othman M, Ali BM (2007). Existing MANET Routing Protocols and Metrics used Towards the Efficiency and Reliability-An Overview. Telecommunications and Malaysia International Conference on Communications, IEEE Int. Confer., pp. 231-236.

Gorantala (2006). Routing Protocols in Mobile Ad-hoc Networks. Master's Thesis in Computing Science, Ume°a University. Department of Computing Science, Sweden, pp. 32-48.

Gupta V, Krishnamurthy SV, Faloutsos M (2002). Denial of Service Attacks at the MAC Layer in Wireless Ad Hoc Networks. In Proc. of MILCOM, pp. 202-215.

IEEE (1997). Wireless LAN Medium Access Control (MAC) and Physical layer (PHY) Specifications. IEEE Std., 802: 11.

Irshad U, Shoaib R (2010). Analysis of Black Hole Attack on MANETs Using Different MANET Routing Protocols. Master thesis report to COM/School of Computing, Blekinge Institute of Technology, Sweden: MEE, 10: 62.

Johnson D, Hu Y, Maltz D (2007). The Dynamic Source Routing Protocol (DSR) for Mobile Ad Hoc Networks for IPv4, p. 4728.

Khalil I, Bagchi S, Shroff N (2005). LITEWORP: a lightweight countermeasure for the wormhole attack in multihop wireless networks. In the International Conference on Dependable Systems and Networks (DSN), Yokohama, Japan, pp. 612-621.

Meka K, Virendra M, Upadhyaya S (2006). Trust based routing decisions in mobile ad-hoc networks. In Proceedings of the Workshop on Secure Knowledge Management (SKM), pp. 41-56.

Miguel P, Ruiz M, Marin RL (2010). Enhanced access control in hybrid MANETs through utility-based pre-authentication control. J. Wireless Comm. and Mobile Comput., pp: 90-96.

Perkins CE, Royer EM (2003). Ad hoc On-Demand Distance Vector (AODV) Routing. IEFT Network Working Group, p. 3561.

Seungjin P, Al-Shurman M, Seong-Moo Y (2004) Black Hole Attack in Mobile Ad hoc Network. ACMSE'04. Huntsville. AL. USA pp: 50-56.

Tamilselvan L, Sankaranarayanan V (2007). Prevention of Blackhole Attack in MANET. Wireless Broadband and Ultra Wideband Communications. AusWireless, pp. 21-21.

Tuch B (1993). Development of WaveLAN, an ISM Band Wireless LAN. AT and T Tech., pp. 27-33.

Venugopal A, Khaleel K, Rahman Ur, Zaman (2008). Performance Comparison of On-Demand and Table Driven Ad Hoc Routing Protocols Using NCTUns. Computer Modeling and Simulation. UKSIM. Tenth Int. Confer., pp. 336-341.

Xiaoqi Li, Michael R. Lyu, Jiangchuan Liu (2004). Trust Model Based Self-Organized Routing Protocol for Ad Hoc Networks. IEEE Aerospace Conference, Big Sky, MT, pp. 2806-2821.

11

Cooperative control and synchronization with time delays of multi-robot systems

Yassine Bouteraa[1,2]*, Asma Ben Mansour[1], Jawhar Ghommam[1] and Gérard Poisson[2]

[1]Research unit on Intelligent Control, design and Optimization of Complex Systems, Sfax Engineering School, University of Sfax, BP W, 3038 Sfax, Tunisia.
[2]Institut Prisme SRI 63 avenue de Lattre de Tassigny 18020 Bourges Cedex, France.

In this article, we investigate the cooperative control and global asymptotic synchronization of Lagrangian system groups, such as industrial robots. The proposed control approach works to accomplish multi-robot systems synchronization under an undirected connected communication topology. The control strategy is to synchronize each robot in position and velocity to others robots in the network with respect to the common desired trajectory. The cooperative robot network only requires local neighbor-to-neighbor information exchange between manipulators and does not assume the existence of an explicit leader in the team. It is assumed that network robots have the same number of joints and equivalent joint work spaces. A combination of the Lyapunov-based technique and the graph theory has been used to establish the multi-robot system asymptotic stability. The developed control combines trajectory tracking and coordination algorithms. To address the time delay problem in the cooperative network communication, the suggested synchronization control law is shown to synchronize multiple robots as well as to track given trajectory, taking into account the presence of the time delay. To this end, Krasovskii functional method has been used to deal with the delay-dependent stability problem. Simulations applied to an illustrative example have shown the effectiveness of the described strategy.

Key words: Cooperative control, decentralized trajectory tracking control, synchronization control, time delays control.

INTRODUCTION

Nowadays, much research have been focusing in group coordination, cooperative control and synchronization problems. In fact, motivated by the profit acquired by using multiple inexpensive systems working together to achieve complex tasks exceeding the abilities of a single agent, cooperative synchronization control has received significant attention. Distributed coordination and decentralized synchronization of multi-agent systems have recently been studied extensively in the context of cooperative control (Soon-Jo and Slotine, 2009; Lin et al., 2004; Jadbabaie et al., 2003; Ogren et al., 2002), to name a few. In particular, design based on graph theory and Laplacian matrix produce interesting results (Mesbahi and Hadaegh, 2001; Olfati-Saber and Murray, 2004; Ren, 2007; Ren et al., 2007). Agreement,

consensus problems in the area of cooperative control of multi-agent systems have been studied in Moreau (2005), Ren and Beard (2005), Olfati-Saber and Murray (2004), Slotine and Wang (2004) and Ren (2007). The coordination control strategies are closely related to the synchronization problem in which control laws are coupled and each agent robot control is updated using local rule based on its own sensors and the states of its neighbors. In this context, one recent representative work (Rodriguez-Angeles and Nijmeije, 2004) shows that we can synchronize the multi-composed system in the case of partial knowledge, that is, only position measuring. A decentralized tracking control law globally exponentially synchronizes an arbitrary number of robots, and represents a generalization of the average consensus problem. This has been presented in Soon-Jo and Slotine (2009). A synchronization approach to trajectory tracking of multiple mobile robots while maintaining time-varying formations has been presented

---

in Dong et al. (2009). Adaptive control strategy to position synchronization of multiple motion axes using cross-coupling technology has been developed in Dong (2003). In many engineering applications, communication delays between subsystems cannot be neglected. Therefore, the problem of time delayed communication in control of multi-robot systems is important in numerous practical applications. Indeed, without control measures of time delays in cooperative task may even cause instability. The problem of time delayed communication in control of multi-agent systems has been studied in several references (Olfati-Saber and Murray, 2004; Nikhil and Mark, 2006; Wang and Slotine, 2006; Tanner and Christodoulakis, 2005). The consideration of time delayed communication in control of multi-robot systems is mainly a practical necessity. In particular, this need occurs when addressing areas which require real-time applications such as operations in unsafe environments and robotic surgery. In the literature, most of earlier works on multi-agent coordination and consensus (Olfati-Saber and Murray, 2004; Lin et al., 2004; Jadbabaie et al., 2003; Zhihua et al., 2008) mainly deal with very simple dynamic models such as linear systems and focuses on an algorithm tacking the form of first-order dynamics (Lawton and Beard, 2002; Olfati-Saber, 2007; Ren and Beard, 2005). In particular, most previous works on consensus and coordination of multi-agent systems using the graph theory and Laplacian (Jadbabaie et al., 2003; Lin et al., 2004; Ren et al., 2007; Olfati-Saber and Murray, 2004) have presented a synchronization to the weighted average of initial conditions but they do not consider multi-agent systems where there is a desired path to follow. Therefore, the aforementioned algorithms cannot give solutions for robot networks, where a desired trajectory is required.

The objective of this paper is to design a control approach that can achieve both synchronization of the robot movements and asymptotic stable tracking of a common desired trajectory. The proposed controller relies principally on a consensus algorithm for systems modeled by nonlinear second-order dynamics and applies the algorithm to the synchronization control problem by choosing appropriately information states on which consensus is reached. The concept key of the new synchronizing controller is the introduction of a state vector that quantifies the coordination degree between a robot manipulator positions and different positions of its neighbors. Moreover, the developed approach achieves not only global asymptotic synchronization of the configuration variables, but also global asymptotic convergence to the desired trajectory. The main contribution of the present work is the use of highly nonlinear system and Langragian dynamics for the derivation of cooperative control law. Notable works have focused on highly nonlinear systems. Their developed strategy requires the coupling feedback of the most adjacent robots (Soon-Jo and Slotine, 2009) or axis (Dong, 2003) for the algorithm. However, the proposed

strategy is based on partial mesh topology in which there are interconnections between all robots, such that all robots have direct influence in the combined dynamics. We provide the use of partial mesh topology, a high degree of reliability due to the presence of multiple paths for data between robots. On the other hand, it is not a fully connected mesh topology and consequently we avoid the expense and the complexity required for a connection between every robot in the network. In this paper, we study the problem of mutual synchronization when there are communication delays in the network. The delays are assumed to be bounded.

Modelling multi-Lagrangian system network

The n degree-of-freedom robot manipulator composed of rigid bodies is expressed based on Newton's and Euler's equations as follows:

$$M_i(q_i)\ddot{q}_i + C_i(q_i,\dot{q}_i)\dot{q}_i + g_i(q_i) = \tau_i \qquad (1)$$

where $q_i \in \mathbb{R}^n$ denotes the joint angles of the ith manipulator; $\dot{q}_i \in \mathbb{R}^n$, and $\ddot{q}_i \in \mathbb{R}^n$ are the vectors of joint velocity and joint acceleration, respectively.

$M_i(q_i) \in \mathbb{R}^{n \times n}$ represents inertia matrix which is symmetric uniformly bounded and positive definite. $C_i(q_i,\dot{q}_i)\dot{q}_i \in \mathbb{R}^n$ is a vector function containing Coriolis and centrifugal forces. $g_i(q_i) \in \mathbb{R}^n$ is a vector function consisting of gravitational forces. Although the above equations of motion are coupled and nonlinear, they exhibit certain fundamental properties due to their Lagrangian dynamic structure. The most important property is the well-known skew-symmetry of the matrix $\dot{M} - 2C$. (Spong and Chopra, 2007). In the present topology, the edge represents bidirectional communication links. This consists fn a group of n manipulators interchanging information that can be viewed as an undirected graph (Figure 1).

CONTROLLER DESIGN

Tracking and Synchronization errors

In this paper, we consider the synchronization of multiple robots following a common time-varying trajectory. We will design decentralized control laws for n robots manipulators such that all joint positions mutually synchronize and track a common desired trajectory. The control objective of the proposed synchronization controller scheme is to synchronize the i-th-joint position and velocity q_i, q_i to the state of any manipulator q_j q_j.

Besides the controller is required to regulate the joint positions q_j to track a desired trajectory q_d. Specifically, the control torque for the i-th-robot is to control the tracking error to converge to zero and at the same time, to synchronize motions of n robots in

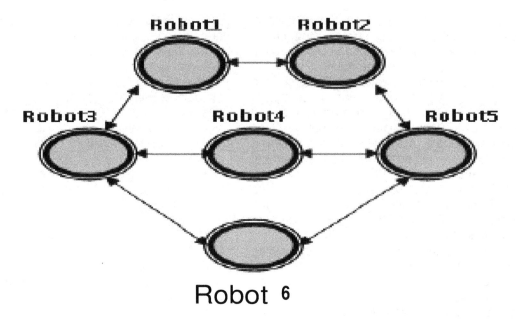

Figure 1. Undirected graph topology structure.

communication so that the synchronization error converges to zero. To this end, we define the measure of the position tracking error of the i-th manipulator as:

$$e_{1i}(t) = \dot{q}_i(t) - q_d(t) + \int_{t_0}^{t} \Lambda_i [q_i(\lambda) - q_d(\lambda)]d\lambda$$

(2)

Where Λ_i is a diagonal positive definite matrix.

Information on the vector e1i will give insight on the convergence of the joint index to the desired trajectory. It is required to know the performance of the controller that is to know how the trajectory of each robot manipulator converges with respect to each other. There are various ways to choose the synchronization error. For example in (Rodriguez-Angeles and Nijmeije, 2004) authors include the error information of all systems involved in the synchronization. Our approach will make use of the graph theory to propose a feasible and efficient synchronization error, which consists of a measure of the synchronization for robot manipulator as defined as follows:

$$e_{2i}(t) = \sum_{j \neq i} K_{ij} \left(q_i - q_j \right)$$

(3)

where, K_{ij} is a coupling term which gives insight on the weighted communication among the robot network.

Feedback control design

The objective of this paper is to design individual tracking controller for n manipulators such that they coordinate their motions and track synchronously a desired trajectory. To this end, we define the global error which encompasses both synchronization error and trajectory tracking error for manipulator i as:

$$e_i = e_{1i} + \int_{t_0}^{t} e_{2i}(\lambda)d\lambda$$

(4)

Under the above strategy, motions of all manipulators are synchronized. The control of each manipulator considers motion responses of the other manipulators for synchronization. It takes into account only robots which make the exchange of information with it. The objective is to design a control law such that the coupling errors, that is, the position errors, velocity errors, and synchronization errors, all converge to zero. For each manipulator, the control law ¿i is defined as follows:

$$\tau_i = C_i(q_i, \dot{q}_i)\dot{q}_i + g_i(q_i) + M_i(q_i)[\ddot{q}_d - K_{pi}e_i - K_{di}\dot{e}_i - \Lambda_i(\dot{q}_i - \dot{q}_d)] + M_i(q_i)[\sum_{j \neq i} K_{ij}(e_{2i} - e_{2j}) + \Lambda_i e_{2i}]$$

(5)

where q_d is a common trajectory reference to be tracked, which is a smooth time varying trajectory and for which the first and the second derivative exist for all $t \geq 0$. K_{di} is a symmetric positive matrix. K_{ij} is a matrix containing element from the Laplacien matrix of a connected graph; It's a symmetric positive matrix.

Stability analysis

Substituting (5) into (1) yields;

$$M_i(q_i)\ddot{q}_i = M_i(q_i)[\ddot{q}_d - K_{pi}e_i - K_{di}\dot{e}_i - \Lambda_i(\dot{q}_i - \dot{q}_d)] + M_i(q_i)[\sum_{j \neq i} K_{ij}(e_{2i} - e_{2j}) + \Lambda_i e_{2i}]$$

(6)

This result;

$$\ddot{q}_i = \ddot{q}_d - K_{pi}e_i - K_{di}\dot{e}_i - \Lambda_i(\dot{q}_i - \dot{q}_d) + [\sum_{j \neq i} K_{ij}(e_{2i} - e_{2j}) + \Lambda_i e_{2i}]$$

(7)

which can be written as follows:

$$\ddot{e}_i = -K_{pi}e_i - K_{di}\dot{e}_i + \sum_{j\neq i}K_{ij}\left(e_{2i} - e_{2j}\right) + \Lambda_i e_{2i} + \dot{e}_{2i} \tag{8}$$

Using the expression of the synchronization error e_{2i} and its first derivative gives:

$$\ddot{e}_i = -K_{pi}e_i - K_{di}\dot{e}_i + \sum_{j\neq i}K_{ij}\left(e_{2i} - e_{2j}\right) + \sum_{j\neq i}\left[K_{ij}(\dot{q}_i - \dot{q}_d) - (\dot{q}_j - \dot{q}_d)\right] +$$
$$\sum_{j\neq i}\Lambda_i K_{ij}\left[(q_i - q_d) - (q_j - q_d)\right] \tag{9}$$

Further calculation, will result in:

$$\ddot{e}_i = -K_{pi}e_i - K_{di}\dot{e}_i + \sum_{j\neq i}K_{ij}\left(\dot{e}_i - \dot{e}_j\right) \tag{10}$$

Equation (10) represents the closed loop synchronized system for the i ₋ th manipulator. In the sequel we proceed to analyze the stability properties of the proposed synchronized control scheme and ultimately to show that control goals: the position errors, velocity errors, and synchronization errors, all converge to zero. To prove the stability of the overall synchronized system, we define:

$$e^T = \left[e_1^T, e_1^T, ..., e_n^T\right]^T$$

Using (10) we obtain the synchronized error dynamics;

$$\ddot{e} = -K_p e - K_d \dot{e} + K_c \dot{e} \tag{11}$$

where $K_p = diag(K_{pi})$, $K_d = diag(K_{di})$ and K_c is given by

$$\begin{pmatrix} \sum_{j\neq 1}K_{1j} & \cdots & -K_{1j} & \cdots & -K_{1n} \\ \cdots & \cdots & \cdots & \cdots & \cdots \\ -K_{i1} & \cdots & \sum_{j\neq i}K_{ij} & \cdots & -K_{in} \\ \cdots & \cdots & \cdots & \cdots & \cdots \\ -K_{n1} & \cdots & -K_{nj} & \cdots & \sum_{j\neq n}K_{nj} \end{pmatrix}$$

Note that K_c is symmetric and positive semi-definite matrix, since we have an undirected graph, that is, $K_{ij} = K_{ji}$. The synchronized error dynamics (11) is a linear time invariant system described by a second order linear differential equation. A sufficient condition for the error dynamics to be stable is that the matrices K_p

and $K_d - K_c$ are positive definite. In particular, matrices K_{di} can be diagonal satisfying:

$$K_{di} > 2\sum_{i\neq j}K_{ij}.$$

To analyze the stability properties of the closed-loop error dynamics (Rodriguez-Angeles and Nijmeije, 2004), we take the following definite and radially unbounded Lyapunov function candidate;

$$V = \dot{e}^T\dot{e} + e^T K_p e \tag{12}$$

Its derivative to respect to time is:

$$\dot{V} = -\dot{e}^T(K_d - K_c)\dot{e} \leq 0 \tag{13}$$

It follows by direct application of Lasalle's invariance principle that the origin $(e, \dot{e}) = (0,0)$ is globally asymptotically stable and $\lim \dot{e} \to 0$ for $t \to \infty$. Referring to the expression of the global error (equation 4

$$e_i = q_i - q_d + \int_{t_0}^t \Lambda\left[q_i(\lambda) - q_d(\lambda)\right]d\lambda + \int_{t_0}^t \sum_{j\neq i}\beta_{ij}\left(q_i - q_j\right)d\lambda \tag{14}$$

as $\dot{e} = 0$ we have

$$\dot{q}_i - \dot{q}_d = -\Lambda_i(q_i - q_d) - \sum_{j\neq i}\beta_{ij}(q_i - q_j) \tag{15}$$

Setting $\varepsilon_i = q_i - q_d$, then Equation (15) can be written as:

$$\dot{\varepsilon}_i = -\Lambda_i\varepsilon_i - \sum_{j\neq i}\beta_{ij}\left(\varepsilon_i - \varepsilon_j\right) \tag{16}$$

Our objective is to show that $\lim \varepsilon_i = 0$ for $t \to \infty$. To this end, we define $\varepsilon = [\varepsilon_1, \varepsilon_2, ..., \varepsilon_n]^T$ and $\Lambda = [\Lambda_1, ..., \Lambda_n]^T$. Then Equation (16) can be written as:

$$\dot{\varepsilon} = A.\varepsilon \tag{17}$$

Where matrix A is given by:

$$\begin{pmatrix} -\Lambda_1 - \sum_{j\neq 1}K_{1j} & \cdots & K_{1j} & \cdots & K_{1n} \\ \cdots & \cdots & \cdots & \cdots & \cdots \\ K_{i1} & \cdots -\Lambda_i - \sum_{j\neq i}K_{ij} \cdots & & K_{in} \\ \cdots & \cdots & \cdots & \cdots & \cdots \\ K_{n1} & \cdots & K_{nj} & \cdots -\Lambda_n - \sum_{j\neq n}K_{nj} \end{pmatrix}$$

We set the Lyapunov function candidate as:

$$v(t) = \varepsilon^T.\varepsilon \tag{18}$$

Differentiating $v(t)$ with respect to time yield;

$$\dot{v} = 2\sum_{i=1}^n \varepsilon_i \dot{\varepsilon}_i \tag{19}$$

$$\dot{v} = 2\sum_{i=1}^n \varepsilon_i \left(-\Lambda_i\varepsilon_i - \sum_{j\neq i}\beta_{ij}\left(\varepsilon_i - \varepsilon_j\right)\right) \tag{20}$$

$$\dot{v} = -2\sum_{i=1}^n \Lambda_i\varepsilon_i^2 - 2\sum_{i=1}^n\sum_{j\neq i}\beta_{ij}\left(\varepsilon_i - \varepsilon_j\right)\varepsilon_i \tag{21}$$

$$\dot{v} = -2\sum_{i=1}^n \Lambda_i\varepsilon_i^2 - 2\sum_{i=1}^n\sum_{j\neq i}\beta_{ij}\varepsilon_i^2 + 2\sum_{i=1}^n\sum_{j\neq i}\beta_{ij}\varepsilon_i\varepsilon_j \tag{22}$$

Knowing that;

$$\sum_{i=1}^{n} \sum_{j\ne i} \beta_{ij}\, \varepsilon_i^2 = \sum_{i=1}^{n} \sum_{j\ne i} \beta_{ji}\, \varepsilon_j^2 \tag{23}$$

Consequently;

$$\dot{v} = -2\sum_{i=1}^{n} \Lambda_i\, \varepsilon_i^2 - \sum_{i=1}^{n}\sum_{j\ne i} \beta_{ij}\left(\varepsilon_i - \varepsilon_j\right)^2 \le 0 \tag{24}$$

It follows by direct application of Lasalle's invariance that the origin is globally asymptotically stable. Consequently we obtain $\lim \varepsilon_i(t) \to 0$ for $t \to \infty$. Then $q_i \to q_d$ and $\dot{q}_i \to \dot{q}_d$ for $t \to \infty$.

Referring to the equation (15), we show that $q_i \to q_j$ for $t \to \infty$.

Coordination with time delays

We study the coordination control problem taking into account time delays of communication channels. As a first assumption, we suppose that these delays can be justified by the fact that data information sent by the neighboring vehicles $j \ne i$ reaches vehicle i after a time-delay due to the short range communication channels. To take into account the time delay produced during the communication among the robots, we introduced in a coordination error expression a term τ which represents the same time delay due to the short range communication channels. Therefore, a coordination error, in the time delay context, will be presented as the well known classical time delayed model of multi-agent network:

$$e_{2i}(t) = \sum_{j\ne i} K_{ij}\left[q_i(t-\tau) - q_j(t-\tau)\right] \tag{25}$$

Consequently, the controller implanted in each Lagrangian system among the network take the following expression:

$$\tau_i = C_i(q_i,\dot{q}_i)\dot{q}_i + g_i(q_i) + M_i(q_i)\left[\ddot{q}_d - K_{pi}e_i(t) - K_{di}\dot{e}_i(t) - \Lambda_i(\dot{q}_i - \dot{q}_d)\right] + M_i(q_i)\left[\sum_{j\ne i} K_{ij}\left(e_{2i}(t-\tau) - e_{2j}(t-\tau)\right) + \Lambda_i e_{2i}(t-\tau)\right] \tag{26}$$

It will be shown that the behavior of the coordinated system under the effect of time delay changes significantly.

Stability analysis

Substituting (26) into (1) yields;

$$M_i(q_i)\ddot{q}_i = M_i(q_i)\left[\ddot{q}_d - K_{pi}e_i - K_{di}\dot{e}_i - \Lambda_i(\dot{q}_i - \dot{q}_d)\right] + M_i(q_i)\left[\sum_{j\ne i} K_{ij}\left(e_{2i}(t-\tau) - e_{2j}(t-\tau)\right) + \Lambda_i e_{2i}(t-\tau)\right] \tag{27}$$

Multiplying by M^{-1} and adding $\dot{e}_{2i}(t-\tau)$ in both sides yields;

$$\ddot{q}_i - \ddot{q}_d + \Lambda_i(\dot{q}_i - \dot{q}_d) + \dot{e}_{2i}(t-\tau) = -K_{pi}e_i - K_{di}\dot{e}_i + \sum_{j\ne i} K_{ij}\left(e_{2i}(t-\tau) - e_{2j}(t-\tau)\right) + \Lambda_i e_{2i}(t-\tau) + \dot{e}_{2i}(t-\tau) \tag{28}$$

Using the expression of the synchronization error e2i and its first derivative gives:

$$\ddot{e}_i = -K_{pi}e_i - K_{di}\dot{e}_i + \sum_{j\ne i} K_{ij}\left(e_{2i}(t-\tau) - e_{2j}(t-\tau)\right) + \sum_{j\ne i} K_{ij}\left((\dot{q}_i - \dot{q}_d) - (\dot{q}_j - \dot{q}_d)\right) + \sum_{j\ne i}\Lambda_i K_{ij}\left((q_i - q_d) - (q_j - q_d)\right) \tag{29}$$

Further calculation, we obtain the synchronized error dynamics;

$$\ddot{e} = K_p e - K_d \dot{e} + K_c \dot{e}(t-\tau) \tag{30}$$

where K_p, K_d and K_c are the same matrices already defined (stability analysis). By the Leibnitz formula, we have;

$$\dot{e} - \dot{e}(t-\tau) = \int_{t-\tau}^{t} \ddot{e}(\lambda)\, d\lambda \tag{31}$$

Substituting 31 into 30 leads to;

$$\ddot{e} = K_p e - K_d \dot{e} + K_c\left(\dot{e} - \int_{t-\tau}^{t} \ddot{e}(\lambda)\, d\lambda\right) \tag{32}$$

Setting $\check{e} = [e,\dot{e}]^T$ Therefore Equation 32 can be written as:

$$\ddot{e} = \begin{pmatrix} 0 & I \\ K_p & -K_d + K_c \end{pmatrix} - \begin{pmatrix} 0 & 0 \\ 0 & K_c \end{pmatrix}\int_{t-\tau}^{t}{}'(\lambda)\, d\lambda \tag{33}$$

This yields the following form;

$$\ddot{e} = \beta_0 - \beta_1 \int_{t-\tau}^{t}{}'(\lambda)\, d\lambda \tag{34}$$

with $\beta_0 = \begin{pmatrix} 0 & I \\ K_p & -K_d + K_c \end{pmatrix}$ and $\beta_1 = \begin{pmatrix} 0 & 0 \\ 0 & K_c \end{pmatrix}$.

To analyze the stability of the global system, we consider the following Lyapunov-Krasovskii functional (LKF):

$$v(t) = v_1(t) + v_2(t) + v_3(t)$$

$$v_1(t) = {}^T(t)P(t)$$

$$v_2(t) = \int_{t-\tau}^{t}{}^T(\lambda)R(\lambda)\, d\lambda$$

$$v_3(t) = \int_{-\tau}^{0}\int_{t-\tau}^{t}{}^T(\alpha)Z(\alpha)\, d\alpha\, d\lambda \tag{35}$$

where $P = P^T > 0; R = R^T > 0; Z = Z^T > 0$ are weighting matrices of appropriate dimensions.

A straightforward computation gives the time derivative of $v(t)$ along the solution of (34) as:

$$\dot{v}(t) = \delta^T[2N^T PM + N^T RN - Q^T RQ + \tau M^T ZM]\delta - \int_{t-\tau}^{t} \check{e}^T(\lambda)Z\dot{e}(\lambda)\, d\lambda$$

where $\delta = [{}^T(t), {}^T(t-\tau)]^T$; $N = [\beta_0, \beta_1]$; $M = [I, 0]$; $Q = [0, I]$.

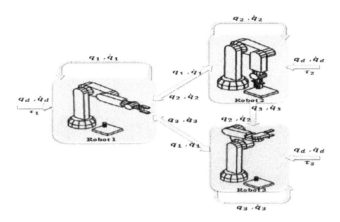

Figure 2. Robot network using bidirectional communication.

The Jensen's inequality gives a suitable bound for the last term of (36).

$$\delta = [\dot{e}^T(t), \dot{e}^T(t-\tau)]^T; \ N = [\beta_0, \beta_1]; \ M = [I, 0];$$
$$Q = [0, I].$$

$$-\int_{t-\tau}^{t} \dot{\tilde{e}}^T(\lambda) Z \dot{\tilde{e}}(\lambda) d\lambda \le \int_{t-\tau}^{t} \dot{\tilde{e}}^T(\lambda) d\lambda (Z/\tau) \int_{t-\tau}^{t} \dot{\tilde{e}}(\lambda) d\lambda$$
$$\le -\tilde{e}^T T^T (Z/\tau) T \tilde{e}$$ 37

with $T = [I, -I]$. The time derivative of the LKF (Equation 35) can thus be bounded by

$$\dot{v}(t) \le \delta^T \xi \delta,$$

Where

$$\xi = 2N^T PM + N^T RN - Q^T RQ + \tau M^T ZM - 1/\tau T^T ZT$$

. Then if the LMI ξ < 0 is satisfied, the derivative of the Lyapunov-Krasovskii functional is negative definite. To ensure that matrix $\xi < 0$ is negative definite, we select appropriate control gains $K_p > K_p^*$ and $K_d - K_c > K^*$ through processing Matlab's LMI solver such that;

$$2N^T PM + N^T RN - Q^T RQ + \tau M^T ZM - \frac{1}{\tau T^T ZT} < 0$$ (38)

Then, if the LMI $\xi < 0$ is satisfied, the derivative of the Lyapunov-Krasovskii functional is therefore negative definite. In consequence the origin $= 0$ is asymptotically stable.

This results in $e \to 0$ for $t \to \infty$ and $\dot{e} \to 0$ for $\to \infty$. The proof for asymptotic convergence of the coordinated tracking error is not sufficient to prove the convergence to zero of both error e1 and e2. Our concern now is to show that coordination is successfully realized for a specific time delay τ_c. The proof pursued the same line reasoning as the proof of stability analysis. Consequently, we obtain the following equation derived from the global error expression.

$$\dot{\varepsilon}_i = -\Lambda_i \varepsilon_i - \sum_{j=i} K_{i,j} \left(\varepsilon_i(t-\tau) - \varepsilon_j(t-\tau) \right)$$ (39)

Rewriting all states of (39) into a compact representation and applying the Laplace transform leads to;

$$s \ \varepsilon(s) - \varepsilon(0) = -\Lambda \varepsilon(s) - e^{-\tau s} K_c \varepsilon(s)$$ (40)

This can be written as:

$$\varepsilon(s) = (sI + \Lambda + e^{-\tau s} K_c)^{-1} \varepsilon(0)$$ (41)

If the characteristic equation $P(s, \tau): det |sI + \Lambda + e^{-\tau s} K_c| = 0$ has all its zeros in the left half complex plan then the system is stable and one can easily concludes about the convergence of q_i to q_d. Since the ordinal system, free from time delay $(i.e, \tau = 0)$ is stable and that $P(s, \tau)$ is a continuous function of τ, then using the D-Decomposition, the minimal positive solution to the following equation;

$$\tau_{ci} = \frac{arcos(-\Lambda_i/K_{ci})}{\sqrt{K_{ci}^2 - \Lambda_i^2}}$$

which would make all the zeros of the characteristic equation in the left half complex plane. Therefore if we select $\tau \in [0, \tau_c]$, where $\tau_c = sup(\tau_{ci}) \ \forall 1 \le i \le n$, solutions of (41) converge to zero and consequently $q_i \to q_d$ for $t \to \infty$, $\dot{q}_i \to \dot{q}_d$ for $t \to \infty$ and $q_i \to q_j$ for $t \to \infty$.

SIMULATION RESULTS

To show the effectiveness of the proposed synchronizing controller we provide some simulation results. These simulations were proposed for a network of 3 identical robot manipulators interconnected under a cooperative scheme as shown in Figure 2.

Let the communication structure among the robots described by an undirected strongly connected graph topology as shown in Figure 3. We set Joint Initial Conditions (JIC), coupling and control gains for the three robots as discussed below (Table 1). Simulations are performed on Matlab/Simulink Figure 4 illustrates the synchronization of robots that follow a common trajectory. This proves that the tracking and synchronization objectives are attained by the proposed controller.

Figures 5 and 6 show respectively the convergence of error positions to zero and the convergence of synchronizing errors to zero, explaining how robots, while tracking the desired trajectory, synchronize their positions. The effect of time delays on the coordination of

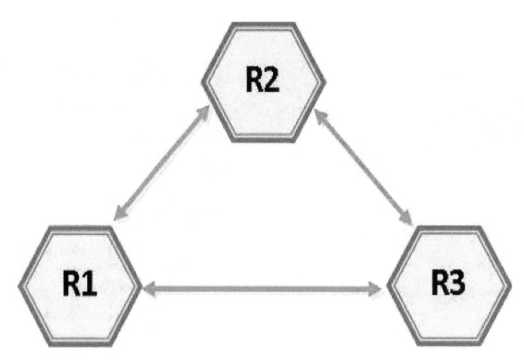

Figure 3. The topology model of the robots in simulation.

Table 1. Control gains.

Control Gains and JIC	Robot 1	Robot 2	Robot 3
k_d	diag{20}	diag{15}	diag{25}
K_p	diag{18}	diag{10}	diag{15}
K_{12}	diag{0.8}	diag{0.8}	
K_{13}	diag{0.5}		diag{0.5}
K_{23}	diag{0.2}	diag{0.2}	
JIC	(2.5,2.5)	(-2, -2)	(1.5, 1.5)

robots is shown in the following write-up.

Firstly, the delay-free case is presented in Figure 7 in which it is shown how the three angular positions asymptotically synchronize. Next, we consider the time delay in communication. Synchronization while tracking periodic trajectory are shown in Figures 8 and 9. From these figures, it is seen that the robots do not have the same starting positions. The speed for achieving agreement depends essentially on the time-delay communication channels. Figures10 and 11 illustrate that the behavior of the coordinated system changes significantly, under the effect of time delay.

Conclusions

This paper has considered the synchronization problem in distributed multi-Lagrangian systems. The aim of this work was to find out a decentralized controller, which individually applied to each Lagrangian system, the

synchronization in position and velocity is therefore met. Reaching synchronization stability of highly nonlinear robot dynamics constitutes one of the main contributions of this paper. The proposed control law ensures the robots' states synchronization while tracking a common desired trajectory. Another aspect of robots coordination and trajectory practically interconnections between all the systems, such that all systems have influence on the overall dynamics. The proposed algorithm works under cooperative scheme in the sense that it does not require any explicit leaders in the team. The studied topology is connected under an undirected interaction graph. To deal with time delays problem in communication between robots, the proposed decentralized control guarantees that the information variables of each robot reach agreement even in the presence of communication delay. Illustrative examples have shown the effectiveness of the described strategy. Future work will address the coordination control of under actuated Lagrangian systems.

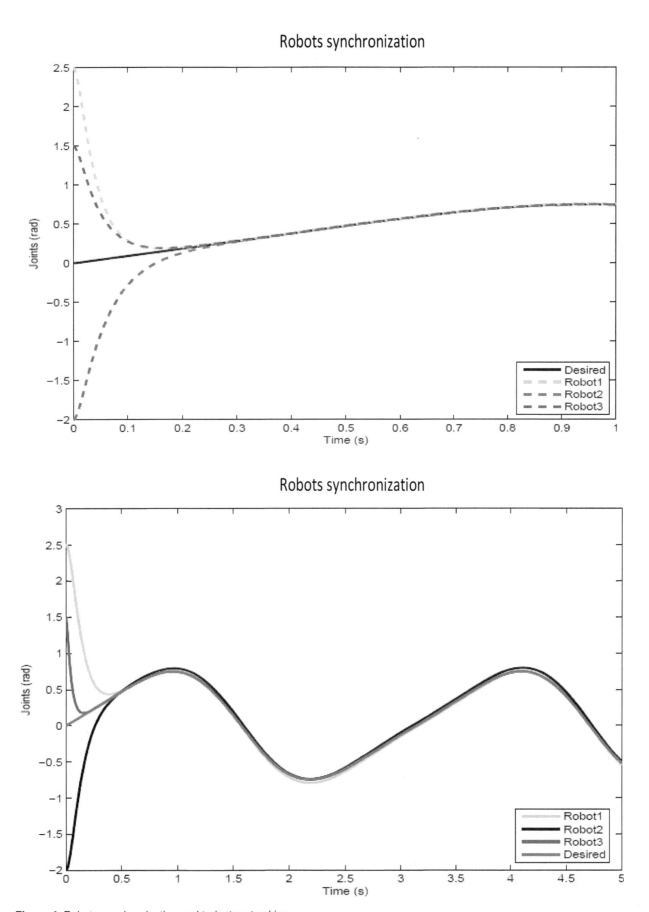

Figure 4. Robots synchronization and trajectory tracking.

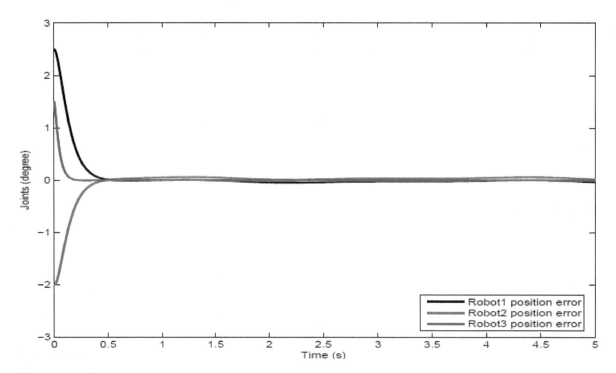

Figure 5. Position errors.

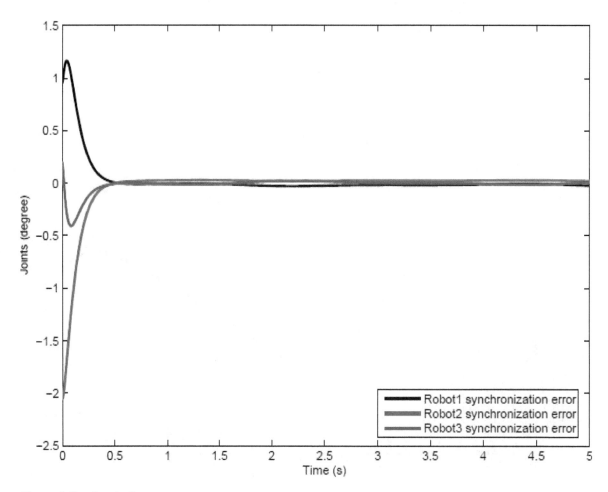

Figure 6. Synchronization errors.

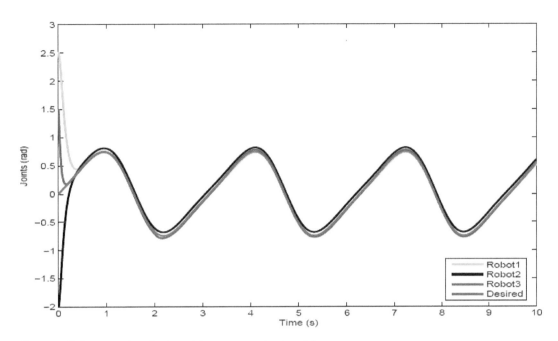

Figure 7. Robots synchronization without communication delay.

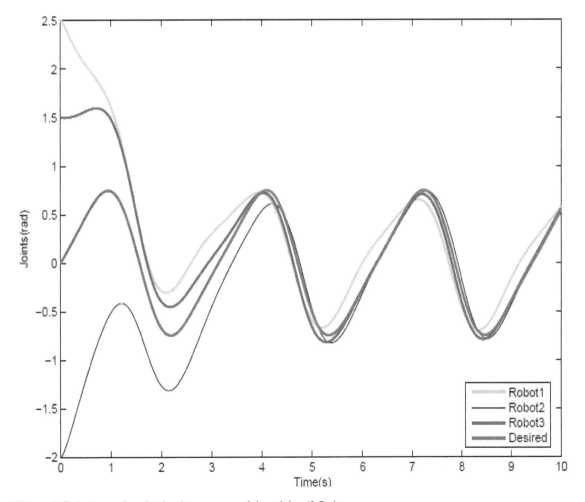

Figure 8. Robots synchronization in presence of time delay (0.5 s).

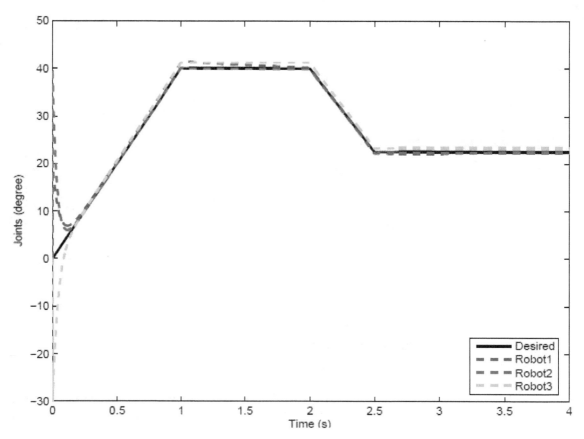

Figure 10. Robots synchronization without time delay.

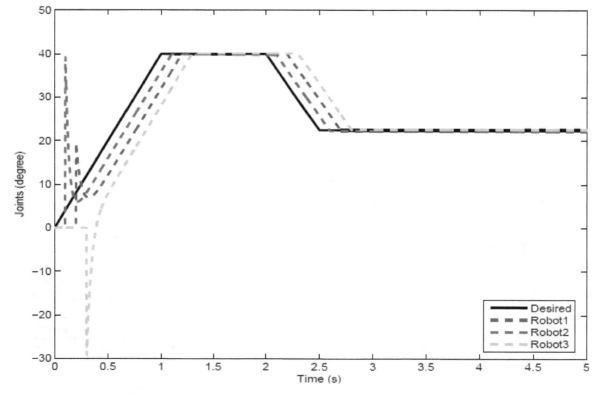

Figure 11. Robots synchronization in presence of time delay.

REFERENCES

Alejandro R-A, Henk N (2004). "Mutual Synchronization of Robots via Estimated: State Feedback: A Cooperative Approach" IEEE Trans. Control Syst. Technol., 12(4).

Dong S (2003) "Position synchronization of multiple motion axes with adaptative coupling control", Automatica, 39(6): 997-1005.

Dong S, Can W, Wen S, Gang F (2009). A Synchronization Approach to Trajectory Tracking of Multiple Mobile Robots While Maintaining Time-Varying Formations, IEEE TRANSACTIONS ON ROBOTICS, 25(3).

Jadbabaie J, Li, Morse AS (2003). "Coordination of groups of mobile autonomous agents using nearest neighbor rules." IEEE Trans. Automatic Control, 48(6), Pp: 988-1001.

Lawton JR, Beard RW (2002). "Synchronized multiple spacecraft rotations", Automatica, 38(8): 1359-1364.

Lee D, Spong MW (2006). "Stable °ocking of multiple inertial agents on balanced graph, Proc. of the 2006 American Control Conf., 52, pp: 1469-1475.

Lin Z, Broucke M, Francis B (2004). "Local control strategies for groups of mobile autonomous agents," IEEE Trans. Automatic Control, 49(4): 622-629.

Mesbahi M, Hadaegh FY (2001). "Formation °ying of multiple spacecraft via graphs, matrix inequalities, and switching," J. Guidance, Control, Dynamics, 24(2): 369-377.

Moreau L (2005). Stability of multi-agent systems with time-dependent communication links. IEEE Trans. Automatic Control, 50(2):169-182,.

Nikhil C, Mark WS (2006). "Output Synchronization of Nonlinear Systems with Time Delay in Communication", Proceedings of the 45th IEEE Conference on Decision and Control Manchester Grand Hyatt Hotel San Diego, CA, USA, pp. 13-15

Ogren P, Egerstedt M, Hu X (2002). "A control Lyapunov function approach to multiagent coordination," IEEE Trans. Robotics Automation, 18(5): 847-851.

Olfati-Saber (2007). "Consensus and Cooperation in Networked Multi Agent Systems" invited paper, 95(1), Proceedings of the IEEE.

Olfati-Saber R, Murray RM (2004). "Consensus problems in networks of agents with switching topology and time-delays," IEEE Trans. on Automatic Control, 49(9): 1520-1533.

Ren W (2007). "Multi-vehicle consensus with a time-varying reference state,"Syst. Control Lett., 56(7-8): 474-483.

Ren W, Beard RW (2005). Consensus seeking in multi-agent systems using dynamically changing interaction topologies. IEEE Trans. Automatic Control, 5(5): 655-661.

Ren W, Beard RW, Atkins E (2007). "Information consensus in multivehicle cooperative control: collective group behavior through local interaction," IEEE Control Syst. Mag., 27(2): 71-82.

Rodriguez-Angeles A, Nijmeijer H (2001). Coordination of two robot manipulators based on position measurements only, Int. J. Control, 74(13): 1311 - 1323,

Slotine JJE, Wang W (2004). A study of synchronization and group cooperation using partial contraction theory. In V. Kumar, N. E. Leonard, and A. S. Morse, editors, Cooperative Control, 309 of Lecture Notes in Control and Information Sciences,.

Soon-Jo Chung, Slotine JJE (2009) "Cooperative Robot Control and Concurrent Synchronization of Lagrangian Systems". IEEE Trans. Robotics, 25(3): 686 – 700.

Soon-Jo Chung, Slotine JJE (2009). Cooperative Robot Control and Concurrent Synchronization of Lagrangian Systems, IEEE Trans. Robotics, 25(3): 686 - 700.

Spong MW, Chopra N (2007). "Synchronization of Networked Lagrangian Systems," In Lagrangian and Hamiltonian Methods for Nonlinear Control 2006, F. Bullo and K. Fujimoto (Eds.), Lecture Notes in Control and Information Sciences, 366, Springer Verlag, pp. 47-59.

Tanner HG, Christodoulakis DK (2005). State synchronization in local interaction networks is robust with respect to time delays, IEEE Conference on Decision and Control.

Wei Wang, Slotine JJE (2006). Contraction analysis of time-delayed communications and group cooperation, IEEE Trans. Automatic Control, 51(4): 712-717.

Zhihua Qu, Jing Wang, Hull RA (2008). "Cooperative Control of Dynamical Systems With Application to Autonomous Vehicles" IEEE Trans. Automatic Control, 53(4): 894-911.

12

New approaches to automatic headline generation for Arabic documents

Fahad Alotaiby[1]*, Salah Foda[1] and Ibrahim Alkharashi[2]

[1]Department of Electrical Engineering, College of Engineering, King Saud University, Riyadh, Saudi Arabia.
[2]Computer Research Institute, King Abdulaziz City for Science and Technology, Riyadh, Saudi Arabia.

A headline is considered a condensed summary of a document. The necessity for automatic headline generation has been on the rise due to the need to handle a huge number of documents, which is a tedious and time-consuming process. Instead of reading every document, the headline can be used to decide which ones contain important and relevant information. There are two major approaches to automatic headline generation. The first is linguistic, in which the knowledge about the structure of the language itself is considered. The second approach is statistical and it comprises all quantitative approaches to automated language processing. However, the Arabic language has a different statistical structure than the English language, and requires special treatment to generate Arabic headlines, especially when there is no dedicated technique for the Arabic language. Therefore, two new statistical methods in automatic headline generation have been developed to create representative headlines for textual documents in the Arabic language. The first is an extractive method based on character cross-correlation, and the second one is an abstractive method based on the hidden Markov model (HMM). The extractive method achieved ROUGE-L of (0.1938) and the HMM method achieved ROUGE-L of (0.2332). In addition, both techniques were assessed via human examiners who evaluated the resulting headlines.

Key words: Summarization, automatic headline generation, hidden Markov model, language model.

INTRODUCTION

Headline generation is an important field of natural language processing (NLP), which includes language analysis, understanding, and synthesis. Thus, generating a headline for a textual document requires analyzing the document, understanding the main idea of the document, and creating a headline that reflects the content of the document. Therefore, the problem of headline generation concerns complex language processing. A headline is a condensed summary of a document that accurately represents the main idea of that document. From this definition, it is obvious that headline generation is a compressed version of summarization, and thus the study of headline generation is a part of the summarization field. The increased amount of information emerging in the modern digital world has created an information overload (Yang et al., 2003). Information overload refers to the difficulty in understanding a topic and making decisions because of the presence of too much information. Therefore, the necessity of automatic headline generation has been raised due to the need to manually review huge numbers of documents, which is a tedious and time-consuming process. Instead of reading every document, the headline can be used to decide which of them contains important or relevant information. Automatic headline generation can be classified according to several dimensions, such as linguistic versus statistical or extractive versus abstractive.

*Corresponding author. E-mail: falotaiby@hotmail.com.

Abbreviations: CCC, Character cross correlation; **DUC,** document understanding conference; **EWM,** exact word matching; **HMM,** hidden markov model; **HTK,** hidden markov model toolkit; **LDC,** linguistic data consortium; **LM,** language model; **MSA,** modern standard Arabic; **NIST,** national institute of standards and technology; **NLP,** natural language processing; **ROUGE,** recall-oriented understudy for gisting evaluation.

In the extractive approaches, the most suitable text unit is extracted from the original document, and then it may be trimmed to the proper size. However, in abstractive headline generation, the original document is analyzed and proper headline words are selected and ordered to represent a consistent and readable headline. On the other hand, statistical approaches include all quantitative approaches to automatically processing the document and generating a headline (Manning and Schütze, 1999). In contrast, the linguistic approaches include the use of knowledge about the structure of the language itself to analyze the document and generate the headline (Allen, 1995). This paper presents two new methods. The first is an extractive approach that employs character cross-correlation to extract the best headlines and overcome the complex morphology of Arabic language. The second is a statistical abstractive approach that utilizes the HMM and statistical language model (LM) to automatically construct a headline for Arabic documents containing news stories. The resulting headlines are evaluated using Recall-Oriented Understudy for Gisting Evaluation (ROUGE) (Lin, 2004a), in addition to human evaluation by a group of examiners. The next section presents related work in the area of automatic headline generation. Then, a brief introduction about the Arabic language, used datasets and headline length is presented, followed by description of the presented approaches and experimental designs. Finally, the results are presented with comments and discussions.

RELATED WORK

There are several systems that automatically generate headlines for documents in languages other than Arabic. Some of them are extractive (Songhua et al., 2010; Lloret and Palomar, 2011) and some others are abstractive (Reddy et al., 2011). For the Arabic language, there is only one system dedicated to generating very short summaries (headlines), *Lakhas* (Douzidia and Lapalme, 2004). *Lakhas* was one of the systems presented at the Document Understanding Conference in 2004 (DUC, 2004), which the American National Institute of Standards and Technology (NIST) organized. Task 3 in this conference was to generate a very short summary of a machine-translated text from Arabic into English. In contrast to the systems in the Document Understanding Conference (2004), *Lakhas* first summarizes the original Arabic document and then applies machine translation to the summary only. Therefore, the published results were not for the Arabic headline, but for the translated headline into English. On the other hand, Conroy and Leary (2001) used HMM to extract sentences from the document in English to form a summary. Only one HMM model was used with $2s+1$ states, where s represents the number of sentences in the summary. In addition, three main features were utilized: position of the sentence, number

of terms in the sentence, and the likelihood of the sentence terms given the document terms. In a similar way, HMM Hedge (Zajic et al., 2002) is an algorithm for selecting headline words from a document based on a standard "noisy channel" model of processing with a subsequent decoder for producing headline words from stories. In HMM Hedge, there is only one HMM. It has two types of states: headline state or gap state. The HMM is constructed with states for only the first N words of the story, where N is a constant (60) or the number of words in the first sentence.

ARABIC LANGUAGE

The Arabic language is a Semitic language spoken by more than 280 million people. Arabic was originally an oral language. For that reason, the classical Arabic writing system was originally consonantal. Each of the 28 letters in the Arabic alphabet represents a single consonant. To overcome the problem of different pronunciations of consonants in Arabic text, graphical signs, known as diacritics, were invented in the seventh century. Currently in Modern Standard Arabic (MSA), diacritics are almost always omitted from written text. As a result, this omission increases the number homographs (words with the same written form). However, Arab readers normally differentiate between homographs by the context of the script. Arabic is a morphologically complex language. An Arabic word may be constructed from a stem as well as affixes and clitics. Furthermore, some parts of the stem may be deleted or modified when appending a clitic to it according to specific orthographical rules. As a final point, different orthographic conventions exist across the Arab world (Buckwalter, 2004a). As a result of omitting diacritics, complex morphology, and different orthographical rules, two of the same stem words may be regarded as different if compared literally.

In Arabic, clitics are attached to a stem or to each other without any orthographic marks (that is, an apostrophe). A clitic is a linguistic unit that is pronounced and written like an affix, but it is grammatically independent. Linguistically speaking, if one can parse an Arabic linguistic unit attached to a stem, it should be considered a clitic. This covers most of the clitics, except the definite article {Al ال}. It is important to mention that the transliteration used in this work is based on the style proposed by Buckwalter (2004b). The number of clitics in Arabic is limited. However, when concatenated, clitics can generate a chain of up to four clitics before the stem (proclitics) and three clitics after the stem (enclitics) (Alotaiby et al., 2010). Clitics and affixes attached to stems make a direct comparison between words impractical. Therefore, this work employed character cross-correlation to extract the best headlines and overcome the Arabic language's complex morphology.

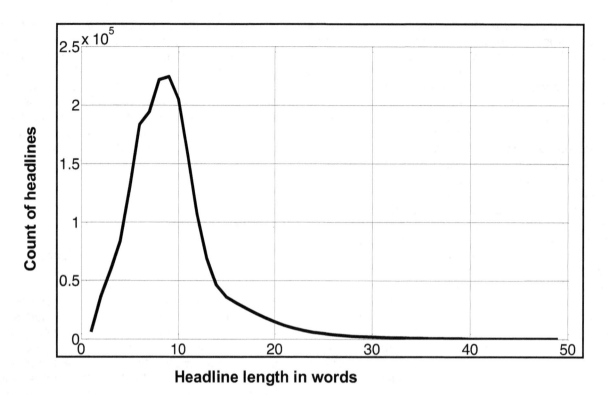

Figure 1. Original headline length distribution in the Arabic Gigaword corpus.

DATASETS

Datasets used in this work were extracted from the Arabic Gigaword (Graff, 2007). The *Arabic Gigaword* is a collection of text data extracted from newswire archives of Arabic news sources, and their titles that have been gathered over several years by the Linguistic Data Consortium (LDC) at the University of Pennsylvania. Text data in the *Arabic Gigaword* were collected from four newspapers and two press agencies. The *Arabic Gigaword* corpus contains almost 2 million documents with nearly 600 million words. However, there are some problems with this dataset, such as spelling mistakes, inconsistent use of punctuation and documents that have no headlines. Yet, simple problems in this corpus such as the presence of odd control characters and word binding were automatically corrected. A common problem in the Arabic corpus is the omission of white spaces between main tokens that end with graphically non-connecting characters, as in the following paragraph: {... *and fighting the spread of nuclear weapons pointing ..., ...* ... مشيرا ومكافحةانتشارالاسلحةالنوويةمشيرا}, which contains five connected words.

HEADLINE LENGTH

In the Document of Understanding Conference in 2004 (DUC, 2004), an evaluation of the very short summary was done on the first 75 bytes of the summary. Knowing that the average word size in Arabic is five characters (Alotaiby et al., 2009) in addition to space characters, the specified summary size in Arabic words will be roughly equivalent to 12 words (assuming each byte represents a single character). In the meantime, the average length of the original headlines in the *Arabic Gigaword* corpus was approximately 9.5 words. Figure 1 shows the headline length distribution in the words used in the corpus. In this work, a 10-word headline is considered as an appropriate length.

BASELINE HEADLINES

Since there are neither official Arabic datasets for automatic headline generation nor published results on Arabic documents as per the knowledge of the authors, it is important to find some ways to assign the resulting evaluation scores a meaning. Therefore, two techniques (besides the original headline that comes with every document under the test) are used to show the upper, lower, and baseline scores for evaluating the proposed techniques. The first baseline technique is a headline-generation system that randomly selects 10 words from the document (Rand-10). This headline represents the worst-case headline. In contrast, the headline is generated by the author of the document (Original) represents the best-case headline. These two headlines

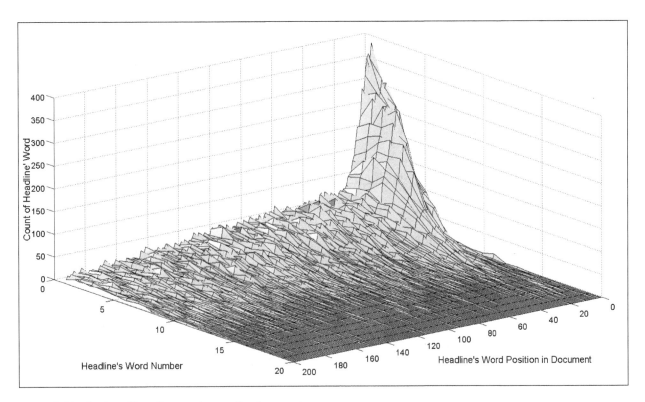

Figure 2. Distribution of headline words over the document.

are the extreme ranges of any evaluation scores. Summarization researchers have observed that the lead sentence of an English news story is often an appropriate summary of the text. Therefore, some of the headline generation systems utilize only the first sentence to generate a headline (Zajic et al., 2002). Those observations are based on English document stories. Therefore, to ensure that this is also the case in Arabic, a statistical study on headline words in Arabic Gigaword was performed to determine the distribution of headlines words among the documents words. Figure 2 shows the distribution of where the words of the headlines appear in the documents in Al-Hayat newspaper stories. It is clear that the first 60 words of the stories contain most of the headline words and that most of the headlines contain fewer than 10 words. As a result, the first 10 words of the document were selected as a baseline headline (Lead-10). It is important to mention that these 10 words are taken in the same sequence as they appear in the document; this gives headline more credit when it is evaluated, especially using automatic evaluation systems such as ROUGE.

EVALUATION TOOLS

Correctly evaluating the automatically generated headlines is an important phase. Automatic methods for evaluating machine-generated headlines are preferred to

human evaluations because they are faster, more cost-effective, and can be performed repeatedly. However, they are not trivial because of various factors such as the readability of headlines and consistency of the headlines (whether the headlines indicate the main content of the news story). Hence, it is difficult for a computer program to judge. However, some automatic metrics are available for headline evaluation. BLEU (Papineni et al., 2002) and ROUGE (Lin, 2004a) are the main metrics used. The evaluation of this experiment was performed using Recall-Oriented Understudy for Gisting Evaluation (ROUGE). ROUGE is a system used for measuring the quality of a summary by comparing it to a correct summary created by human. ROUGE provides four different measures: ROUGE-n (usually n = 1, 2, 3 and 4), ROUGE-L, ROUGE-W, ROUGE-S, and ROUGE-SU. Lin (2004b) showed that ROUGE-1, ROUGE-L, ROUGE-SU, and ROUGE-W were very reliable measures in the short summaries category, and they will be recorded for this work.

PROPOSED APPROACHES

Two main approaches are presented with different technical variations in each of them. The first is an extractive method of automatic headline generation that utilizes the cross-correlation of letters to overcome the heavy existence of clitics and affixes in Arabic. The

Table 1. An example of headline nomination.

a	ارتبطت نشأة المخطوطات العربية في السودان ببروز معالم الثقافة العربية الإسلامية،
	The emergence of the Arabic manuscripts in Sudan was associated with the rise of the Arabic-Islamic culture
b	ارتبطت نشأة المخطوطات العربية في السودان ببروز معالم الثقافة العربية
	The emergence of the Arabic manuscripts in Sudan was associated with the rise of the Arabic culture
c	نشأة المخطوطات العربية في السودان ببروز معالم الثقافة العربية الإسلامية
	The emergence of the Arabic manuscripts in Sudan ... with the rise of the Arabic-Islamic culture

second is an abstractive method in which the hidden Markov model and different statistical language models are used to build a meaningful headline that represents the corresponding document. The following subsections provide details of the proposed approaches.

Extractive automatic headline generation

The main idea of the used method is to extract the most appropriate set of consecutive words (phrase) from a document body, which should represent an adequate headline for the document. Then, those headlines are evaluated by calculating the ROUGE score against a set of three reference headlines. To do so, a list of nominated headlines was first created from the document body. After this, four different evaluation methods were applied to choose the best headline that reflects the idea of the document among the nominated list. The aim of these methods is to determine the most suitable headline that matches the document. The idea here is to choose the headline that contains the largest number of the most frequent words in the document, while ignoring stop words and giving more weight to earlier sentences in the documents.

Nominating a list of headlines

A window of a length of 10 words was passed over the paragraphs word by word to generate chunks of consecutive words (sentences) that could be used as headlines. Moving the window one word at a time may corrupt the fluency of the sentences. A simple approach to reduce this issue is to minimize the size of the paragraphs. Therefore, the document body was divided into smaller paragraphs at new-line, comma, colon and period characters. This step increased the number of nominated headlines with a proper start and end. The result is a nominated list of headlines with a length of 10 words. In the case of a paragraph containing fewer than 10 words, there will be only one nominated headline of the same length for that paragraph. Table 1 shows an example of a nominating headline list, where *a* is the

selected paragraph, *b* is the first nominated headline, and *c* is the second nominated headline.

Calculating word matching score

In this step every word in the nominated headlines will be compared to all words in the document to calculate matching scores. The very basic process of making a matching score between every two words in the nominated headline and document body is to assign a score of 1 if the two words match exactly or 0 if there is even one mismatched character. This basic step is called exact-word matching (EWM). Unfortunately, the Arabic language contains clitics and is morphologically rich. This means that the same word may appear with a single clitic attached to it and yet be considered a different word in the EWM method. Therefore, the idea of using the character cross-correlation (CCC) method emerged, in which a variable score in the range of 0 to 1 is calculated depending on how many characters match each other. For example, if the word {*and he wrote it*, وكتبها } is compared with the word {*he wrote*, كتب} using the EWM method, the resulting score will be 0. However, when using the CCC method, it will be 0.667. The CCC method comes from signal cross-correlation, which measures the similarity of two waveforms. In this method, the score is calculated according to the following equation:

$$CCC_{w_i,w_j} = \frac{2 \max_n c[n]}{M+N} \quad (1)$$

And

$$c[n] = \sum_{m=-(N-1)}^{M-1} w_i[m] * w_j[n+m] \quad (2)$$

Where w_i is the first word containing M characters, w_j is the second word containing N characters, and the operation *result is 1 if the two corresponding characters match each other and 0 otherwise.

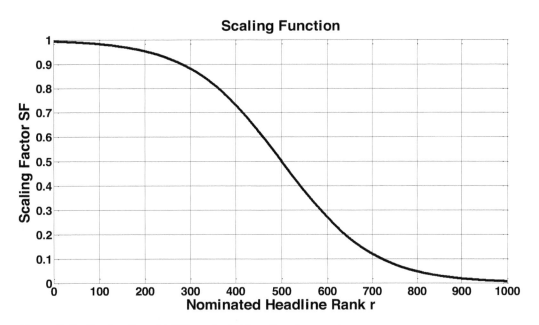

Figure 3. Scaling function of 1,000 nominated headline documents.

Calculating best headline score

After preparing the matching score of the two tables of words, they will be utilized in the selection of the best headline. Except stop words, every word in the document body (w_d) will be matched with every word in the nominated headline (w_h) using the CCC and EWM methods, and a score will be registered for every nominated sentence. A simple stop word list consisting of approximately 180 words was created for this purpose. Calculating a matching score for every sentence is also performed in two ways. The first way is the SUM method, which is defined in the following equation:

$$SUM_p = \sum_{i=1}^{L} \sum_{j=1}^{K} CCC w_d, w_j$$

(3)

Where SUM_p is the score using the SUM method for the nominated headline p, K is the number of unique words in the document body, and L is the number of words in the nominated headline (except stop words). In this method, a summation of the cross-correlation score of every word in the document body and every word in the headline is totaled. In a similar way, in the other method MAX_p the maximum score between every word in the document body and the nominated headline is added up. Therefore, for every word in the document, its maximum matching score will be added in either case, CCC or EWM. It can also be defined in the following equation:

$$MAX_p = \sum_{i=1}^{L} \max_j CCC_{w_d, w_j}$$

(4)

SUM_p and MAX_p were calculated using EWM and CCC method, resulting in four different variations of the algorithm, namely SUM-EWM, SUM-CCC, MAX-EWM, and MAX-CCC.

Weighing early nominated headlines

In the case of news articles, the early sentences usually absorb the subject of the article. To reflect that, a nonlinear multiplicative scaling factor was applied. With this scaling factor, late sentences are penalized. The suggested scaling factor is inspired by the hyperbolic tangent function (*tanh*) and described in the following equations:

$$SF = -\left(\frac{e^z - 1}{e^z + 1} - 1 \right) / 2$$

(5)

Where

$$z = 5\left(\frac{2r}{s} - 1 \right),$$

(6)

r is the rank of the nominated headline, and S is the total number of sentences. According to the nominating mechanism, hundreds of sentences could be nominated as possible headlines.

Figure shows the scaling function of 1,000 nominated headlines. After applying the scaling factor, the headline

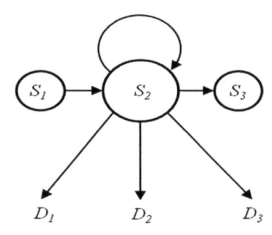

Figure 4. Single state with one entry (S1) and one exit (S3) state HMM used in the AHG system.

with the maximum score was chosen.

HMM-BASED AUTOMATIC HEADLINE GENERATION

HMM-based automatic headline generation systems use one model for the document and up to four features as observation. In the proposed approach, HMM is utilized for every word in the headline with 10 features as the observation vector. The words are also connected together through a bigram probabilistic language model built up from different resources. What follows is a more detailed description of the approach. The document consists of a sequence of words ($D=D_1, D_2 \ldots D_p$), where each document word is represented by a sequence of word observation vector D_t as follows:

$$D_t = d_1, d_2, d_3, \ldots, d_M$$
(7)

Where d_m is the document word features observed, so $M = 10$. The headline consists of a sequence of words $H = h_1, h_2, \ldots, h_n$, and the automatic headline-generation system determines the most probable word sequence H, given the observed document vector D ($argmax_H$ $P(H|D)$).

To do this, Bayes rule is used to decompose the required probability $P(H|D)$ into two components:

$$H = \arg\max_H P(H \mid D)$$

$$= \arg\max_H \frac{P(D \mid H) P(H)}{P(D)}$$

$$= \arg\max_H P(D \mid H) P(H)$$
(8)

This equation indicates that in order to find the most likely word sequence H, the word sequence that maximizes the product of $P(H)$ and $P(D|H)$ must be found. The first term represents the a priori probability of observing H, independent of the observed document, and this probability is determined by a language model. The second term represents the probability of observing the vector sequence D, given some specified word sequence H. This probability is determined by the HMM. The process of the proposed HMM-based automatic headline generation system for determining (recognizing) headlines is as follows: a word sequence H is *assumed* and the language model computes its probability $P(H)$. For each headline word (h_i), there is a corresponding HMM model. The sequence of HMMs needed to represent the assumed headline is concatenated to form a single composite model, and the probability of that model generating the observed sequence D is calculated. This is the required probability $P(D|H)$. In principle, this process can be repeated for all possible word sequences, and the most likely sequence is selected as the recognizer output.

An important factor to make this approach successful is the assumption that the words appearing in the headline must appear in the document body and in the same sequence, but not as concatenated as in the headline. Every HMM used is a simple HMM consisting of one state besides the entry and exit states, as shown in Figure 4. Single state with one entry (S1) and one exit (S3) state HMM used in the AHG system.

Converting the above design idea into a practical system requires the solution to a number of challenging problems. First, a front-end parameterization (feature extraction) technique is needed, which can extract all the necessary information from the document words in a compact form compatible with the HMM-based statistical model. Secondly, the HMM models must accurately represent the distribution of each headline word. Furthermore, the HMM parameters must be estimated from a sufficient number of samples. Thirdly, the language model must be designed to give accurate word predictions based on the preceding history. However, regarding the HMMs, insufficient data that cover all word sequences is an ever-present problem, and the language model must be able to deal with word sequences for which no examples occur in the training data. Finally, the process outlined above for finding H by enumerating all possible word sequences is impractical. Instead, possible word sequences are explored in parallel, discarding the hypothesis as soon as they become improbable. This process is called decoding.

Feature extraction

One of the most important modules in statistical headline-generation systems is the feature extraction process, in which document words are converted into some type of

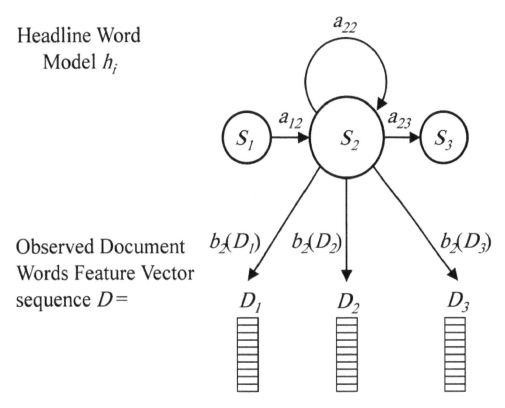

Figure 5. Headline word model used.

parametric representation for further processing. This part is important because the choice of an appropriate feature set influences the accuracy of the headline-generation process. The proposed features of the document words cover a wide range of word characteristics that have a statistical influence. The proposed features are as follows:

1. Position of the word in the current document.
2. Character length of the current word.
3. Word frequency in the current document.
4. Rank of the word in the current document.
5. Is the word a stop-word?
6. Global word frequency throughout the whole corpora.
7. Global rank of the word.
8. Paragraph number in which the word appears.
9. Global frequency of the word with the next word.
10. Global frequency of the word with the previous word.

The global features of any word are difficult to calculate. It took a long time to parameterize each document. Therefore, two methods were proposed to calculate these features. One of them is quick but less accurate, and it was used in a large text to boot up the training and alignment of features. The other one is more accurate, but it requires more time to complete, and it was used for training a smaller set of samples and for the testing phase.

Headline modeling

The modeling unit in the HMM-based automatic headline-generation system is the document words themselves. The purpose of the headline models in this system is to provide a method of calculating the likelihood of any vector sequence D given a headline word h_j. Each individual headline word is represented by a HMM. The HMM has a number of states connected by arcs. It can be regarded as a random generator of a document's word feature vectors. It consists of a main state, entry state, and exit state connected by probabilistic transitions. It changes to a new state for each new headline word, generating a new document's word feature vector according to the output distribution of that state. Therefore, the feedback transition probability models the durational variability in the document word sequence, and the output probabilities model the variability of the features of the document's words. The HMM word model used has one emitting state and a simple left-to-right topology, as illustrated in Figure 5.

The entry and exit states are provided to make it easy to join the models together. This enables words models to be joined together to form complete headlines. Each time t that a state j is entered, a document's word feature

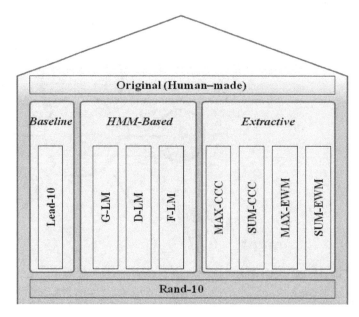

Figure 6. Proposed automatic headline generation methods.

vector D_t (observed at time t) is generated with a probability density $b_j(D_t)$. Furthermore, the transition from state i to j is also probabilistic and governed by the discrete probability a_{ij}. Figure 5 shows an example of this process in which the model moves through the state sequence X = 1, 2, 2, 2 and 4 in order to generate the sequence D_1 to D_3. The joint probability of a vector sequence D and state sequence X given some model (for example h_i, as in Figure 5) is calculated simply as the product of the transition probabilities and the output probabilities. Therefore, for the above state sequence X:

$$P(D, X \mid h_i) = a_{12}\, b_2(D_1)\, a_{22}\, b_2(D_2)\, a_{22}\, b_2(D_3) \quad (9)$$

However, the required probability $P(D|h_i)$ is easily found by summing Equation (9) over all possible state sequences. The determination of the most likely state sequence is the key to generating a headline from an unknown document's word sequence and is computed using the Viterbi algorithm.

Language model

In the proposed approach, $P(H)$ is approximated by a bigram, as shown in the following equation:

$$P(H) = \prod_{i-1}^{m} P(w_i \mid w_1 \ldots w_{i-1}) \approx \prod_{i}^{m} P(w_i \mid w_{i-1}) \quad (10)$$

The bigram language model is used to connect word

pairs of the headline according to the probability of that pair. Language models are typically trained on a large corpus of text from the language so that they can obtain robust estimates of their internal parameters. On the other hand, a large and comprehensive corpus could loosely take a broad view of the language and miss important relations in the story for which the headline is generated. To check this assumption, three bigram language models are proposed in this approach. The first one is a general language model (*HMM-G-LM*), which is computed using the entire *Gigaword* corpora. The second is a document-specific language model (*HMM-D-LM*), which is computed using the document for which the headline is generated. The last one is a flat language model (*HMM-F-LM*) with equal probability between corresponding word pairs.

Complete proposed approaches and techniques

In summary, new extractive and abstractive approaches are introduced. In the extractive approach, the most appropriate sentence is extracted from the document using four different techniques: SUM-EWM, MAX-EWM, SUM-CCC and MAX-CCC. In the abstractive approach, three different techniques of HMM-based automatic headline generation are implemented, and they depend on different language models HMM-G-LM, HMM-D-LM and HMM-F-LM.

Figure 6 shows a block diagram of the proposed headlines. It is clear that *Rand-10* is the lowest-limit headline and original i the highest-limit N headline and the extractive and HMM-based techniques will compete against the baseline technique, which is Lead-10.

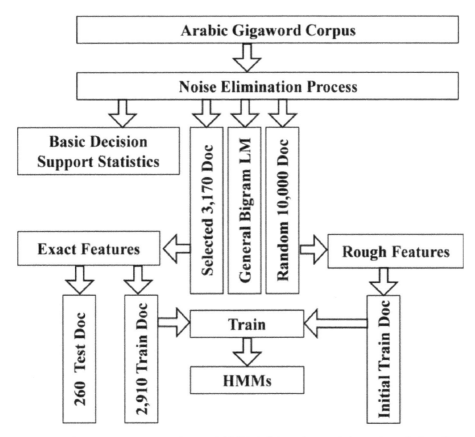

Figure 7. The dataset preparation and HMM training phase of the automatic headline-generation systems.

EXPERIMENTAL DESIGN

The experiment is divided into three main phases: the datasets preparation and training phase, the testing phase and the results evaluation phase. The application used to generate headlines is self-developed software around the Hidden Markov Model Toolkit (HTK) version 3.4 (HTK, 2009). The HTK is a free and portable toolkit for building and manipulating hidden Markov models primarily for speech recognition research. However, HTK has been widely used for other topics such as speech synthesis (Tokuda et al., 2000), character recognition (Khorsheed, 2007), and deoxyribonucleic acid (DNA) sequencing (Grundy, 1997). The main activities performed within the HTK are training, alignment and decoding. In contrast, feature extraction, feature file format conversion, Arabic text transliteration, building HMMs, evaluation and others were developed outside HTK.

Preparing and training phase

The first process in the implementation was the preparation of the *Arabic Gigaword* corpus. It included noise elimination, document investigation and document selection. In noise elimination, simple automatic corrections were applied, as described in datasets. In the document investigation, basic statistics about headlines and corresponding documents were computed to aid in the next phase. In document selection, three datasets were built from the corpus.

The first contained all the documents and was used to generate general statistical bigram and unigram language models. The

second contained 10,000 documents and was used to initially train the HMMs with a less-accurate estimate of global features, because global features calculations needed greater processing time. The last dataset contained 3,170 documents with a headline size that varies from 7 to 15 words. This dataset was selected from documents that have informative headlines. Descriptive and eye-catching headlines were avoided. This dataset was divided into a training dataset of 2,910 documents and a test set of 260 documents. All features of the 3,170 documents were accurately estimated. However, two documents of the test set were discarded because of some mistakes in the assessment made by the human examiners. Since the extractive approach does not require training, the resulting 258 test documents were directly processed to generate the four extractive headlines (SUM-EWM, MAX-EWM, SUM-CCC and MAX-CCC).

Figure shows an illustrating block diagram of the dataset preparation and training phase.

Testing phase

In the testing phase, the extractive headline generation system directly generated headlines for the test documents using the four different approaches described earlier. Conversely, the already trained HMMs were utilized to generate different headlines for the test documents using three different language models. The first language model was a general bigram language model (HMM-G-LM) computed from the entire *Arabic Gigaword* corpus. The second

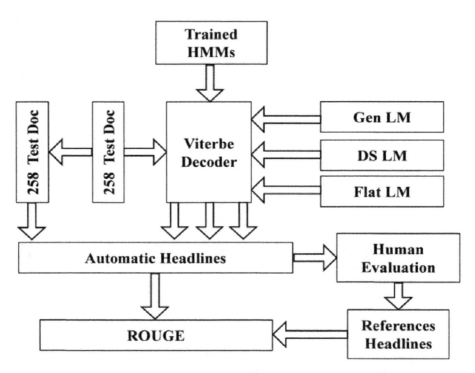

Figure 8. The testing and evaluation phases of the automatic headline-generation systems.

language model was a document-specific bigram language model (HMM-D-LM) computed from the document for which the headline is generated. Finally, the last one was a flat language model (HMM-F-LM) in which the probability of each word pair is the same. Therefore, the contribution of the language model in the *HMM-F-LM* case was almost negligible.

Systems evaluation phase

The evaluation of the resulting headlines was performed using ROUGE version 1.5.5, which generates three scores (recall, precision and F-measure) for each evaluation. Before this version, only one score was generated (recall). For consistency issues, the recall scores will be used. A stemmer is available in ROUGE. The idea of using the stemmer is to compare bare words in the reference headline and the generated headline, ignoring the morphological variation in the words. Unfortunately, the Arabic language is morphologically complex and ROUGE 1.5.5 does not support it. Therefore, the registered scores are expected to be higher if an Arabic stemming is applied in ROUGE 1.5.5. The parameters used in ROUGE 1.5.5 are as follows:

1. Confidence interval is 95%.
2. Computes skip bigram (ROGUE-S) co-occurrence with no gap length limit.
3. Maximum n-gram is 4.
4. Uses only the first 10 words in the automatically generated and reference headlines.
5. The rest of the parameters are the default ones.

As no reference system uses the same dataset, the automatic evaluation metric is more suitable for comparing systems rather than assigning an abstract universal score. Thus, three human examiners were hired to evaluate one set of generated headlines. They work in the field of manual document classification. Their task

was to examine the readability and consistency of two generated headlines (HMM-D-LM and MAX-CCC) in addition to the original document headline, and generate three headlines (one from each examiner) so that they can be used as references in the ROUGE tool.

Figure 8 shows a brief description of the testing and evaluation phases. As described to the human examiners, the readability score represents the grammatical correctness of the headline despite its meaning, while the consistency score represents how closely the headline reflects the main content of the document, regardless of its syntax. The allowed range of scores varies from 1 to 10. The examiners were told to follow strict instructions to preserve as stable an evaluation as possible. For this purpose, a software tool was specially developed to manually evaluate the headlines. Figure shows the user interface of the manual evaluation tool. The examiner should read the document carefully, suggest an appropriate headline and then evaluate the three headlines. This process should be performed one at a time for each document, and it is advisable to evaluate a large number of headlines in every session to reduce the number of stop periods throughout the entire process.

RESULTS AND DISCUSSION

The evaluation results of the proposed automatic headline-generation systems are presented. The evaluation contains two parts. The first is the automatic evaluation using ROUGE. While the second is the manual evaluation, which was performed by a set of three examiners. The aim of the evaluation results is to compare the proposed approaches against some baseline headlines and the human examiners' evaluation.

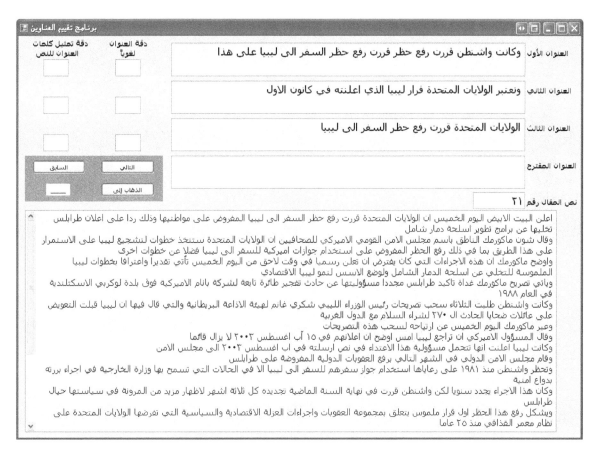

Figure 9. User interface of the manual evaluation tool.

Table 2. ROUGE scores of all headlines.

System	R-1	R-L	R-W	R-SU
Original	0.37683	0.36329	0.21867	0.22498
HMM-D-LM	0.24369	0.2332	0.14689	0.11305
MAX-CCC	0.20367	0.19384	0.12898	0.09001
SUM-CCC	0.18974	0.17944	0.11944	0.08368
Lead-10	0.18353	0.17592	0.11434	0.08761
MAX-EWM	0.18279	0.17252	0.11458	0.07360
HMM-G-LM	0.14184	0.13092	0.08106	0.0423
SUM-EWM	0.11006	0.10624	0.07247	0.04941
HMM-F-LM	0.09428	0.08772	0.05507	0.02193
Rand-10	0.08153	0.07081	0.04491	0.01521

Automatic evaluation

The aim of the evaluation results is to compare the proposed methods against each other and against the results of some baseline headlines. The reference headlines used in ROUGE were the three headlines generated by the human examiners. A total of 10 headlines were used in this evaluation, three of which are the baselines (Original, Lead-10 and Rand-10), three of which are HMM-based (HMM-G-LM, HMM-D-LM and HMM-F-LM), and four of which are the extractive methods (SUM-EWM, MAX-EWM, SUM-CCC and MAX-CCC). Lead-10 can be considered a main baseline, since it produces a meaningful headline with less effort. The other two baseline headlines are introduced to show the highest and lowest score. Although ROUGE-1, ROUGE-L, ROUGE-W-1.2 and ROUGE-SU scores are registered in this section, the ROUGE-L score will be used as a main score for comparison. Table 2 shows the ROUGE scores of the extractive, HMM - based and baselines

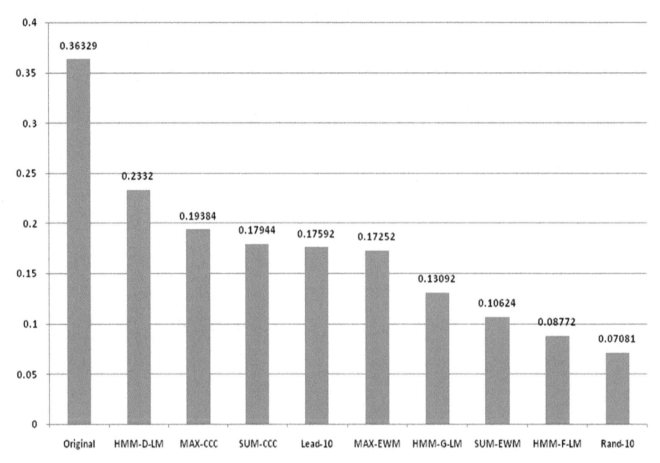

Figure 10. ROUGE-L scores of all headlines.

headlines. On the other hand, Figure 10 shows the ROUGE-L scores of all headlines. From the registered results, the MAX-CCC scores the highest result among the extractive methods. It is clear that MAX-CCC has overcome the problem of the rich existence of clitics and morphology. Character cross-correlation was a valuable procedure in choosing the best headline from the nominated sentences in Arabic documents.

The advantage of using character cross-correlation is that it can overcome the concatenation of clitics to the Arabic words. In this experiment, MAX-CCC produced ROUGE-L = 0.19384 and it outperformed the MAX-EWM, which registered ROUGE-L = 0.17252. Therefore, character cross-correlation can be an effective method for comparing words in morphologically complex languages such as Arabic. As shown in Figure ,

it is obvious that HMM-D-LM is the best automatically generated headline among the systems presented. As predicted, a general language model, one way or another, ignores important relationships in the story and may capture general relationships, but not correct ones for the specific document. In fact, the performance of the system with general language is worse than the Lead-10, which is the baseline system. As predicted, no method

registered scores above the original headlines or below Rand-10.

To utilize a language model in an efficient way, a language model scale factor can be applied. The language model scale factor is the amount by which the language model probability is scaled before it is utilized in generating headlines. Unfortunately, the value of the scale factor can be found only by trial-and-error methods. To investigate the effect of the langue model contribution in the HMM-D-LM method, the LM scale factor was varied from 0 (no effect of the language model) to 14, with a step of 1. At each scale factor value, the system is rerun and results are recorded.

Figure m is rerun and results are recorded. Figure shows the change of the ROUGE-L scores for the HMM-D-LM automatic headline-generation system with different values of the LM scale factor. When the LM scale factor is 0, the system is equivalent to the HMM-F-LM because the probabilistic relationships between word pairs were completely ignored.

The best performance was achieved at the LM scale factor of 11 (ROUGE-L = 0.2332). But it can be seen that the system performance settled after the LM scale factor of 6. It is worth mentioning that all results of HMM-based

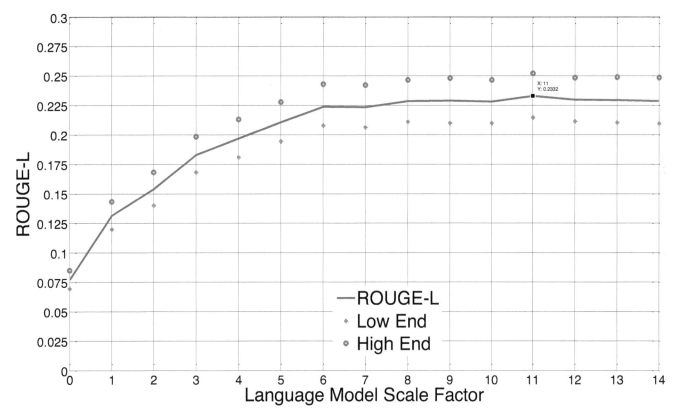

Figure 11. ROUGE-L scores for different values of LM scale factor.

Table 3. Overall evaluation results of the human examiners.

Headline source	Readability (%)	Consistency (%)	Overall (%)
Original	97.90	94.40	96.15
HMM-D-LM	62.20	76.30	69.25
MAX-CCC	77.00	69.20	73.10

systems in Table 2 were generated with a language model scale factor of 11.

Manual evaluation

One of the main criticisms of automatic evaluation metrics is that they do not give a global absolute score. However, they provide a reliable indication when used to compare systems. Therefore, the 258 Original, HMM-D-LM and MAX-CCC headlines were evaluated according to the readability and consistency of the headline. As a result, ROUGE scores become more interpretable. The examiners were asked to assign a score from 1 to 10 for readability and consistency; in which 1 is the lowest score and 10 is the highest. Table 3 shows the overall results of the human evaluation. Few original headlines contained grammatical or spelling mistakes that made them less readable. At the same time, more of them did not

perfectly represent the corresponding documents. Obviously, the *HMM-D-LM* headlines were less accurate than the originals, but it is remarkable that their consistency score is higher than their readability score. Since the MAX-CCC headlines were extractive, their readability score is high. The trimming of the MAX-CCC headlines to 10 words is the major factor that reduces their readability. After reviewing the human evaluation in detail, it seems that the examiners could not completely discriminate between readability and consistency. The less readable headline received a lower consistency score, even if it is constructed out of well-represented words.

In this paper, the effectiveness of using character cross-correlation in choosing the best headline from nominated sentences in Arabic documents has been shown. The advantage of using character cross-correlation is that it can overcome the complex morphology of the Arabic language. In the comparative experiment, character cross-correlation registered ROUGE-L = 0.19384 and outperformed the exact word match, which registered ROUGE-L = 0.17252. Therefore, we can conclude that character cross-correlation is effective when comparing words in morphologically complex languages such as Arabic. Also a new HMM-based approach to automatic headline generation for Arabic news stories was proposed. In this approach, headline words were modeled. In addition, 10 features for every observed word in the document were used as observation vectors. The proposed approach was applied using three different language models. The HMM-based approach with a bigram language model computed from the document for which the headline was generated gave the best score among other automatic systems. The registered ROUGE-L scores were 0.2332 for HMM-D-LM, 0.13092 for HMM-G-LM and 0.08772 for HMM-F-LM. The increase in scores from Flat-LM to Gen-LM to DS-LM shows the strong effect of the language model in building a statistical automatic headline-generation system. Therefore, introducing a higher level of statistical language models than bigram language models may produce a great improvement in the readability of the final headline.

ACKNOWLEDGEMENT

This work has been supported by a direct grant from His Excellency the Rector of King Saud University, Prof. Abdullah Bin Abdulrahman Al-Othman and by a grant from the Research Center, College of Engineering, King Saud University.

REFERENCES

Allen J (1995). Natural Language Understanding. Benjamin/Cummings Pub. Co., Michigan, USA.

Alotaiby F, Alkharashi I, Foda S (2009). Processing large Arabic text corpora: Preliminary analysis and results. In Proceedings of the Second International Conference on Arabic Language Resources and Tools. Cairo, Egypt, pp. 78-82.

Alotaiby F, Foda S, Alkharashi I (2010). Clitics in Arabic language: a statistical study. In Proceedings of Pacific Asia Conference on Language, Information and Computation 24 (PACLIC 24). Sendai, Japan, pp. 595-602.

Buckwalter T (2004a). Issues in Arabic orthography and morphology analysis. In Proceedings of the Workshop on Computational Approaches to Arabic Script-based Languages. Geneva, Switzerland.

Buckwalter T (2004b). Buckwalter Arabic morphological analyzer version 2.0, Linguistic Data Consortium (LDC) catalogue number LDC2004L02, ISBN 1-58563-324-0, Philadelphia, USA.

Conroy JM, O'Leary DP (2001). Text summarization via hidden Markov models. In Proceedings of SIGIR 2001. New York, USA, pp. 406-407.

Douzidia F, Lapalme G (2004). Lakhas, an Arabic summarization system. In Proceedings of Document Understanding Conference (DUC), Boston, MA, USA.

DUC Document Understanding Conference (2004). http://duc.nist.gov/duc2004/tasks.html.

Graff D (2007). Arabic Gigaword (3rd ed.). Linguistic Data Consortium. Philadelphia, USA.

Grundy WN (1997). Modeling biological). Linguistic Data Consortium. Philadelphia, USA.

Grundy WN (1997). Modeling biological sequences using HTK. Technical report prepared for Entropic Research Laboratory, Washington, DC.

HTK, Hidden Markov Model Toolkit version 3.4 (2009). http://htk.eng.cam.ac.uk/index.shtml.

Khorsheed M (2007). Offline recognition of omnifont Arabic text using the HMM Toolkit (HTK). Journal of Pattern Recognition Letters, 28(12), Elsevier Science Inc. New York, USA.

Lin CY (2004a). ROUGE: a package for automatic evaluation of summaries. In Proceedings of the Workshop on Text Summarization Branches Out. Barcelona, Spain, pp. 56-60.

Lin CY (2004b). Looking for a few good metrics: ROUGE and its evaluation. In Proceedings of the Fourth NTCIR Workshop on Research in Information Access Technologies, Information Retrieval, Question Answering and Summarization. Tokyo, Japan.

Lloret E, Palomar M (2011). Analyzing the use of word graphs for abstractive text summarization. In Proceedings of The First International Conference on Advances in Information Mining and Management (IMMM 2011), Barcelona, Spain, pp. 61-66.

Manning CD, Schütze H (1999). Foundations of Statistical Natural Language Processing. The MIT Press, Cambridge, MA, USA.

Papineni K, Roukos S, Ward T, Zhu WJ (2002). BLEU: a method for automatic evaluation of machine translation. In Proceedings of the 40th Annual Meeting of the Association for Computational Linguistics (ACL). Philadelphia, USA.

Reddy PV, Vardhan BV, Govardhan A, Babu MY (2011). Statistical translation based headline generation for Telugu. Int. J. Comput. Sci. Netw. Security, 11(6): 295-299.

Songhua X, Shaohui Y, Francis CM (2010). Keyword extraction and headline generation using novel word features. In Proceedings of the Twenty-Fourth AAAI Conference on Artificial Intelligence (AAAI-10), Georgia, USA, pp. 1461-1466.

Tokuda K, Yoshimura T, Masuko T, Kobayashi T, Kitamura T (2000). Speech parameter generation algorithms for HMM-based speech synthesis. In Proc. ICASSP 2000. Istanbul, Turkey, pp. 1315-1318.

Yang C, Chen H, Honga K (2003). Visualization of large category map for internet browsing. J. Decis. Support Syst., 35(1): 89-102.

Zajic D, Dorr B, Schwartz R (2002). Automatic headline generation for newspaper stories. In Workshop on Automatic Summarization. Philadelphia, USA, pp. 78-85.

13

Hybrid time-frequency domain adaptive filtering algorithm for electrodynamic shaker control

Martino O. A. Ajangnay

Electrical Engineering Department, College of Engineering and Architecture, University of Juba, South Sudan.
E-mail: Ajangnay16@hotmail.com.

In this paper, adaptive filtering algorithm for control of the vibration force applied on the specimen in testing control systems is presented. Application for adaptive filtering especially in time domain is associated with a high computational complexity. This complexity is mitigated by using frequency-domain adaptive filtering scheme. In this paper, adaptive filtering algorithm in association with fast fourier transformation (FFT) was proposed. The algorithm was implemented using digital signal processor (DSP). The proposed algorithm show significant reduction in computational complexity as shown in results and discussion.

Key words: Hybrid frequency-time, adaptive filtering algorithm, electrodynamics shaker.

INTRODUCTION

Vibration design and control, aims either to eliminate or to reduce the undesirable vibration effects that may cause human discomfort and hazards, structural degradation and failure, performance deterioration and malfunction of machinery and processes. When a mechanical or electronic system is exposed to a vibration force, it causes the system to vibrate, producing an output response as a result of the vibratory excitation force. The control objective, in such a case, is to suppress the output response to a level that is acceptable. In an adaptive vibration control system, the vibration responses are explicitly sensed through transducers. This sensed response is fed to the controller producing the force that counteracts the effect of the vibration source, suppressing vibration at the sensing location. This force is applied to the system through the actuator. In this paper the electrodynamic shaker, with a permanent magnetic field, is used as a vibration exciter and the control algorithm adopted is a variant of adaptive control.

The application of adaptive control for shaker is motivated by the fact that some parameters of the shaker are time-varying (for example, coil inductance is frequency dependent, and the coil resistance may change with time as the result of skin effect and temperature). Also the specimen or load characteristic is usually unknown beforehand and it may be nonlinear. The shaker control algorithms proposed in the literature

(George, 1997; George and Dave, 2001), have been derived based on a linear shaker model or on the assumption that the load nonlinearity and variation of shaker parameters with time can be neglected. The performance of these controllers degraded when the shaker dynamics are time-varying or the load is highly nonlinear. Besides, the frequency domain adaptive filtering algorithm studied in IMV Corporation Japan, 2001 (Frain, 1977) suffers from high computational complexity and long time delay resulting from the utilization of the block frequency domain method. The limitations of these algorithms were addressed in this paper by utilizing a time and frequency block partitioning adaptive filtering algorithm to reduce the computational complexity, convergence time and the time delay. The electro-dynamic shaker's main function is to deliver a force proportional to the current applied to its armature coil. These devices are used in such diverse activities as product evaluation, stress screening, squeak-and-rattle testing, and modal analysis.

The shakers may be driven by sinusoidal, random or transient signals, depending on the application. They are invariably driven by an audio-frequency power amplifier and may be used 'open loop' (as in most modal testing) or under closed-loop control, where the input to the driving amplifier is servo-controlled to achieve a desired motion level in the device under test. There are three

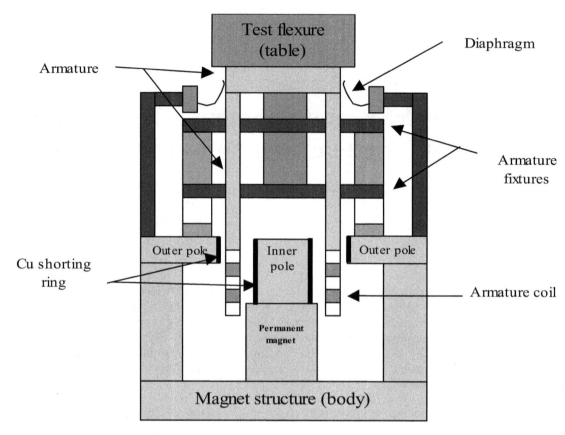

Figure 1. Electrodynamic shaker cross-section.

major shaker types widely used (Hydraulic, Inertial and Electrodynamic Shakers) in vibration testing. However, electrodynamic shakers have many advantages compared to the other types due to their high output bandwidth and moderate input power requirements. In the vibration control system with the shaker used as an exciter, it is essential to characterize the shaker dynamic model and to compute the shaker mechanical and electrical parameters that will be used in the simulation stage. An initial experiment is performed by monitoring the voltage input to the power amplifier or the current delivered by the power amplifier, and measuring the dynamic response of the shaker (accelerometer signal) with a bare shaker table, then with a known table load (George, 1997; De Silva, 2000).

The schematic depicted in Figure 1 shows a sectioned view of a permanent magnet electrodynamic shaker with emphasis on the magnetic circuit and the suspended driving table. At the heart of the shaker is a single-layer armature coil of copper wire, suspended in a uniform radial magnetic field. When a current is passed through the coil, a longitudinal force F is produced in proportion to; the current I flowing in the coil, the length l of the coil in the magnetic field, and the strength B of the field flux. This force is transmitted to the table structure to which the device under test is attached. The generated force in

the armature coil is mathematically expressed as (Frain, 1977).

$$F = BlI \qquad (1)$$

Where, F, is the armature coil force, (N); B, is the magnetic flux density, (T); l, is the length of armature coil in the field, (m); I, is the armature coil current, (A).

SYSTEM MODELLING OF ELECTRODYNAMIC SHAKER

The electrodynamic shaker can be expressed as a current driven or voltage, transfer function. In the current driven transfer function mode, the acceleration frequency response is plotted as current supplied by the power amplifier against the shaker acceleration response. In this case, the effect of electromagnetic damping is not evidenced. The frequency response plot reflects only the structural damping terms, those that could be measured with external excitation applied to the shaker with its drive coil un-terminated. The same low damping factors are usually evident when a current amplifier drives the shaker. In contrast, the voltage driven transfer function (voltage applied to the shaker system against the acceleration, reflects the significant electromagnetic damping applied

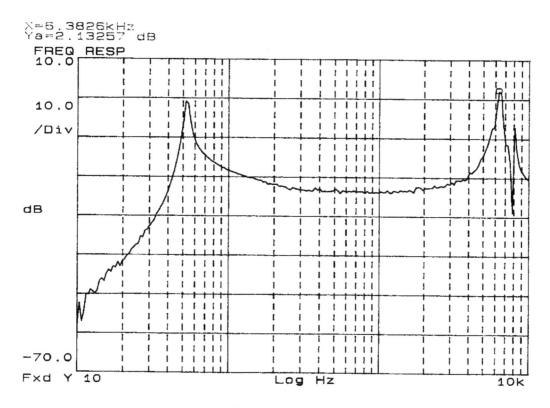

Figure 2. Current driven transfer function of the unloaded electrodynamic shaker.

by the cross-coupling terms between the electrical and mechanical components of the system (George, 1997; Haykin, 2002). The force provided by the shaker is given by $F = Bll$. Figures 2 and 3 show, respectively, the current–driven and voltage-driven frequency response when the swept sine signal of amplitude 0.7 v was applied to shaker power amplifier. The shaker mechanical model is modelled by assuming the armature structure is elastic rather than rigid.

This gives the shaker mechanical model three degrees-of-freedom. This is achieved by modelling the coil and table as separate masses connected by springs and dampers (George, 1997; George and Dave, 2001). In order to compute the mechanical and electrical parameters of the electrodynamic shaker and the associated load, a swept sine test is conducted to compute the frequency response function as the ratio between the shaker's output response (accelerometer signal), and the input supply voltage (voltage mode). The resonance frequencies in the operating range and the half-power points are recorded. These are used in mathematical formulas (Equation 1), to estimate the masses, damping constant, spring stiffness, and electrical impedance. Some of the parameters are tuned using trail and error during simulation, so that the simulated frequency response matches the measured frequency response shape. The mathematical equations used to deduce the mechanical and electrical parameters

from the frequency response, are given by IMV Corporation Japan (2001).

$$M_e = \frac{M_a f_a}{f_n^2 - f_a^2}$$

$$K = \left(2\pi f_n\right)^2 M_e \qquad (2)$$

$$D = 2\pi \Delta f_{3dB} M_e$$

Where;

M_e	effective mass of the shaker system
M_a	mass of the load
K	spring stiffness
D	damping factor
f_n	resonance frequency when the shaker has no load (6.38 kHz)
f_a	resonance frequency when the shaker is loaded
Δf_{3dB}	half-power (-3dB) points bounding resonance frequency f_n

Electrical equivalent model

The electrical model of the electrodynamic shaker consists of the coil resistance R and inductance L. The electrical impedance of the shaker coil reflects the

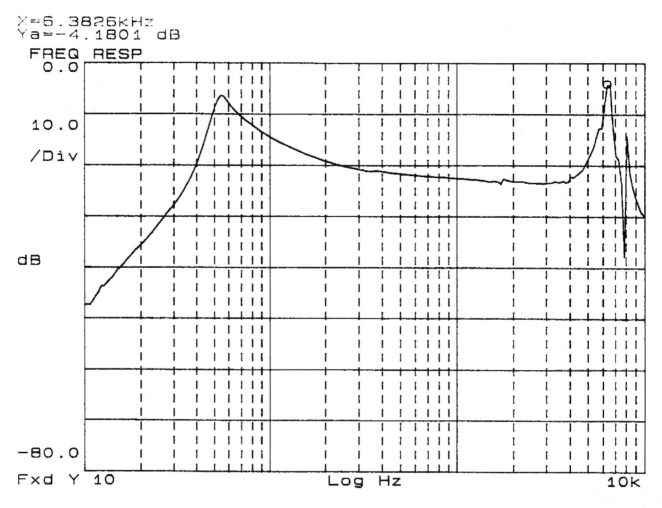

Figure 3. Voltage driven transfer functions of the unloaded electrodynamic shaker.

mechanical motion of the shaker table. When the coil moves in the magnetic field, a voltage is generated across the coil proportional to the motion velocity ($E = Bl$ $u = \alpha u$). Thus the voltage at the coil terminals may be written in terms of the flowing current i and the velocity u as:

$$v = Ri + L\frac{di}{dt} + \alpha u \qquad (3)$$

Where $\alpha = Bl$ is constant, called the transduction factor. The mechanical mobility (velocity/force) of the shaker mechanical components may be represented by a driving-point frequency response function H_{fu}, so that

$$u = H_{fu}F \qquad (4)$$

The coil produces an axial force, acting on the shaker mechanical elements, in proportion to the applied current.

$$F = \alpha i \qquad (5a)$$

Combining equations (3, 4 and 5), yields the impedance Z exhibited by the coil.

$$Z = \frac{v}{i} = R + j2\pi fL + \alpha^2 H_{fu} \qquad (5b)$$

The minimum coil impedance is determined by the differential (dc) resistance, which is real-valued. The coil inductance contributes an imaginary (90° phase-shifted) ac component that increases in direct proportion to frequency. The mechanical mobility contributes frequency-dependent terms that exhibit a real maximum at each mechanical resonance. These can significantly increase the impedance in a narrow frequency band. The effective resistance and inductance of the coil can be measured by clamping the fixture table (locked rotor test). The equivalent circuit is shown in Figure 4 where R_1 and L_1 are the resistance and leakage inductance of the moving coil, R_2 and L_2 are the resistance and leakage inductance of the copper pole-plating, and L_m is the moving coil magnetizing inductance. Using current mesh

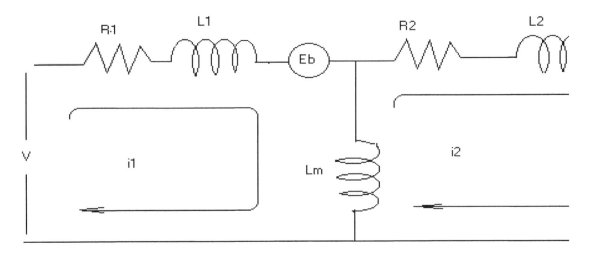

Figure 4. Moving coil T-circuit showing the short-circuit secondary.

analysis, the mathematical equations for the shaker electrical model can be derived from Figure 3 as

$$v = R_1 i_1 + L_1 \frac{di_1}{dt} + L_m \left(\frac{di_1}{dt} - \frac{di_2}{dt} \right) + \alpha \frac{dl_1}{dt}$$

$$0 = R_2 i_2 + L_2 \frac{di_2}{dt} + L_m \left(\frac{di_2}{dt} - \frac{di_1}{dt} \right)$$

(6)

Mechanical equivalent model

The shaker mechanical system includes a means for storing potential energy (spring), a means for storing kinetic energy (mass or inertia), and a means by which energy is gradually lost (dampers). The mechanical model of the shaker consists of two distinct elements, the moving coil and the fixture table. The fixture table is suspended by a suspension flexure to the shaker body assembly. The fixture table can be modelled as a pair of masses M_2 and M_3, with flexure stiffness, K_2 and K_3, and damping coefficients, D_2 and D_3. The moving coil of mass M_1 is adhered to the fixture table by an adhesive bonding, which also can be characterized by a spring with a finite stiffness K_1 and a damping element with coefficient D_1. Thus Figures 4 and 5 can represent the unloaded shaker electrical and mechanical systems, respectively. The mechanical system and mathematical equations can be expressed as:

$$\alpha i_1 = M_1 \frac{d^2 l_1}{dt^2} + K_1 (l_1 - l_2) + D_1 \left(\frac{dl_1}{dt} - \frac{dl_2}{dt} \right)$$

$$K_1 (l_1 - l_2) + D_1 \left(\frac{dl_1}{dt} - \frac{dl_2}{dt} \right) = M_2 \frac{d^2 l_2}{dt^2} + K_2 (l_2 - l_3) + D_2 \left(\frac{dl_2}{dt} - \frac{dl_3}{dt} \right)$$

(7)

$$K_2 (l_2 - l_3) + D_2 \left(\frac{dl_2}{dt} - \frac{dl_3}{dt} \right) = M_3 \frac{d^2 l_3}{dt^2} + K_3 l_3 + D_3 \frac{dl_3}{dt}$$

$$\alpha i_1 = M_1 \frac{d^2 l_1}{dt^2} + K_1 (l_1 - l_2) + D_1 \left(\frac{dl_1}{dt} - \frac{dl_2}{dt} \right)$$

$$K_1 (l_1 - l_2) + D_1 \left(\frac{dl_1}{dt} - \frac{dl_2}{dt} \right) = M_2 \frac{d^2 l_2}{dt^2} + K_2 (l_2 - l_3) + D_2 \left(\frac{dl_2}{dt} - \frac{dl_3}{dt} \right)$$

(7)

$$K_2 (l_2 - l_3) + D_2 \left(\frac{dl_2}{dt} - \frac{dl_3}{dt} \right) = M_3 \frac{d^2 l_3}{dt^2} + K_3 l_3 + D_3 \frac{dl_3}{dt}$$

PARTIALLY HYBRID TIME-FREQUENCY DOMAIN ADAPTIVE FILTERING ALGORITHM

In vibration testing control systems, the shock test is conducted to simulate the effect of the shock that a specimen is expected to be subjected to, during its lifetime. To prevent testing damage, it is essential that the test be controlled such that the shaker output converges smoothly to the intended reference shock pulse. Usually, in shaker vibration control, the load dynamics are not well defined before hand. Thus, the control algorithm must be designed with the following consideration:

(1) The controller should be able to update its parameters to cope with load uncertainty.
(2) The controller must have a fast response, especially when the pulse used is a shock pulse; and
(3) The controller must be robust, such that it can adapt to a large range of load variations.

The following give a brief description of inverse adaptive filtering, time domain adaptive filtered-x filtering and hybrid time-frequency domain adaptive filtering algorithms.

Inverse adaptive filtering algorithm

For tracking control or servo-control systems, the inverse

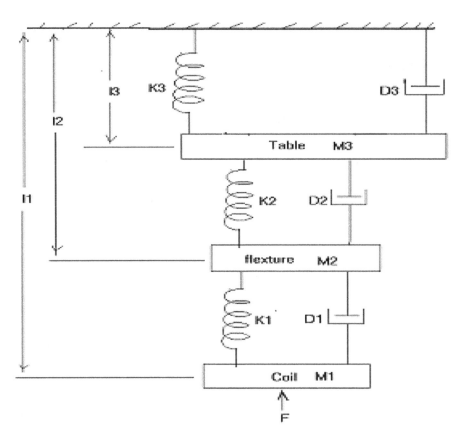

Figure 5. Mechanical equivalent circuit of the unloaded electrodynamic shaker.

of the system dynamics can be employed as a controller such that, when the inverse model is cascaded with the system dynamics, the overall system output converges to the reference input. This configuration of the inverse model and system dynamics constitutes a feed-forward control system. Adaptive feed forward techniques have been used widely in the active control of sound and vibration (Olmos et al., 2002; Valoor et al., 2000). The application of the shaker inverse model as a controller has been reported in Macdonald (1994), where the shaker and controller were modelled in the frequency domain. Cascading the adaptive filter with the unknown system causes the adaptive filter to converge to a solution that is the inverse of the unknown system. Therefore, inverse modelling is motivated by the fact that, when the transfer function of the unknown system is $W(z)$ and the adaptive filter transfer function is $C(z)$, then error measured between the desired signal and the signal from the cascaded system reaches its minimum when the product of $W(z)$ and $C(z)$ is 1.

$$W(z)C(z) = 1 \qquad (8)$$

For the previous relation to be true, $W(z)$ must be equal $[C(z)]^{-1}$, the inverse of the transfer function of the unknown system. In practice, it is sometimes essential to

have prior knowledge of the system dynamics, so that an accurate inverse of the dynamic system can be obtained. For example, if the system under investigation is known to be minimum-phase, that is, has all of its zeros inside the unit circle in the z-plane, then the inverse will be stable with all its poles inside the unit circle. When the plant is non-minimum-phase, then some of the poles of the inverse will be outside the unit circle and the inverse will be unstable. It is also essential to consider the effect of transport delay in the system. For instance, when the unknown system is cascaded with the filter, the output signal from the cascaded system reaches the summation points after it has been delayed by a time equal to the unknown system delay plus the filter delay.

To prevent the adaptive filter from trying to adapt to a signal it has not yet seen (equivalent to predicting the future), the desired signal is delayed, with the number of samples equivalent to half the length of the adaptive filter. Figure 6 shows the block diagram for modelling the inverse of the electrodynamic shaker using a finite impulse response (FIR) filter. Assuming the shaker and the payload are linear, then the commutation rule applies, such that the controller and plant position can be interchanged. Assuming the input signal $r(n)$ is applied to the shaker and a payload, the acceleration response Output $a(n)$ will act as the input to the FIR filter. The

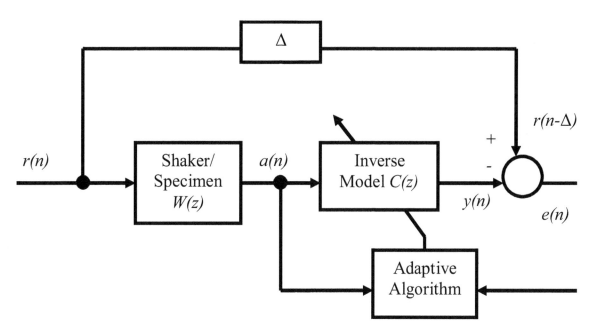

Figure 6. Inverse adaptive modelling block diagram.

output response of the cascaded system is given by

$$y(n) = \sum_{i=0}^{L-1} c_i(n)a(n-i) \qquad (9)$$

Where L is the number of weights in the FIR filter and $c_i(n)$ is the ith weight of the adaptive filter at iteration n. The error between the delayed input signal and the output of the cascaded system is

$$e(n) = r(n-\Delta) - y(n) \qquad (10)$$

Where Δ is the sample delay, equal to $L/2$. Using the Least mean squares (LMS) algorithm, the weights of the inverse adaptive filter are updated using the following formula

$$c(n+1) = c(n) + \mu e(n)a(n) \qquad (11)$$

Where μ is the step-size, and the weight vector $c(n)$ and filter regression input vector $a(n)$ are given by equations (5a) and (5b), respectively.

$$c(n) = [c_0(n), c_1(n), ..., c_{L-1}(n)]^T \qquad (12)$$

$$a(n) = [a(n), a(n-1), ..., a(n-L+1)]^T \qquad (13)$$

Filtered-x adaptive filtering algorithm

The filtered-x algorithm has been extensively applied in

the active control of sound and vibration. The design is carried out in two phases. In the first phase, the model of the dynamic system to be controlled is computed. In the second phase, the controller weights are updated, and the optimal values found are implemented to control the dynamic system. The main feature of the filtered-x algorithm is that the signal used in the controller weights adaptation, is produced by filtering the reference input signal, via the system model weights. Figure 7 illustrates the block diagram of the filtered-x adaptive filtering algorithm for the electrodynamic shaker. Assume the model of the shaker and the specimen has been computed. Let the number of weights in the shaker/specimen model and the control filter be L_c and L_p, respectively. The output response of the FIR filter controller is computed as a convolution of the FIR filter weights and the input reference signal.

$$u(n) = \sum_{i=0}^{L_c-1} c_i(n)r(n-i) \qquad (14)$$

The FIR filter output is applied to the shaker/specimen, generating the acceleration output of $a(n)$. The error signal is computed as the difference between the delayed input signal and the shaker/specimen acceleration output response.

$$e(n) = r(n-\Delta) - a(n) \qquad (15)$$

Where Δ is the time delay. The input reference signal is filtered through the shaker model weights to generate the

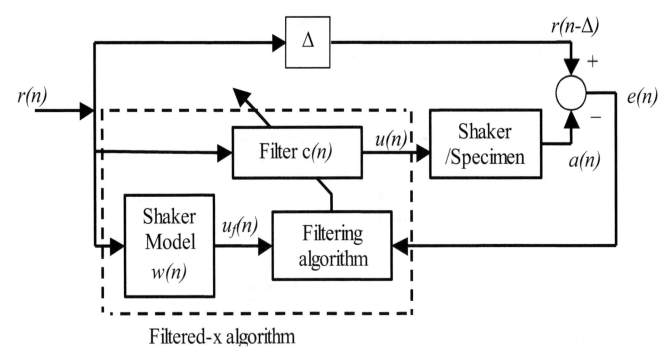

Figure 7. Filtered-x adaptive filtering block diagram.

filtered signal $u_f(n)$ given by

$$u_f(n) = \sum_{i=0}^{L_p-1} w_i(n)r(n-i) \qquad (16)$$

Using the LMS algorithm, the controller weights are updated using

$$c(n+1) = c(n) + \mu e(n)u_f(n) \qquad (17)$$

Where μ is the step-size, $c(n)$ is the controller weight vector, and $u_f(n)$ is the regression vector.
The controller weight vector is given by

$$c(n) = \begin{bmatrix} c_0, c_1, \ldots, c_{L_c-1} \end{bmatrix}^T \qquad (18)$$

The regression vector is defined as

$$u_f(n) = \begin{bmatrix} u_f(n), u_f(n-1), \ldots, u_f(n-L_p+1) \end{bmatrix}^T \qquad (19)$$

Partially hybrid time-frequency domain adaptive filtering (PHTFDAF) algorithm

Here, partially hybrid time-frequency domain adaptive filtering (PHTFDAF) algorithms are described for modelling and controller design for the shock control of the electrodynamic shaker. The model and inverse model

of the electrodynamic shaker are modelled by an FIR filter. Experimental results show that the model and inverse model of the shaker required thousands of FIR weights to represent the dynamic system (shaker and load attached) effectively. This large number of filter taps results in complex computation and implementation and in real-time requires large resources, in terms of memory. As a result, it is impractical to use time-domain filtering methods to find the model and inverse model of the electrodynamic shaker and its load. Computational complexity and convergence speed of the FIR model's weights to their optimal values was addressed using the frequency domain adaptive filtering algorithm studied in partially hybrid time-frequency domain adaptive filtering (PHTFDAF) algorithm. However, the conventional frequency domain adaptive filtering algorithm has a drawback of inherent delay between the block input and the system output response, especially during the initial stages while the input block data collection is processing.

The problem of the long delay in frequency domain adaptive filtering was addressed by splitting the time domain filter weights sequentially into non-overlapping partitions (Olmos et al., 2002; Valoor et al., 2000). Although partitioning of the filter weights results in a small input block size, it does not completely eliminate the system time delay. A delay less frequency domain adaptive filtering algorithm was proposed in Bendel et al. (2001), where the system delay is eliminated by adapting the first partition weights using a time domain algorithm and adapting the remaining partitions using a frequency domain adaptive filtering algorithm. Although this method

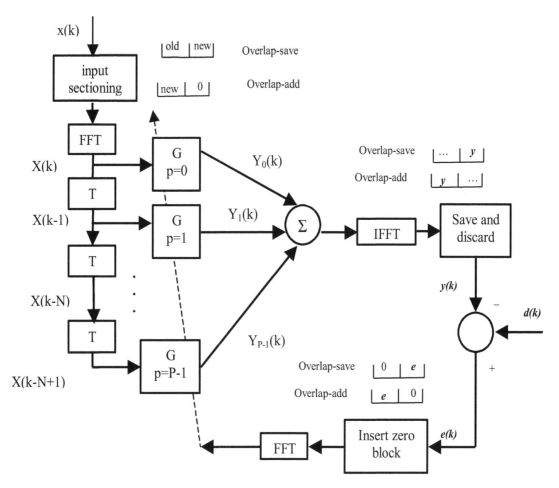

Figure 8. Partitioned frequency domain adaptive filtering block diagram.

eliminates the time delay in adaptation, it increases computational complexity due to the use of the time domain adaptive filtering method in updating the first partition weights. To reduce the computational complexity of partitioned frequency domain adaptive filtering, the PHTFDAF algorithm was proposed. In the PHTFDAF algorithm, the time domain filter weights are sequentially divided into non-overlapping partitions. The first partition weights are adapted using the time domain only during the initial stage. Then these weights are adapted using the frequency domain algorithm as well as the other partition's weights.

This method of partially updating some weights in the time domain and then in the frequency domain reduces the computational complexity of the whole adaptation process, as well as minimising the time delay in the adaptation process. The proposed algorithm for adaptive control is different from the one reported in Olmos et al. (2002), and Bendel et al. (2001). The time domain adaptive filtering of the model and its inverse are sequentially split into non-overlapping partitions and the first partition weights are updated only in the time domain during the first block input data collection, then they are

adapted in the frequency domain in the remaining adaptation periods along with the other partitions weights.

PBFDAF algorithm

The computational complexity and long time-delay problems, associated with the conventional frequency domain adaptive filtering algorithm, can be minimized by using the partitioned block frequency domain adaptive method, in which the weights of the FIR filter are sequentially split into non-overlapping partitions. Then the frequency domain adaptive algorithm is applied to each partition. The main advantage of PBFDAF over the non-partitioned algorithm is that a small processing block size is required; consequently, the delay of the PBFDAF is small. Figure 8 shows the PBFDAF block diagram. To derive the equations that govern the PBFDAF algorithm, assume that the FIR filter has M weights, divided into P partitions, each partition containing N weights. Therefore the output of the blocks of N samples is given by

$$y_k = [y(kN),...,y(kN+N-1)]^T = \sum_{p=0}^{P-1} A(k-p)[w_{pN}(kN),...,w_{(p+1)N-1}(kN)]^T \quad (20)$$

Where $A(k)$ is an *NxN* matrix whose *i,j* element is given by

$$A_{i,j}(k) = x(kN + i - j), \qquad i,j = 0,1,...,N-1$$

The output of each partition is a circular convolution of the partition input with the weight vector of the partition at the kth time, where for example, the input of the partition (overlap-save) and weight vector per partition are, respectively.

$$\mathbf{x}(k-p) = [x([k-p-1]N),..., x([k-p])N,..., x([k-p+1]N-1)]^T \quad (21)$$
$$\mathbf{w}_p(k) = [w_p(kN),..., w_{(p+1)N-1}(kN),0,....,0]^T$$

Thus the input and partition weight vector in the frequency domain are defined as

$$X(k-p) = diag(F\mathbf{x}(k-p)), \qquad p = 0,1,...P-1$$
$$W(k) = F\mathbf{w}_p(k) \qquad\qquad p = 0,1...,P-1 \quad (22)$$

Where F denotes the discrete Fourier transform (DFT) operator of order *2N*. For the overlap-save method of the block sectioning, the adaptive filter output in the time domain is

$$\mathbf{y}_k = [y(kN),..., y(kN+N-1)]^T = [0_n I_n]F^{-1}\sum_{p=0}^{P-1} Y_p(k) \quad (23)$$
$$where \quad Y_p(k) = X(k-p)W_p(k)$$

where $[0_N I_N]$ is *Nx2N*, is the output projection matrix used to force the first element of the output vector to zero as a result of the application of the overlap-save sectioning on the input block. The weight update of each partition is defined as

$$W_p(k+1) = W_p(k) + 2\mu F\left(\begin{bmatrix} I_N & 0_N \\ 0_N & 0_N \end{bmatrix}F^{-1}\{X^*(k-p)E(k)\}\right) \quad (24)$$

Where $E(k)$ is the error vector in the frequency domain and is defined as

$$E(k) = F(e(k)) = F[0,0,...,0,e(kN),...,e(kN+N-1)]^T \quad (25)$$

EXPERIMENTAL SETUP

In this paper, the loaded shaker was characterized using a swept sine signal, generated from the HP 3562A Dynamic Signal Analyzer Figure 15. The signal, swept from 10 Hz to 10 kHz, was applied to the shaker/specimen via the power amplifier. The acceleration output response was measured via a charge amplifier, whose output was connected to the 2nd channel of the Dynamic Signal

Analyzer. The frequency response was computed as the ratio between output acceleration measured by charge amplifier and the input swept sine signal of 0.7 v rms amplitude. The charge amplifier sensitivity and scale values were set to 80 pC/g and 5 g/V, respectively. From the measured transfer function of the unloaded shaker (Figure 9a), the upper resonance frequency occurs at 6.38 kHz and low resonance at 54.32 Hz. The resonance frequency values from Figure 9a and the half-power values were used to compute masses, and springs and damper constants of the mechanical system. Some electrical components were measured. The remaining electrical and mechanical parameters were approximated using trail-and-error, by tuning the simulation program till the frequency response matched the measured frequency response. The frequency response of the unloaded shaker model is shown in Figure 9b.

RESULTS AND DISCUSSION

The shaker model represented by the FIR adaptive filter is identified using the partially hybrid frequency domain adaptive filtering algorithm described in partially hybrid time-frequency domain adaptive filtering algorithm. The FIR filter representing the model has 1024 weights. The time-domain weights are divided into two partitions, each of 512 taps, as is explained in the previous sections. The weights of the first partition are adapted using the non-block time domain filtering algorithm only in the first block input stage $(n = 0,1,...,511)$. In subsequence block input iterations, the weights in the first partition and the weights of the other partitions are updated using the frequency domain adaptive filtering algorithm. After the shaker model is computed, the model weights are used in the PHTFDAF FIR controller model, such that when the resultant FIR controller is connected in cascade with the shaker, the shaker output tracks the reference input signal. That is, the control objective can be stated as: given the desired input reference signal and the shaker model, it is required to compute the FIR controller model such that when cascaded with the shaker, the output of the shaker tracks the reference input signal (Figure 10).

The transition of the shaker controlled output response to the input reference signal should occur in a short time (due to the shock pulse width, usually 2 to 20 ms) and converge smoothly (no overshoot). The control model is represented by an FIR filter of 1024 weights. The weights are divided into two partitions, each of 512 weights, as in the case of the system identification of the shaker model. Using the filtered-x method in the time and frequency domains, the shaker output tracks the reference signal. The adaptation process converges to the optimal values after 20 block input iterations. The input reference signal and shaker controlled output responses are shown in Figures 11 and 12, respectively. From comparison of the desired input reference signal (Figure 11) and the shaker-controlled output (Figure 12), it is seen that the shaker output tracks the input reference signal. The control algorithm implementation results in a reduction in the ringing of the shaker output response. The rise time and

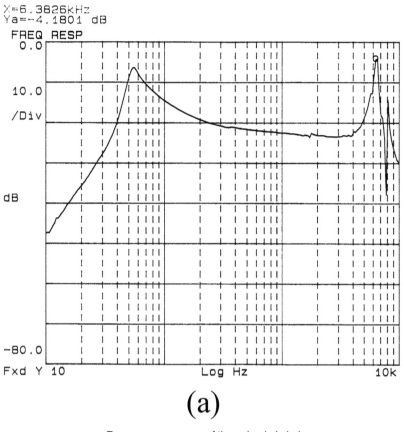

(a)

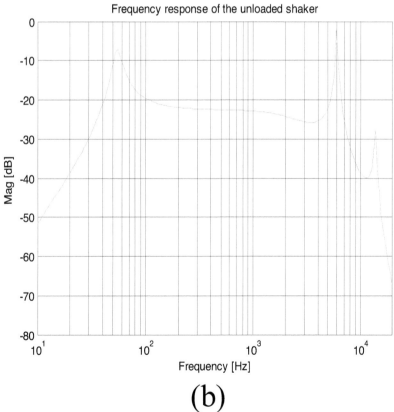

(b)

Figure 9. Frequency response of the unloaded shaker: (a) practical and (b) simulation.

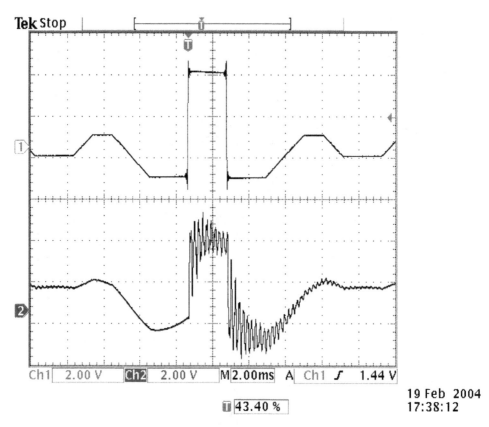

Figure 10. Shaker input reference and shaker output response.

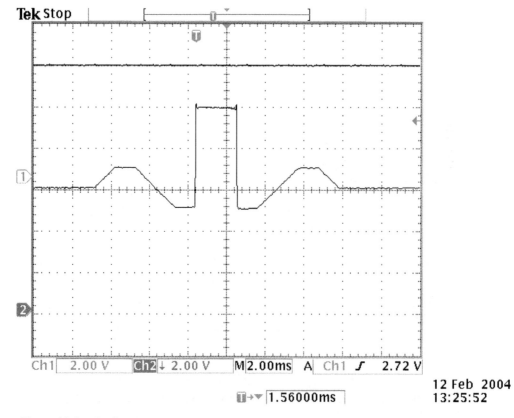

Figure 11. Input reference.

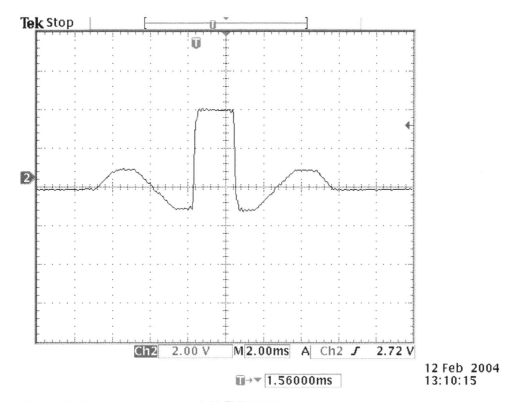

Figure 12. Shaker controlled output (with PHTFDAF).

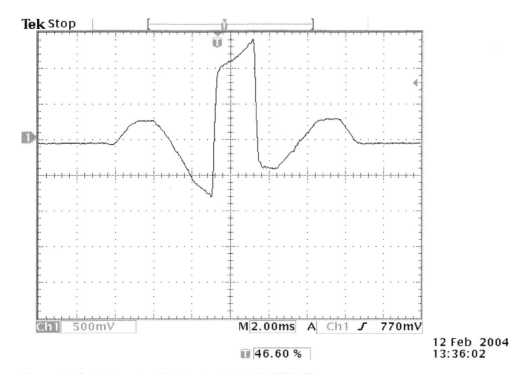

Figure 13. Controller output (Shaker input- (with PHTFDAF).

settling time achieved are 0.05 and 0.85 ms, respectively. The controller output signal (shaker input) is shown in Figure 5. Figures 13 to 15 shows the shaker performance with conventional adaptive time domain Filtered-x

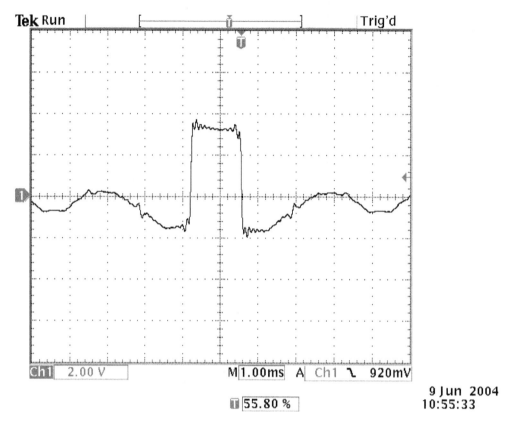

Figure 14. Shaker controlled output (with Filtered-X).

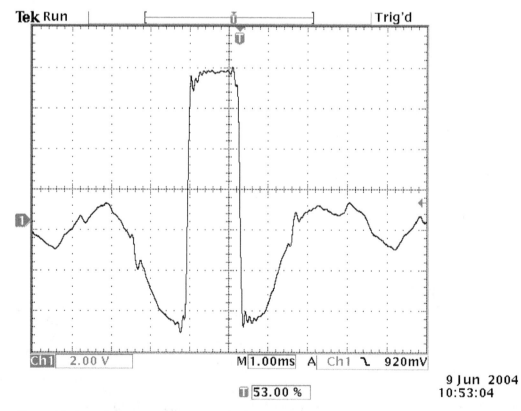

Figure 15. Controller output (shaker input-with Filtered-x).

algorithm used to implement control design for shaker system. During simulation it is found that the PHTFDAF algorithm converges to the desired signal faster than with the conventional frequency domain adaptive filtering (FDAF) method.

REFERENCES

George FL (1997). Electrodynamic Shaker Fundamentals, Sound and Vibration, Data Physics Corporation, San Jose, California. pp. 1-8.

George FL, Dave S (2001). Understanding the Physics for Electrodynamic Shaker Performance, Dynamic reference issue, Sound and Vibration, Data Physics Corporation, San Jose, California. pp. 1-9.

De Silva CW (2000). Vibration fundamentals and Practice, CRC press.

Frain WE (1977). Shock wave testing on an Electrodynamic Vibrator, Applied Physics Laboratory, The Johns Hapkins University Laurel Maryland.

George FL (1997). Electrodynamic Shaker Fundamentals, Sound and Vibration, Data Physics Corporation, San Jose, California.

George FL, Dave S (2001). Understanding the Physics for Electrodynamic Shaker Performance, Dynamic reference issue, Sound and Vibration, Data Physics Corporation, San Jose, California.

IMV Corporation Japan (2001), Instruction Manual.

Macdonald HM (1994). Analysis and Control of an Electrodynamic Shaker, PhD Thesis, Heriot-Watt University, Edinburgh.

Haykin S (2002). Adaptive Filter Theory, Prentice-Hall.

Olmos S, Sornmo L, Laguna P (2002). Block Adaptive Filters with Deterministic Reference Inputs for Event-Related Signals: BLMS and BRLS, IEEE Tran. Sig. Proc., 50(5): 1102-1112.

Bendel Y, Burshtein D, Shalvi O, Weinstein E (2001). Delayless Frequency Domain Acoustic Echo Cancellation, IEEE Trans on Speech and Audio Proc., 9(5): 589-597.

Valoor MT, Chandrashekhara K, Agarwal S (2000). Active Vibration control of smart composite plates using self-adaptive neuro-controller, Smart Mater. Struct., Vol. 9, IOP Publishing Ltd, pp. 197-204.

14

Interference reduction in mobile ad hoc and sensor networks

Maaly A. Hassan* and Ibrahim S. Abuhaiba

Department of Electrical and Computer Engineering, The Islamic University of Gaza, Gaza, Palestine.

There are still a lot of open questions in the field of mobile ad hoc networks (MANETs) and sensor networks. If a topology incurs a large interference, either many communication signals sent by nodes will collide, or the network may experience a serious delay at delivering the data for some nodes, and even consume more energy. So, we reach the conclusion that interference imposes a potential negative impact on the performance of wireless networks. In the last few years, researchers actively explored topology control approaches for such networks. The motivation of topology control (TC) is to maintain the connectivity of the network, reduce the node degree and thereby reduce the interference, and reduce power consumption in the sensor nodes. Some literatures have pointed out that a node can interfere with another node even if it is beyond its communication range. To improve the network performance, designing topology control algorithms with consideration of interference is imminent and necessary. Since, it leads to fewer collisions and packet retransmissions, which indirectly reduces the power consumption and extends the lifetime of the network. In this paper, we propose a new interference-aware connected dominating set-based (IACDS) topology construction algorithm, namely, IACDS algorithm, a simple, distributed, interference-aware and energy-efficient topology construction mechanism that finds a sub-optimal connected dominating set (CDS) to turn unnecessary nodes off while keeping the network connected and providing complete communication coverage with minimum interference. IACDS algorithm utilizes a weighted distance-energy-interference-based metric that permits the network operator to trade off the lengths of the branches (distance) for the robustness and durability of the topology (energy and interference).

Key words: Interference, mobile ad hoc networks (MANETs), topology control, connected dominating set (CDS), wireless sensor network (WSN), interference-aware connected dominating set-based (IACDS) algorithm.

INTRODUCTION

A mobile ad hoc network (MANET) is a temporary self-organizing multi-hop system of wireless mobile nodes which rely on each other to keep the network connected without the help of any preexisting infrastructure, pre-defined topology, or central administrator. These networks are generally formed in environments where it is difficult to find or settle down a network infrastructure Santi (2005). In this type of networks, nodes must collaborate and organize themselves to offer both basic network services as routing and management services as security. A wireless sensor network (WSNs) is a wireless network consisting of spatially distributed autonomous

devices using sensors to cooperatively monitor physical or environmental conditions, such as temperature, sound, vibration, pressure, motion, or pollutants, at different locations (Roemer et al., 2004; Westhoff et al., 2006).

Wireless sensor networks (WSNs) are a particular type of ad hoc networks, in which the nodes are sensors equipped with wireless transmission capability. Hence, they have the characteristics, requirements, and limitations of an ad hoc network (Santi, 2005). The term ad hoc network describes a type of wireless network without a fixed infrastructure. Conventional wireless networks including WiFi and cellular networks have supporting backbones and are hierarchical. Nodes communicate with each other via the base stations. In an ad hoc network the nodes can communicate with each other directly via multi-hops paths. Usually the network

*Corresponding author. E-mail: maaly_awad@hotmail.com.

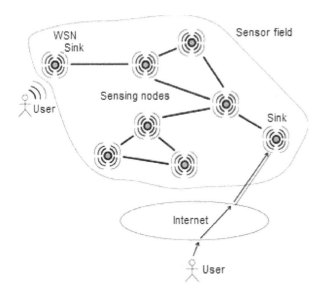

Figure 1. Basic structure of a wireless sensor network.

does not have any coordinating node and hence, ad hoc networks are decentralized, self-organized, and self-healing. Messages may be duplicated on the way to the base station to provide extra resilience (Akyildiz et al., 2002).

A WSN is usually composed of a large number of sensing nodes in the order of tens, hundreds, or even thousands scattered in a sensor field and one or a few base stations/ sinks, which connect the sensor networks to the users via the internet or other networks. Sensor nodes are equipped with sensing, data processing, and communicating components to accomplish their tasks. Each of the sensor nodes is capable of collecting data and routing the data back to the sink by multi-hopping, as illustrated in Figure 1.

Interference in MANETs and sensor networks

One of the main challenges of wireless communication is interference. Unfortunately, research in this area is so young that researchers have to investigate different ideas regarding the identification of a universal measure of network interference. According to the Glossary of Telecommunication Terms - Federal Standard 1037C, interference is defined as a coherent emission having a relatively narrow spectral content, for example, a radio emission from another transmitter at approximately the same frequency, or having a harmonic frequency approximately the same as another emission of interest to a given recipient, and which impedes reception of the desired signal by the intended recipient.

Informally speaking, a node u may interfere with another node v if u's interference range unintentionally covers v. Consequently, the amount of interference experienced by

a node v corresponds to the amount of interference produced by nodes whose transmission range covers v.

Interference reduction in MANETs and sensor networks

In frequency division multiplexing cellular networks, reducing the amount of interference results in fewer channels, which in turn, can be exploited to increase the bandwidth per frequency channel. In systems using code division multiplexing, small interference helps in reducing coding overhead. In the context of ad hoc and sensor networks, there is an additional motivation for keeping interference low. In these networks consisting of battery driven devices, energy is typically scarce and the frugal usage of it is critical in order to prolong system operability and network lifetime. In addition to enhancing throughput, minimizing interference may help in lowering node energy dissipation by reducing the number of collisions (or amount of energy spent in an effort of avoiding them) and consequently retransmissions on the media access layer.

Interference can be reduced by having nodes send with less transmission power. The area covered by the smaller transmission range will contain fewer nodes, yielding less interference. On the other hand, reducing the transmission range has the consequence of communication links being dropped. However, there is surely a limit to how much the transmission power can be decreased. In ad hoc networks, if the node's transmission ranges become too small and too many links are abandoned, the network may become disconnected. Hence, transmission ranges must be assigned to nodes in such a way that the desired global network properties are maintained.

Topology control

Topology control (TC) is one of the most important techniques used in wireless ad hoc and sensor networks to reduce energy consumption (which is essential to extend the network operational time) and radio interference (with a positive effect on the network traffic carrying capacity). The goal of this technique is to control the topology of the graph representing the communication links between network nodes with the purpose of maintaining some global graph property (for example, connectivity), while reducing energy consumption and/or interference that are strictly related to the nodes' transmitting range. An informal definition of topology control is the art of coordinating nodes, decisions regarding their transmitting ranges, in order to generate a network with the desired properties. Interference-efficient topology control is to find a sub-graph H from the original graph G, representing a network, to minimize interference while preserving fixed properties (connectivity and low power consumption). Topology control is a system-level perspective to optimize the choice of the nodes' transmit power levels to achieve a certain global property while power control is a wireless channel perspective to optimize the choice of the transmit power level for a single wireless transmission, possibly along several hops.

Topology control techniques have the potential to mitigate two important problems occurring in wireless ad hoc networks: node energy consumption and radio interference.

Another major requirement of topology control in MANETs and sensor networks is to maintain connectivity in the network. Once the connectivity is ensured, the second goal is usually to reduce the radio transmission power of individual nodes for two reasons. The first is to reduce the power used for transmitting packets. The second one is to reduce the node degree in the neighborhood. A sparse network is desirable because it can enhance the performance of the MAC protocols. If a CSMA type scheme is used, low network degree means less probability of collisions. If a TDMA scheme is used, slot assignment is easier with fewer nodes and there is less chance of congestion. Moreover, routing is simpler in a sparse network than a dense network because there are fewer routes to consider.

RELATED WORKS

Topology control

Topology construction can be exercised by reducing the transmission range of all nodes by the same minimum amount, or the minimum transmission range for each node (Santi, 2005). Other techniques are based on the assumption that nodes have information about their own positions and the position of their neighbors (Li et al., 2001), or that they have directional antennas that are used to determine the orientation of the nodes (Kumar et al., 2002; Li et al., 2003). Although both assumptions are valid, they are costly and not easy to implement. Other topology control methods, such as the one considered in this paper, are based on the connected dominating set (CDS) paradigm. Here, the idea is not to change the transmission range of the nodes but to turn unnecessary nodes off while preserving important network properties, such as connectivity and communication coverage.

The CDS approach has been utilized in several papers (Kumar et al., 2002; Butenko et al., 2004; Chen et al., 2002; Guha and Khuller, 1998; Wu et al., 1999, 2004, 2006; Yuanyuan et al., 2006). Most CDS-based mechanisms work in two phases: In phase one, they create a preliminary version of the CDS, and in phase two they add or remove nodes from it to obtain a better approximation to the optimal CDS. Two relevant CDS-based mechanisms are the energy efficient CDS

(EECDS) (Wu et al., 1999) and the CDS-Rule-K (Guha and Khuller, 1998) algorithms.

The EECDS algorithm builds a CDS tree creating maximal independent sets (MIS), which are clusters with non-connected clusterheads, and then selects gateway nodes to connect the clusterheads of the independent sets. The EECDS algorithm proceeds in two phases. The first phase begins with an initiator node that elects itself as a clusterhead and announces it to its neighborhood. This set of nodes is now "covered". The now "covered" nodes will pass the message to its uncovered neighbors, 2-hop away from the initiator, which start competing to become clusterheads. Once there is a new clusterhead, the process repeats with the 4-hop away nodes from the initiator, until there are no more uncovered nodes. On the second phase the covered non-clusterhead nodes compete to become gateways between the clusterheads.

The CDS-Rule-K `utilizes the marking algorithm proposed in Wu et al. (1999) and the pruning rule included in Wu et al. (2004). The idea is to start from a big set of nodes that accomplishes a minimum criterion and prune it according to a specific rule. In the first phase, the nodes will exchange their neighbor lists. A node will remain active if there is at least one pair of unconnected neighbors. In the second phase, a node decides to unmark itself if it determines that all its neighbors are covered by marked nodes with higher priority, which is given by the level of the node in the tree: lower level, higher priority. The final tree is a pruned version of the initial one with all redundant nodes with higher or equal priority removed.

Interference reduction via topology control

Here, related works in the field of topology control are discussed with special focus on the issue of interference. Interference reduction is one of the main motivations of topology control besides direct energy conservation by restriction of transmission power. Astonishingly however, all the above topology control algorithms at the most implicitly try to reduce interference. Where interference is mentioned as an issue at all, it is maintained to be confined at a low level as a consequence to sparseness or low degree of the resulting topology graph.

However, Burkhart et al. (2004) reveal that such an implicit notion of interference is not sufficient to reduce interference since message transmission can affect nodes even if they are not direct neighbors of the sending node in the resulting topology. Besides demonstrating the weakness of modeling interference implicitly, Burkhart et al. (2004) introduces an explicit definition for interference in wireless networks. Burkhart et al. (2004) presents a traffic-independent model and defines the interference of a link e = (u, v) as the cardinality of the set of nodes covered by two disks centers at u and v with radius $\|uv\|$, denoted as coverage set of link e, cov(e). This model, named as link-interference via coverage, is chosen from the assumption that whenever a link (u, v) is used for a send-receive transaction all nodes whose distance to node u or node v is less than ||uv|| will be affected in some way.

Moaveni et al. (2005), extend this work and propose node-interference via coverage model. The interference of a node u is defined as the maximum coverage set of links incident on u. However, coverage model is based on the question how many other nodes can be disturbed by a given communication node or link. The definition of interference suggested in Moaveni et al. (2005) is problematic in two respects. First, it is based on the number of nodes affected by communication over a given link. In other words, interference is considered to be an issue at the sender instead of at the receiver, where message collisions actually prevent proper reception. It can therefore be argued that such sender-centric perspective hardly reflects real-world interference. The second weakness of the model introduced in Moaveni et al. (2005) is of more technical nature. According to its definition of interference, adding (or removing) a single node to a given network can dramatically influence the interference measure. Addition of one node to a cluster of roughly homogeneously distributed nodes entails the construction of a communication link covering all nodes in the network, accordingly - merely by introduction of one additional node - the interference value of resulting topology is pushed up from a small constant to the maximum possible value, that is the number of nodes in the network. This behavior contrasts to the intuition that a single additional node also represents one additional packet source potentially causing collisions. Moreover, neglect of the case that a particular node might be influenced by multiple communication links with small coverage set might lead discontented results of the proposed algorithms in Moaveni et al. (2005).

An attempt to correct this deficiency is made by Richenband et al. (2005), where an alternative, receiver-centric, interference model is introduced. In this model, node u will be interfered by v whose distance to v is less than Rv, its distance to reach the farthest neighbor, or {v | ||uv|| ≤ Rv} formally. It is denoted as node-interference via transmission model. Under the assumption that only symmetric edges are considered, it can be proved that nodes set, mentioned earlier, is equivalent to {v | ||uv|| ≤ Ru}. Unfortunately, one fatal drawback is that previous works consider the interference range equals to the transmission range. According to the theoretical analysis of actual cause of interference by Xu et al. (2003), interference range generally differs from transmission range and hidden terminals located within the 1.78d distance (d denotes the communication distance) of the receiver are also disturbing sources, which is neglected in previous works at all times. Researches mistake nodes within the transmission range for the only hidden interfering nodes.

Authors of Meyer et al. (2002) introduce an explicit definition of interference between edges and establish – based on a time-step routing model – a trade-offs between the concepts of congestion, energy consumption, and dilation. This interference definition is based on the current network traffic. In Meyer et al. (2002), more attention is also being paid to the fact that if nodes are capable of adapting their transmission power – an assumption already made in early work that can be considered originators of topology control considerations (Hou et al., 1986; Takagi et al., 1984) – interference ranges correlate with the length of communication links. More precisely the interference range of a link depends on the transmission power levels chosen by the two nodes communicating over the respective link. While Meyer et al. (2002) defines interference based on current network traffic, Burkhart et al. (2004) introduces a traffic-independent notion of interference. Moreover, the latter work shows that the previous statement that graph sparseness or small degree implies low interference is misleading. The interference model described in Burkhart et al. (2004) builds on the question of how many nodes are affected by communication over a given link. This sender-centric perspective can however be accused to be somewhat artificial and to poorly represent reality, interference occurring at the intended receiver of a message. Furthermore, this interference measure is susceptible to drastic changes even if single nodes are added to or removed from a network.

PROPOSED SOLUTION

Interference-efficient topology control is to find a sub-graph H from the original graph G to minimize interference while preserving fixed properties.

Network representation

An ad hoc network is modeled as an Euclidian graph G = (V, E) with vertices in V representing network nodes, and the edges E representing communication links. The Euclidian position of the vertices in the graph corresponds to the physical position of the nodes in the Euclidian two dimensional space, which means that the edge weight, w(u, v), represents the physical distance between nodes u and v. Each node u has a maximum transmission range Ru. In order to prevent existing basic communication between neighboring nodes from becoming unacceptably cumbersome (Prakash, 1999), only symmetric edges are considered. Since only undirected links are considered, a link uv can only exist if the Euclidian distance between the nodes u and v is no larger than min (Ru, Rv). Assume that any node can adjust its transmission power to any value from 0 to its maximum transmission power, depending on the desired

Algorithm 1.

Algorithm 1
Purpose: Calculating the interference amount at the receiver of HM
Inputs: Hello Message HM
Outputs: Total interference amount IA(receiver)

Procedure:
1.   For (i=1 to numberOfNeighbors) {
a.   IR = 1.78 * d (receiver, Neighbors (i))
b.   INS (i) = 0
c.   For (j=1 to numberOfNeighbors) {
i.   If (d (receiver, Neighbors (j)) ≤ IR)
ii.   INS (i) ++
d.   }
2.   }
3.   IA (receiver) = max INS_i

Where:
IR refers to Interference Range
d refers to the Euclidean distance
INS refers to Interference Neighbor Set
IA refers to Interference Amount

---

transmission radius: when transmitting to node v, node u uses the lowest possible transmission power needed to reach v. A common path loss model says that the signal strength received by a node can be described as p/dα, where p is the transmission power used by the sending node, d is the distance between two nodes, and α is a path loss gradient, depending on the transmission environment. Consequently, the energy cost c(u, v) to send a message of fixed length directly from node u to node v is θ(|u, v|α). The energy cost of a path is defined as the sum of the energy costs of all edges in the path.

Measurement of interference

Intuitively, a node in the network G is interfered by others, if messages are received but not intended for it (Zhang et al., 2007). From the perspective of the physical layer, a signal arriving at a receiver is assumed to be valid if the signal to noise ratio (SNR) is above a certain threshold TSNR. Assume a transmission to a receiver with transmitter-receiver d meters apart and at the same time, an interfering node d meters away from the receiver starts another transmission. According to analysis in Xu et al. (2003), a crucial conclusion is made that interference range is $\sqrt[4]{T_{SNR}} * d$, with an approximation value of 1.78*d when TSINR is set to 10 for instance. Previous researchers mistake nodes within the transmission range for the only hidden interfering ones. Distinctly, for a node, all active neighbors within its interference range are potential interfering sources. Consequently, interference amount is defined as the maximum cardinality of active interference neighbors set. Given a network N = (V, E), the interference neighbors set of a node u communicating with v in N, denoted as INS_u^v, is defined as follows:

$$INS_u^v = \{w \in V \mid w \in D(w, \sqrt[4]{T_{SNR}} * \|uv\|)\} \quad (1)$$

Consequently, the interference amount of the node is defined as:

$$IA \text{ (receiver)} = \max INS_i \quad (2)$$

Where D (u, r) denotes the set of nodes located in the circular area centered at node u with radius r, and ||uv|| the communication distance.

The receiver node of a "Hello Message" computes its interference amount using Algorithm 1.

Figure 2 shows an example network consisting of twenty nodes. The interference neighbor set of node u when communicating with node v is seven, while its interference neighbor set when communicating with node w is eleven, and when communicating with node z its interference neighbor set equals to ten. The maximum of its interference amounts is 11. Based on the previous definition node u suffers from interference, and it can be measured as follows:

$$INS_u^v = 7 \quad (3)$$

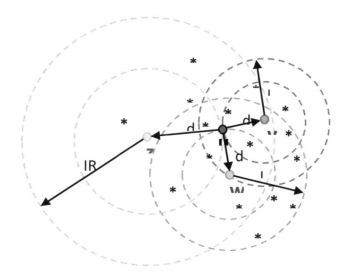

Figure 2. Example network to demonstrate the first interference metric.

$$INS_u^w = 11 \qquad (4)$$

$$INS_u^z = 10 \qquad (5)$$

$$I(u) = \max_{x=v,w,z} INS_u^x \qquad (6)$$

$$I(u) = INS_u^w = 11 \qquad (7)$$

The previous definition is problematic, since it works according to the principle: The global interference in a network depends solely on the local part with the highest interference. Reducing the interference in that part by definition reduces the interference of the entire network. One problem is that the metric does not consider the interference in general; a network with high interference in one place and low interference everywhere else could have the same interference as another network with equally high interference everywhere. We extend the previous work by defining an average interference neighbors set as the sum of the interference neighbors sets divided by the number of neighbors.

$$IA(receiver) = \sum_{i=1}^{|INS|} INS_i / |INS| \qquad (8)$$

Despite the previous extended metric makes a relationship between all local parts of the network, from another point of view it suffers from some weakness: it does not take into account the real distribution of the interference in the network, which means that several networks with different interference amounts in their local parts may have the same global interference. In other words, there will be local parts with higher interference than the global interference of the entire network which is not realistic, for example, a network with high interference in one place and low interference everywhere else.

We propose to form an interference measure which functions with the following properties: creates a relationship between all local parts of the network, and takes into account the maximum interference of the network. This can be achieved by mixing the previous two metrics in one equation.

$$IA(receiver) = \sum_{i=1}^{|INS|} INS_i / |INS| * \max INS_{i=1}^{|INS|} \qquad (9)$$

INTERFERENCE-AWARE CDS-BASED TOPOLOGY CONSTRUCTION ALGORITHM (IACDS)

Topology control is a well-known strategy to save energy and extend the lifetime of wireless mobile ad hoc and sensor networks. In this paper we exploit the benefits of topology control in order to reduce interference in the entire network. So, we propose the IACDS algorithm, a simple, distributed, and energy-efficient topology construction mechanism that finds a sub-optimal connected dominating set (CDS) to turn unnecessary nodes off while keeping the network connected and providing complete communication coverage with minimum interference. IACDS algorithm utilizes a weighted distance-energy-interference-based metric that permits the network operator to trade off the lengths of the branches (distance) for the robustness and durability of the tree (energy and interference).

IACDS algorithm

Interference-efficient topology control is to find a sub-graph H from the original graph G to minimize

Algorithm 2.

Algorithm 2
Purpose: CDS topology such that the resulting topology is connected and with minimal interference.   Inputs: Original network $G = (V, E)$ Outputs: $H_{CDS} = (V_H, E_H)$

Procedure:

1. $V_H = \{sink\}$
2. Start with the sink node: discover its neighborhood NH
3. For each node $v \in NH$, calculate the interference metric
4. Sort nodes in NH in an ascending order of the interference metric
5. While NH is not empty
6. Select $v \in NH$ with minimum interference metric and outside the coverage area of other node in

the neighborhood
- if sink and v are not connected in H_{CDS} then

$V_H = V_H \cup \{v\}$

- end if
- $NH = NH \setminus \{v\}$
7. End while
8. Repeat step 2 with all v's in V_H
9. $H_{CDS} = (V_H, E_H)$

Table 1. Simulation parameters.

Parameter	Simulation 1	Simulation 2	Simulation 3
Deployment area		200 × 200 m	
Number of nodes	100	10, 20, 40, 60, 80, 100	36, 64
Transmission range	28, 42, 56, 70, 84 m	63 m	40 m
Node distribution	Uniform (200, 200)		Grid HV and Grid HVD
Instances per topology		50 instances	
Maximum energy		1 Joule	
IACDS weights		WI = 0.5, WE = 0.5, WD = 0.5	

interference while preserving fixed properties (connectivity and low power consumption) (Algorithm 2).

SIMULATION RESULTS

The following assumptions were made during the simulation:

(1) Nodes are located in a two dimensional space and have a perfect communication coverage disk.
(2) The initial graph is connected.
(3) Distances can be calculated as a metric perfectly proportional to the received signal strength indicator (RSSI).
(4) Idle state energy consumption is assumed negligible.
The networks are constructed by uniformly distributing

nodes in a 200 × 200 square area. Without loss of generality, the mean result is derived from 50 networks randomly generated with a fixed number of nodes and different transmission ranges for the first simulation (changing the node degree) and different number of nodes and fixed transmission range for the second one (changing the node density). Table 1 presents a summary of the simulation parameters used in the performance evaluation of the proposed interference reduction mechanism.

Simulation 1: Changing the node degree

This simulation mainly aims to compare the algorithms when the node degree of the network is changed by increasing the transmission range of the nodes while

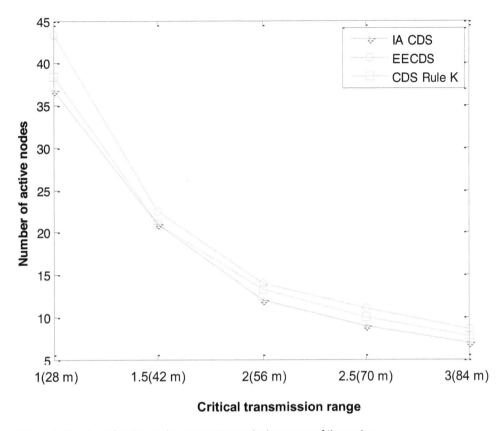

Figure 3. Number of active nodes versus transmission range of the nodes.

maintaining the number of nodes fixed = 100. Given that these algorithms work based on information from neighbors, it is important to measure their performance with neighborhoods of different sizes.

As it can be seen from Figure 3, the three algorithms produce CDSs with almost similar number of nodes. However, IACDS generates fewer nodes in all scenarios. Another note to be seen from this figure, all the algorithms tend to decrease the number of active nodes with the node degree, as expected.

Figures 4 and 5 show two important metrics: the total energy and number of messages used to build the CDSs. In this case, the IACDS mechanism shows its superior performance. IACDS presents an almost constant energy consumption and number of messages compared with the EECDS and CDS-Rule-K algorithms, which show a non-linear increase trend. These results can be easily explained.

The non-linear behavior of the EECDS mechanism is explained by the competition used in both phases of the algorithm. This is due to the fact that with a higher communication range, more nodes are covered, and the network has fewer nodes in higher levels. This, at the same time, reduces the amount of nodes competing to become part of the CDS in the outer regions of the topology.

In the case of the CDS-Rule-K algorithm, the factor that increases the amount of messages (and energy, consequently) is related to its pruning process in which every node must update nodes two hops away when it is unmarked. This overhead increases with the number of neighbors because more nodes will retransmit the message. Also, when the node degree increases, more nodes get unmarked and will produce this extra overhead.

The linearity of IACDS is a consequence of the bounded number of messages that each node needs to transmit, which remains almost identical and never goes over 4n in ideal conditions. The IACDS algorithm uses four types of messages: hello message, parent recognition message, children recognition message, and sleeping message. Figure 6 illustrates the behavior of the proposed interference-aware CDS topology control algorithm, IACDS, in a graphical manner. In this case, the number of nodes is fixed to 100 and the transmission ranges are varied.

Simulation 2: Changing the node density

The main goal of this simulation is to compare the algorithms when the network density is changed by

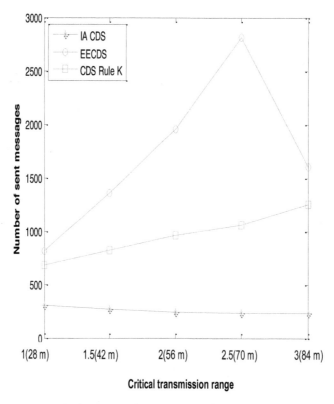

Figure 4. Number of sent messages versus transmission range of the nodes.

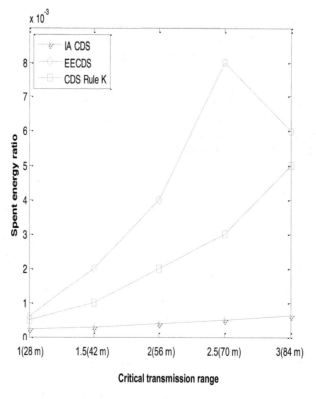

Figure 5. Spent energy ratio versus transmission range of the nodes.

Transmission Range: CTR=28m

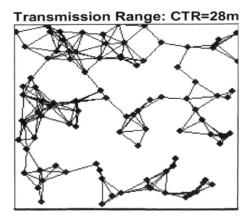

Original network

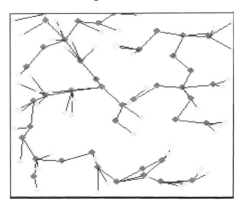

Resulting Network after applying IACDS

Figure 6. Topologies obtained after applying the proposed algorithm.

varying the number of nodes in the deployment area while keeping a fixed communication range of 63. Communication range of 63 is equivalent in this simulation to 1 × CTR (10).

This simulation is important to show how scalable the algorithms are in dense topologies and how the resource usage depends on the number of nodes. The results shown subsequently are similar to the ones shown in simulation 1.

Figure 7 shows that all algorithms need a similar amount of active nodes, although before 35, CDS-Rule-K shows a small advantage over IACDS, after 35 both EECDS and CDS-Rule-K algorithm go above IACDS. After 60 the CDS-Rule-K algorithm goes up to reach its maximum peak at 80, after 80 it goes down, but still above IACDS algorithm.

Figures 8 and 9 show that in terms of the message complexity and energy efficiency, the trends are similar. The EECDS and the CDS-Rule-K algorithms present a non-linear increase, while the IACDS algorithm shows a low and linearly bounded number of messages and energy consumption. This shows that the proposed

algorithm is scalable and is not highly affected by the number of nodes deployed. Figure 10 illustrates the behavior of the proposed interference-aware CDS topology control algorithm, IACDS, in a graphical manner. In this case transmission range is fixed to 63 and the number of nodes is varied.

Simulation 3: Performance using ideal grid topologies

The third simulation considers the ideal grid scenario with two variants of node location distribution: Grid HV and Grid HVD, as shown in Figure 11. This simulation shows the performance of the algorithms in a perfectly homogeneous topology, with ideal condition of density and node degree, which could be considered a predefined scenario. From Figure 11a, it can be seen that the IACDS algorithm shows similar or better results in the number of active nodes metrics, including 58% of the nodes in the Grid HV and 34% in the Grid HVD scenarios, versus 64 and 41% from EECDS, and 61 and

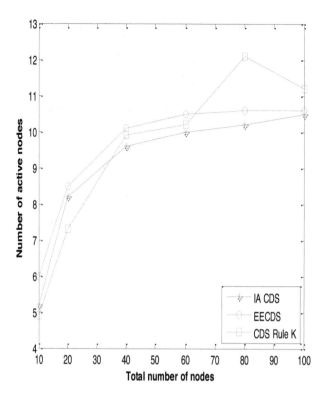

Figure 7. Number of active nodes versus the number of nodes in the area.

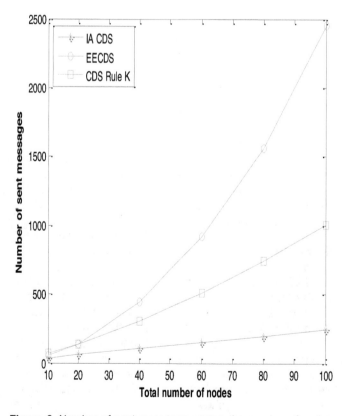

Figure 8. Number of sent messages versus the number of nodes in the area.

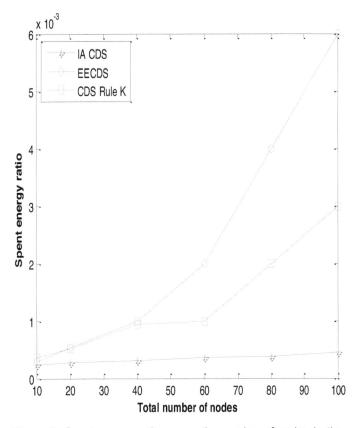

Figure 9. Spent energy ratio versus the number of nodes in the area.

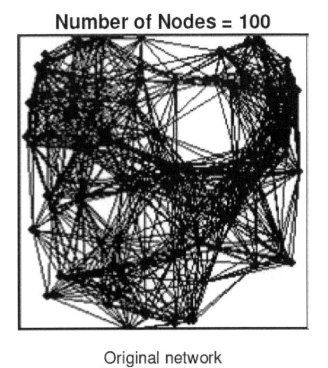

Figure 10. Topologies obtained after applying the proposed algorithm.

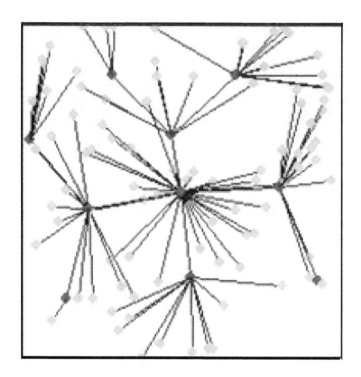

Resulting Network after applying IACDS

Figure 10. Contd.

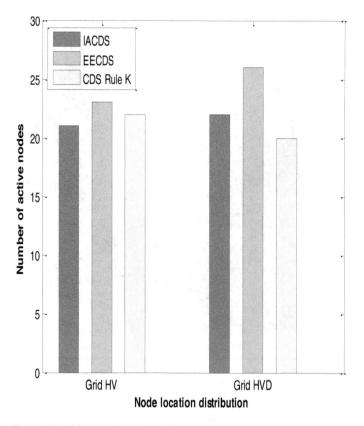

Figure 11a. Number of active nodes.

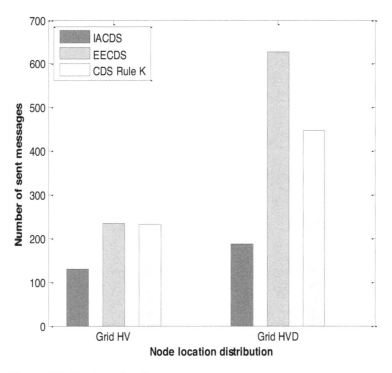

Figure 11b. Number of sent messages.

Table 2. Grid HV and Grid HVD.

Grid H-V	Distribute nodes in the deployment area with a distance of communication radius between nodes, so nodes are adjacent with their vertical and horizontal neighbors.
Grid H-V-D	Distribute nodes in the deployment area with a distance of communication radius $\times \sqrt{2}$ between nodes, so nodes are adjacent with their vertical, horizontal and diagonal neighbors.

31% from CDS-Rule-K algorithms. The other two metrics show an increasing trend for EECDS and CDS-Rule-K while IACDS still shows a bounded cost in overhead and energy as seen in Figures 11b and c, respectively. Table 2 summarizes the parameters that can be defined for a homogeneous family of nodes.

Figure 12a shows graphically the behavior of the proposed IACDS algorithm in the case of Grid HV. The number of active nodes is 20 from original 36 nodes. Nodes are distributed in the deployment area with a distance of communication radius between nodes; nodes are distributed close to each other. Results show that the number of active nodes is large with respect to the total number of nodes.

Figure 12b shows graphically the behavior of the proposed IACDS algorithm in the case of Grid HVD. The number of active nodes is 21 from original 64 nodes. Nodes are distributed in the deployment area with a distance of communication radius $\times \sqrt{2}$ between nodes; nodes are distributed separate from each other. Results

show that the number of active nodes is small with respect to the total number of nodes.

Area of communication coverage

When applying these algorithms, the active nodes determine the communication coverage area. This area is expected to cover as much of the deployment area as possible. Figure 13 shows the average communication area covered by the algorithms using the scenarios from Simulation 2. As it can be seen from this Figure 13, although all algorithms produce an almost similar coverage with the selected active nodes, IACDS is still better; it covers the same or more area but using fewer resources than the others.

CONCLUSION

In this paper, the primary effort has been devoted to

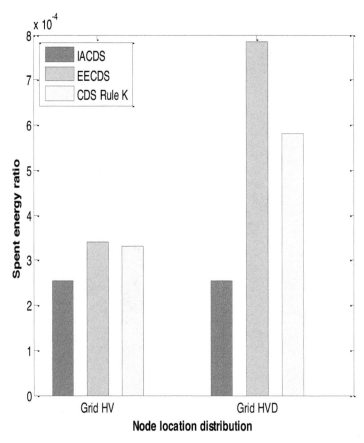

Figure 11c. Spent energy ratio in the CDS creation process.

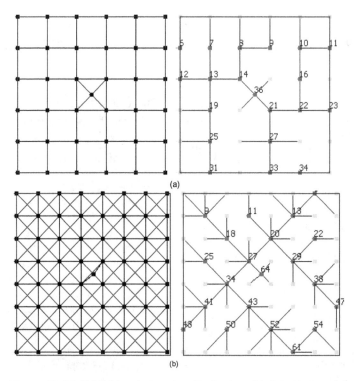

Figure 12. (a) Grid HV node location distribution. (b) Grid HVD node location distribution.

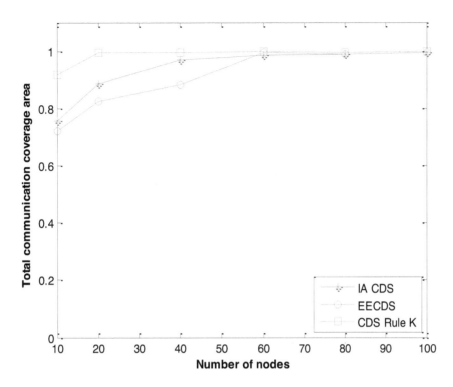

Figure 13. Total communication coverage area.

propose a new topology construction algorithm, namely, IACDS algorithm, a simple, distributed, interference-aware and energy-efficient topology construction mechanism that finds a sub-optimal connected dominating set (CDS) to turn unnecessary nodes off while keeping the network connected and providing complete communication coverage with minimum interference. IACDS algorithm utilizes a weighted distance-energy-interference-based metric that permits the network operator to trade off the lengths of the branches (distance) for the robustness and durability of the CDS (energy and interference). Through extensive simulation experiments, results show the superiority of the IACDS algorithm compared with the existing alternatives, EECDS and CDS-Rule-K algorithms, in terms of number of active nodes needed, message complexity, and energy efficiency.

REFERENCES

Akyildiz I, Su W, Sankarasubramaniam Y, Cayirci E (2002). A survey on sensor networks. IEEE Comm. Mag., 40: 102-114.

Burkhart M, Richenbach P, Wattenhofer R, Zollinger A (2004). Does topology control reduce interference?. Proc. 5th ACM Int. Symp. on Mobile Ad hoc Networking and Computing. pp. 9-19.

Butenko S, Cheng X, Oliveira C, Pardalos P (2004). A new heuristic for the minimum connected dominating set problem on ad hoc wireless networks. Kluwer Academic Publishers, pp. 61-73.

Chen B, Jamieson K, Balakrishnan H, Morris R (2002). Span: an energy-efficient coordination algorithm for topology maintenance in ad hoc wireless networks. ACM Wireless Networks, 8: 481-494.

Guha S, Khuller S (1998). Approximation algorithms for connected dominating sets. Algorithmica, 20: 374-387.

Hou T, Li V (1986). Transmission range control in multihop packet radio networks. IEEE Trans. Commun., 34: 38-44.

Kumar V, Arunan T, Balakrishnan N (2002). E-span: enhanced-span with directional antenna. Proc. of IEEE Conf. on Convergent Technol. for Asia-Pacific Region, 2: 675-679.

Li L, Halpern J, Bahl P, Wang Y, Wattenhofer R (2001). Analysis of a cone-based distributed topology control algorithm for wireless multi-hop networks. Proc. of Ann. ACM Symp. on Principles of Distributed Comput., pp. 264-273.

Li N, Hou J, Sha L (2003). Design and analysis of an mst-based topology control algorithm. Proc. of IEEE INFOCOM. 3: 1702-1712.

Meyer auf de Heide F, Schindelhauer C, Volbert K, Gruenewald M (2002). Energy, congestion and dilation in radio networks. Proc. 14th Ann. ACM Symp. on Parallel Algorithms and Architectures, 230-237.

Moaveni-Nejad K, Li X (2005). Low-interference topology control for wireless ad hoc networks. Ad Hoc and Sensor Wireless Networks. 1: 41-64.

Prakash R (1999). Unidirectional links prove costly in wireless ad-hoc networks. Proc. 3rd Int. Workshop on Discreet Algorithms and Methods for Mobile Comput. and Commun., pp. 15-22.

Richenband P, Schmid S, Wattenhofer R, Zollinger A (2005). A robust interference model for wireless ad-hoc networks. Proc. of IPDPS, 13: 239.

Roemer K, Mattern F (2004). The design space of wireless sensor networks. IEEE Wireless Comm. 11: 54-61.

Santi P (2005). Topology control in wireless ad hoc and sensor networks. ACM Comput. Surv., 37: 164-194.

Santi P (2005). Topology control. Topology Control in Wireless Ad Hoc and Sensor Networks. p. 1.

Takagi H, Kleinrock L (1984). Optimal transmission ranges for randomly distributed packet radio terminals. IEEE Trans. Commun., 32: 246-257.

Westhoff D, Girao J, Sarma A (2006). On Security Solutions for Wireless Sensor Networks, NEC J. Advan. Technol., 1(3): 2-6

Wu J, Cardei M, Dai F, Yang S (2006). Extended dominating set and its applications in ad hoc networks using cooperative communication. IEEE Trans. Parallel Distributed Syst. 17: 851-864.

Wu J, Dai F (2004). An extended localized algorithm for connected dominating set formation in ad hoc wireless networks. IEEE Trans. Parallel and Distributed Syst. 15: 908-920.

Wu J, Li H (1999). On calculating connected dominating set for efficient routing in ad hoc wireless networks. Proc. 3rd ACM int. Workshop on Discrete Algorithms and Methods for Mobile Comput. Commun., pp. 7-14.

Xu K, Gerla M, Bae S (2003). Effectiveness of RTS/CTS handshake in IEEE 802.11 based ad hoc networks. J. Ad Hoc Networks. 1: 107-123.

Xu K, Gerla M, Bae S (2003). Effectiveness of RTS/CTS handshake in IEEE 802.11 based ad hoc networks. J. Ad Hoc Networks. 1: 107-123.

Zhang X, Liu Q, Shi D,Liu Y, Yu X (2007). An average link interference-aware routing protocol for mobile ad hoc networks. In: ICWMC: Proc. Third Int. Con. Wireless Mobile Commun., Washington, DC, USA, IEEE Computer Society, p. 10.

Yuanyuan Z, Jia X, Yanxiang H (2006). Energy efficient distributed connected dominating sets construction in wireless sensor networks. Proc. Int. Con. Wireless Commun. Mobile Comput., pp. 797-802.

15

Optimization of spatial join using constraints based-clustering techniques

V. Pattabiraman

School of Computing Science and Engineering, VIT University - Chennai - 600 048, Tamil Nadu, India.
E-mail: pattabiraman.v@vit.ac.in.

Spatial joins are used to combine the spatial objects. The efficient processing depends upon the spatial queries. The execution time and input/output (I/O) time of spatial queries are crucial, because the spatial objects are very large and have several relations. In this article, we use several techniques to improve the efficiency of the spatial join; 1. We use R*-trees for spatial queries since R*-trees are very suitable for supporting spatial queries as it is one of the efficient member of R-tree family; 2. The different shapes namely point, line, polygon and rectangle are used for isolating and clustering the spatial objects; 3. We use scales with the shapes for spatial distribution. We also present several techniques for improving its execution time with respect to the central processing unit (CPU) and I/O-time. In the proposed constraints based spatial join algorithm, total execution time is improved compared with the existing approach in order of magnitude. Using a buffer of reasonable size, the I/O time is optimal. The performance of the various approaches is investigated with the synthesized and real data set and the experimental results are compared with the large data sets from real applications.

Key words: Spatial data mining, spatial clustering, spatial queries, spatial join.

INTRODUCTION

Spatial join operation is used to cluster two or more dataset with respect to a spatial predicate. Predicate can be a combination of direction, distance, and topological relations of spatial objects. In non spatial join, the joining attributes must be of the same type and in spatial join they can be of different types. Each spatial attribute is represented by its minimum bounding rectangles (MBR).

A typical example of spatial join is "Find all pair of rivers and cities that intersect". For example in Figure 1, the result of join between the set of rivers {R1, R2} and cities {C1, C2, C3, C4, C5} is { (R1, C1), (R2, C5)} (Shashi and Sanjay, 2003).

The spatial objects can be movable and immovable objects. Hash based algorithms focus only on natural join and equi-join. Since spatial objects are multidimensional data, we need new efficient spatial join algorithm. The methods for computing the spatial join are discussed in great detail for quad trees and similar access methods (Shou et al., 2003).

Key concepts

The two steps involved in spatial join are filter step and refine step. In filtering step, tuples whose minimum bounding rectangle (MBR) overlaps with query region are determined. This step is not computationally expensive but it requires at most four computations to determine rectangles intersection. In refine step, the tuples which passed the filter step is fed to the refinement step where exact spatial representation is used and spatial predicate is checked on these spatial representations. Refinement step is computationally expensive, but the number of tuples it processed in this step is less, due to initial filter step. Spatial join algorithm can be classified into three categories: nested Loop, tree matching and partition-based spatial merge join (Brinkhoff et al., 1993).

In general the spatial objects are of two types, namely, movable objects and immovable objects. The process that includes movable objects are like to identify the cell

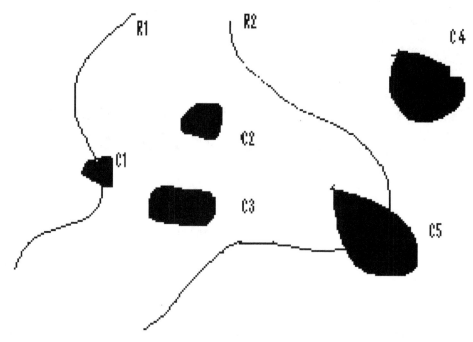

Figure 1. Example of spatial joins (Shashi and Sanjay, 2003).

phone towers of the respective cellular network service provider and in process of immovable object are to find identify the ideal object in the multi spectral image (spatial data). For the movable objects the spatial queries are classified into single scan queries and multi-scan queries.

In this paper, we propose the spatial joins for immovable objects like to find the banks that are nearer to the PSG College of Arts and Science. Initially, with the help of the constraints based spatial clustering algorithm the banks are identified within Coimbatore. Here we use R*-trees for spatial database querying.

Clustering introduction

Clustering is the classification of objects into different groups, or more precisely, the partitioning of a data set into subset (clusters), so that the data in each subset (ideally) shares some common trait-often proximity according to some defined distance measure. Data clustering is a common technique for statistical data analysis which is used in many fields, including machine learning, data mining, pattern recognition, image analysis and bioinformatics. The computational task of classifying the data set into k clusters is often referred to as k-clustering.

Types of clustering

Data clustering algorithms can be:

i. Hierarchical algorithms: Find successive clusters using previously established clusters. Hierarchical algorithms can be agglomerative ("bottom-up") or divisive ("top-down"). Agglomerative algorithms begin with each element as a separate cluster and merge them into successively larger clusters. Divisive algorithms begin with the whole set and proceed to divide it into successively smaller clusters.

ii. Partitioned algorithms: Typically determine all clusters at once, but can also be used as divisive algorithms in the hierarchical clustering.

iii. Density-based clustering algorithms: Are devised to discover arbitrary-shaped clusters. In this approach, a cluster is regarded as a region in which the density of data objects exceeds a threshold. DBSCAN and OPTICS are two typical algorithms of this kind.

iv. Two-way clustering, co-clustering or biclustering: Are clustering methods where not only the objects are clustered but also the features of the objects, that is, if the data is represented in a data matrix, the rows and columns are clustered simultaneously.

Another important distinction is whether the clustering uses symmetric or asymmetric distances. A property of Euclidean space is that distances are symmetric (the distance from object A to B is the same as the distance from B to A).

Spatial database system is a database system for managing spatial data. There is a rapid growth in number and the size of spatial databases for applications such as geo-marketing, traffic control, and environmental studies (Orenstein, 1986). Spatial data mining, or knowledge discovery in spatial databases refers to the extraction from spatial databases of implicit knowledge, spatial relations, or other patterns that are not explicitly stored (Shashi and Sanjay, 2003).

Clustering analysis for data in a 2-D space is considered as spatial data mining and its applications are geographic information systems, pattern recognition, medical imaging, marketing analysis, weather forecasting, etc. Clustering in spatial data is an active research area and most of the research focus on effectiveness and scalability.

RELATED WORK

Historical background

In 1986, Orenstein used grid based technique to perform spatial join. It is the first known technique to solve spatial join operation. Using a multidimensional grid, spaces are divided into smaller blocks, known as pixels. Then, z-ordering is used to order the pixels. Each object is approximated by the pixels which intersect with its MBR. As pixels are ordered by z-ordering, each object is represented by a set of z-values which are one-dimensional. Now, any one-dimensional indexing (e.g., B+-tree) can be used to sort them and by using sort-merge, spatial join operation is done. The performance of this technique solely depends on the granularity of the grids. The finer grids gives the accurate results but with higher memory consumption. Later on to remedy this problem, multidimensional indices (e.g., R-tree), which can directly handle spatial data, were devised. Various new spatial join algorithms (e.g., R-tree join, sort and match, spatial hash join, slot index hash join etc.) based on multi-dimensional index appeared (Brinkhoff et al., 1993).

Base work

In the base paper, data file is in (xls) format and used for the spatial join1 algorithm. Data is read into buffers with different last recently used (LRU) size in bytes 0, 8, 32, 128, 256 and 512 and compared with data in the size 1KB, 2KB, 4KB and 8KB (while inserting in the buffer) to find the optimal comparisions time.

In spatial join2 algorithm, before taking the buffer for the comparisions, apply the sorting technique to arrange the data(line shape) in order. For example each areas are identified with the unique identified code namely FID and it is sorted in order using nearby locations with detailed information like name of the place. Then use the spatial join1 algorithm for further process.

In spatial join3 algorithm, based on spatial ordering this algorithm creates a sequence of pairs of intersectional rectangles. Obviously, this sequence can also be used to determine the read schedule of the spatial join.

Partition clustering

K-means clustering

The K-means algorithm assigns each point to the cluster whose center (also called centroid) is the nearest. The center is the average of all the points in the cluster, that is, its coordinates are the arithmetic mean for each dimension separately over all the points in the cluster. For example, a data set has three dimensions and the cluster has two points: $X = (x_1, x_2, x_3)$ and $Y = (y_1, y_2, y_3)$. Then, the centroid Z becomes $Z = (z_1, z_2, z_3)$, where $z_1 = (x_1 + y_1)/2$ and $z_2 = (x_2 + y_2)/2$ and $z_3 = (x_3 + y_3)/2$.

The algorithm steps are:

i. Choose the number of clusters, k.
ii. Randomly generate k clusters and determine the cluster centers, or directly generate k random points as cluster centers.
iii. Assign each point to the nearest cluster center.
iv. Recompute the new cluster centers.
v. Repeat the two previous steps until some convergence criterion is met (usually that the assignment has not changed).

The main advantages of this algorithm are its simplicity and speed which allows it to run on large datasets. Its disadvantages are not yielding the same result with each execution, since the resulting clusters depend on the initial random assignments. It minimizes intra-cluster variance, but does not ensure that the result with global minimum of variance.

Quality threshold (QT) clustering algorithm

QT clustering is an alternative method of partitioning data, invented for gene clustering. It requires more computing power than k-means, but need not to specify the number of clusters in prior, and also it returns the same result when several executions takes place. The algorithm is:

i. The user chooses a maximum diameter for clusters.
ii. Build a candidate cluster for each point by including the closest point, the next closest, and so on, until the diameter of the cluster surpasses the threshold.
iii. Save the candidate cluster with the most points as the first true cluster, and remove all points in the cluster from further consideration. Must clarify what happens if more than 1 cluster has the maximum number of points?
iv. Recurse with the reduced set of points.

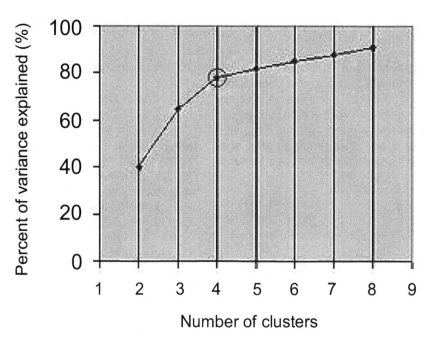

Figure 2. Percent of variance with the number of clusters.

The distance between a point and a group of points is computed using complete linkage, that is, as the maximum distance from the point to any member of the group.

Locality-sensitive hashing

Locality-sensitive hashing can be used for clustering. Feature space vectors are sets, and the metric used is the Jaccard distance. The feature space can be considered high-dimensional. The min-wise independent permutations LSH scheme (sometimes MinHash) is then used to put similar items into buckets. With just one set of hashing methods, there are only clusters of very similar elements. By seeding the hash functions several times (e.g. 20), it is possible to get bigger clusters.

Graph-theoretic methods

Formal concept analysis is a technique for generating clusters of objects and attributes, giving a bipartite graph representation for relations between the objects and attributes. Other methods for generating overlapping clusters are also discussed.

Determining the number of clusters

If the number of the clusters is not apparent from prior knowledge, it should be chosen in some way (Figure 2).

Several methods for this have been suggested within the statistical literature where one rule of thumb sets the number to:

$$k \approx (n/2)^{1/2} \qquad (1)$$

Where n is the number of objects (data points).

The "elbow" is indicated by the red circle. The number of clusters chosen should be 4. Another thumb rule looks at the percentage of variance explained as a function of the number of clusters: We should choose a number of clusters so that adding another cluster does not give much better modeling of the data. More precisely, if we graph the percentage of variance explained by the clusters against the number of clusters, the first clusters will add much information (explain a lot of variance), but at some point the marginal gain will drop, giving an angle in the graph. The number of clusters chosen at this point is "elbow criterion". This "elbow" cannot always be unambiguously identified. Percentage of variance explained is the ratio of the between-group variance to the total variance. A slight variation of this method plots the curvature within group variance.

Other ways to determine the number of clusters use Akaike's information criterion (AIC) or Bayesian information criterion (BIC), if it is possible to make a likelihood function for the clustering model. For example, the k-means model is almost a Gaussian mixture model and thus also determine AIC and BIC values.

In a Geographic Information System (GIS) application, studying the movement of pedestrians to identify optimal bank machine placements, for example, the

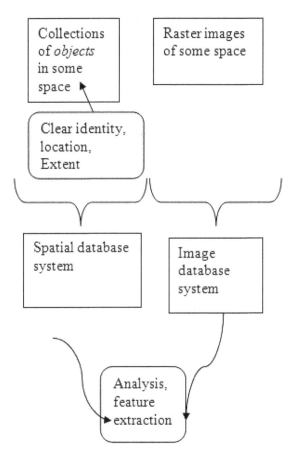

Figure 3. An example of a spatial database.

Table 1. Sample spatial data set.

FID	Shape	Division	School no	School name
0	Point	1	1	Alvernia Matric School
1	Point	6	2	Alwyn English Primary School
2	Point	12	3	Avila Matric School
3	Point	10	4	A.L.G Matriculation School
4	Point	6	5	Bharathi Vidya Bhavan

A spatial database may contain.

presence of a highway hinders the movement of pedestrians and should be considered as an obstacle. To the best of our knowledge, the following clustering algorithms for clustering spatial data with the constraints are DBRS, DBRS+, COD_CLARNS, AUTOCLUST, AUTOCLUST+, DBCluc, IKSCOC, GKSCOC and PSOCOC.

SPATIAL DATABASE

Spatial database is a system related to some space (Shashi and Sanjay, 2003). It should contain the collection of objects related to space of different types (Figure 3).

The different objects of spatial database

1. Point: represents a single location like city or particular place (Table 1)
2. Line: moving through space, connections in space (River, Highways).

3. Region: is an abstraction of an object with extent (forest, Lake, City).

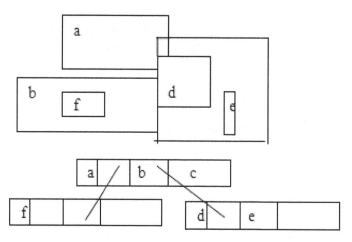

Figure 4. Data structure of R-tree.

Fundamental operations on spatial data (Algebra): i. Spatial selection, ii. Spatial join, iii. Spatial function application, iv. Other set operations,

Spatial selection - selection based on a spatial predicate. Example queries are given below:

a. "Find all schools in Coimbatore." – School select [center inside Coimbatore],
b. "Find all rivers intersecting a query window." - rivers select [route intersects Window],
c. "Find all big Municipal cities no more than 100 km from Coimbatore." - cities select[dist(center, Coimbatore 100 and pop > 500 000].

Spatial join - join based on a predicate comparing spatial attribute values (Mamoulis, 2001). Example queries are given below:

a. "Combine Municipal cities with their districts." – municipal cities districts join[center inside area],
b. "For each river, find all municipals cities within less than 50 km." – municipal cities rivers join[dist(center, route) < 50] a REGION value and a POINT value.

Spatial function application - We use operations of a spatial algebra computing new SDT values by regions lines and lines intersection:

a. In selection conditions.
b. Object algebra operators allow one to apply functions to each member of a set: i. Filter operator (FAD), ii. Replace, iii. Map and iv. Extend.

Example queries are given below:

"For each river going through Coimbatore, return the name, the part inside Coimbatore and the length of that part." - rivers select[route intersects Coimbatore] extend[intersection(route, Coimbatore) {part}] extend[length(part) {plength}] project[rname, part, length] (Ralf, 1994).

Spatial query processing

Since spatial database contains different objects, we need excellent access methods to handle the data. In traditional cases minimum bounding rectangle (MBR) concept was used (An and Sivasubaramainam 2001). In this case, two techniques are used:

(i) Filter step: Find all objects whose MBR intersects the query rectangle.
(ii) Refinement step: For those objects, check whether they really fulfill the query condition (if necessary, make use of the exact representation).

The basic idea of these methods is to decompose the data space into non-overlapping cells which can be computed by recursively cutting the space into two or four parts of equal size (Corral, 2000). Cells can be identified by a location code, called z-value, and a size code, called level. In R*-trees also, we should not give the redundant values (Guttmann, 1984).

R*-Tree

An R-tree is a B*-tree like access method that stores multidimensional rectangles as complete objects without clipping them or transforming them to higher dimensional points. Until now, the most efficient variant of the R-trees is experimentally shown to be the R*-tree. The R*-tree uses more sophisticated insertion and splitting algorithms than the original R-tree (Figure 4). However, there is

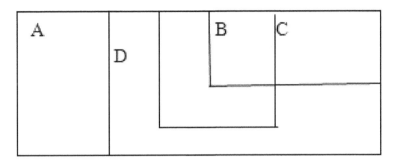

Figure 5. Example of spatial joins.

almost no difference in the data structure (Samet, 1990).

Advantage: Spatial object (or key) in a single bucket.
Disadvantage: Multiple search paths due to overlapping regions.

Spatial joins using R*-tree

The Central Processing Unit (CPU) time is calculated by using the floating point comparison.
Algorithm: (An and Sivasubaramainam, 2001)
SpatialJoinl (R, S: R_Node); (* height of R is equal height of S *)
FOR (all Es € S) DO
FOR (all E_R € R with E_R.rect o Es.rect # Ø) DO
IF (R is a leaf page) THEN
   (* (S is also a leaf page)*)
   Output E_R,E_S
ELSE
   ReadPage(E_R.ref); ReadPage(Es.ref);
   SpatialJoinl E_R.ref, E_S.ref
END
END
END
END SpatialJoin 1;

Here B and C are joined with D.
   We have to consider each and every point, that is, A with B, C, D and B with A, B, and C and so on (Figure 5). This will take the comparison more (n^2). So this is not effective for more spatial joins. Sorting the objects belonging to their category can be done in prior to Spatial Joins for time optimization of CPU process.

The proposed spatial join algorithm:

Step 1: Read the spatial objects with the constraints.
Step 2: Cluster the spatial objects based on the constraints.
Step 3: Sort the clustered spatial objects.

Step 4: Compare the nodes of the spatial objects with the relationship.

The objects may be in single relation or multiple relations (Manli, 2005). For example, combining the highways in Coimbatore city. This is simple relation. Combining the highways that are connecting the universities is multiple relations. Likewise the complexity may get increased.

CONSTRAINTS BASED SPATIAL JOIN
The proposed spatial joins with the constraints manipulate whole sets of spatial objects in a special way. The spatial join operation is a conceptual unit which aims to address the constraints based spatial objects.

K-medoids clustering under spatial data with obstacle constraints

This is because in spatial data, there are two kinds of objects namely movable and immovable objects. To identify the moving and non-moving objects, here we use K-medoids clustering with the obstacle using edge detection method. This helps to cluster the data with the obstacle constraints to identify movable and immovable objects under spatial data (images). It is easy and less time consumption (An and Sivasubaramainam, 2001). K-Medoids clustering generates the clusters with much related data.

Spatial joins for datasets

After K-Medoids, it is easy to join our spatial data. By using the modified spatial join algorithm we can combine our datasets (Faloutsos, 2000).

Spatial joins for images

If the images are spatial images then it is possible to cluster by using image clustering algorithms. After that,

Table 2. CPU and I/O time tunning.

The data were implemented by taking the buffer size of 1024 and the objects are all point shape					
		Size of pages			
		1 KByte	2 KByte	4 KByte	8 Kbyte
	0	24,727	12,479	5720	2837
	8	20318	12010	5720	2837
Size of buffer	32	13803	9589	5454	2822
	128	11359	6299	4474	2676
	512	10372	4964	2768	2181
	1024	9589	4372	1084	1027

we can use the modified Spatial join algorithm. Hence, to identify the movable objects we can use K-NN (K-nearest neighnour algorithm) and for immovable objects Spatial Joins Algorithm. The above process are most essential for applying spatial joins under the spatial data (images).

Spatial joins with points

With the help of clustering algorithm in data mining, it is possible to group the data under spatial objects (images). Consequently, we can use K-mediods constraint based clustering algorithms under the spatial data to find the cluster with the shapes like (point, line, polygon) based on the constraints like river, mountain, highway and buildings (Koudas, 2001). After finding the clusters under the spatial data we can apply spatial joins for easy identification of locations in geographical area (Yannis, 2005). The spatial joins are applicable only for the idle objects namely city, school, college and banks, etc. in the spatial objects. In base paper, they did not focused on clustering by assuming that the cluster already exist. Hence, straight away they have taken towards spatial joins. But in our work first we use clustering technique to identify the clusters under the spatial data, then it is taken for the spatial query processing and also for spatial joins.

The only data which is taken for the spatial join in the existing papers is the line objects. But we have taken various objects points namely: city, school, college and banks etc., in the spatial objects (image) to find the spatial joins between these object points. Likewise in future, it is possible to take the following combinations of spatial objects like point-point, line-line, polygon-polygon, point-line, line-point, point-polygon, polygon-line to find the spatial joins between them (Mamoulis, 2001).

In the base paper, without using algorithms with the properties, they have taken two files namely R and S for R* tree comparison. But it has high time consumption for comparison. The proposed spatial join algorithms will take the optimum time for the comparison. If we are applying the above strategies under the spatial data (image), it is very easy to identify or locate the exact geographical area which is needed for the user.

RESULTS AND DISCUSSION

Performance comparison of CPU and I/O time tunning

Table 2 shows the CPU and I/O time tuning based on the buffer size 1024KB and the objects are all point shape. In addition to preserve spatial locality in the buffer, this approach can be used without any extra cost. Hence, call this approach as local plane-sweep order and the corresponding join algorithm as spatial join3. Note that it is assumed in the algorithm sorted intersection test does not use sequences of rectangles as introduced originally, but sequences of entries for input and output and also assume that the spatial data to be taken for spatial join after applying the constraints based spatial clustering. Compared with the existing algorithm, the proposed method provide less complexity with the best improvement of CPU time using R*-tree spatial joins with the constraints.

Figure 6 shows the performance comparison chart based on the size of the pages with the size of the buffer. Comparing with the existing method, the proposed one gives better result without any extra cost and also the chart represents the multiples of bytes in terms of size of the pages with the buffer size.

One of the key applications of spatial join is to find all the objects which either intersect or overlap with each other. Some variants of spatial join (e.g., distance join) are used in data mining for data analysis and clustering. It can also be used to process closest-pairs query, k-nearest neighbors query, and ε-distance query. Figure 7 shows the comparison chart of processor based on the size of the pages with the size of the buffer. The Anthon 64FX, Pentium 4 (III, "Prescott") shows competent performance compare to other processor.

FUTURE WORK

There are some issues in spatial join that require further attention from research community. For processing spatial join queries, we usually follow filter and refine step

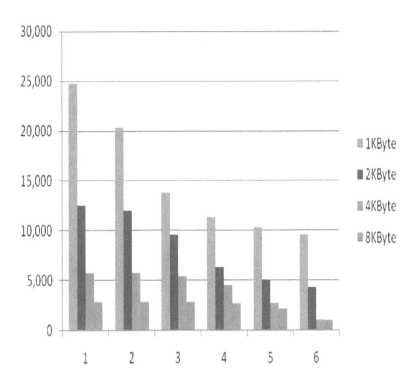

Figure 6. Size of pages in buffer vs. buffer size.

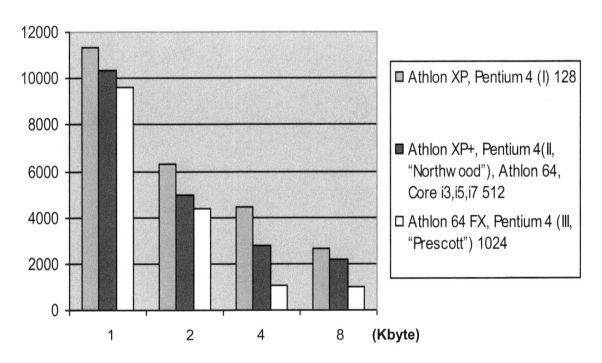

Figure 7. Comparison of processor, size of buffer and pages.

in order. In some cases, some variants of this (e.g., interleaving) may give us more benefit. We can explore where probable variants can be beneficial and what information we need to collect for this. Although, intersection join algorithms (e.g., R-tree join) can be directly extended for other types (e.g., distance join), it causes inefficient performance benefit. Various optimization techniques can be applied to rectify this.

Extending existing intersection join algorithms with various optimization criteria to other domain, it will be an interesting area for research.

Conclusion

In this paper, the discussion was focused on the spatial join effects with the constraints-based spatial data without any extra cost. The constraint-based spatial clustering reduces the time taken to identify the required objects under the spatial image. The R*-tree concept reduce the number of search pages to combine spatial objects. By using this, CPU utilization time increases, the number of comparison of spatial objects can be reduced and also reduces the I/O time.

REFERENCES

An NY, Sivasubaramainam A (2001). Selectivity estimation for Spatial Joins" Proceedings of the IEEE ICDE Conference. pp. 368-375.

Brinkhoff T. Kriege H, Seeger B (1993). Efficient processing of spatial joins using R-trees" Proceeding of ACM SIGMOD Conference. pp. 237-246.

Brinkhoff T, Kriegel H, Seeger B (1996). Parallel processing of spatial joins using R-trees" Proceeding of ICDE Conference. pp. 258-265.

Corral A, Manolopoulos Y, Theodorisdis Y. Vassilakopoulos M (2000). Closest pair queries in spatial databases", Proceedings of the ACM SIGMOD Conference. pp. 189-200.

Faloutsos C, Seeger B, Traina A, Traina C (2000). Spatial Join Selectivity Using Power Laws", Proceedings of the ACM SIGMOD Conference, pp. 177-188.

Guttmann A (1984). R-trees: A dynamic index structure for spatial searching", Proceedings of the ACM SIGMOD Conference. pp. 47-57.

Koudas N, Sevcik K (2000). High Dimensional Similarity Join", Proceedings of the ACM SIGMOD Conference. pp. 324-335.

Mamoulis N, Papadias D (2001). Multi-way Spatial Joins", "ACM Transactions on Database Systems. 26(4): 424 - 475.

Mamoulis N, Papadias D (2003). Slot Index Spatial Join", IEEE Transactions on Knowledge and Data Engineering. 15(1): 211-231.

Manli Z, Dimitris P, Jun Z, Dik Lun L (2005). Top-k Spatial Joins", IEEE Transactions on Knowledge and Data Engineering, 17(4): 567-579.

Orenstein JA (1986). Spatial Query Processing in an Object-Oriented Database System", Proceeding of ACM SIGMOD Int. Conf. on Management of Data, Washington D.C. pp. 326-333.

Patel JM, Dewitt DJ (1996). Partition Based Spatial-Merge Join", Proceedings of ACM SIGMOD Conference. pp. 259-270.

Agrawal R and Srikant R (1994). Fast Algorithms for Mining Association Rules," Proceeding of Very Large Data Bases Conference. pp. 487-499.

Samet H (1990). The Design and Analysis of Spatial Data Structures", Addison Wesley, 1990.

Shashi S, Sanjay C (2003). Spatial Databases A Tour", First Edition, Prentice Hall, 2003.

Shou Y, Mamoulis N, Cao H, Papadis D, Cheung DW (2003). Evaluation of Iceberg Distance Joins", Proceedings of the Eighth International Symposium on Spatial and Temporal Databases, 2003, pp. 270 - 288.

Yannis RM, Apostolos P, Michel Gr. Vassilakopulous (2005). Spatial Databases, Technologies, Techniques and Trends", IDEA Group Publishing.

Ralf HG (1994). An Introduction to Spatial Database Systems", Special Issue on Spatial Database Systems of the VLDB Journal, 3(4): 357-399.

16

The Writing-Pal tutoring system: Development and design

Jianmin Dai, Roxanne B. Raine, Rod Roscoe, Zhiqiang Cai and Danielle S. McNamara*

Institute of Intelligent Systems, Department of Psychology, University of Memphis
38152 Memphis, USA.

Writing-Pal is an intelligent tutoring system designed to offer high school students writing strategy instruction and guided practice to improve their essay-writing skills. Students are taught to use writing strategies via interactive lessons, games, and essay-writing practice. This paper presents an overview of Writing-Pal's foundations and design, which are based on key pedagogical and educational-technology, and design principles. These considerations are important for the efficacy of the system, as well as its stability and portability in diverse settings, such as the laboratory, classroom, or students' homes. We expect this paper to be of interest to educational developers, as well as other developers who may face similar goals and challenges.

Key words: Writing-pal, writing strategy training, architecture, design, intelligent tutoring system, essay-writing skills, vicarious learning, pedagogy, strategy instruction.

WRITING STRATEGY INSTRUCTION

Effective written communication is an essential skill with critical importance for educational and professional success. Research has indicated that students' writing abilities not only affect their acceptance into college, but are also key predictors of success once enrolled (Geiser and Studley, 2001; Kellogg and Raulerson, 2007; Powell, 2009). The value of writing does not decline after college; professionals in nearly every field report that writing is a significant aspect of gaining employment, day-to-day work, and attaining promotions (Light, 2001; Porter, 1997; Sharp, 2007). Unfortunately, the National Commission on Writing (NCW, 2004; 2008) and National Assessment of Educational Progress (NAEP, 2002) have found that many students tend to be very poor writers. Given the near universal importance of writing, these findings are of grave concern.

The improvement of students' writing via instruction has been a goal of decades of research (e.g., de la Paz, 2007; Graham and Perin, 2007; Hillocks, 1984). One of the major factors that emerge from such reviews is the importance of scaffolded strategy instruction with guided practice. In terms of pedagogical design principles,

instructional interventions need to a) teach specific and explicit strategies for planning, drafting, and revising text, b) teach the background knowledge needed to understand and implement those strategies, and c) provide opportunities to practice those strategies over time with ample individualized feedback. For example, de la Paz and Graham (2002) trained adolescents to use a "PLAN and WRITE" strategy. The PLAN strategy helped students plan their essays by attending to the prompt, generating main ideas and supporting ideas, and organizing these ideas. The WRITE strategy helped students to compose their essays by remembering to utilize their plans and goals, and trying to use more varied sentence structure and vocabulary. The strategy instruction took place over a lengthy period (6 weeks) and several stages, including explicit discussions of how and why to use the strategies, teacher-led demonstrations and modeling, and opportunities for supported and independent practice. This training program, typical of strategy-based writing instruction interventions, resulted in student essays that were greater in length, used a more sophisticated and varied vocabulary, and were of higher overall quality. These positive effects persisted over time (that is, after a one month delay).

Although effective, a clear challenge for such strategy instruction is that it requires a tremendous amount of time

*Corresponding author. E-mail: dsmcnamara1@gmail.com.

and effort on the part of teachers - teachers who must already juggle the demands of grading multiple essay drafts from multiple classes, along with other curricular goals such as literacy and literary analysis. Many teachers, especially in the upper grades, may not be able to devote weeks or months to the remediation of "students" poor writing skills. One solution that has been effectively implemented in other learning domains is incorporating intelligent tutoring systems (ITSs) into the curriculum. ITSs programs typically use complex algorithms and/or interactive designs to teach content and strategies in a dynamic and adaptive manners similar to expert human tutors. Indeed, when designed well, these computer systems can support meaningful learning gains comparable to one-on-one human tutoring (Graesser et al., 2005; McNamara et al., 2004; Quintana et al., 2004; VanLehn et al., 2007). Moreover, by providing supplemental instruction inside or outside of the classroom, ITS use can reduce teachers' burden of assisting struggling students (or enriching advanced students) while also adhering to broader curricular constraints. In terms of educational technology design principles, such systems need to be a) accessible to as many students as possible, b) interactive, c) flexible and reconfigurable, and d) able to trace and respond to students' learning processes.

Numerous ITSs have been developed, most often in science (e.g., Graesser et al., 2004; VanLehn et al., 2005) and mathematics (e.g., Aleven and Koedinger, 2002; Beal, et al., 2010). A handful of systems have targeted reading skills (e.g., McNamara et al., 2006). However very few have addressed writing strategies. Summary Street (Wade-Stein and Kintsch, 2004) assists students with writing text summaries. The system initially provides guidelines and examples, and then employs Latent Semantic Analysis (LSA) algorithms to judge whether students' summaries are of sufficient length and relevance. Strategy practice using this software has resulted in significantly improved student summaries. However, Summary Street does not address whole essay composition. Several commercially-available computer technologies focus on giving detailed, extensive feedback on essay quality with automated essay scoring. For example, WPP Online implements the Process Essay Grade (PEG) scoring system developed by Ellis Page (Page and Petersen, 1995; Shermis et al., 2001). WPP Online provides feedback on a variety of dimensions, including sentence structure, word choice, mechanics, and organization. Many skills can be reviewed and practiced in brief animated tutorials. However, the central focus is on essay writing and scoring. The Criterion system developed by the Educational Testing Service (ETS) also offers extensive automated essay scoring (Burstein et al., 2004; Burstein et al., 2003). As with WPP Online, Criterion can rate essays based on usage, grammar, mechanics, and certain elements of style and structure.

The Criterion system does not currently offer any direct strategy instruction, although students do receive ample feedback that contains tips and guidance for future writing. In these kinds of essay scoring systems, students are encouraged to review their feedback and strive to improve their scores. Although such systems may satisfy the pedagogical principle of practice and feedback, they often do not adequately address principle of scaffolded strategy instruction. As such, they may neglect one of the critical elements that are known to effectively improve students' writing skills. In contrast, such instruction is the central aim of Writing-Pal (W-Pal), an intelligent tutor for writing strategies. W-Pal teaches specific strategies used by competent writers. It then encourages students to practice increasingly difficult essay-writing tasks that incorporate these strategies. Essay scoring algorithms are used to provide the feedback students need to gauge and improve their performance.

WRITING-PAL FRAMEWORK AND PRINCIPLES

W-Pal provides scaffolded strategy instruction via a series of Writing Strategy Modules corresponding to three broad phases of the writing process: prewriting, drafting, and revising. The prewriting modules (Freewriting and Planning) teach strategies to help students access their prior knowledge, generate potential arguments and evidence, and organize these elements into a structured essay plan. The drafting modules (Introduction Building, Body Building, and Conclusion Building) cover strategies for providing a clear and engaging start to an essay, developing one's arguments in several body paragraphs, and then finishing with a strong conclusion that ties the essay together. Finally, the revising modules (Paraphrasing, Cohesion Building, and overall Revising) are designed to assist students with finding better and more diverse ways to clearly and coherently express themselves and carefully review their work to make sure it meets the requirements of a thorough essay. Each module comprises an instructional Lesson and several practice Challenges. More detail about the content and rationale of individual modules is provided elsewhere (McNamara et al., in press), but a brief overview is provided here with an example of one of the modules.

Each lesson is developed using a similar overall narrative and context: lessons take place in a virtual classroom in which a "teacher" agent named Dr. Julie discusses writing strategies with two "student" agents, Sheila and Mike. Each agent is a computer-simulated character with a distinct appearance, voice, and personality. Thus, rather than purely didactic tutorials in which information is merely delivered to students, each module is a highly interactive dialog between the three agents. Research on vicarious learning with animated pedagogical agents (Craig et al., 2004; Johnson et al., 2000) has shown that this can be a powerful means of making content and strategy instruction available to students. For example, the iSTART system, which effectively improves students' reading comprehension via self-explanation strategies, relies on a similar arrangement of agents and vicarious learning (McNamara et al., 2004). Within each lesson, students are provided background knowledge about the target essay goal and specific strategies for achieving those goals. Often, these strategies and requirements are summarized by a mnemonic device that serves as a checklist students can use to guide their writing process. Many examples are provided throughout the lesson. Also included within each lesson are a series of quiz-like or game-like "checkpoints." Some checkpoints ask multiple-choice questions to probe recall of recently covered information. Others ask students to apply the strategies or generate small samples of text. Pedagogically, these checkpoints help to focus and maintain students' attention on key concepts, while providing immediate opportunities for practice with feedback. They also serve as assessment points to identify how well students are progressing through the lesson.

Strategy instruction and practice are not limited to the lessons and checkpoints. Each strategy lesson is complimented by numerous challenges. These challenges are game-like opportunities for extended practice with feedback from the system. Others have proposed that the important factors influencing the success of edutainment environments are storytelling, challenge, interactivity, and interface (Embi, 2005). To address these needs, each of our challenges contain a narrative and/or immersive challenge, scaffolded difficulty, feedback, and are designed within the same interface framework. More specifically, we expect that our challenges meet the edutainment requirements set forth by Embi (2005) in their possession of these features. The narrative or immersive aspects of the challenges are achieved through maintaining underlying themes within each activity, many of which recur throughout numerous activities and across lessons. Underlying themes provide an underlying storyline to provoke student interest. The inclusion of scaffolded difficulty within each challenge serves to prod students in a way that should build off of the knowledge students should have obtained by viewing each challenge's corresponding lesson. Interactivity is enhanced by personalized artificial intelligence and feedback. This feedback is provided in the form of direct and immediate responses to the students' particular answers to questions, and should aid in further scaffolding their knowledge as well as increase the interactivity of the system. Finally, the inclusion of these challenges within the familiar W-Pal interface is expected to provide ease of use and control for students with regard to navigating and understanding the game design. Embi's (2005) requirements and W-Pal's strategy for addressing these requirements are explained below in further detail.

Underlying themes

Some challenges ask students to identify and classify examples (e.g., identify an appropriate thesis statement) whereas others ask students to manipulate information (e.g., sort argument and evidence sentences into an outline) or generate text (e.g., write a conclusion paragraph for an essay). Although each challenge includes a storyline, the challenges are diversified enough to differ in the extent to which they are puzzle-like or narrative. One narrative game is "Speech Writer," in which students are placed in the role of a speech editor for a politician. Depending on their proficiency in the task, they may hear the crowd cheer at the end of their speech, or they may hear cricket noises if they have performed poorly. A more puzzle-based game is "Ready, Sets, Go," which is a card game that resembles Gin Rummy, wherein students match strategies with their associated lessons.

Scaffolding and games

Each challenge game builds off of the knowledge students are expected to have obtained within the challenges' corresponding lessons. Thus, they are a slight degree more difficult than the checkpoint quizzes and activities within the lessons themselves. Furthermore, many of the challenge games have more than one version. As such, students who have mastered the easier versions of these challenges can move on to more difficult challenges. For example, in the first version of "Ready, Sets, Go" that is described above, students get a "hand" of cards that have strategies and their associated lessons written on the cards. They are to match these strategy/lesson cards with lesson cards that appear at the top of their screens. In the more difficult version of this game, many of the cards in the students' hand do not have the lesson printed on them. Rather, they have the strategy listed without the lesson and must match the strategy card to its corresponding lesson relying on their recollection of content presented within the W-Pal system. In this way, the first game allows the student to become familiarized with the task and to receive further exposure to the content, whereas the second, more difficult version of the game, tests this associative knowledge between strategies and lessons.

Interactivity and feedback

In many of the W-Pal challenges, feedback on students' responses is generated based on Natural Language Processing (NLP) algorithms. Students practice strategies and skills taught in the lessons as they play the challenges. By making strategy practice game-like, we hope to maintain greater student engagement, and thus

Figure 1. From this page, students can easily navigate from one section of Writing-Pal to another.

increase the amount of time that students choose to practice (Gee, 2003; 2008). In this way, we address two important aspects of educational games: pedagogy and game design components (Tan et al., 2007).

Interface and design

The interface of W-Pal (shown in Figure 1) is self-contained, intended to be used over a long period of time (6 months to one year and beyond), supplemented by tutorial videos (The student tutorial video is available on YouTube: http://youtu.be/bKovhZ-6mNY) for "teachers" or students, sufficiently consistent across tasks, easily accessed locally or remotely on any browser or operating system, and quick to load with minimal storage and processing demands. The details behind these requirements and how they are met are explained in the fourth section of this paper, wherein we discuss the design of our system.

WRITING-PAL STRATEGY LESSONS AND TRAINING

To provide a more concrete example of W-Pal's instructional content, consider the Writing Strategy Module for learning how to begin an essay, "Introduction Building." The Introduction Building lesson begins with a discussion among the agents about the importance of beginning an essay well and the rhetorical goals that a good introduction must satisfy. This is summarized using

the "TAG" mnemonic and checklist: (T)hesis statement, (A)rgument preview, and (G)rab the reader's attention. Students are then taught how to write a thesis statement that clearly states the author's position and connects to the main supporting arguments. Next, students are taught to preview their arguments in more detail, making clear to the reader what the essay will be about without explaining the evidence yet. Finally, students are presented with several techniques they can use to try to engage the reader's interest, such as sharing a personal anecdote, asking leading questions, or using an illustrative historical example. Interspersed with these strategies are several checkpoints in which students are asked to judge or identify examples. A simple quiz-like checkpoint is shown in Figure 2. Another set of checkpoints within the Introduction Building module is framed as a game, "Mission to the Moon." In this game, students collect moon rock samples by correctly identifying the attention-grabbing technique used in a paragraph. Students receive points for each correct answer and a final score at the end.

The Introduction Building lesson discusses the requirements of introductory paragraphs along with strategies for fulfilling those requirements. Although there are opportunities to practice within the lesson, the majority of the practice is situated within several game-like challenges. New games are continuously being developed, but here we will highlight two cases. The first challenge, "Essay Launcher," (Figure 3) revisits the "Mission to the Moon" checkpoint narrative, except that now the player is returning their spaceships home to

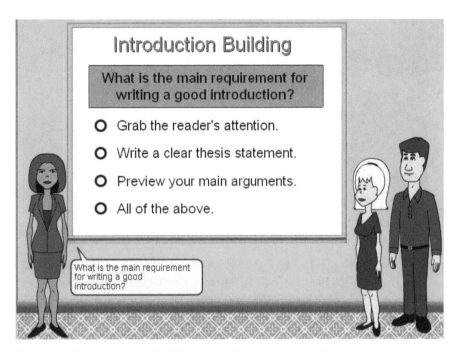

Figure 2. The Introduction Building lesson includes checkpoints that are intended to keep the students' attention during the lessons.

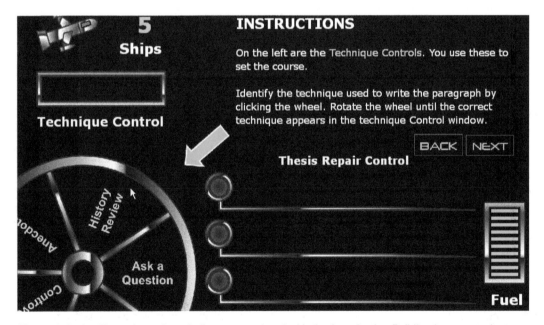

Figure 3. In the Essay Launcher challenge associated with the Introduction Building lesson, students are required to identify the technique used in a given introductory paragraph and chose the best thesis sentence for the given paragraph.

Earth. To successfully pilot five ships home, students must perform two tasks: 1) identify the attention-grabbing technique used to write the paragraph (from a list of five techniques), and 2) choose a thesis statement that would be most appropriate for that paragraph (from a list of three options). In this challenge, students are exposed to many introduction examples and asked to think critically about their defining features. For example, what cues or information indicates that a historical example is being used? What kinds of language are used when the Set a Scene technique is employed? What is the basic structure of a higher quality, relevant thesis statement?

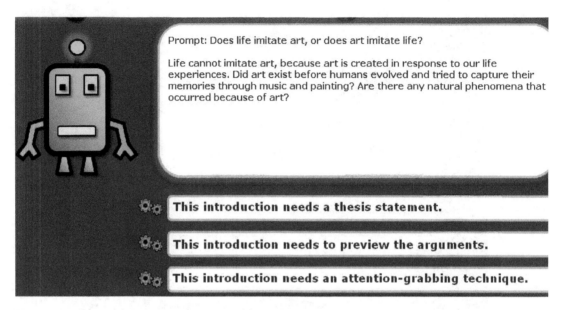

Figure 4. In the challenge Fix It, students must identify problems with introductory paragraphs.

A second challenge, called "Fix It," (Figure 4) does not possess a story-like narrative, but is instead more like a game-show. In the "Regular Round," students are presented with an example introduction and asked to identify what is wrong with the paragraph, if anything. That is, does the paragraph lack a thesis statement, an argument preview, an attention-grabber, or is the paragraph complete? This evaluation task helps students practice using the TAG mnemonic to evaluate the completeness of an introduction, which is a skill they must learn to apply to their own writing. Students earn points for making correct answers with few mistakes and are given feedback on right or wrong answers. After identifying a problem in the Regular Round, students enter a "Bonus Round" in which they are asked to choose (from a list of two options) a piece of text that will fix the paragraph. If a thesis statement was missing, students must choose an appropriate thesis, and so on. After completing six Regular Rounds, students who have achieved a high score are rewarded with access to a "Super Bonus Round." In this round, students are shown a flawed introduction, told what the flaw is, and then must generate the missing text. For example, if the paragraph lacks an argument preview, the students will need to fix the paragraph by generating plausible arguments. NLP algorithms determine whether students' generated text is adequate (see McNamara et al., in press). Via this challenge, students' skills in both self-evaluation and generation of essay introductions are practiced and reinforced.

It is important to note that writing strategies are not practiced only componentially via targeted challenges such as Essay Launcher and Fix It. Students also practice writing full essays using the Essay Writing tools. At any time or when assigned an essay by a teacher,

students can write an essay on one of many pre-set prompts and receive feedback (generated via NLP) on various aspects of their writing. Writing feedback first focuses on basic concerns such as length, relevance, and paragraph structure. Students are asked to revise to improve their essays. Once basic elements are in place, essays receive holistic scores along with feedback targeting the weakest areas. For example, if a student writes a "Good" essay (rating of 4 out of 6), they will be reminded of specific revising strategies and given additional feedback on two areas that could benefit from focused revision (that is, introductions, body paragraphs, conclusions, or mechanics). This process is iterative. For assigned essays, students may revise as many times as allowed by their instructor. For purely practice essays, students may revise as many times as they wish.

Overall, the content and design of the Strategy Module Lessons follow the pedagogical design principles outlined above. By participating in the full series of eight modules, students are taught a variety of explicit strategies for all three phases of the writing process - prewriting, drafting, and revising. Each lesson provides students with the background knowledge needed to enact the strategies, as well as opportunities for immediate practice and feedback. Further strategy practice is offered in the form of engaging games that allow students to practice every strategy, with automated feedback, whenever the students desire. Finally, the essay writing interface and feedback allows students to combine and integrate these skills in the process of composing complete essays. While writing and revising, students can freely return to the various lessons and challenges for review and practice. In fact, students are often encouraged to do so in the feedback they receive. As mentioned above, these lessons and training components are presented in a user-

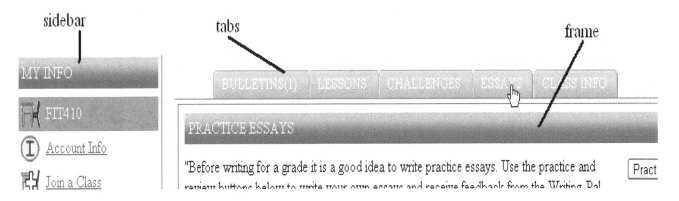

Figure 5. The W-Pal interface's navigability is enhanced by the use of frames and a consistent sidebar. The current activity appears in a frame (the Practice Essay activity is pictured above), whereas the tabs above the frame and the sidebar remain constant while the user is in W-Pal. Some other activities appear in a pop-up window with the W-Pal interface in the background behind the window.

friendly way with an all-inclusive desktop workspace, which is intended to facilitate the student's ease of use with the system. W-Pal is designed to achieve the interface needs of an educational system. The details behind W-Pal's design and how it accommodates ease-of-use within its interface are described below.

WRITING-PAL DESIGN

W-Pal's is designed to provide a powerful learning environment that has an easy-to-master navigational logic. By streamlining the users' interactions with the system, the teachers can dedicate their time and efforts to more important tasks (e.g., actual teaching), and the students can spend more time learning about essay-writing (as opposed to learning how to use the computer program itself). However, this is not the only consideration that should be fundamental to an ITS's design. Other features needed in an optimized educational environment include accessibility, relative consistency, pedagogically motivated and accurate feedback methods and algorithms, and flexible configurability. Our solutions to these obstacles to comprise of a number of design features that, although certainly not novel, we expect to be of interest and useful to other designers, whether they be pedagogically-oriented or pleasure-based gaming interface designers. Below, we discuss each of these features in turn: navigability and consistency, accessibility, feedback accuracy, and flexible configurability.

Navigability and consistency

Navigability refers to the ease with which one can retrieve useful and desired information from a system. Tried and true measures of navigation success include time spent getting from one's current state to a desired goal location, self-reported ease of use, amount of support needed to learn the aspects of a system, and the degree to which features within a system are used or visited (e.g., Palmer, 2002; Pitkow and Kehoe, 1996). Consistency, on the other hand, regards the system's overall coherence and presentation style (Nielson, 1993). For example, in a consistent multiple-paged interface, the user will know where to look for links to desired pages by virtue of having previously visited other pages with similar presentation styles. That is, if a system has sufficient consistency, users should have greater ease in navigating the system because components are presented similarly throughout the interface for the entire system. Thus, although navigability and consistency are entirely different aspects of a virtual environment, it is appropriate to discuss them in tandem as consistency can contribute so greatly to the system's navigability.

Consistency within W-Pal is achieved in a number of ways. First, the overarching frame of W-Pal is constant throughout one's W-Pal experience. The outer frame of the system is comprised of a tabulated button list at the top of the screen, situated over an embedded window and a sidebar containing various other links. This frame-like structure allows the user to navigate through many aspects of the system without the framing area changing at all. The window within the frame is where pages such as class bulletins, lesson lists, game choices, and scoreboards can appear. Thus, many aspects of the W-Pal system are accessed through a window that is embedded within the main W-Pal frame. A sidebar also remains constant, which provides links to other classes in which the user might be enrolled, links to printable PDF handouts for students (or answer keys to these handouts for teachers), and other such supplementary system tools (Figure 5).

However, there are aspects of W-Pal that are best experienced when not embedded within the overarching

W-Pal frame. Namely, the lessons, challenges, and essay-writing practice components and tests are more immersive if they appear in their own windows as opposed to the alternative option of presenting them embedded within the frame, which might be distracting to users who are engaging in an interactive task. As such, these activities appear in a pop-up window. This solution optimizes the consistency of the system without compromising its immersive potential. While students have a pop-up window open, they are prevented from engaging in other tasks. However, they are free to close the current pop-up window at any time. If they close a lesson video before completing it, they can return to their desired spot in the lesson videos up to their level of progress in that particular lesson. For example, if a student were interrupted after watching 75% of the Introduction Building lesson, the student would return to that 75% marker when the lesson was resumed. Furthermore, the student could then return to any point in that lesson from 0 to 75% (any point up to the point at which the video had been watched). After viewing a lesson in its entirety, students are able to access any point in the lesson at any time in the future. This feature of resuming where one left off and unlocking as one progresses is achieved by an XML-Binding mechanism that bridges the modules and their components. The lesson record is updated to the server every 5 seconds, which provides accuracy in assessing the student's real-time progress within the ITS.

This use of framing and pop-up windows does not only serve to strengthen the system's configurability and navigability. Rather, the combination of an outer frame, an embedded window and supplementary pop-up windows also contribute to W-Pal's overall usability. As Shneiderman (1998) points out, user interfaces should be well organized (Fang and Holsapple, 2007). These features, along with a clear presentation, help ease cognitive load demands on users. Other aspects of the W-Pal experience should also aid the users with finding their way around. Namely, the system's consistency is enhanced by the long-term usage with which its clients will be exposed. That is, once they have learned the links within its constant external shell, they will be repeatedly exposed to this exact same frame each and every time they use any part of the W-Pal program. In any case, all users are provided with a quick and clear tutorial video in their first exposure to the system. These aspects of configurability and hence navigability are expected to contribute to the user's experience in W-Pal based on prior research showing that configurability and navigability are substantial factors influencing usability (Palmer, 2002).

Accessibility

W-Pal's accessibility arises from its ease of use across platforms, as well as its functionality in environments with internet connectivity limitations. There is an online version that can be deployed to a web server, as well as a downloadable version that is compatible with Mac or Windows operating systems. An important consideration in the development of systems that are intended for use in classrooms is the availability of (or lack of) a network connection. The W-Pal system is designed to run smoothly with or without a network connection. All actions relying on network connections can be recorded into a network log in the case that a network connection is not available. The network data service layer has been designed to provide the connection managing, XML-RPC and real-time message services. This Connection Managing Service monitors the network connecting state. This prevents network disconnections from hindering the students' learning processes. Because user interactions depend on the network connection, the connection managing service ensures that all interaction data is saved to a local database.

Additionally, a Database Service Component provides the JDBC-driven SQL interface for the students to store or query the learning data (including record of their progress and achievements) from MySQL database on the server. For example, a Freewriting Feud game, the final score needs to be stored to the database after finishing the game, and the day's top 5 leaders are displayed via a database query. Local data is uploaded to a centralized server through calling Database Service when the network is connected. An auto-restore mechanism is incorporated in the system so students can continue from their previous break point by retrieving the current state from the data server.

Feedback accuracy

W-Pal achieves its capacity to provide immediate and personalized feedback via NLP tools, such as a lemmatizer, syntax parser, WordNet utility, and Latent Semantic Analysis, among others (McNamara et al., in press). Although NLP is computationally costly, it is necessary for providing the level of analysis and precision of feedback that W-Pal aims to achieve. Certainly, as shown above, others have found systems similar to this one are quite effective in other domains (e.g., Litman and Silliman, 2004). In Freewriting Feud, students are asked to freewrite on a topic. Based on our experiments with freewrites, we have determined a number of words that appear frequently in freewrites that human raters scored high, but do not appear in freewrites that received low scores from human raters. As such, once the student has freewritten on a topic, we can assume that their freewrite would be scored highly by human raters if they used the words that are unique to highly scored freewrites. Thus, in the Freewrite Feud game, the appearances of six keywords in the user's freewrite are the basis for their success in the Freewrite Feud challenge. Once the student has completed a freewrite, these key words flip one-by-one in 1-second intervals.

W-Pal has required an extensive amount of corpora collection in order to develop lessons and practice modules. For example, the corpus of introductions is a collection of essay introductions used in the Dungeon Escape game. For each lesson, corpora must be collected to determine correlations between essay features and human-rated quality. To date, we have collected nearly 1,000 essays which have been scored by expert human raters. Additionally, these human ratings have been correlated with our Coh-Metrix features (see McNamara et al., in press) to determine automated algorithms for providing feedback on individuals' essay and freewrite inputs to the system. Aside from the value added to our system in terms of correlations between computational assessments of essay features and human ratings, our corpora of sample essays also inform our system design in a number of ways. For example, the freewriting corpus provides a collection of writing assignments, prompts, and examples of good and poor freewriting texts. Based on our studies with human subjects, we have determined effective freewriting instructions that depend on the user's preexisting essay-writing skill level. Higher skilled writers do not benefit from the same kind of practice as lesser skilled writers. This corpus has also helped us to determine differences in freewrite content between higher and lower skilled writers. With this knowledge, we can make more educated decisions about how to structure our practice exercises and challenges as we continue to improve our system.

NLP algorithms play a critical role in W-Pal, both during the mini- and full practice lessons as well as during the final phase of writing complete essays (see McNamara et al., in press). Supplying adequate and online feedback to the students about their writing is one of the most challenging aspects and most important features of the system. Algorithms are needed to assess students' input during practice as well as their writing quality and the strategies they have used when writing full essays. These NLP tools include a lemmatizer, part-of-speech tagger, syntactic parser, Latent Semantic Analysis, and WordNet. These tools are deployed on the high-speed server. Each module in W-Pal can access these tools using a client-server socket connection.

Configurability

W-Pal is highly configurable in two regards. First, it is highly configurable from a designer's perspective, allowing for quick modification to the system throughout its development and deployment. Second, it also provides its teachers with a great deal of power in personalizing their courses on a global level (that is, all of their classes) as well as a local level (that is, for particular classes). The W-Pal lessons are constructed with Media Semantics' Character Builder software (www.mediasemantics.com), enhanced by Loquendo text-to-speech engine technology (www.loquendo.com). The Loquendo text-to-speech technology gives a substantial amount of control over the agents, such as playing, pausing, resuming, and stopping the agent dialogue, as well as dispatching the event to callback when completing one of the XML-formatted scripts. This design allows for ease in changing dialogue speech scripts as well as control over the flow at each speaking end-point. To achieve these implementations, W-Pal currently relies on Character Builder software to produce flash files of the lessons and feedback dialogue speeches.

W-Pal includes numerous basic components that are presented via the flash lesson player, including the agents' dialogue, the interface and avatar animations, a variety of games' background music, and various other sound effects. In order to incorporate such a diverse collection of features in the W-Pal user interface, a common library is required. This library is comprised of components for converting, loading and playing multimedia, parsing corpora, designing animations, and designing the dialogue system. Because the common library is independent from many of the interactive activities, they can easily be replaced and modified. Another advantage of the use of this common library throughout the system relates to the system's accessibility. By drawing from a common library, many sound events in the games and other components of the ITS can occur by issuing a call back action to a single file. Each time an event happens that should invoke that sound effect (or video, image, etc.), only one audio file needs to be stored and accessed. The reuse of sound effects within the common library reduces memory requirements for those running the system locally by downloading it on their computers and it also minimizes load time for those accessing the system online. An additional component of the ITS stores the lessons. More specifically, the Strategy Lesson Training Index XML file stores the strategy lessons. A training index xml file is used to store the strategy lessons in order to easily add, delete, or update the strategy lesson without having to make revisions to the program codes. All corpora are described in XML format. Therefore an XML Corpus Parser has been built to easily reuse these corpora for different purposes.

Aside from W-Pal's configurability capabilities for the designer and future designers who might modify the system, it is also highly configurable for each individual teacher as well. For example, teachers may create their own essay-writing assignments or tests, choose to have these essays timed or untimed, proof-readable or required to be completed by the students in one sitting, and other such specifications. The teachers may also choose to provide a particular assignment to all of their classes or to individual classes. Due dates can easily be assigned within the system as well. Teachers can add other instructors, delete and add students to their databases, evaluate and modify scores on essay assignments, track students' progress throughout the system on an individual basis or for the class as a whole, create assignments, adjust W-Pal grades, make bulletins, and designate tasks as priorities that must be completed before students are allowed to navigate to any other part of the system.

DISCUSSION

W-Pal has been in the development process for over a year. Although it is not the only writing tutorial program, it is indeed different from those currently available, commercially or otherwise. W-Pal includes strategy instruction that is soundly based in empirical studies found throughout ITS disciplines, as well as pedagogically effective components such as scaffolded training, game-based learning, and feedback-enhanced practice. W-Pal includes feedback on a number of levels and provides a number of different types of learning experiences for students. In addition, it incorporates a number of important design principles that have been shown to substantially increase usability and overall user experience. The underlying themes give it conceptual consistency, whereas the games are scaffolded to provide enough variation with the game play without overwhelming the students. NLP and empirical studies inform the feedback mechanisms, which provide personalized interactivity.

Furthermore, the interface and design of the system are informed by numerous usability studies (many of which are still in progress), that aim for navigability and consistency to make the system easier to manage, reduce cognitive load on the users, and allow more time to be allocated towards writing tasks. The system is highly accessible, with multi-platform compatibility and on- or off-line capabilities. W-Pal's architecture renders it easy to define system requirements with writing strategy XML schema, and easily expandable. It also minimizes processing needs with the capacity to reuse the common components. It is also highly configurable for designers as well as instructors.

There are certainly a number of ways to implement and incorporate all of these features within a system. The methodology used in designing W-Pal is not necessarily novel in that the approaches chosen in creating this system have each been used in other contexts. However, to our knowledge, the incorporation of all of these features within one system has not been done before in this way and for this purpose. As such, this paper should be valuable to other designers and engineers who face

similar challenges.

ACKNOWLEDGEMENTS

This work is supported by the Institute of Education Science Research Grant (IES R305A080589). The authors would also like to thank the W-Pal research group for their contributions to this project. We are particularly thankful to Adam Renner, Tanner Jackson, Kyle Dempsey, Jennifer Weston, Scott Crossley, Phil McCarthy, Loel Kim, Art Graesser, Randy Floyd, and Vasile Rus.

REFERENCES

Aleven V, Koedinger KR (2002). An effective meta-cognitive strategy: Learning by doing and explaining with a computer-based cognitive tutor. Cognitive Science, 26: 147-179.

Beal C, Arroyo I, Cohen P, Woolf B (2010). Evaluation of animal watch: An intelligent tutoring system for arithmetic and fractions. J. Interactive Online Learning, 9: 64-77.

Burstein J, Chodorow M, Leacock C (2004). Automated essay evaluation: The criterion online writing service. AI Magazine, 25: 27-36.

Burnstein J, Marcu D, Knight K (2003). Finding the WRITE stuff: Automatic identification of discourse structure in student essays. IEEE Intelligent Systems, 18: 32-39.

Craig S, Driscoll D, Gholson B (2004). Constructing knowledge from dialog in an intelligent tutoring system: Interactive learning, vicarious learning and pedagogical agents. J. Edu. Multimedia and Hypermedia 13: 161-183.

de la Paz S (2007). Managing cognitive demands for writing: Comparing the effects of instructional components in strategy instruction. Reading and Writing Quarterly, 23: 249-266.

de la Paz S, Graham S (2002). Explicitly teaching strategies, skills and knowledge: Writing instruction in middle school classrooms. J. Edu. Psychol. 94: 687-698.

Embi ZC (2005). A case study on the implementation of framework for edutainment environment. Cyberjaya, Malaysia: Multimedia University.

Fang X, Holsapple CW (2007). An empirical study of web site navigation structures' impacts on web site usability. Decision Support Systems, 43: 476-491.

Gee JP (2003). What video games have to teach us about learning and literacy. New York, NY: Palgrave/Macmillan.

Gee JP (2008). Learning and games. In K. Salen (Ed.), The ecology of games: Connecting youth, games and learning (pp. 21–40). Cambridge, MA: The MIT Press.

Geiser S, Studley R (2001). Relative contribution of high school grades, SAT I and SAT II scores in predicting success at UC: Preliminary findings. Unpublished manuscript, University of California.

Graesser AC, Lu S, Jackson GT, Mitchell H, Ventura M, Olney A, Louwerse MM (2004). AutoTutor: A tutor with dialogue in natural language. Behavioral Research Methods, Instruments and Computers, 36: 180-193.

Graesser AC, McNamara DS, VanLehn K (2005). Scaffolding deep comprehension strategies through PointandQuery, AutoTutor and iSTART. Educational Psychologist, 40: 225-234.

Graham S, Perin D (2007). A meta-analysis of writing instruction for adolescent students. J. Edu. Psychol. 99: 445-476.

Hillocks G (1984). What works in teaching composition: A meta-analysis of experimental treatment studies. Ame. J. Edu. 93: 133-170.

Johnson WL, Rickel J, Lester JC (2000). Animated pedagogical agents: Face-to-face interaction in interactive learning environments. Int. J. Artificial Intelligence in Edu. 11: 47-78.

Kellogg R, Raulerson B (2007). Improving the writing skills of college students. Psychonomic Bulletin and Review, 14: 237-242.

Light R (2001). Making the most of college. Cambridge, MA: Harvard University Press.

Litman D, Silliman S (2004). ITSPOKE: An intelligent tutoring spoken dialogue system. In Proceedings of the Human Language Technology Conference of the 4th Meeting of the North American Chapter of the Association for Computational Linguistic. Boston, MA: HLT/NAACL.

McNamara DS, Levinstein IB, Boonthum C (2004). iSTART: Interactive strategy trainer for active reading and thinking. Behavioral Research Methods, Instruments, and Computers, 36: 222-233.

McNamara DS, O'Reilly T, Best R, Ozuru Y (2006). Improving adolescent students' reading comprehension with iSTART. J. of Edu. Compt. Res. 34: 147-171.

McNamara DS, Raine R, Roscoe R, Crossley S, Jackson GT, Dai J, Cai Z, Renner A, Brandon R, Weston J, Dempsey K, Lam D, Sullivan S, Kim L, Rus V, Floyd R, McCarthy PM, Graesser AC (in press). The Writing-Pal: Natural language algorithms to support intelligent tutoring on writing strategies. In P.M. McCarthy and C. Boonthum (Eds.), Applied natural language processing and content analysis: Identification, investigation and resolution. Hershey, PA: IGI Global.

National Assessment of Educational Progress (2002). The nation's report card: Writing 2002. Retrieved from http://nces.ed.gov/nationsreportcard/pubs/main2002/2003529.asp

National Commission on Writing (2004). Writing: A ticket to work...or a ticket out. College Board.

National Commission on Writing (2008). Writing: A ticket to work...or a ticket out: A survey of business leaders. College Board.

Nielson J (1993). Usability engineering. New York, NY: Morgan Kaufmann.

Page, EB, and Petersen, NS (1995). The computer moves into essay grading: Updating the ancient test. Phi Delta Kappan, 76, 561-565.

Palmer JW (2002). Web site usability, design and performance metrics. Information Systems Research, 13: 151-167.

Pitkow J, Kehoe C (1996). Emerging trends in the WWW user population. Communications of the ACM, 39: 106-108.

Porter LR (1997). Creating virtual classroom: Distance learning with the Internet. New York, NY: Wiley.

Powell P (2009). Retention and writing instruction: Implications for access and pedagogy. College Composition and Communication, 60: 664-682.

Quintana C, Reiser BJ, Davis EA, Krajcik J, Fretz E, Duncan RG, Kyza E, Edelson D, Soloway E (2004). A scaffolding design framework for software to support science inquiry. Journal of the Learning Sciences, 13: 337-386.

Sharp DB (2007). Learn to write. ISA Career website. http://www.isa.org/Template.cfm?Section=CareersandTemplate=/ContentManagement/ContentDisplay.cfmandContentID=5328

Shermis MD, Mzumara HR, Olson J, Harrington S (2001). Online grading of student essays: PEG goes on the world wide web. Assessment and Evaluation in Higher Education, 26: 247-259.

Shneiderman B (1998). Designing the user interface: Strategies for effective human-computer interaction. Reading, MA: Addison-Wesley.

Tan P, Ling S, Ting C (2007). Adaptive digital game-based learning framework. In K. K. W. Wong, L. Fung, and P. Cole, (Eds.), Proceedings of the 2nd International Conference on Digital interactive Media in Entertainment and Arts, pp. 142-146. New York, NY: ACM.

VanLehn K, Graesser AC, Jackson GT, Jordan P, Olney A, Rosé C (2007). When are tutorial dialogues more effective than reading? Cognitive Science, 31: 3-52.

VanLehn K, Lynch C, Schulze K, Shapiro JA, Shelby R, Taylor L, Treacy D, Weinstein A, Wintersgill M (2005). The Andes physics tutoring system: Lessons learned. International Journal of Artificial Intelligence in Education, 15: 147-204.

Wade-Stein D, Kintsch E (2004). Summary Street: Interactive computer support for writing. Cognition and Instruction, 22: 333-362.

17

Comparison and performance analysis of reactive type DSR, AODV and proactive type DSDV routing protocol for wireless mobile *ad-hoc* network, using NS-2 simulator

Shrikant Upadhyay*, Pankaj Joshi, Neha Gandotra and Aditi Kumari

Department of Electronics and Communication Engineering, Dehradun Institute of Technology, Dehrdun-248002, India.

Routing in MANET is a critical task due to highly dynamic environment. A routing protocol is needed whenever a packet needs to be transmitted to destination via number of nodes and numerous routing protocols have been proposed for *ad-hoc* network. In this paper we try to judge the impact of both reactive as well proactive type protocols by increasing the density of nodes in the network, keeping source node fixed and move the destination node and lastly, keeping the destination node fixed and move source node. In all the three cases, the performance of the routing protocol have been analyzed to improve and select efficient routing protocol for network setup and its designing for practical scenario. The performance matrix includes delivery fraction, packet loss and end to end delay.

Key words: Wireless mobile, routing protocols, mobile *ad hoc* networks.

INTRODUCTION

Mobile ad hoc networks (MANETs) are rapidly evolving as an important area of mobile mobility. MANETs are infrastructure less and wireless in which there are several routers which are free to move arbitrarily and can mange themselves in same manners. MANETs as shown in Figure 1 have characteristics that network topology changes very rapidly and unpredictably in which many mobile nodes moves to and from a wireless network without any fixed access point where routers and hosts move, so topology is dynamic. It has to support multihop path for mobile nodes to communicate with each other and can have multiple hops over wireless links; also connection point to the internet may also change. If mobile nodes are within the communication range of each other, then source node can send message to the destination node otherwise it can send through intermediate node.

Nowadays mobile ad hoc networks have robust and efficient operation in mobile wireless networks as it can include routing functionality into mobile nodes which is more than just mobile hosts and reduces the routing overhead and saves energy for other nodes. Hence, MANETs are very useful when infrastructure is not available (Pucha et al., 2007), impractical, or expensive because it can be rapidly deployable, without prior planning or any existing infrastructure.

And it's an autonomous system in which mobile hosts connected by wireless links are free to be dynamic and sometimes act as routers at the same time. All nodes in a wireless ad hoc network act as a router and host as well as the network topology is in dynamically, because the connectivity between the nodes may vary with time due to some of the node departures and new node arrivals.

The special features of Mobile Ad Hoc Network (MANET) bring this technology great opportunity together with severe challenges (MANET is explained in details in

---

*Corresponding author. E-mail: shri.kant.yay@gmail.com.

Abbreviations: DSR, Dynamic source routing; **AODV,** *ad-hoc* on demand distance vector routing; **DSDV,** destination sequenced distance vector routing; **MANET,** mobile *ad hoc* networks; **NS,** network simulator.

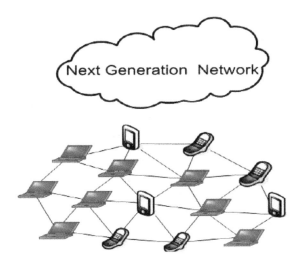

Figure 1. Mobile Ad-hoc Networks (MANETs).

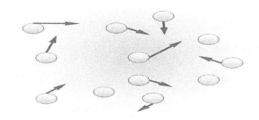

Figure 2. Nodes move randomly in different speed and different direction.

the Appendix). All the nodes or devises responsible to organize themselves dynamically the communication between the each other and to provide the necessary network functionality in the absence of fixed infrastructure or we can call it ventral administration, It implies that maintenance, routing and management, etc. have to be done between all the nodes. This case Called Peer level Multi Hopping and that is the main building block for Ad Hoc Network. In the end, conclude that the Ad Hoc Nodes or devices are difficult and more complex than other wireless networks. Therefore, Ad Hoc Networks form sort of clusters to the effective implementation of such a complex process. Figure 2 shows some nodes forming ad hoc networks, and there are some nodes more randomly in different direction and different speeds.

Reactive and proactive protocol

On demand/reactive routing protocol

On-demand routing protocols were designed to reduce the overheads in proactive protocols by maintaining

information for active routes only. This means that routes are determined and maintained for nodes that require sending data to a particular destination. Route discovery usually occurs by flooding a route request packets through the network. When a node with a route to the destination (or the destination itself) is reached a route reply is sent back to the source node using link reversal if the route request has traveled through bidirectional links or by piggy-backing the route in a route reply packet via flooding. Reactive protocols can be classified into two categories: source routing and hop-by-hop routing. In source routed on-demand protocols, each data packets carry the complete source to destination address. Therefore, each intermediate node forwards these packets according to the information kept in the header of each packet. This means that the intermediate nodes do not need to maintain up-to-date routing information for each active route in order to forward the packet towards the destination. Furthermore, nodes do not need to maintain neighbor connectivity through periodic beaconing messages. The major drawback with source routing protocols is that in large networks they do not perform well. This is due to two main reasons; firstly as the number of intermediate nodes in each route grows, then so does the probability of route failure. The advantage of this strategy is that routes are adaptable to the dynamically changing environment of MANETs, since each node can update its routing table when they receiver fresher topology information and hence forward the data packets over fresher and better routes. Under this category Dynamic Source Routing (DSR) protocol requires each packet to carry the full address (every hop in the route), from source to the destination (Khatri et al., 2010).

DSR (Dynamic source routing)

DSR allows the network to be completely self-organizing and self-configuring, without the need for any existing network infrastructure or administration. The protocol is composed of the two main mechanisms of "Route Discovery" and "Route Maintenance", which work together to allow nodes to discover and maintain routes to arbitrary destinations in the ad hoc network. However, this protocol has a number of advantages over routing protocols such as AODV, LMR and TORA and in small to moderately size networks (perhaps up to a few hundred nodes), this protocol may perform better. An advantage of DSR is that nodes can store multiple routes in their route cache, which means that the source node can check its route cache for a valid route before initiating route discovery and if a valid route is found there is no need for route discovery. This is very beneficial in network with low mobility. Since they routes stored in the route cache will be valid longer. Another advantage of DSR is that it does not require any periodic beaconing (or hello message exchanges), therefore nodes can enter sleep node to conserve their power. This also saves a considerable amount of bandwidth in the network (Khatri et al., 2010).

AODV (Ad-Hoc on demand distance vector routing)

AODV is a modification of the DSDV algorithm. When a source node desires to establish a communication session, it initiates a path-discovery process to locate the other node. The source node broadcasts a RREQ packet with its IP address, Broadcast ID (BrID), and the sequence number of the source and destination. While, the BrID and the IP address is used to uniquely identify each request, the sequence numbers are used to determine the timeliness of each packet. Receiving nodes set the backward pointer to the source and generates a RREP unicast packet if it is the destination or contains a route to the destination with a sequence number greater than or equal to the destination sequence number contained in the original RREQ. As the RREP is routed back to the source, forward pointers are setup by the intermediate nodes in their routing tables. The deletion of a route would occur if an entry was not used within a specified lifetime. Link failures are propagated by a RREP message with infinite metric to the source node where route discovery would again occur. An optional feature of AODV is the use of hello messages to maintain the connectivity of neighboring nodes. The hello protocol yields a greater knowledge of the network and can improve the route discovery process.

Proactive routing protocol/table driven routing protocol

It maintains the routing table using the routing information learnt from neighbors on periodic basis. Main characteristics of these protocols include: distributed, shortest-path protocols, maintains routes between every host pair at all times, based on periodic updates of routing table and high routing overhead and consumes more bandwidth (Walaia and Singh, 2011). In table driven protocols, each node maintains one or more tables containing routing information to every other node in the network. All nodes keep on updating these tables to maintain latest view of the network (Taneja and Kush, 2008).

DSDV (Destination sequenced distance vector routing)

The distance vector algorithm described is a classical Distributed Bellman-Ford (DBF) algorithm (Vetrivelan and Reddy, 2008; Basagni et al., 1998). DSDV is a distance

vector algorithm which uses sequence numbers originated and updated by the destination, to avoid the looping problem caused by stale routing information. In DSDV, each node maintains a routing table which is constantly and periodically updated (not on-demand) and advertised to each of the node's current neighbors. Each entry in the routing table has the last known destination sequence number. Each node periodically transmits updates, and it does so immediately when significant new information is available. The data broadcasted by each node will contain its new sequence number and the following information for each new route: the destination's address the number of hops to reach the destination and the sequence number of the information received regarding that destination, as originally stamped by the destination. No assumptions about mobile hosts maintaining any sort of time synchronization or about the phase relationship of the update periods between the mobile nodes are made. Following the traditional distance-vector routing algorithms, these update packets contain information about which nodes are accessible from each node and the number of hops necessary to reach them. Routes with more recent sequence numbers are always the preferred basis for forwarding decisions. Of the paths with the same sequence number, those with the smallest metric (number of hops to the destination) will be used. The addresses stored in the route tables will correspond to the layer at which the DSDV protocol is operated.

METHODOLOGY

In this paper the different routing protocols have been analyzed by using simulator tool called network simulator (NS). We are using NS-2.27 for the performance analysis of these protocols. In your first scenario the total number of nodes is 10 and the source node 0 is fixed and destination node 9 is in movement while in second scenario the number of nodes is same but, here source node 0 is in mobility and destination node 9 is fixed (Figures 3, 4 and 5). The final scenario is based on increasing the density of nodes in the network and tries to judge the impact of such scenario with different simulation time 10, 50 and 100 ms. Table 1 shows the main characteristics used for scenario. The analysis result helps the network designer to choose right protocol.

Simulation tool

Software used for the performance analysis of taken protocol is based on NS-2 version 2.27. NS Simulator based on two languages: an object oriented simulator, written in C++, and a OTcl (an object oriented extension of Tcl) interpreter, use to execute users command scripts. There are two classes hierarchies: the complied C++ hierarchy and the interpreted OTcl one, with one two one correspondence between them. The complied C++ hierarchy allows us to achieve efficiency in the simulation and faster execution times. This is in particular useful for the detail definition and operation of protocols. This allows one two reduce packet and event processing time. OTcl script provided by the user, and can define a particular Network Topology, the specific protocols and applications that we wish to stimulate (who behavior is already

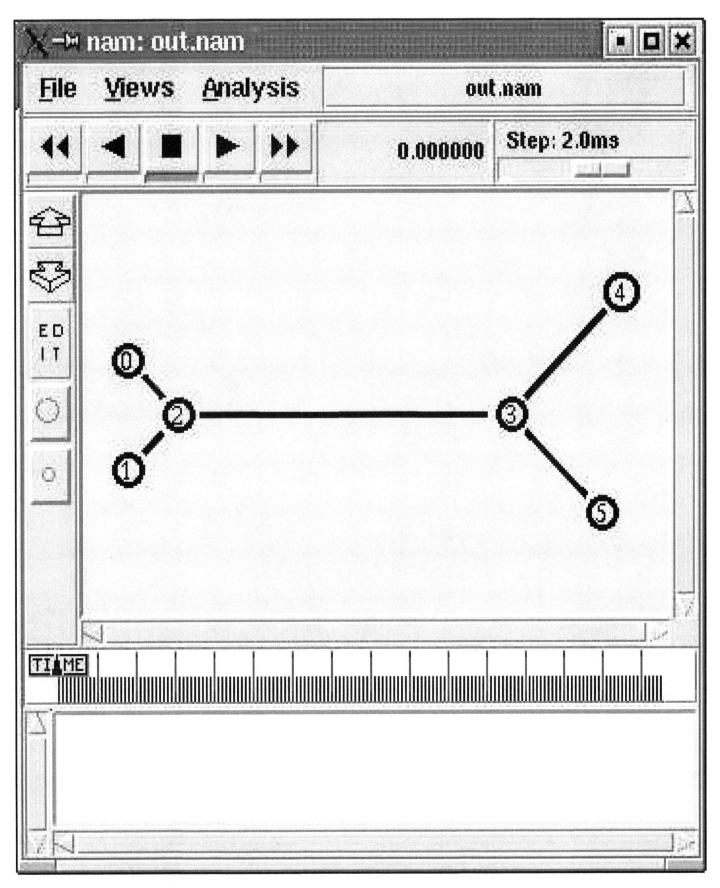

Figure 3. Example for creating file nam: nam. out.

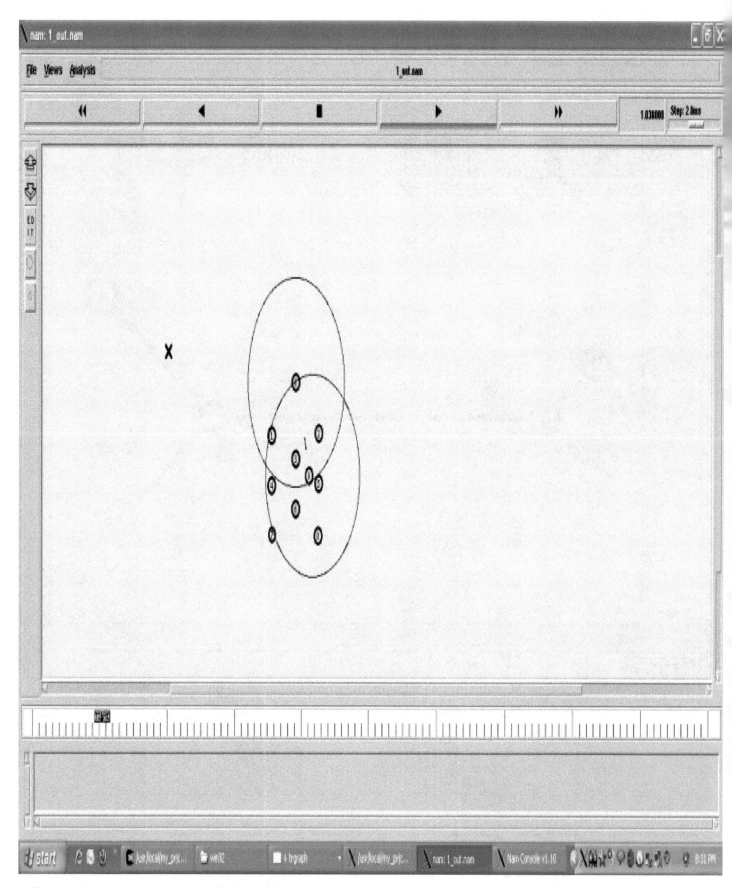

Figure 4. Scenario for source and destination variation.

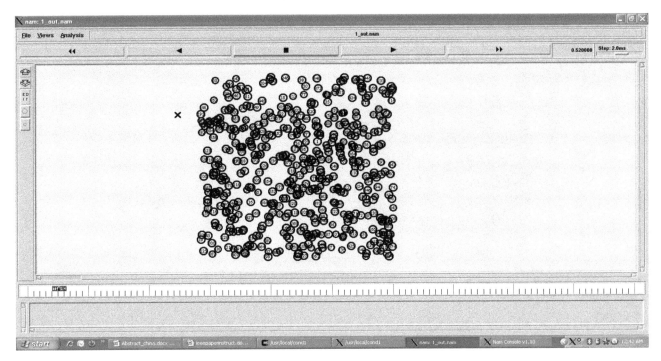

Figure 5. Scenario for node density increase.

Table 1. Main Characteristics of scenario.

Statistic	Value
Simulator	NS-2.27
Protocol studied	DSR, AODV, DSDV
Scenario size	1000 × 1000 m
Number of nodes	10, 100
Node mobility (m/s)	10
Traffic type	CBR
Node movement model	Random Waypoint
Transmit power (W)	0.005
Simulation time (min)	10, 50, 100

defined in the complied hierarchy) and the form of output that we wish to obtain from the simulator. The OTcl can make use of the object complied in C++ through an OTcl linkage (done using tclCL) that creates a matching of the OTcl objects for each of the C++. NS is a discrete event simulator, where the advance of time depends on the timing of events which are maintained by a scheduler. An event is an object in the C++ hierarchy with a unique, a scheduled time and the pointer to an object that handles the events.

The schedulers keeps an ordered data structure (there are four, but by default NS use a simple linked- list) with the events to be executed and fires them one by one, invoking the handler of the event. The otcl script used in this simulator is defined in the following manner:
Otcl Script:

#Create a simulator object
set ns [new Simulator]
#Open the trace file(s)
set nf [open out.nam w]

$ns namtrace-all $nf
#Define a 'finish' procedure
proc finish {} {
global ns nf
$ns flush-trace
close $nf; #Close the trace file
exec nam out.nam & #Execute nam on the trace file
#(optional)
exit 0
}
.nam file is generated by.tcl file and we can visualize the network scenario by this.

RESULTS

The calculated result will be in the form of trace file and it

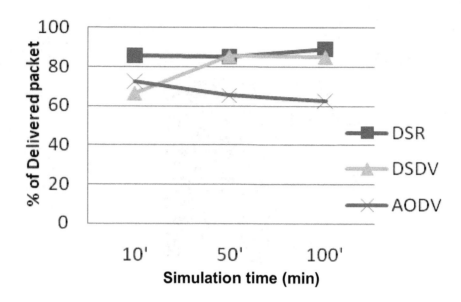

Figure 6. Packet Delivery Fraction.

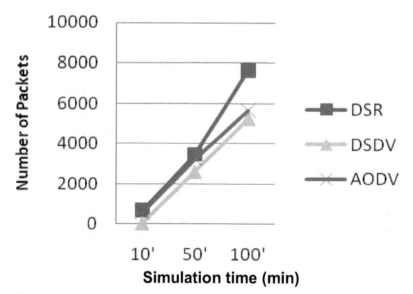

Figure 7. Packet loss.

is plotted with the help of Microsoft Excel 2007 tool. Figures 6, 7 and 8 shown result of the network when the source node 0 is fixed at one place and destination node 10 is in movement. The analysis results are shown in Figures 6, 7 and 8.

The result plotted for the three routing protocols DSR, DSDV and DSR respectively for the first scenario having 10 nodes.

The simulated result is of second scenario when the source node 0 is in movement and destination node 9 is fixed or constant in the network. The analysis result is shown in Figures 9, 10 and 11. The result plotted for the

three routing protocols DSR, DSDV and AODV respectively for the second scenario having 10 nodes.

The simulated result is of third and final scenario of node density increase shown in Figures 12, 13 and 14.

Conclusion

This paper does the realistic comparison of three routing protocols DSR, AODV and DSDV in node mobility and node density increase in the network. In first scenario keeping source node fixed and destination node variation

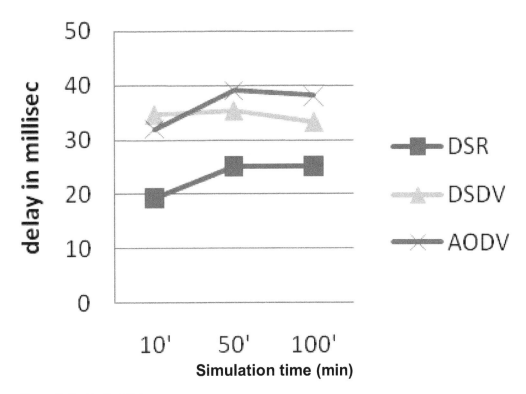

Figure 8. End to End Delay.

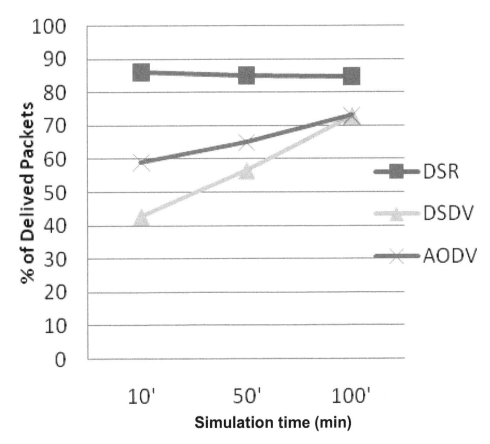

Figure 9. Packet delivery fraction.

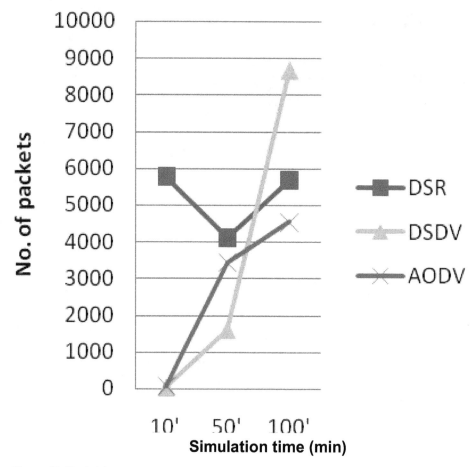

Figure 10. Packet loss.

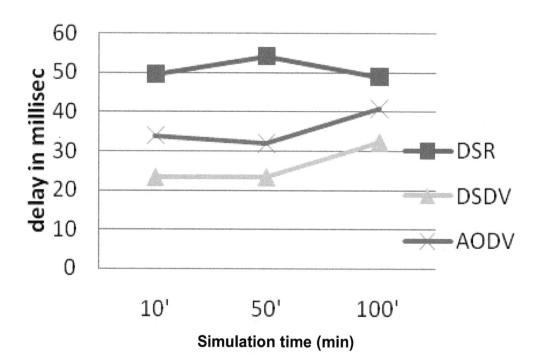

Figure 11. End to End Delay.

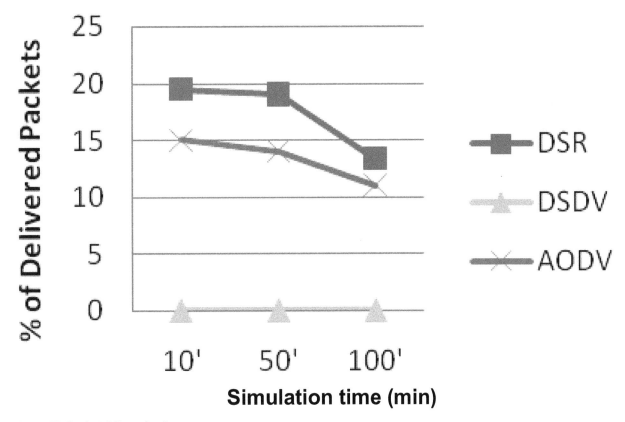

Figure 12. Packet delivery fraction.

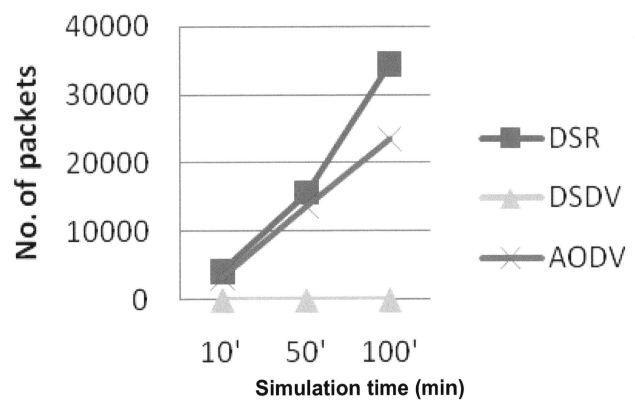

Figure 13. Packet loss.

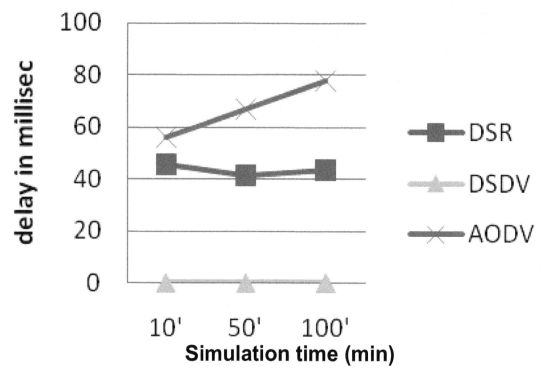

Figure 14. End to end delay.

DSR routing protocol performance is quite well compared to AODV and DSDV. While keeping the destination node fixed and source node variation we again conclude that DSR performance improves much better compared to AODV as well as DSDV routing so, in second scenario DSR performs efficient for the network. And the loss would be much in DSDV routing protocol. Finally, in the last scenario of your work when the node density increases then DSDV performance deteriorate poorly and it goes nearly to zero value. Also, here the performance of DSR routing protocol is much better than AODV and DSDV. So, under high traffic condition DSR performs well and is good for engineers while designing any ad-hoc real scenario network.

REFERENCES

Basagni S, Chlamtac I, Syrotiuk VR, Woodward BA (1998). A distance routing effect algorithm for mobility(dream). Proceedings of the IEEE/ACM International conference on mobile computing and networking (MOBICOM'98).

http://www.comp.brad.ac.uk/~sburuha1/wirelessadhoc.html.
Khatri P, Rajput M, Shastri A, Solanki K (2010). Performance study of ad-hoc reactive routing protocols. J. Comput. Sci., 6(10): 1130-1134.
Pucha H, Das SM, Hu YC (2007). The Performance impact of traffic patterns on routing protocols in mobile ad hoc network. Journal (COMNET), 51(12): 3595-3616.
Taneja S, Kush A (2008). A survey of routing protocols in mobile ad hoc networks. Int. J. Innov., manage. Technol., 1(3).
Vetrivelan N, Reddy AV (2008). Performances analysis of three routing protocols for varying MANET size. Proceeding international multiconference of engineers and computer scientists, IMECS, (2): 19-21.
Walaia GK, Singh C (2011). Simulation based performance evaluation and comparison of proactive and reactive routing protocols in mobile ad-hoc networks. International journal of computer science and technologies, 2(3): 1235-1239.

APPENDIX

Mobile ad hoc networks (MANET) represent complex distributed systems that comprise wireless mobile nodes that can freely and dynamically self organize into arbitrary and temporary ad hoc network topologies. Ad-hoc networks are autonomous systems which comprise a collection of mobile nodes that use wireless transmission for communication. They are self organized, self-configured and self-controlled infrastructure-less networks. This type of network can be set up or deployed anywhere and anytime because it poses very simple infrastructure set up and no or minimal central administration. These networks are mainly used by community users such as military, researchers, business, students and emergency service. Because of the frequent changes of mobile nodes, routing has always been one of the most challenging problems for MANET's designers. And routing protocol play an important role to find a suitable route for packet delivery and delivery the packet to the correct destination.

18

Dynamic task scheduling using service time error and virtual finish time

S. V. Kasmir Raja[1] and Daphne Lopez[2]*

[1]SRM University, Kattangulathur, Tamil Nadu, India.
[2]VIT University, Vellore, Tamil Nadu, India.

The computational grid has emerged as an attractive platform to tackle various science and engineering problems. One of the challenging issues in the grid associated with the effective utilization of the heterogeneous resources is scheduling. This paper designs and implements a task-scheduling algorithm considering the dynamicity of the resources and the tasks. We explain the concept of queue's virtual time and combine it with virtual finish time and the service time error to allocate resources to the tasks for improved fairness and better throughput. The detailed performance evaluation of virtual finish time driven scheduling algorithm is carried out through a series of simulations by varying the number of tasks and processors of different capacities to optimize the cost and execution time of the tasks to achieve fairness.

Key words: Computational grid, heterogeneous resources, dynamicity, task-scheduling.

INTRODUCTION

Despite efforts that current grid schedulers with various scheduling algorithms have made to provide comprehensive and sophisticated functionalities, they have difficulty guaranteeing the quality of schedules they produce. The single most challenging issue that they encounter is the dynamicity of resources, that is, the availability and capability of a grid resource change dynamically (Foster and Kesselman, 1999a, b). Although a resource may be participating in a grid, its main purpose is for use by local users of the organization that it belongs to. Therefore, the load on the resource imposes a great strain on grid scheduling. Though there are a number of scheduling algorithms existing, identifying the best algorithm in a grid environment is complex and critical. All the tasks that are submitted to the grid will have to be executed in the stipulated time and its complexity increases due to dynamic change of the resources. An important issue in practical scheduling is fairness in user service. The scheduling policies could be preemptive or non-preemptive as shown in Figure 1.

Non-preemptive scheduling is performed only when processing the previous task is completed and is attractive due to the simplicity of its implementation for it

is not necessary to maintain a distinction between an unserviced task and a partially serviced one. Preemptive scheduling (Jackson and Rouskas, 2002) involves the interruption of the task after it has executed for its time quantum and added to queue of pending requests. Irrespective of the type of policy, the objective function is to reduce the execution time and cost associated with the execution of the job, which increases the throughput of the system.

Proportional share resource management provides a flexible and useful abstraction for multiplexing scarce resources among users and applications.

Virtual time is a paradigm for organizing and synchronizing distributed systems which can be applied to such problems as distributed discrete event simulation and distributed database concurrency control. Virtual time provides a flexible abstraction of real time in much the same way that virtual memory provides an abstraction of real memory. This paper introduces virtual time (Mattern, 1989), a concept that allows a distributed system to be organized around a linear global clock; rather than maintain a synchronized clock, it achieves efficiency by having each node maintain its own local virtual time and performing rollback when a node receives a message in the past. Although not widely adopted, it has served as an influential model of a general system with optimistic results.

---

*Corresponding author. E-mail: daphnelopez@vit.ac.in.

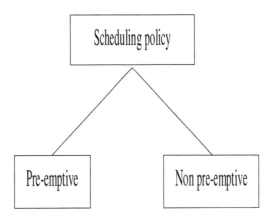

Figure 1. Scheduling policy.

RELATED WORK

Proportional fair is a compromise-based (Kushner and Whiting, 2004) scheduling algorithm. It is based upon maintaining a balance between two competing interests: This concept is basically applied to networks in the context to maximize total wireless network throughput, while at the same time allowing all users at least a minimal level of service. Fair queuing (Doulamis et al., 2007; Hosaagrahara and Sethu, 2008) can be interpreted as a packet approximation of generalized processor sharing (GPS). This is done by assigning each data flow a data rate or a scheduling priority (depending on the implementation) that is inversely proportional to its anticipated resource consumption. Demers et al. (1989) propose fair queuing for network packet scheduling as Weighted Fair Queueing (WFQ), with a more extensive analysis provided by Parekh and Gallager (1993), and later applied by Waldspurger (1995) to CPU scheduling as stride scheduling. Fair queuing in network emulates fairness of bitwise round-robin (Shreedhar and Varghese, 1996) sharing of resources among competing flows. Elshaikh et al. (2006) propose a fair new weighted fair queuing algorithm used in networks where two types of queues and the queue length is used as a parameter incalculating the virtual time, to ensure that the flows or aggregates are not punished for using uncounted bandwidth.

Doulamis et al. (2007) uses a max-min fair sharing approach for providing fair access to users. When there is no shortage of resources, the algorithm assigns to each task enough computational power for it to finish within its deadline. When there is congestion, the main idea is to fairly reduce the CPU rates assigned to the tasks so that the share of resources that each user gets is proportional to the user's weight. All tasks whose requirements are lower than their fair share CPU rate are served at their demanded CPU rates which they define as fairness. Distributed scheduling algorithms with multiprocessor systems (Ramamritham et al., 1990) and metascheduler (Shreedhar and Varghese, 1996) is also

proposed.

In order to reduce the computational load, the concept of virtual time is introduced. Weighted fair queuing introduces the idea of a virtual finishing time (VFT) to do proportional sharing scheduling. The virtual finish time is dependent on the virtual time. Virtual time of a task is defined as the degree to which a task has received its proportional allocation relative to other tasks. Given a task's virtual time, the virtual finish time (VFT) is the virtual time the task has after executing for one time quantum. Virtual time round robin is another scheduling algorithm that uses the virtual finish time parameter in Linux to achieve fairness.

Sanjay and Vadhiyar (2008) calculated the time taken to execute parallel application by considering the problem size, the varying number of processors and the transient CPU and network characteristics respectively. The execution time is split into two, one for representing the computation and the other for communication costs.

DYNAMIC VIRTUAL TIME FAIR QUEUE ALGORITHM

Grid model

The grid model consists of a number of computational nodes and each node consists of a number of processors of varying capacity. Once the user is issued, an acceptance of the task it belongs to the grid administrator.

The resources are discovered that are capable of executing the tasks that are submitted to the site. The resources that do not meet the tasks requirements are moved to the other site.

The tasks are placed in the task queue and move to the active state. Tasks in the active state are scheduled and ready for execution. When the task is allocated, the resources transits to the execution state and on expiry of the time quantum the task is either moved to the end of the queue or removed from the queue if it is not ready for the second time quantum. On successful completion the tasks enters a finished state and is moved to the user's site.

Problem formulation

The problem of task scheduling in a grid G basically consists of a dynamic set of T independent tasks to be scheduled on a dynamic set of N computational nodes (resources).

An instance of the problem consists of:

1. A set of T independent tasks to be scheduled. Each task has associated with it a workload (in million of instructions). Every task must be entirely executed in a unique machine.
2. A set of M number of processors which has its corresponding computing capacity (in MIPS).

ALGORITHM

The user submits the task to the grid environment. The grid scheduler allocates the submitted tasks to the computational nodes. A queue is maintained for each computational node and the queue size depends on the number of tasks submitted initially in the grid environment. The size may not be equal at all intervals of time because of the dynamic nature of the grid.

In this algorithm, a task has six values associated with its execution state: share, service time error, virtual finishing time, time counter, task identity and the run state. A task's share value identifies its resource rights. Share is allocated to the task based on the price the user pays. *Perfect fairness* is an ideal state in which each task has received service exactly proportional to its share at all intervals of time. Denoting the share of a task as S and the service received by task during a time interval t_1, t_2 as W, the perfect fairness of a task is represented as:

$$W(t_1, t_2) = (t_2 - t_1)S / \sum_{i=1}^{n} S$$

(1)

The service time error is calculated as the difference between the amount of service time allocated to the task during interval (t_1, t_2) under the given algorithm, and the amount of time that would have been allocated under an ideal scheme that maintains perfect fairness for all clients over all intervals:

$$E = st(t_1, t_2) - w(t_1, t_2)$$

(2)

The virtual time of a task is a measure of the degree to which a task has received its proportional allocation relative to other tasks. Virtual time is represented as:

$$VT = W(t) / S$$

(3)

Given a task's virtual time, the task's virtual finishing time (VFT) is defined, as the virtual time the task would have after executing for one time quantum. A task's VFT advances at a rate proportional to its resource consumption divided by its share. The VFT is used to decide the position of the task in the queue and that the task in the beginning of the queue would be allocating the resources. A task's time counter measures the number of allocations for that particular task in order to measure the fairness at the end of each scheduling cycle. Information about the scheduler as the time quantum, queue, total shares and the queue virtual time is also maintained. The total shares are the sum of the shares of all the tasks that are ready to run.

Dynamic considerations

Initially when the execution starts, the tasks are sorted to their share values and tasks would not have consumed any time quantum so the task's implicit virtual time is set to be the same as the queue virtual time (QVT). Virtual finish time of a new task is calculated as

$$VFT(t) = QVT(t) + Q / S$$

(4)

If the executable task is not in an active state, it is simply removed from the queue and the service time error for the current and the next task is calculated and is allotted the resource. The task that is in an inactive state lies somewhere in the queue then the task is removed and the pointer values are appropriately modified in the linked lists. This way, the tasks can be preempted and used. The pseudocode is given in Figure 2. The time complexity is $O(n^2)$.

Arrival model

The tasks arrival is modeled as an application of a queuing system. They are allowed up to Q seconds of time and are fed back to the queue if they have not completed their processing. We assume that the task resumes its operation when it gets the processor for the next time quantum. We also assume that the arrival times are independent of each other. λ is the rate at which the jobs arrive at the system, μ is the rate at which the jobs are serviced. Assuming $\rho = \lambda / \mu$.

Modeling each queue as an M/D/1 system, it can be shown that the average length of the queue:

$$Q = \frac{\rho^2}{2(1 - \rho)}$$

(5)

Input: A set of taks T, a set of N computational nodes with multiple processors

Output: A schedule of T onto N

1. Create a set Q of N queues qsize = T/N

2. Each user is associated with the broker entity and the resource characteristics are identified

3. Assign shares to the tasks, a positive value (depends on how much the user pays for his service)

4. Remove qsize tasks in T and enqueue them to q_i

5. SCHEDULING: (a) Assign shares to the tasks in each queue. SORT is performed (Arrange the tasks in decreasing order of their shares) Repeat c & d for one scheduling cycle

(b) The first task in queue is executed initially for the required time quantum

(c) Compute the service time error for the task in execution and the task in the head of the queue

(d) Schedule the job which has the least value

6. VIRTUAL TIME: Compute the virtual time and the virtual finish time and store the values in the counters.

7. Schedule the task with a negative value

8. Change position: After every scheduling cycle the order of the tasks are based on their virtual finish time. The task with the smallest Virtual Finish Time is first chosen.

9. Repeat steps 5c through 5d for the current scheduling cycle

10. RESULT: Return the result set to the user

Figure 2. Pseudocode for dynamic virtual time fair queuing.

While the average waiting time is given by:

$$W = \frac{\rho}{2\mu(1-\rho)} \quad (6)$$

And the total time for task completion is:

$$t = \frac{2-\rho}{2\mu(1-\rho)} \quad (7)$$

Objective function

The objective function is to minimize the service time error. Minimization of error uses root mean square method as given in Equation (8):

$$Z = \sqrt{\frac{\sum_{n-1 \, to \, m}\left(W_n - \{t_{2n} - t_{1n}\} * S_n / \sum_{n-1}^{m} S_n\right)^2}{m}} \quad (9)$$

SIMULATION EXPERIMENT SETUP

GridSim requires the creation of resources with different capacities. We model the application as Gridlets and define all the parameters associated with the task. Then a GridSim user entity is created, that interacts with the resource broker scheduling entity to coordinate the execution of the tasks. Finally we implement a resource broker entity that performs scheduling on grid resources. The resources with their attributes used in scheduling are listed in Tables 1 and 2.

Table 1. The grid resources attributes.

Parameter	Value	Notation
Total number of resources R_0 to R_{20}	1-20	Machines
Speed	200-400	Million instructions per second
Number of processors	4-6	Processing elements
Resource manager type	Time-shared	

Table 2. Workload attributes.

Parameter	Value	Notation
Total number of tasks	100-500	
Length of a task	1,000-5,000	Million instructions (MI)
Number of processors required	4-6	Million instructions per second (MIPS)

Table 3. Experimental results for number of tasks 100 and 4 processing elements in each machine.

Parameter	Cost	Execution time	Min. error	Max. error
FCFS	461452.0	19342	-26.20000	25.54433
Round robin	422050 .9	17509	-25.80999	23.83333
Dynamic virtual time fair queue	300139.0	10766	-16.15	17.13205

Table 4. Experimental results for number of tasks 300 and 6 processing elements in each machine.

Parameter	Cost	Execution time	Min. error	Max. error
FCFS	521252.2	21251.93	-37.46000	37.21818
Round robin	495897.3	19690.05	-36.45126	36.63650
Dynamic virtual time fair queue	401112.19	14389.11	-29.7989	30.97099

Table 5. Experimental results for number of tasks 500 and 6 processing elements in each machine.

Parameter	Cost	Execution time	Min. error	Max. error
FCFS	656040.5	28765.54	-42.7814	42.72
Round Robin	615497.6	25721.15	-39.100	39.4535
Dynamic virtual time fair queue	551960.17	18435.12	-29.7576	28.4557

EXPERIMENTAL RESULTS

We perform simulations to implement fairness by using service time error as one parameter and using the virtual time fair queue performing simulations with 100 to 500 numbers of tasks. The experiment is carried out for FCFS (First Come First Serve), round robin and dynamic virtual time fair queuing. It minimizes error as well as using the virtual finish time it maximizes fairness. The experimental results in terms of cost, execution time, minimum and

maximum error are shown in Tables 3 to 5, for number of tasks 100, 300 and 500, respectively. A comparison of execution time with tasks, maximum error with tasks and cost with tasks is given in Tables 6 to 8 respectively. Corresponding graphical representations are also shown in Figure 3 to 5. Maximum error for the number of tasks ranging from 100 to 500 is tabulated in Table 9. It guarantees that all the tasks are considered for execution.

The experimental results show that the maximum error reaches a maximum value and starts declining even

Table 6. Comparison of execution time with number of tasks.

No. of task	Execution time		
	FCFS	RR	Dynamic virtual time fair queue
100	19342	17509	10766
300	21251.93	19690.05	14389.11
500	28765.54	25721.15	18435.12

Table 7. Comparison of maximum error with number of tasks.

No. of task	Maximum error		
	FCFS	RR	Dynamic virtual time fair queue
100	25.54433	23.83333	17.13205
200	37.21818	36.63650	30.97099
300	42.72	39.4535	28.4557
500	48.96457	45.68740	25.16666

Table 8. Comparison of cost with number of tasks.

No. of task	Cost		
	FCFS	RR	Dynamic virtual time fair queue
100	461452.0	422050 .9	300139.0
200	521252.2	495897.3	401112.19
300	656040.5	615497.6	551960.17
500	721460.3	701412.3	591209.8

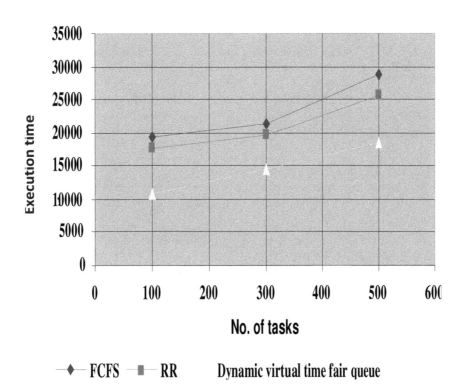

Figure 3. Execution time versus number of tasks.

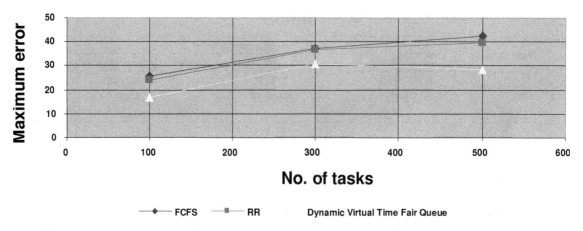

Figure 4. Maximum error versus number of tasks.

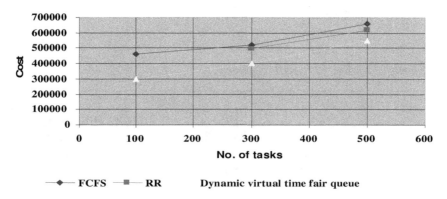

Figure 5. Cost versus number of tasks.

Table 9. Maximum error values for number of tasks 100 to 500.

No. of tasks	Max error
100	17.13205
200	18.002
300	20.013
400	21.1201
500	19.0

when the number of tasks increases. This is due to the consideration of the virtual finish time in the allocation of resources. The algorithm has proved to give the best results of all the algorithms even after considering the dynamic submission of the jobs. When new job arrives, the queue's virtual time is the virtual time of the job. In this way, after every scheduling cycle even, a new job that has arrived recently gets a proportional allocation of the resource. Even with dynamic considerations, virtual time fair queue algorithm shows a 50% higher performance than FCFS and round robin.

Conclusion

We discussed the use of service time error and virtual finish time for devising scheduling strategies for high end tasks on distributed resources. We simulated and evaluated the performance of scheduling algorithms in terms of error, cost and time for a variety of scenarios. This algorithm can be used to study the performance of various real time applications and can be embedded in a metascheduler also for enabling global scheduling. It is proposed to scale it up to the cloud infrastructure.

REFERENCES

Foster I, Kesselman C (1999a). "The Grid: Blueprint for a Future Computing Infrastructure". San Francisco, CA: Morgan Kaufmann Publishers, pp. 21-26

Foster I, Kesselman C (1999b). "The Grid: Blueprint for a new computing infrastructure". Chapter "The Globus toolkit", 1st edition, San Francisco, CA: Morgan Kaufmann Publishers Inc., pp. 259-278.

Demers A, Keshav S, Shenker S, (1989). "Analysis and simulation of a Fair Queuing Algorithm". In Proc. ACM SIGCOMM '89, New York, NY: ACM, pp. 1-12.

Doulamis ND, Varvarigos E, Varvarigou T (2007). "Fair Scheduling Algorithms in Grids". IEEE Trans. Parallel Distrib. Syst., 18(11): 1630-1648.

Hosaagrahara M, Sethu H (2008). "Max-Min Fair Scheduling in Input-Queued Switches". IEEE Trans. Parallel Distrib. Syst., 19(4): 462-475.

Elshaikh MA, Othman M, Shamala S, Desa J (2006). "A New Fair Weighted Fair Queuing Scheduling Algorithm in Differentiated Services Network". Int. J. Comput. Sci. Netw. Security, 6(11): 267-271.

Mattern F (1989). "Virtual Time and Global States of Distributed Systems". J. Parallel Distrib. Algorithms. pp. 215-226.

Shreedhar M, Varghese G (1996). "Efficient Fair queuing using Deficit Round Robin", IEEE Trans. Netw., 4(3): 375-385.

Waldspurger CA (1995). "Lottery and Stride Scheduling: Flexible Proportional-Share Resource Management". PhD thesis, Department of Electrical Engineering and Computer Science, Massachusetts Institute of Technology, pp. 12-34

Sanjay HA, Vadhiyar S (2008). "Performance modeling of parallel applications for grid scheduling," J. Parallel Distrib. Comput., 68: 1135-1145.

Ramamritham K, Stankovic JA, Shiah PF (1990). "Efficient Scheduling Algorithms for Real-Time Multiprocessor Systems". IEEE Trans. Parallel Distrib. Syst., 1(2): 184-194.

Kushner HJ, Whiting PA (2004). "Convergence of proportional-fair sharing algorithms under general conditions". IEEE Trans. Wireless Commun., 3(4): 1250-1259.

Parekh AK, Gallager RG (1993). "A Generalized Processor Sharing Approach to Flow Control in Integrated Services Networks: The Single-Node Case". IEEE/ACM Trans. Netw., 1(3): 344-357.

19

Statistical modeling and computer simulation of corrosion growth in aluminum alloy

E. Ogala* and D. O. Aideyan

Department of mathematical science, Kogi State University, Anyigba, Kogi State, Nigeria.

An extension of a brick wall model was used to describe corrosion of aluminum alloys. The extended model simulates the behavior of corrosion paths at intersections of grain boundaries within the metal sample. Situations considered include the cases where a corrosion path might assume an upward turn, skip an intersection (not turn) or split into branches. The splitting of a corrosion path results in a smaller median of the minimum order statistic while the other factors increase the median of the minimum order statistic. Moreover, a larger number of grain layers increases the minimum path length for a sample with given thickness. With a proper combination of these factors, the extended model is able to provide a good fit to the experimental data developed by the foil penetration technique.

Key words: Intergranular corrosion (IGC), extended brick wall model, corrosion, computer simulation algorithm, intersection.

INTRODUCTION

High strength aluminum alloys such as AA2024-T3 are widely used in aerospace applications. They are resistant to uniform corrosion but highly susceptible to localized corrosion. Localized corrosion, usually in the forms of intergranular corrosion, pitting corrosion, crevice corrosion, exfoliation and stress corrosion cracking (Davis, 1999), is unpredictable in terms of the exact places of initiation and initiation time. With traditional deterministic approaches, such as the electrochemical theory of corrosion, localized corrosion cannot be well explained due to the scattering of the corrosion data. On the other hand, considering localized corrosion as rare events, statistical approaches could provide an appropriate way to describe the mechanism of corrosion (Shibata, 1996), potentially to evaluate quantitatively localized corrosion behavior. Among all the forms of localized corrosion in high strength aluminum alloys in aqueous environment, IGC and pitting attack are two common forms that have received a good deal of attention. IGC is a preferential attack of grain boundaries or nearby adjacent regions without appreciable attack of the grain matrix, while

pitting corrosion occurs at the intermetallic particles or in the grain matrix. Both forms of attack are similar from an electrochemical point of view (Galvele et al., 1970; Muller et al., 1977). However, IGC might have very different growth kinetics from pitting. For predictive modeling of corrosion propagation, it is important to understand these growth kinetics independently. In this paper, we describe a model predicting the growth kinetics of IGC in aluminum alloy.

There are many factors that determine the resistance and susceptibility of an alloy to IGC, such as alloy composition, microstructure and the environment (Davis, 1999; Scully et al., 1992; Scully, 1999). The exact role of each of these factors is still unclear. For example, even though there are a few reports on quantitative measurements of IGC in aluminum alloys, little is known about the relationship between alloy microstructure and IGC growth kinetics. Zhang and Frankel (2000) made quantitative measurements of localized corrosion kinetics in AA2024-T3 using the foil penetration technique. They reported that the growth kinetics of localized corrosion in this type of alloy exhibit a strong anisotropy as a result of anisotropy in the microstructure of the wrought aluminum alloy. AA2024-T3 has a typical laminated structure with grains elongated in the longitudinal (rolling) and long

*Corresponding author. E-mail: emmainfotech@yahoo.com.

transverse directions relative to their dimension in the short transverse (through-thickness) direction. The time for intergranular corrosion to penetrate a given distance along the longitudinal or long transverse direction is much less than the time to penetrate the same nominal distance in the short transverse direction (Zhang and Frankel, 2000). The ratio of nominal penetration rates for the longitudinal direction to that for the short transverse direction was found by Zhang (Zhang and Frankel, 2000) to be 4.29. The local intergranular growth rate should not depend on the direction of growth, though it is likely a function of total path length from the surface exposed to the bulk solution. The difference in nominal growth rate with through-thickness direction relative to the rolling direction is a result of the anisotropic grain dimensions and the resulting difference in path length. Any intergranular path in the through thickness direction of a plate with an elongated microstructure will be very convoluted, resulting in nominal rate of penetration that is much less than the local rate of intergranular growth. It is of interest to be able to determine the influence of a grain structure with a particular size and shape anisotropy on the kinetics of intergranular growth in the through thickness direction. Ruan et al. (2004) proposed a statistical model to describe the relationship between the microstructure and the IGC growth rate based on foil penetration data and quantification of the microstructure of AA2024-T3. In the model, a brick wall represents the laminated microstructure of AA2024-T3. The distributions of the grain size (both width and length) are approximated by gamma distributions. Since the grain size in the longitudinal or rolling direction is much larger than that in the long transverse direction, the problem can be simplified into two dimensions, the short and long transverse dimensions. IGC in the longitudinal direction is assumed not to contribute to penetration in the short transverse direction. Given the length and the width of the grain, the distance that a corrosion path travels along a given grain is assumed to be uniformly distributed. Then, a Matlab program was used to simulate the distribution of the minimum order statistic of the corrosion path length. The simulation gives estimates with a small amount of underestimation compared to the actual result from Zhang's experiments (Zhang, 2001).

The brick wall model relates the growth kinetics of AA2024-T3 aluminum alloy to the microstructure of the alloy. It provides a simple way to quantitatively evaluate the growth kinetics of IGC for a given microstructure in AA2024-T3. However, the brick wall model was based on a series of simplified assumptions, which do not provide a totally accurate description of the corrosion propagation process. In particular, there are two cases that were not accounted for in the model. First, corrosion was assumed to turn toward the bottom surface (away from the environment) at every intersection with a vertical grain boundary. However, a corrosion path might actually skip an intersection and not turn. Moreover, when a corrosion path does make a turn, it might turn up toward the top surface (toward the environment) or down toward the bottom surface of the metal strip depending on the nature of the three-way intersection. When a corrosion path turns upward and reaches the top surface, the propagation can be assumed to end up. Second, a corrosion path was assumed not to split at any intersection while it might actually split into two corrosion paths at an intersection. Each of these two corrosion paths might propagate independently in the metal. Accordingly, the number of corrosion paths increases. Based on the above considerations of corrosion behavior, a more realistic brick wall model is discussed in this paper.

MODELING CORROSION GROWTH AT AN INTERSECTION

Basic assumptions

Consider a strip of metal with thickness T and a total of k grain layers across the thickness. The widths bj of the grains are taken to be common within a given layer but they are permitted to vary across different layers. That is,

$$T = \sum_{j=1}^{k} b_j.$$

2.1

Let denote grain length and assume that it has a distribution with pdf f(a) (probability density function). As stated in the previous paper (Ruan et al., 2004), both the grain length and width are reasonably modeled by gamma distributions with appropriate parameter values α and β. suppose there are m corrosion initialization points on the surface of the metal. For i = 1;... m, let Wi;D denote the distance that the ith initial corrosion path travels to reach a fixed depth, say D, of the metal. If the corrosion path reaches the bottom surface, Wi;D corresponds to Wi;T. Assume these m corrosion paths are independent. Figure 1 is a graphical representation of a brick wall model that represents an aluminum sample with a simplified layered microstructure. The corrosion path initiated from the top surface travels along a grain boundary that is perpendicular to the surface. It propagates along the grain boundary until it meets an intersection. Then, it might turn to a horizontal direction (either left or right on the figure), or it might split into two horizontal corrosion paths. In the former case, it propagates along the length direction of the grains until it meets another intersection. Depending on the nature of this new three-way intersection, it might turn upward, or downward or might skip the intersection and continue propagation along the horizontal direction. Since the widths of the grains are small compared to the lengths of the grains, it is reasonable to assume that a corrosion path will always make a turn toward a horizontal direction at the end of a vertical step. If a corrosion path turns

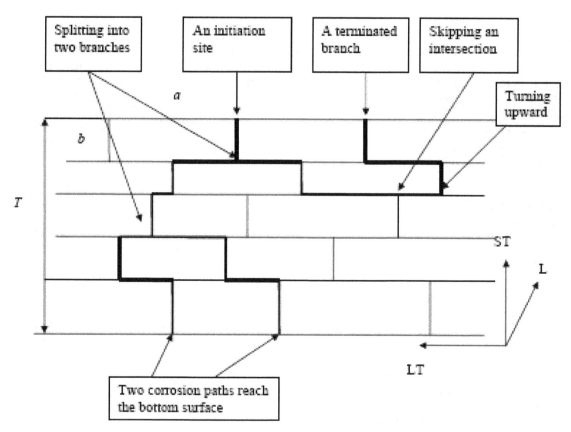

Figure 1. A graphical representation of the growth behavior of a corrosion path at a three-way intersection in a strip of metal with k = 5 grain layers. The bold line represents Wi;D and a and b are random variables representing the length and width, respectively, of a grain model. (Note: ST-short-transverse direction; LT—long-transverse direction; L-longitudinal direction).

upward and reaches the top surface again, it is considered to be a terminated path since IGC corrosion does not propagate on the surface of the alloy. Additionally, it is assumed that a corrosion path cannot terminate anywhere except the top or bottom surface of the metal strip. In the case where a corrosion path splits into two horizontal pieces at an intersection, these pieces are viewed as two corrosion paths having initiated from the same place on the top surface with a common previous path length. These paths are then assumed to propagate independently in the remainder of the metal sample under the previously described assumptions. However, in the case of such a split, the total number of corrosion paths increases.

The foil penetration technique measures the time taken by the fastest corrosion growth path to reach the bottom surface. With the vital assumption that the local corrosion growth rate is identical in all directions, the fastest corrosion growth corresponds to the shortest corrosion path length (Zhang, 2001; Zhang et al., 2003). Correspondingly, any path that terminates before reaching the bottom surface should not be considered the shortest corrosion growth path (minimum order statistic) for our purposes. When a horizontal corrosion path meets an

intersection, it can either continue to propagate in the horizontal direction or turn toward a vertical direction that is perpendicular to the surface. There are two types of intersections, represented by '$\perp$' and '$\top$' For the "$\perp$" type intersection, the horizontal corrosion path can turn downward toward the bottom surface. For the "$\perp$" type intersection, the horizontal corrosion path can turn upward toward the top surface. Therefore, the probability that a horizontal corrosion path turns upward depends on the proportion of the "$\perp$" type intersections among all the intersections it meets. Similarly, the probability that a corrosion path turns downward depends on the proportion of "$\top$" type intersections among all the intersections it meets. Let $p\perp$ and $p_\top$ denote these two proportions, respectively. Then,

$$p_\perp + p_\top = 1.$$

2.2

Let p_{skip} represent the probability that a horizontal corrosion path skips an intersection and let p_{up} and p_{down} be the probabilities that it turns upward and downward, respectively. Then, according to our previous assumptions, we have:

$$p_{up} + p_{down} + p_{skip} = 1.$$ 2.3

If a horizontal corrosion path is known to make a turn at an intersection, the two conditional probabilities $p_{up}/(1 - p_{skip})$ and $p_{down}/(1 - p_{skip})$ describe the likelihood that a corrosion path would turn upward and downward, respectively, corresponding to the proportions of the "⊥" and "⊤" types of intersections, respectively. That is,

$$p_\perp (1 - p_{skip}) = p_{up},$$

$$p_\top (1 - p_{skip}) = p_{down}.$$ 2.4

Further, let psplit denote the probability that a corrosion path splits into two branches at an intersection at the end of a vertical step. We assume all of these probabilities are identical for each intersection.

We consider a total of m initial corrosion sites on the top surface of a metal strip. Propagation with possible splitting results in (m + u) path lengths, where u ≥ 0 is the total number of branches resulting from splitting of corrosion paths. Among these lengths, we let v ≥ 0 be the number of paths terminated on the top surface instead of the bottom surface. Therefore, the (m + u – v) paths lead to a random number of corrosion path lengths and the minimum of these lengths is recorded as a random observation Wmin; T from the distribution of the minimum path length for a metal strip of thickness T. The minimum order statistic for the corrosion path lengths is thus given by

$$W_{min,T} = \min_{i=1,\ldots,m+u-v} W_{i,T}, \quad i = 1,\ldots,m+u-v,$$ 2.5

Where $W_{i;T}$ is the length of the ith corrosion path.

Let Wi;D; horizontal and Wi;D ;vertical represent the total horizontal distance and the total vertical distance, respectively, traveled by the ith corrosion path, so that

$$W_{i,D} = W_{i,D,vertical} + W_{i,D,horizontal}, \quad i = 1,\ldots,m+u.$$ 2.6

Let Ti (j) be the vertical distance that the ith corrosion path travels along the width of the jth grain before it turns toward a horizontal direction. That is,

$$W_{i,D,vertical} = \sum_j T_i(j), \quad i = 1,\ldots,m+u.$$ 2.7

Where j ∈{1; 2;... k}, and k is the total number of grain layers across the thickness. Since corrosion paths might turn upward and travel on previous layers again, the total vertical distance for a given corrosion path might not exactly equal the thickness T. Each Ti(j) is, however,

equal to the width of the jth layer. Since the width of the grain in each layer is modeled by a gamma distribution, all the Ti(j)s have a common gamma distribution. Let Di(j) represent the horizontal distance that the ith corrosion path travels on the bottom surface of the jth layer of the metal, for j ∈ {1; : : : ; k – 1}, where k is the total number of grain layers across the thickness. Note that no corrosion paths propagate on either the top surface of the first layer or on the bottom surface of the kth layer. Then,

$$W_{i,D,horizontal} = \sum_j D_i(j), \quad i = 1,\ldots,m+u.$$ 2.8

When a corrosion path skips an intersection and keeps propagating in the horizontal direction, the associated Di(j) would include at least two horizontal pieces. In Fig. 2, we show such a situation where a corrosion path skips three successive intersections on the bottom surface of the first layer leading to four horizontal pieces that add up to Di(1). The corrosion path turns downward at the fourth intersection. (Note that other grains randomly on either the top or bottom surface might intercept a grain.) Given the length of the grain, the first piece of Di(1) is modeled by a uniform distribution and is denoted by Hi(1). The unconditional distribution of this random variable was discussed in detail in Ruan et al. (2004). BrieGy, the pdf (Probability density function), h(d), of Hi(1) is given by the following:

$$h(d) = \int_d^\infty \frac{1}{a} \frac{1}{\Gamma(\alpha)\beta}$$

$$= \frac{1}{(\alpha - 1)\beta} \int_d^\infty$$

$$\vdots a^{\alpha-1}e^{-a/\beta} \, da$$

$$\frac{1}{\Gamma(\alpha - 1)\beta^{\alpha-1}} a^{\alpha-2}e^{-a/\beta} \, da, \quad 0 < d < \infty$$ 2.9

Where α > 0 and β > 0 are the parameters of the gamma distribution used to model the distribution of grain lengths in the metal.

Once a corrosion path skips an intersection, however, the remaining horizontal pieces on the grain layer are modeled solely by the gamma distribution without use of a conditional uniform distribution (Figure 2). We denote these pieces by [Gi(1)]s; s = 1;... m + u - v, where n is the total number of such complete horizontal pieces. We note that this is actually an upper bound approximation since the last piece of the horizontal distance might not cover an entire grain length before the path turns again. However, during propagation, we believe that a horizontal corrosion path is likely to meet many more "⊤" type intersections than "⊥" type intersections. Therefore, the probability that a corrosion path turns downward is likely to be greater than the probability that it turns upward. As a result, the upper bound approximation from using these

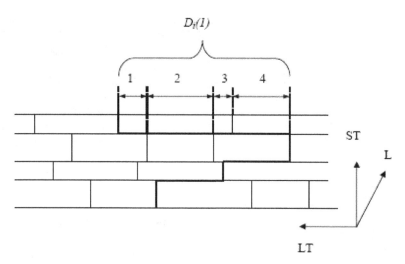

Figure 2. The bold line represents a corrosion path Wi;D. Di(1) is the horizontal distance that the ith corrosion path travels in the second grain layer.

complete horizontal gamma distances when a corrosion path skips an intersection should not result in serious overesti-mation. With this notation, we have

$$D_i(1) = H_i(1) + \sum_{s=l}^{n} [G_i(1)]_s.$$

2.10

COMPUTER SIMULATION

Under the discussed assumptions, we used a Matlab algorithm to simulate the distribution of the minimum path length. First, the thickness of each layer, bj; j =1;... k, is generated from a gamma distribution. The parameters of the gamma distribution are estimated via the method of moments (Ruan et al., 2004). The sum of this set of random numbers is subject to the constraint

$$T = \sum_{j=1}^{k} b_j.$$

We must adjust the width of the last grain layer to accommodate For a corrosion path, the first step is always taken to be a vertical step Ti(1), which is equal to b1. Next, the first Hi(1) from the distribution with pdf (2.9) is generated. Then, probabilities pup, pdown, pskip and psplit are assigned. As an example, consider pdown = 0:8 and pskip = 0:1 so that pup = 1 – pdown – pskip = 0:1 by (2.3). A random number w is generated from the uniform (0; 1) distribution. If w < 0:1, the corrosion assumes an upward turn. Accordingly, a vertical step is generated with the distance b1, the thickness of the first grain layer. If w > 0:9, the corrosion skips the intersection and a random number Gi(1) is generated. If w falls between 0.1 and 0.9, the corrosion path assumes a downward turn and the vertical step takes the value of b2, the thickness of the second grain layer.

An indicator variable, X, is used to record the layer number that the corrosion path is currently on. The initial value of X is zero. When the corrosion path makes a downward turn, X is increased by 1. When the corrosion path makes an upward turn, X is reduced by 1. Otherwise, X retains its current value. X = 0 (except initially) corresponds to a corrosion path that is terminated at the top

surface. Similarly, X = k if a corrosion path reaches the bottom surface. The minimum path length is obtained from those corrosion paths that reach the bottom surface. Starting from the first vertical step, it is necessary to consider whether a corrosion path might split into two branches. For example, assume psplit = 0.2. A random number r is generated from the uniform (0; 1) distribution. If r > 0.2, the corrosion path is split into two horizontal pieces. Each of the branches is then simulated separately from this point on. The total number of branches and the number of the current layer where the splitting occurs are recorded. For branch 1, the horizontal and vertical distances it travels are simulated accordingly given the known probabilities pup, pdown, pskip and psplit. If there is another split somewhere along the path, the layer number and the number of total splits are again recorded. After branch 1 reaches the bottom surface or terminates at the top surface, the program starts to simulate branch 2. This branch has a portion overlapping with the first one, so the new simulation starts from the layer where the split occurs until the second branch is also terminated. This entire procedure is repeated until all of the branches have been simulated. The entire set of corrosion paths constitutes a random sample from the distribution of Wi;D; i = 1; ..., m + u. Using the indicator variable X which records the current layer of the corrosion path, a random sample is generated from the distribution of Wi;T; i = 1; ..., m + u – v; that is, from the distribution of corrosion path lengths that reach the bottom surface. The number of corrosion initialization sites, m, is estimated to be in the order of 10^3 for this type of aluminum foil penetration samples (Ruan et al., 2004). However, m is assumed to be 100 in this paper in order to reduce the amount of computation and still illustrate the application of the simulation procedure. The minimum of these lengths is recorded as a random observation Wmin;T from the distribution of the minimum path length. A sufficient number (e.g., sample size = 100) of minimum path length values are generated by repeating the above procedure. The algorithm of the computer program is summarized in Figure 3.

SIMULATION RESULTS AND DISCUSSION

We use the method of moments (Shibata, 1996) to estimate the parameters of the gamma distributions in order to simulate the grain sizes. From previous work

Table 1. Comparism of the result for gamma (2, 0.0255) and gamma (3, 0.017).

	Median of minimum path length (Pdown=1, Pup = 0, Pskip = 0, psplit = 0 (mm)	Median of minimum path length (pdown=0.94, Pup = 0.05, Pskip = 0.01, Psplit = 0.03 (mm)
gamma (2, 0.0255)	1.296	1.325
gamma (3, 0.017)	1.294	1.385

The number of sum is m=100 and the number of layer is k = 12. A random sample of size 100 was taken from the distribution of the minimum path length for each model.

(Ruan et al., 2004), the method of moments estimators for the parameters a and β for grain length of the AA2024-T3 sample tested by Zhang (2001) are 4 and 0.075, respectively. In addition, from Zhang (2003), the sample mean and standard deviation of the grain thickness measurements are 0.05 and 0:032 mm, respectively. Assuming that the thickness of the grains is distributed as a gamma (a^1, β^1) distribution, it follows from the method of moments that solving

$$a'\beta' = 0.05$$

and

$$a'\beta'^2 = 0.032^2 \qquad\qquad 3.1$$

Simultaneously yields

$\hat{a}' = 2.44$ and $\hat{\beta}' = 0.02$.

However, since a^1 must be an integer for the gamma distribution in our model, we could use either gamma (2; 0:0255) or gamma (3; 0:017) to simulate the distribution of grain thickness. In the case that a corrosion path can only assume a downward turn, these two sets of parameters give close results in terms of the median from the distribution of the minimum path length, as shown in Table 1. In the case when pup = 0:05, pskip = 0:01 and psplit = 0:03, however, the agreement between these two sets of parameters is not as good as the previous case, since the median for gamma (2; 0:0255) is 1.325 while the median for gamma (3; 0:017) is 1.385. This small deference is most likely due to the randomness of the simulation rather than the deference in the parameters, that is, the number of times that a corrosion path skips an intersection or splits into two pieces is deferent from path to path.

Hence, either gamma (2; 0:0255) or gamma (3; 0:017) can be used to model the distribution of the grain width. For the rest of our study, we use only gamma (2; 0:0255) to simulate the distribution of the grain thickness. Using the algorithm described above, the influences of turning upward, skipping an intersection and splitting into two branches on the minimum corrosion path lengths are investigated separately and the results are summarized in Tables 2 - 4, respectively. The thickness of the grain is

simulated by a gamma (2; 0:0255) distribution. The number of corrosion initialization sites is m = 100, the number of layers is k = 12 and the sample thickness T is assumed to be 0:4 mm. A random sample of size 100 is taken from the distribution of the minimum path length and the median of these observations M is computed, along with the normalized ratio, given by the expression:

Normalized ratio = M/N   3.2

This ratio is expected to be close to 4.29 for the sample of AA2024-T3 tested by Zhang (2001). Table 2 summarizes the simulation results for the setting where a corrosion path can turn up or down but not skip or split at an intersection (pskip = 0; psplit = 0). The probability of turning upward, pup, varies from 0 to 0.5 in steps of 0.05. As pup increases, the median of the minimum path length tends to increase. For pup between 0 and 0.5, the median M increase is roughly linear in the range of 0.1-0.3 but the increase is more dramatic for pup > 0:3 (Figure 4). When pup = 0, some undere-stimation exists in the estimated median minimum path length because the normalized ratio is smaller than the target 4.29. When pup is large, the model overestimates this nominal median minimum path length as the normalized ratio increases dramatically. The increase in simulated median minimum path length can be attributed to two factors. When a corrosion path assumes an upward turn, it propagates along a more tortuous route than those paths that do not turn upward. On the other hand, some corrosion paths that turn upward might terminate at the top surface of the metal strip, thus decreasing the total number of paths reaching the bottom surface. In this case, the minimum order statistic is likely increased. However, the influence of m on minimum order statistic is small (Zhang et al., 2003).

Table 3 summarizes the simulation results for the setting where a corrosion path can assume a downward turn at an intersection or skip the intersection but it cannot turn upward or split (pup = 0; psplit =0). The probability of skipping an intersection, pskip, varies from 0.05 to 0.5 in steps of 0.05. As pskip increases, the median of the minimum path length tends to increase. We note that when the two probabilities pup and pskip are small, they have similar on both the median of the minimum path length and the normalized ratio. They demonstrate similar amounts of random variation with

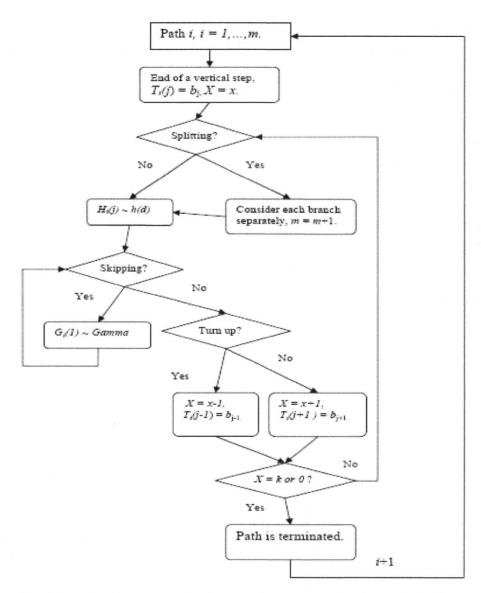

Figure 3. A flow chart representing the computer simulation algorithm of Ogala, E and Aideyan D.O.

Table 2. Simulation result minimum corrosion path length when a corrosion path turn upward or downward but not skip an intersection or split into branches (Pskip = 0, Psplit = 0).

Sample	Pdown	Pup	Median of minimum path length (mm)	Normalized ratio
1	1.00	0.00	1.296	3.24
2	0.95	0.05	1.358	3.39
3	0.90	0.10	1.438	3.59
4	0.85	0.15	1.485	3.71
5	0.80	0.20	1.580	3.95
6	0.75	0.25	1.701	4.25
7	0.70	0.30	1.828	4.57
8	0.65	0.35	2.123	5.31
9	0.60	0.40	2.275	5.69
10	0.55	0.45	2.787	6.97
11	0.50	0.50	3.686	9.22

Table 3. Simulation result minimum corrosion path length when a corrosion path turn downward or skip an intersection or split into branches (Pup = 0, Psplit = 0).

Sample	Pdown	Pskip	Median of minimum path length (mm)	Normalized ratio
12	0.95	0.05	1.362	3.40
13	0.90	0.10	1.435	3.59
14	0.85	0.15	1.486	3.72
15	0.80	0.20	1.586	3.96
16	0.75	0.25	1.701	4.25
17	0.70	0.30	1.812	4.53
18	0.65	0.35	1.955	4.89
19	0.60	0.40	2.124	5.31
20	0.55	0.45	2.246	5.61
21	0.50	0.50	2.488	6.22

Table 4. Simulation result minimum corrosion path length when a corrosion path can split into two branches at the of a vertical step, but not turn upward or skip an intersection (Pup = 0, Pskip = 0).

Sample	Pdown	Psplit	Median of minimum path length (mm)	Normalized ratio
22	0.95	0.05	1.232	3.08
23	0.90	0.10	1.196	2.99
24	0.85	0.15	1.154	2.89
25	0.80	0.20	1.142	2.86
26	0.75	0.25	1.092	2.73
27	0.70	0.30	1.054	2.63
28	0.65	0.35	1.042	2.60
29	0.60	0.40	1.016	2.54
30	0.55	0.45	0.991	2.48
31	0.50	0.50	0.960	2.40

slightly increasing trends. When both probabilities are large, pup is more influential than pskip, when a corrosion path skips an intersection and continues to propagate in the horizontal direction, the total horizontal distance it travels will increase. However, when a corrosion path assumes an upward turn, both its horizontal distance and vertical distance traveled will increase. Additionally, pskip does not have the potential to decrease the number of corrosion paths that reach the bottom surface as does pup.

Table 4 summarizes the simulation results for the setting where a corrosion path can split into two branches at an intersection at the end of any vertical step but it cannot turn upward or skip an intersection (pup = 0; pskip = 0). As with other settings, the probability of splitting at an intersection, psplit, varies from 0.05 to 0.5 in steps of 0.05.

As psplit increases, the median of the minimum path length tends to gradually decrease linearly (Figure 4). The psplit is relatively small compared to the influences of pup and pskip. The decrease in the median of the minimum path length is due to the fact that the minimum

order statistic is likely to decrease as the number of paths reaching the bottom surface increases. In the case that pup and pskip are both equal to zero, the total number of paths that reach the bottom surface is the sum of the number of initial corrosion sites m and the number of splits that occurred during corrosion propagation. However, the effect of the total number of paths on the minimum order statistic is relatively small compared to the effects of pup and pskip. Figure 4 shows a representative sample of the number of splits that occurred for each psplit. As psplit increases from 0.05 to 0.5, the observed number of splits changes from a magnitude of 10^2 to 10^4, but the variation in the median of the minimum path length is less than 0:3 mm, as shown in Table 4.

Conclusions

In this paper, we discuss an extension of the brick wall model proposed by Ruan et al. (2004). The basic brick wall model underestimates the minimum path length that

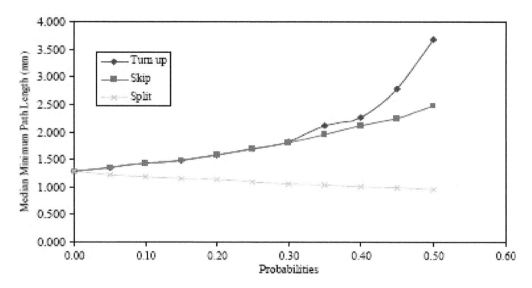

Figure 4. Effect of probabilities (pup; pskip; psplit) on the median of the minimum path length.

a corrosion path travels along grain boundaries in an aluminum alloy sample. This problem is addressed by modeling the behavior of corrosion paths at intersections of grain boundaries. Situations considered include the cases where a corrosion path might assume an upward turn, skip an intersection or split into branches. We found that small percentage changes in the probabilities of any of these options can result in significant changes in the median of the minimum order statistic and the normalized ratio.

However, with a proper combination of these probabilities, the extended model is able to obtain a good fit to the experimental data. This extension of the brick wall model represents a more precise description of the growth kinetics for AA2024-T3. Even though it is still unknown in practice which values are reasonable to assign to these probabilities for this type of alloy, the simulation of such phenomena can provide useful quantitative insights into the understanding of the corrosion kinetics in AA2024-T3. If deemed necessary for a given metal alloy, further refinement of this model is also possible. For example, a corrosion path might have positive probabilities to turn to one direction or split into two branches no matter whether it is at a horizontal or vertical step. That is, even at the end of a horizontal step the corrosion path might split into two branches, where one branch skips the intersection and the other turns to a vertical direction. Also, it is reasonable to allow a corrosion path to terminate within the metal when it meets another corrosion path from an opposite direction.

REFERENCES

Davis JR (Ed.) (1999). Corrosion of Aluminum and Aluminum Alloys. ASM International, Materials Park, OH.

Galvele JR, De Micheli SM (1970). Mechanism of intergranular corrosion of Al–Cu alloys. Corrosion Sci., 10: 795-807.

Muller IL, Galvele JR (1977). Pitting potential of high purity binary aluminum alloys-I, Al-Cu alloys. Pitting and intergranular corrosion. Corrosion Sci., 17: 179-193.

Danny B. Lange , Mitsuru O (1999). Seven good reasons for mobile agents. Communications of the ACM, 42(3): 88-89.

Muller G, Moura B, Bellard F, Consel C (1997). Harissa: A flexible and efficient Java environment mixing bytecode and compiled code. In Proceedings of the Third Conference on Object-Oriented Technologies and Systems, pp. 1-20.

Seth S (1999). Nortel plans new product to bolster optical networks. The New York Times.

Scully JR (1999). Environment-assisted intergranular cracking. Mat. Res. Soc. Bull. 24: 36-42.

Permissions

List of Contributors

Ali Heidari
Department of Civil Engineering, Shahrekord University, Shahrekord, Iran

Mehdi Delshad Chermahini
Department of Material Science and Engineering, Kerman University, Kerman, Iran

Mohammad Heidari
Islamic Azad University, Aligodarz Branch, Aligodarz, Iran

Miguel Sánchez Sotelo
Universidad Autonóma del Estado de México, Centro Universitario Valle de Chalco, Hermenegildo Galena No.3, 56615, Valle de Chalco, México

Rosa María Valdovinos Rosas
Universidad Autonóma del Estado de México, Centro Universitario Valle de Chalco, Hermenegildo Galena No.3, 56615, Valle de Chalco, México

Roberto Alejo Eleuterio
Tecnológico de Estudios Superiores de Jocotitlan, Carr. Toluca-Atlacomulco Km 44.8, 50700, Jocotitlan, México

Edgar Herrera
Instituto Nacional de Investigación Nuclear ININ, Carr. Mexico-Toluca s/n, 52750, La Marquesa, Mexico

Eduardo Gasca
Instituto Tecnológico de Toluca, Av. Tecnológico s/n, 52140, Metepec, Mexico

Ladislav Zjavka
Faculty of Management Science and Informatics, University of Žilina, Univerzitná 8215/1, 010 01 Žilina, Slovakia

Tsu-Wang (David) Shen
Department of Medical Informatics, Tzu Chi University, Hualien, Taiwan 701, Sec. 3, Jhong-Yang Rd., Hualien, 97004, Taiwan

Willis J. Tompkins
Department of Biomedical Engineering, University of Wisconsin, Madison, WI, USA

Yu Hen Hu
Department of Electrical and Computer Engineering, University of Wisconsin, Madison, WI, USA

Jiacai Wang
Department of Mechanical Science and Engineering, Tokyo Institute of Technology, Japan

Lirong Wang
Institute of Advanced Integration Technology, Shenzhen Institute of Advanced Technology, Chinese Academy of Science, China

Jinzhu Li
Insigma China, Beijing, China

Ichiro Hagiwara
Department of Mechanical Science and Engineering, Tokyo Institute of Technology, Japan

Parag Jain
Bhagwant University, India.
Computer Applications Department, Roorkee Institute of Technology, Roorkee, India

S. C. Gupta
Department of Electronics and Computer, Indian Institute of Technology, Roorkee, India

R. H. Laskar
Department of Electronics and Communication Engineering, National Institute of Technology, Silchar, India

F. A. Talukdar
Department of Electronics and Communication Engineering, National Institute of Technology, Silchar, India

Biman Paul
Department of Electronics and Communication Engineering, National Institute of Technology, Silchar, India

Debmalya Chakrabarty
Department of Electronics and Communication Engineering, National Institute of Technology, Silchar, India

Shebel Asad
Department of Mechatronics, Faculty of Engineering Technology (FET), Al Balqa Applied University (BAU), P. O Box 15008. Amman - Jordan

Maazouz Salahat
Department of Mechatronics, Faculty of Engineering Technology (FET), Al Balqa Applied University (BAU), P. O Box 15008. Amman - Jordan

Mohammad Abu Zalata
Department of Mechatronics, Faculty of Engineering Technology (FET), Al Balqa Applied University (BAU), P. O Box 15008. Amman - Jordan

Mohammad Alia
Department of Mechatronics, Faculty of Engineering Technology (FET), Al Balqa Applied University (BAU), P. O Box 15008. Amman - Jordan

Ayman Al
Department of Mechatronics, Faculty of Engineering Technology (FET), Al Balqa Applied University (BAU), P. O Box 15008. Amman - Jordan

Rawashdeh
Department of Mechatronics, Faculty of Engineering Technology (FET), Al Balqa Applied University (BAU), P. O Box 15008. Amman - Jordan

F. Laib
CEVITAL Group, Algiers, Algeria

M. S. Radjef
LAMOS laboratory, Department of Operational Research, University of Bejaia, Algeria

H. S. H. Jassim
College of Engineering, Universiti Tenaga Nasional, KM 7, Jalan kajang puchong, 43009 Kajang, Selangor, Malaysia

S. K. Tiong
College of Engineering, Universiti Tenaga Nasional, KM 7, Jalan kajang puchong, 43009 Kajang, Selangor, Malaysia

S. Yussof
College of Information Technology, Universiti Tenaga Nasional, KM 7, Jalan kajang puchong, 43009 Kajang, Selangor, Malaysia

S. P. Koh
College of Engineering, Universiti Tenaga Nasional, KM 7, Jalan kajang puchong, 43009 Kajang, Selangor, Malaysia

R. Ismail
College of Information Technology, Universiti Tenaga Nasional, KM 7, Jalan kajang puchong, 43009 Kajang, Selangor, Malaysia

Yassine Bouteraa
Research unit on Intelligent Control, design and Optimization of Complex Systems, Sfax Engineering School, University of Sfax, BP W, 3038 Sfax, Tunisia
Institut Prisme SRI 63 avenue de Lattre de Tassigny 18020 Bourges Cedex, France

Asma Ben Mansour
Research unit on Intelligent Control, design and Optimization of Complex Systems, Sfax Engineering School, University of Sfax, BP W, 3038 Sfax, Tunisia

Jawhar Ghommam
Research unit on Intelligent Control, design and Optimization of Complex Systems, Sfax Engineering School, University of Sfax, BP W, 3038 Sfax, Tunisia

Gérard Poisson
Institut Prisme SRI 63 avenue de Lattre de Tassigny 18020 Bourges Cedex, France

Fahad Alotaiby
Department of Electrical Engineering, College of Engineering, King Saud University, Riyadh, Saudi Arabia

Salah Foda
Department of Electrical Engineering, College of Engineering, King Saud University, Riyadh, Saudi Arabia

Ibrahim Alkharashi
Computer Research Institute, King Abdulaziz City for Science and Technology, Riyadh, Saudi Arabia

Martino O. A. Ajangnay
Electrical Engineering Department, College of Engineering and Architecture, University of Juba, South Sudan

Maaly A. Hassan
Department of Electrical and Computer Engineering, The Islamic University of Gaza, Gaza, Palestine

Ibrahim S. Abuhaiba
Department of Electrical and Computer Engineering, The Islamic University of Gaza, Gaza, Palestine

V. Pattabiraman
School of Computing Science and Engineering, VIT University - Chennai - 600 048, Tamil Nadu, India

Jianmin Dai
Institute of Intelligent Systems, Department of Psychology, University of Memphis 38152 Memphis, USA

Roxanne B. Raine
Institute of Intelligent Systems, Department of Psychology, University of Memphis 38152 Memphis, USA

Rod Roscoe
Institute of Intelligent Systems, Department of Psychology, University of Memphis 38152 Memphis, USA

Zhiqiang Cai
Institute of Intelligent Systems, Department of Psychology, University of Memphis 38152 Memphis, USA

Danielle S. McNamara
Institute of Intelligent Systems, Department of Psychology, University of Memphis 38152 Memphis, USA

Shrikant Upadhyay
Department of Electronics and Communication Engineering, Dehradun Institute of Technology, Dehrdun-248002, India

Pankaj Joshi
Department of Electronics and Communication Engineering, Dehradun Institute of Technology, Dehrdun-248002, India

Neha Gandotra
Department of Electronics and Communication Engineering, Dehradun Institute of Technology, Dehrdun-248002, India

Aditi Kumari
Department of Electronics and Communication Engineering, Dehradun Institute of Technology, Dehrdun-248002, India

S. V. Kasmir Raja
SRM University, Kattangulathur, Tamil Nadu, India

Daphne Lopez
VIT University, Vellore, Tamil Nadu, India

E. Ogala
Department of mathematical science, Kogi State University, Anyigba, Kogi State, Nigeria

D. O. Aideyan
Department of mathematical science, Kogi State University, Anyigba, Kogi State, Nigeria